PATTERN-ORIENTED SOFTWARE ARCHITECTURE

PATTERN-ORIENTED SOFTWARE ARCHITECTURE

On Patterns and Pattern Languages

Volume 5

Frank Buschmann,
Siemens, Munich, Germany

Kevlin Henney,
Curbralan, Bristol, UK

Douglas C. Schmidt,
Vanderbilt University, Tennessee, USA

John Wiley & Sons, Ltd

Other Wiley Editorial Offices

John Wiley & Sons Inc., 111 River Street, Hoboken, NJ 07030, USA

Jossey-Bass, 989 Market Street, San Francisco, CA 94103-1741, USA

Wiley-VCH Verlag GmbH, Boschstr. 12, D-69469 Weinheim, Germany

John Wiley & Sons Australia Ltd, 42 McDougall Street, Milton, Queensland 4064, Australia

John Wiley & Sons (Asia) Pte Ltd, 2 Clementi Loop #02-01, Jin Xing Distripark, Singapore 129809

John Wiley & Sons Canada Ltd, 22 Worcester Road, Etobicoke, Ontario, Canada M9W 1L1

Wiley also publishes its books in a variety of electronic formats. Some content that appears in print may not be
available in electronic books.

British Library Cataloguing in Publication Data

A catalogue record for this book is available from the British Library

ISBN-13: 978-0-471-48648-0

Typeset in 10/13 Bookman-Light by Laserwords Private Limited, Chennai, India
Printed and bound in Great Britain by Antony Rowe Ltd, Chippenham, Wiltshire
This book is printed on acid-free paper responsibly manufactured from sustainable forestry
in which at least two trees are planted for each one used for paper production.

Table of Contents

Foreword by Richard P. Gabriel

†'Software patterns have significantly changed the way we design...' is how POSA5 starts out—its preface, its self-explanation, maybe its justification. But design: what happens when we design? Is design about problems or about beauty? Does resolving forces while solving a problem force beauty into the design? Or can beauty and ideal problem solving emerge only after a (pattern) language has been tooled over the raw material? Someone once told me that any establishment where the entrance is obvious is not worth visiting.

The Oxford English Dictionary, second edition, informs us about design as follows:

> 1. A mental plan.

> 1.a. a plan or scheme conceived in the mind and intended for subsequent execution;...the preliminary conception of an idea that is to be carried into effect by action; a project;

In Guy Steele's 1998 talk at OOPSLA, 'Growing a Language,' he said:

> A design is a plan for how to build a thing. To design is to build a thing in one's mind but not yet in the real world—or, better yet, to plan how the real thing can be built.

I once wrote:

> Design is the thinking one does before building.

Carliss Baldwin and Kim B. Clark define design like this:

> Designs are the instructions based on knowledge that turn resources into things that people use and value.

> —*Between 'Knowledge' and 'the Economy': Notes on the Scientific Study of Designs*

Each of these definitions and characterizations revolve around ideas, plans, knowledge, problems, values and purposes, and hint at a before-building time. Very rational-sounding and the way we would like design to go—reliable, the trusty well-educated mind working things out: you can feel safe walking across the real thing because it will not sway and fall down. But let's think a little about who *we*[†] is.

People have been 'designing and building' cities for millennia, using, perhaps, tools and concepts like Christopher Alexander's pattern languages. Such artifacts are huge and hugely complex. It's hard to say where the mental plan is, because the imagining that might take place is surely scattered across the years, decades, centuries, and sometimes millennia it takes to fashion a proper city—a city like Athens, Rome, Berlin, London, Istanbul, or even New York or San Francisco and surely Boston. Thus the '*we*' in the up-noted sentence[†] must refer to a more recent set of *us*-es—namely software designers, who, one could argue, have gravitated toward the more conservative or possibly less realistic ideas of design reflected in the quotes above. Even in my quote—where I was trying to leave room for the interweaving of design, building, and reflection that cities, for example, enjoy as part of their design journey—it is hard to not see the before-building thrust into the forefront: *the thinking one does before building.*

That design has a landscape of meanings and nuances brings to mind a set of characterizations of design by Adrian Thompson at the University of Sussex. I call these characterizations *design metaheuristics,* meaning they are approaches to how to think about design, like the approach of using patterns and pattern languages. There are three design metaheuristics. Here's the first:

> **Inverse model is tractable**: If there is a tractable 'inverse model' of the system, then there is a way of working out in advance a sequence of variations that brings about a desired set of objective values.

Here a design is a plan, like a blueprint, and the inverse model is this: once the thing to be designed is imagined, there is a way to work out the blueprint or a plan for how to build the thing. This is the essential up-front design situation, which works best when designing something that has been built at least once before, and typically dozens or thousands of times. Alexander knows of this style of working: the ideas behind patterns and pattern languages evolved from the notion that people who built, for example, Swiss barns knew Swiss-barn patterns and pattern languages naturally—as a result of seeing them every day, working in them, and helping build them as children. In this sense the inverse model is well established: the image in the head is not unlike the barn next door, and the steps to build it are known with perhaps only modest modification. A pattern language (implicit or explicit) can guide the designer/builder along, and the little adjustments that are always needed are just building as usual. This leads to Thompson's second design metaheuristic:

> **Inverse model is not tractable, but forward model is**: In this case, we can predict the influence of variations upon the objective values, but the system is not tractably invertible so we cannot derive in advance a sequence of variations to bring about a desired set of objective values. This implies an iterative approach, where variations carefully selected according to the forward model are applied in sequence. This kind of iterative design-and-test is a common component of traditional approaches.

Design a little, build a little, reflect a little—this is how I explain this heuristic. It is the essence behind the agile methodologies, I think, evolutionary design/programming, and Alexander's 'Fundamental Process.' From the Agile Manifesto:

> Welcome changing requirements, even late in development. Agile processes harness change for the customer's competitive advantage.

> Deliver working software frequently, from a couple of weeks to a couple of months, with a preference to [sic] the shorter timescale.

> …

> The best architectures, requirements, and designs emerge from self-organizing teams.

> —http://agilemanifesto.org/principles.html

Alexander's 'Fundamental Process' is how he describes designing and building in *The Nature of Order*. In this massive four-volume book, he talks about how **centers**—places of interest and attention in space— are structured to create **wholeness**. Here are steps 1, 2, 4, 6, and 8:

> 1. At every step of the process—whether conceiving, designing, making, maintaining, or repairing—we must always be concerned with the whole within which we are making anything. We look at this wholeness, absorb it, try to feel its deep structure.

2. We ask which kind of thing we can do next that will do the most to give this wholeness the most positive increase of life.

4. As we work to enhance this new living center, we do it in such a way as also to create or intensify (by the same action) the life of some larger center.

6. We check to see if what we have done has truly increased the life and feeling of the whole. If the feeling of the whole has not been deepened by the step we have just taken, we wipe it out. Otherwise we go on.

8. We stop altogether when there is no further step we can take that intensifies the feeling of the whole.

Pattern languages are used like this, both by Alexander and by software developers. Such usage reflects, merely, the realization that the first design metaheuristic applies only to cases in which designs are being (mostly) repeated. In such cases, there are often models that can be used to simulate the design-a-little / build-a-little pattern the 'Fundamental Process' describes. Either there is literally a model—physics and mathematics and science—that is the boss of the design, and pretend designs can be tried out, or else we fool ourselves into thinking that large steps in the fundamental process—releases of version 1, then version 2, then version 3—are each actually full-blown designs. We are fooled because we don't want to zoom out to the larger scale. Alexander's 'Fundamental Process' is also a good description of the various agile methodologies, although one would expect refactoring to be more explicitly mentioned.

The book you either are about to read, are reading, or have finished reading—the one in which this foreword is embedded—is about pattern languages largely in this context. *The thinking one does before building* can be described by steps 1, 2, & 4. In this context, design really is a sort of problem solving. As Jim Coplien says:

> Design is a process of intentional acts to the end of moving from some conception of a problem to the reduction of that problem. A problem is the difference between a current state and desired state.

This seems to miss two aspects that seem (to some) central to design: beauty and newness. A very fine wine glass is both functional and beautiful, it is made from an exquisite and exotic material, its shape—each type of wine has a preferred wineglass shape to concentrate the aroma best, to direct the wine to the best part of the mouth for its flavor components, to prevent too much warming from the hands—presents the wine to its best effect, while also pleasing the eye with its elegance and line. Instead of 'newness' I almost wrote 'novelty,' but 'novelty' implies an intellectual or academic newness that misses the point. It isn't that the design is an invention full of brand new workings, it's the pleasure and surprise of seeing something you've never seen before. I'm thinking about the Cord Model 810 automobile introduced in 1936:

> The body design of the Cord 810 was the work of designer Gordon M. Buehrig and his team of stylists that included young Vince Gardner. The new car caused a sensation at the 1936 New York Auto Show in November. The crowds around the 810 were so dense, attendees stood on the bumpers of nearby cars to get a look. Many orders were taken at the show...
>
> —Wikipedia

People had never seen a car like this before—coffin-shaped nose, headlights hidden, exhaustpipes (one per cylinder) chromesnakes jutting out the sides, the smooth curved shelf at the front—it even was designed by stylists not designers. Notable about both its appearance, engineering, and user experience were the recessed headlights and the fact that the transmission came out the front of the engine, so that the floor of the passenger compartment could be lower and flatter than was usual at the time. Some say the design of the Cord 810 remains the most distinctive of the twentieth century. In 1996, American Heritage magazine proclaimed the Cord 810 sedan 'The Single Most Beautiful American Car.'

For example.

I find it hard to say that the Cord is the result of the reduction of a problem to a final outcome: something else is happening. Rebecca Rikner names this 'something else':

> Design is not about solving a problem. Design is about seeing the beauty.

Many would guess I'm done with Thompson's metaheuristics, but there's a third. And it's the third which is the topic of his research.

> **Neither forward nor inverse models are tractable**: There is neither a way of discerning which variations will give improvements in the objective values, nor a way of predicting what will be the effects of variations upon the objective values. Without evolution all is lost.

> —*Notes on Design Through Artificial Evolution: Opportunities and Algorithms*

Evolution!

Thompson's work includes the design of an analog circuit that can discriminate between 1kHz and 10kHz square waves using a field-programmable gate array designed using a genetic algorithm.[1] The result is described as 'probably the most bizarre, mysterious, and unconventional unconstrained evolved circuit yet reported,' in large part because the researchers were unable, in the end, to understand how the circuit works. It's not important to understand the details of the following remarks from their paper—just take a look at the expressions of incredulity:

> Yet somehow, within 200ns of the end of the pulse, the circuit 'knows' how long it was, despite being completely inactive during it.

> This is hard to believe, so we have reinforced this finding through many separate types of observation, and all agree that the circuit is inactive during the pulse.

Research in genetic algorithms, genetic programming, neuro-evolution, neural nets, and statistical/aleatoric methods all demonstrate surprising results—some of them displaying a puzzling illusion of design, like the antenna designed and tested by NASA and designed by artificial evolution. The size of an infant's hand, the elements bend off in a crazy cryptosymmetry like a small black bush half-frozen after a frost. It doesn't look like something a person would design, but it has better antenna-crucial characteristics in some ways, and so it is a good design—in terms of *reducing a problem*.

---

1. Adrian Thompson et al, *Explorations in Design Space: Unconventional Electronics Design Through Artificial Evolution*.

But do we *feel* that it is a good design? What do we make of this evolution stuff? How does artificial evolution work? In short, a population is subjected to artificial reproduction in which some characteristics from one parent are combined with others from another. The resulting characteristics are subjected to a small amount of random mutation, and the resulting population—which can include the original parents in some algorithms—is tested for fitness against a fitness function. Assuming the characteristics are related to aspects of design, this reduces to taking some design elements from one not-so-bad solution and combining them with design elements from another not-so-bad solution, making some small changes, and seeing how that goes. Aside from the random part, this doesn't sound so random.

If you take it from me that some of the things 'designed' this way have interesting characteristics, we need to ask whether this approach is a form of design. Some people would say that without a human designer, there can be no design, that the 'intentional' in Coplien's characterization and the 'mind' in the OED definition are essential features. Where are the 'instructions based on knowledge'? If Pierre Menard[2]

---

2. *Pierre Menard, Author of The Quixote*, by Jorge Luis Borges. In this story, a twentieth century writer (Menard) puts himself in a frame of mind to rewrite, word for word, part of Cervantes' *Don Quixote de la Mancha*, but not as a transcription, but as a coincidence. Enjoy:

> *It is a revelation to compare Menard's Don Quixote with Cervantes'. The latter, for example, wrote (part one, chapter nine):*
>
>> *...truth, whose mother is history, rival of time, depository of deeds, witness of the past, exemplar and adviser to the present, and the future's counselor.*
>
> *Written in the seventeenth century, written by the 'lay genius' Cervantes, this enumeration is a mere rhetorical praise of history.*
>
> *Menard, on the other hand, writes:*
>
>> *....truth, whose mother is history, rival of time, depository of deeds, witness of the past, exemplar and adviser to the present, and the future's counselor.*
>
> *History, the mother of truth: the idea is astounding. Menard, a contemporary of William James, does not define history as an inquiry into reality but as its origin. Historical truth, for him, is not what has happened, it is what we judge to have happened. The final phrases—exemplar and adviser to the present, and the future's counselor—are brazenly pragmatic.*
>
> *The contrast in style is also vivid. The archaic style of Menard—quite foreign, after all—suffers from a certain affectation. Not so that of his forerunner, who handles with ease the current Spanish of his time.*

were to dream up the FPGA tone discriminator or the weird antenna, such doubters might declare the result a design—or perhaps further, human-sensible explanations of the design are required to make that leap.

This brings to my mind the idea of canalization, described like this:

> A developmental outcome is canalized when the developmental process is bound to produce a particular end-state despite environmental fluctuations both in the development's initial state and during the course of development.
>
> —(adapted from) Andre Ariew, *Innateness is Canalization:*
> *In Defense of a Developmental Account of Innateness*

A thing produced is canalized when once it falls into a tributary of a river, by the process of its production it ends up in the river. 'Canalized' comes from the word 'canal'—once in the canal, you cannot escape. Strange attractors in complexity science are canalizations. Artificial evolution doesn't care whether a design—or at least a thing it produces—is beautiful, elegant, understandable, parsimonious, maintainable, extendable, sleek, slick, simple, superfluous, silly, or human. All it cares about is that it fits what the fitness function dictates. The design is not canalized by those things—those human things—as just about all human designs are and most likely must be.

Facing it in another direction, the design of, say, the antenna looks strange because it is not what a person would ever design. We are incapable of exploring a full design space, only those parts that look pretty to us.

This book is about design viewed through the lens of patterns and pattern languages. As you read it, permit your mind to drift closer to ideas of design and perhaps later on, further away. Permit yourself to wonder about design in all its glories and incarnations. The three design metaheuristics might very well represent points on a coherent continuum, and if they do, there also is a point where the human becomes non-human or, maybe worse, post-human.

Pattern languages can encompass lots of design space. They are part of our software design and construction toolboxes. They work by helping people design better. Reflection on good design is how pattern languages are written down. Design, design, design, design.

Richard P. Gabriel

Foreword by Wayne Cool

Way back I fell in with a bunch hot on the trail of a revolution in programming, hefting on their backs the unwieldy and orthodoxless ideas of a mad architect himself bent on revving the future by reviving the past in the splendor of its design sense[1] but not its design [Ale79]. This cool group holed up in retreats and self-concocted workshops, never in a mainstream meet-up but in contrast to official miracles, in a far-off locale, some backwater or Podunk which although unverifiable is visitable.[2] Unlike the madman who crowed 'beauty beauty beauty,' this crew worked the nuts, oiled the bolts, screwed together a practice and a program, a practicality and a precision straight-aimed at the practitioner and around the corner from theory.

Along the way I hopped from PLoP to PLoP, café to bar, beer to Starbucks; I was there when Beck proclaimed, when the workshops wound up, when the rainstorm first came up on the parquet Allerton floor, when the sun rose at Irsee, when the trail rides ended and the dust settled in Wickenberg; I was there when the books were written, reviewed, printed, and praised. Through all this I watched the interest grow in design and the structure of man-made things, in the strength of the written word aimed at the creation of a built-up world made of ideas and abstractions but felt like the built world of wood and shellac, stone and metal rods.

And this is what I want to come to: the realm of software patterns converts the world of surfaces—a world where mechanism is hidden beneath impenetrable covers—to one of exposed innards and plain working; the hidden becomes the object of a craftsmanship that can be defined as the desire to do something well—for its own sake, for no reward, for the pride of skill applied with discernment and in reflection, taking a long time and going deeply into it. For those who build

---

1. Or 'scents,' as the agile would proclaim.
2. Apologies to Bill Knott.

Foreword by Wayne Cool

this way, it matters little that the craft is buried under a user interface—because one day someone must peek underneath and see. The surfaces matter but they don't hide.

Art. Craft. Engineering. Science. These are the swirling muses of design patterns. Art and science are stories; craft and engineering are actions.

Craft is midway between art and science; art and craft stand over against engineering and science. Art is the unique example, the first thing, the story as artifact condensing out of talent and desire. Craft is reliable production of quality. A craftsman[3] might be disappointed but rarely fails. A work of craft is the product of a person and materials. Engineering is reliable and efficient production of things for the use and convenience of people. Science is a process of making a story that can be used for engineering. A book called 'The Art of X' is about the mystery of the rare individual who can make an X. 'The Craft of X' is about the sweat and training endured by those who make Xs one at a time. 'The Engineering of X' is about discipline and long days planning and making Xs for institutional customers. 'The Science of X' is a maths book.

But the roles of science and craft have been misdiagnosed. Most believe (deeply) that science precedes, as they believe it must, craft and engineering; that building requires abstract knowing. As in: to design a steam engine you need a (correct) theory of thermodynamics. But when the steam engine was developed, scientists believed the 'caloric theory:' that there is a 'subtle fluid' called *caloric* that is the substance of heat. The quantity of this substance is fixed in the universe; it flows from warmer bodies to colder. Good story. The caloric theory explained a lot, but the mechanics who built the first steam engines didn't know the theory or didn't care about it. Working with boilers, they noticed relations between volume, pressure, and temperature and they built steam engines. Maybe the scientists even used observations of steam engines to come up with 'modern' thermodynamics.

---

3. Today I choose the pretty word.

Craftsmen know the ways of the substances they use. They watch. Perception and systematic thinking combine to formulate understanding. A well-developed craft gives rise to technological developments. And science. Sure: there are feedback loops between science and engineering, but neither is queen—and hands-on dominates sit-and-think.

This is about building, and all building requires planning and execution. Planning is the thinking one does before building. Execution is understanding the plan and producing something from it. Since the early twentieth century management science has pushed for the separation of planning from execution. Frederick Winslow Taylor said it with art and poetry this way:

> All possible brain work should be removed from the shop and centered in the planning or lay-out department.
>
> —Principles of Scientific Management

Sweet.

Planning and execution merge in art but stand wide apart in engineering; somewhere in between for craft. Science is in the realm of thought and ideas.

Separation of planning from execution is not about efficiency. Not about getting the most value per hour. Maybe it will; maybe it won't. Planning takes thinking; thinking costs money. If you can think a little, build a lot, you can make money. Thinking while executing is replaced by process; education is replaced by training—the way Dancing Links and Algorithm X[4] can solve Sudoku. With Dancing Links and Algorithm X, Sudoku needs a computer, not a person. Separating planning from execution is about cost.

And this is not about quality. The best quality cars are not built on blind robotic assembly lines. Cost.

If cost is pressure toward engineering, patterns is the push-back toward craft and art.

---

4. Dancing Links is a technique suggested by Donald Knuth to efficiently implement Algorithm X, a recursive, nondeterministic, depth-first, brute-force algorithm that finds all solutions to the exact cover problem.

Patterns. Craftsmanship: we think of it arising from the texture of the built world. A world where quality and attention to detail is visible on the surface of materials, in the gaps between things, in methods of joining without friction but with shape and convolution. A world where talent sits besides knowledge and intelligence. Read this description of the problem of making *felloes*—sections of rim on a wooden carriage wheel—in *The Wheelwright's Shop* by George Sturt:[5]

> Yet it is in vain to go into details at this point; for when the simple apparatus had all been gotten together for one simple-looking process, a never-ending series of variations was introduced by the material. What though two felloes might seem much alike when finished? It was the wheelwright himself who had to make them so. He it was who hewed out that resemblance from quite dissimilar blocks, for no two felloe-blocks were ever alike. Knots here, shakes[6] there, rind-galls[7], waney[8] edges, thicknesses, thinnesses, were for ever affording new chances or forbidding previous solutions, whereby a fresh problem confronted the workman's ingenuity every few minutes. He had no band-saw (as now [1923]) to drive, with ruthless unintelligence, through every resistance. The timber was far from being prey, a helpless victim, to a machine. Rather it would lend its own special virtues to the man who knew how to humour it.
>
> —The Wheelwright's Shop

You can feel the wood as equal partner to craftsman.

The work of patterns is the work of people who have systematic encounters with code, going deeply into it, dwelling for long periods of time on the tasks of design and coding to get them right, people who don't believe planning can be separated from execution. People who work this way are having the sort of encounter that gives rise to science. This is not mere trafficking in abstractions; it is thinking. Patterns don't push

---

5. First published in 1923.

6. A crack in timber caused by wind or frost.

7. A damage the tree received when young, so that the bark or rind grows in the inner substance of the tree.

8. A sharp or uneven edge on a board that is cut from a log not perfectly squared, or that is made in the process of squaring.

toward art and craft but are the tools of people who do. To be resisted is the automation of patterns which is the separation of planning and execution.

Computer scientists stand at the chalkboard—write and erase, squint and stare, remark and declaim. Patterns people, like mechanics, bend at the waist and peer into the code, their arms are drenched in code up to the elbows. It's what they work on: knots here, shakes there, rind-galls, waney edges, thicknesses, thinnesses forever affording new chances or forbidding previous solutions. They see programming almost as manual work—muscled arms, sleeves rolled tight against biceps, thought bright behind the eye linking mind and hand.

I was there when the patterns community started. I sat the hillside; I huddled in the redwoods; I ran the beach; I hiked Mt Hood; I kayaked, did the ropes course, gazed on the Sun Singer at sunset; I sweated in the sauna; I rode the big horse, Bigfoot; I sang with the cowboy over steaks and corn. But I didn't add a single idea, not even one sentence, nor one dot of punctuation to what the patterns people thought, wrote, and built. I'll bet, though, you know exactly what I think about it.

Wayne Cool, Venice Beach

About the Authors

Frank Buschmann

Frank Buschmann is Senior Principal Engineer at Siemens Corporate Technology in Munich, Germany. His research interests include object technology, software architecture, product-lines, model-driven software development, and patterns. He has published widely in all these areas, most visibly in his co-authorship of three POSA volumes [POSA1] [POSA2] [POSA4]. Frank was a member of the ANSI C++ standardization committee X3J16 from 1992 to 1996, initiated the first EuroPLoP conference in 1996, co-edited several books on patterns [PLoPD3] [SFHBS06], and serves as an editor of the Wiley Series in Software Design Patterns. In his development work at Siemens, Frank has led architecture and implementation efforts for several large-scale industrial software projects, including business information, industrial automation, and telecommunication systems.

When not at work Frank spends most of his time enjoying life with his wife Martina and daughter Anna, having fun riding his horse Eddi, watching the time go by in Munich beer gardens, getting excited when watching his favorite soccer team, Borussia Dortmund, dreaming when listening to a performance at the Munich opera, and relaxing with rare Scotch single malts before bedtime.

Kevlin Henney

Kevlin Henney is an independent consultant based in Bristol, UK. His work involves teaching, mentoring, and practicing across his areas of interest, which include programming languages and techniques, software architecture, patterns, and agile development. His clients range from global firms to smaller startups, involved in the worlds of systems software, telecommunications, embedded systems, middleware development, business information, and finance.

Kevlin is a regular speaker at software conferences, and has also been involved with the organization of many conferences, including EuroPLoP. He has participated in the C++ standardization process, through the BSI and ISO, as well other language standardization efforts. Kevlin is also known for his writing, which has included a POSA volume [POSA4], conference papers, and regular (and irregular) columns for many publications, including *C++ Report*, *C/C++ Users Journal*, *Java Report*, *JavaSpektrum*, *Application Development Advisor*, *The Register*, *EXE*, and *Overload*.

In what passes for spare time, Kevlin enjoys spending time with Carolyn, his wife, and Stefan and Yannick, their two sons. This time takes in Lego, toy fixing, reading, and the odd beer or glass of wine.

Douglas C. Schmidt

Doug Schmidt is a Professor of Computer Science and Associate Chair of the Computer Science and Engineering program at Vanderbilt University, Nashville, Tennessee, USA. His research focuses on patterns and pattern languages, optimization principles, and empirical analysis of techniques that facilitate the development of quality of service (QoS)-enabled component middleware and model-driven engineering tools that support distributed real-time and embedded systems.

Doug is an internationally-recognized expert on patterns, object-oriented frameworks, real-time middleware, modeling tools, and open-source development. He has published over 300 papers in top technical journals and conferences, has co-authored books on patterns [POSA2] [POSA4] and C++ network programming [SH02] [SH03], and has also co-edited several popular books on patterns [PLoPD1] and frameworks [FJS99a] [FJS99b]. In addition to his academic research, Doug has led the development of ACE, TAO, CIAO, and CoSMIC, which are widely used open-source middleware frameworks and model-driven engineering tools that contain a rich set of reusable components implemented using the patterns presented in this book.

In his rare spare time Doug enjoys spending time with his wife Lori and their son Bronson, as well as weight-lifting, guitar playing, debating world history and politics, and driving Chevy Corvettes.

About this Book

Software patterns have significantly changed the way we design, implement, and think about computing systems. Patterns provide us with a vocabulary to express architectural visions, as well as examples of representative designs and detailed implementations that are clear and to the point. Presenting pieces of software in terms of their constituent patterns also allows us to communicate more effectively, with fewer words and less ambiguity.

Since the mid-1990s many software systems, including major parts of the Java and C# programming languages and libraries, were developed with the help of patterns. Sometimes these patterns were applied selectively to address specific challenges and problems. At other times they were used holistically to support the construction of software systems from the definition of their baseline architectures to the realization of their fine-grained details. Today the use of patterns has become a valuable commodity for software professionals.

Over the past decade and a half, a large body of literature has been created to document known patterns in a wide range of areas related to software development, including organization and process, application and technical domains, and best programming practices. This literature provides concrete guidance for practicing software engineers and increasingly influences the education of students. Each year new books and conference proceedings are published with yet more patterns, increasing the depth and breadth of software development knowledge codified in pattern form.

In the same way, the knowledge of, and experience with, *applying* patterns has also grown steadily, along with our knowledge about the pattern concept itself: its inherent properties, different flavors, and relationships with other technologies. In contrast to the ever-growing number of documented and refactored *concrete* patterns, however, publications *about* patterns and the pattern concept have been updated only sparsely and in selected areas since the mid-1990s, despite the enormous increase of conceptual knowledge in the software patterns community. The introduction to software patterns in *A System of Patterns* [POSA1] and *Design Patterns* [GoF95], and the white paper on *Software Patterns* [Cope96], remain the most relevant sources about the pattern concept. Furthermore, only relatively recently have publications started to discuss and document pattern sequences explicitly [CoHa04] [PCW05] [Hen05b].

To summarize the current state of affairs, no complete and up-to-date work on the pattern concept is available. Moreover, knowledge of the latest advances in the conceptual foundations of patterns remains locked in the heads of a few experts and thought leaders in the patterns community. Mining this knowledge and documenting it for consumption by the broader software development community is the intention of this book, *On Patterns and Pattern Languages*, which is the fifth and final volume in the *Pattern-Oriented Software Architecture* series.

In this book we present, discuss, contrast, and relate the many known flavors and applications of the pattern concept: stand-alone patterns, pattern complements, pattern compounds, pattern stories, pattern sequences, and—last but not least—pattern languages. For each concept flavor we investigate its fundamental and advanced properties, and explore insights that are well-accepted by the pattern community, as well as perspectives that are still the subject of discussion and dispute. We also discuss how patterns support and interact with other technologies commonly used in software development. In a nutshell, we provide an overview of the current state of knowledge and practice in software patterns.

Note, however, that while we are general and broad regarding the elaboration and discussion of the pattern concept itself, the concrete examples we use to illustrate or motivate different aspects of the concept focus mostly on software design patterns—as opposed to other types of patterns such as organizational patterns, configuration-management patterns, and patterns for specific application domains. The reason for this (self-)restriction is twofold. First, the majority of all documented software patterns are software design patterns, so we have a wealth of material for our examples. Second, the largest group of software pattern users are architects and developers—thus our focus on software design patterns allows us to explain the 'theory' behind patterns using practical examples with which this group is most familiar.

Intended Audience

The main audience of the book are software professionals interested in the conceptual foundations of patterns. Our primary goal is to help such professionals broaden, deepen, and complete their knowledge and understanding of the pattern concept so that they know what and how patterns can contribute to their projects. Our other goals are to help them avoid common misconceptions about patterns, and apply concrete patterns more effectively in their daily software development work.

This book is also suitable for undergraduate or graduate students who have a solid grasp of software engineering, programming languages, runtime environments, and tools. For this audience, the book can help them to learn more about what patterns are and how they can help with the design and implementation of high-quality software.

Structure and Content

The book is structured into three main parts, which are surrounded and supported by several smaller chapters that motivate and complete its vision and content.

Chapter 0, Beyond the Hype, reflects on the original definitions of the pattern concept and discusses how these definitions are received and understood by the software community. Our analysis suggests that some adjustments and enhancements are useful to avoid misconceptions when understanding patterns, and to help prevent the misapplication of patterns in software projects. This introductory chapter provides the foundation for the three main parts of the book, which elaborate and discuss these adjustments and enhancements in greater detail to provide a more complete and consistent picture of the pattern concept.

Part I, *Inside Patterns*, reflects on the use of stand-alone patterns, and presents and discusses the insights into patterns we have collectively gained over the last decade. These insights complement existing pattern definitions, helping us to understand patterns at a deeper level.

Part II, *Between Patterns*, moves outside individual patterns to explore the relationships between patterns: sometimes a set of patterns represent alternatives to one another, sometimes they are adjuncts to one another, and sometimes they are bound together as a tightly-knit group. Beyond the common, passive notion of a collection, this part of the book also considers how patterns can be organized as a sequence, with patterns applied one after another in a narrative flow, thereby adding an active voice to the use of patterns in the design process.

Part III, *Into Pattern Languages*, builds on the concepts and conclusions of the first two parts by introducing pattern languages. Compared with individual patterns and pattern sequences, pattern languages provide more holistic support for using patterns in the design and implementation of software for specific technical or application domains. They achieve this goal by enlisting multiple patterns for each problem that arises in their respective domains, weaving them together to define a generative and domain-specific software development process.

Chapter 14, From Patterns To People, picks up the discussion about the concept of patterns from the first three parts of the book, to conclude that despite all technology within patterns and the support they provide for other software technologies, the prime audience of patterns is people.

Chapter 15, The Past, Presence, and Future of Patterns, revisits our 2004 forecast on where we expected patterns to go that was published in the third volume of the *Pattern-Oriented Software Architecture* series. We discuss the directions that patterns have actually taken during the past three years and analyze where patterns and the patterns community are now. Based on this retrospection, we revise our vision about future research and the application of patterns and pattern languages.

This book is the last volume we plan to publish within the POSA series—at least for now. *Chapter 16, All Good Things...*, therefore wraps up and concludes our more than fifteen years of work on, and experience with, patterns, and examines the five volumes of the POSA series that we have written during this time.

The book ends with a summary of all the pattern concepts we discuss, a chapter with thumbnail descriptions of all the patterns we reference in the book, an extensive list of references to work in the field, a pattern index, a general subject index, and an index of names that lists everyone who helped us shape this book.

There are undoubtedly properties and aspects of the pattern concept that we have omitted, or which will emerge over time with even greater understanding of patterns and their use in practical software development. If you have comments, constructive criticism, or suggestions for improving the style and content of this book, please send them to us via e-mail to `siemens-patterns@cs.uiuc.edu`. Guidelines for subscription can be found on the patterns home page at `http://hillside.net/patterns/`. This link also provides an important source of information on many aspects of patterns, such as available and forthcoming books, conferences on patterns, papers on patterns, and so on.

Acknowledgments

It is a pleasure for us to thank the many people who supported us in creating this book, either by sharing their knowledge with us or by reviewing earlier drafts of its parts and providing useful feedback.

First and foremost, we want to thank John Vlissides, to whom we also dedicate this book. John was one of the most brilliant minds in the software patterns community—as ground-breaking thought leader and co-author of the legendary and seminal Gang-of-Four book [GoF95], and as 'discoverer' and mentor of many now well-known and world-class pattern experts. The inspirations and foundations from his work have significantly influenced and helped shape the pattern concept we elaborate and discuss in this book.

Champion review honors go to Wayne Cool, Richard P. Gabriel, Michael Kircher, James Noble, and Linda Rising, who reviewed all our material in depth, focusing on its correctness, completeness, consistency, and quality. Their feedback significantly increased the quality of material in the book. Wayne Cool also contributed many ideas and thoughts that we explore in depth in the book.

In addition, we presented parts of the material in the book at four EuroPLoP pattern conferences and also to several pattern experts. Alan O'Callaghan, Lise Hvatum, Allan Kelly, Doug Lea, Klaus Marquardt,

Tim O'Reilly, Michael Stal, Simon St. Laurent, Steve Vinoski, Markus Völter, Uwe Zdun, and Liping Zhao provided us with extensive feedback, which led to many minor and also some major revisions of various aspects of the pattern concept and their presentation.

Many thanks also go to Mai Skou Nielsen, who permitted us to use photos from her collection in the book.

Special thanks go to Lothar Borrmann and Reinhold Achatz for their managerial support and backing at the software engineering labs of Corporate Technology of Siemens AG, Munich, Germany.

Very special thanks go to our editor, Sally Tickner, our former editor Gaynor Redvers-Mutton, and everyone else at John Wiley & Sons who made it possible to publish this book. On a sunny evening at EuroPLoP 2002, Gaynor convinced us to write this POSA volume, and she also accompanied the first two years of its creation. Sally, in turn, had an enormous amount of patience with us during the two additional and unplanned years we spent completing the manuscript. Very special thanks also go to Steve Rickaby, of WordMongers Ltd, our copy editor, for enhancing our written material. Steve accompanied all five volumes of the POSA series with his advice and support.

Last, but not least, we thank our families for their patience and support during the writing of this book!

Guide to the Reader

This book is structured and written so that the most convenient way to read it is from cover to cover. If you know where you want to go, however, you can choose your own route through the book. In this case, the following hints can help you decide which topics to focus on and the order in which to read them.

A Short Story about Patterns

This book provides an in-depth exploration of the pattern concept. Starting with a popular—yet brief and incomplete—pattern definition, we first motivate, examine, and develop the inherent properties of stand-alone patterns. A solid understanding of what a stand-alone pattern is—and what it is not—helps when applying individual patterns effectively in software development.

We next explore the space 'between' patterns. Patterns are fond of company and can connect to one another through a variety of relationships: they can form alternatives to one another, or natural complements, or define a specific arrangement that is applied wholesale. Patterns can also line up in specific sequences that, when applied, generate and inform the architectures of concrete software systems. Knowing about and understanding the multifaceted relationships that can exist between patterns supports the effective use of a set of patterns in software development.

Finally, we enrich the concept of stand-alone patterns with the various forms of relationships between patterns, to elaborate the notion of pattern languages. Pattern languages weave a set of patterns together to define a generative software development process for designing software for specific applications or technical domain. Pattern languages realize the vision and goal of pattern-based software development that we had in mind when we started the *Pattern-Oriented Software Architecture* series over ten years ago.

All the concepts we explore and develop build on one another. The various types of relationships between patterns take advantage of the properties of stand-alone patterns. Pattern languages further build on and take advantage of the relationships between patterns. Starting with an informal and intuitive characterization of what a pattern is, we progressively mine and elaborate the different properties and facets of the pattern concept, until we have developed a more complete and consistent picture of what patterns are, what they are not, how they can support you when developing software, and how they relate to other software technologies and techniques.

Patterns Viewed from Specific Angles

If you prefer to take a different route through the book—for example to focus on a specific perspective on the pattern concept—we suggest you read the respective parts and chapters in an order that is most interesting or relevant for you. Note, however, that each part of the book, and each chapter within a part, builds on the concepts investigated and developed in the preceding chapters and parts. If you are unfamiliar with a specific aspect referenced in the chapters you are reading, the *Pattern Concept Summary* at the end of the book provides a condensed description of all aspects of the pattern concepts we explore in this book. If you are unfamiliar with any pattern we mention, *Referenced Patterns* at the end of the book cites the sources for each pattern referenced and includes a brief description of it.

All About Patterns from One Source

Since we follow a grass roots approach to investigating the pattern concept, you can read and comprehend the book even if this is your initial exposure to patterns. We also build on and integrate the earlier works on the pattern concept published in the mid to late 1990s: the fundamental concepts and terminology related to patterns for software architectures and designs outlined in *A System of Patterns* [POSA1] and *Design Patterns* [GoF95], and the elaboration of the pattern language concept in Jim Coplien's white paper on *Software Patterns* [Cope96]. If you are familiar with these works you will find what you already know about patterns being reinforced, extended, and—we hope—fulfilled in this book.

0 Beyond the Hype

Use missteps as stepping stones to deeper understanding and greater achievement.

Susan L. Taylor, journalist

This chapter revisits our pattern definition from 1996, which was presented in *A System Of Patterns*, the first volume of the *Pattern-Oriented Software Architecture* series, and subjects it to a careful and thorough examination. Our analysis suggests that some adjustments and enhancements are useful, even necessary, to avoid misconceptions in understanding patterns, and therefore to help prevent the misapplication and misappropriation of patterns in software projects.

0.1   Beginnings...

A key event in the emergence and adoption of patterns within software was the 'birds of a feather' session run by Bruce Anderson at ECOOP in 1990. It was entitled *Towards an Architecture Handbook*, and led to workshops at the next three OOPSLA conferences, where the Gang-of-Four (GoF) first met [GoF95]:

> Our first collective experience in the study of software architecture was at the OOPSLA '91 workshop led by Bruce Anderson. The workshop was dedicated to developing a handbook for software architects. (Judging from this book, we suspect 'architecture encyclopedia' will be a more appropriate name than 'architecture handbook.')

These OOPSLA workshops were also where some of the earliest *Pattern-Oriented Software Architecture* work was presented. The assembly of a handbook or encyclopedia of software architecture is an ambitious project, and one that has inspired many within the patterns community to dig deeply into their experience. Most notably, Grady Booch has done field studies to survey software systems actively in search of sound patterns of practice [Booch].

Enthusiasm for patterns has increased since the release of the seminal work by the Gang-of-Four [GoF95]. Its successors, which include collections of selected patterns from the Pattern Languages of Programming (PLoP) conferences [PLoPD1] [PLoPD2] [PLoPD3] [PLoPD4] [PLoPD5] and the first four volumes from the *Pattern-Oriented Software Architecture* series [POSA1] [POSA2] [POSA3] [POSA4], further kindled the interest in patterns sparked by the Gang-of-Four book and earlier work on software idioms [Cope92] and user-interface patterns [BeCu87].

Ever since the publication of the GoF book in 1994, software developers around the world have embraced this 'new idea,' with the hope that patterns would help them untangle tricky problems into well-knit solutions—something with elegance, directness, and versatility. The pattern concept and many specific patterns found their way into the vocabulary and code of many software development projects, books, and university courses. A movement had begun. It was, and still is, thriving.

0.2   A Story of Success... with Some Exceptions

One reason for the success of patterns is that they constitute a grass roots initiative to build on and draw from the collective experience of skilled software designers. Although each development project is new and distinct in its own way, such projects rarely tackle genuinely new problems that demand truly novel solutions. Developers may sometimes arrive at similar solutions independently, or they often recall a similar problem they once solved successfully in a different situation, reusing its essence and adapting its details to resolve a new problem. Expert architects and developers can draw on a large body of these 'solution schemes' to address design problems that arise when developing new systems and maintaining existing ones.

Distilling commonality from this pairing of application-specific design problems and their solutions leads comfortably to a central theme of the pattern concept: each pattern captures a solution and its relationship to the corresponding problem, framing it in a more readily accessible form. Patterns can teach novices many of the concepts they need to work on projects of modest complexity, helping them to act with greater confidence in selecting appropriate designs and employing suitable practices. Patterns can similarly support experts in the development of more complex software systems, offering them alternative perspectives on familiar problems and enabling them to learn from the experience of other experts. Few other concepts in the world of software development have similar or comparable properties.

Consequently there are many pattern success stories to tell: stories about systems whose architectures and development benefited from being designed and refined consciously and carefully with patterns, including tales from telecommunications [Ris98], business information systems [KC97], industrial automation [BGHS98], warehouse management [Bus03a], network management [KTB98] [Sch98], network protocols [HJE95], communication middleware [SC99], and other industrial-strength systems [BCC+96].

Naturally, the role of patterns, and their successes, extends beyond the realm of software design. Patterns have been mined, championed, and applied explicitly in many other domains, including patterns for introducing change into organizations [MaRi04], patterns for organizational structure [CoHa04], patterns for development practices [Cun96], patterns for teaching [PPP], patterns for configuration management [BeAp02], patterns for security [SFHBS06], patterns for documentation [Rüp03], and even patterns for writing patterns [MD97]! Many diverse examples of patterns and their application have captured and related successful strategies effectively in a domain for others to use.

Under Observation

Alas, success is neither universal nor unconditional. There are also many tales of failure to relate: stories about systems in which patterns were used intentionally and explicitly in design, but whose architectures were penalized by unnecessary and accidental complexity. Consider the following case:

> In a development project a problem arose where some components were dependent on the information provided by another component. Whenever information maintained by the information provider was modified, it was necessary to restore data consistency with the information consumers. The team knew about the OBSERVER pattern, and it seemed like the 'right' solution to the problem—with the information provider as a subject and the information consumers as observers. The team therefore applied the OBSERVER pattern to resolve the problem.

> One information consumer implemented as an observer also served as an information provider for another set of components. The OBSERVER pattern, therefore, could be applied a second time. This, however, raised a 'problem.' The pattern's description in the Gang-of-Four book [GoF95] does not specify a class that is both a subject *and* an observer. How could such a component then be built without 'violating' the pattern?

> The project's solution was to introduce three classes for this component. The first class implemented the component's observer functionality and the second class its subject part. The third class was derived from both these classes via multiple inheritance and provided functionality for coordinating state and computation of its two superclasses.

In other words, in both cases where OBSERVER was applicable, the project team faithfully transliterated the OBSERVER class diagram pictured in the Gang-of-Four book and connected the two island implementations with an additional glue component. A single coherent responsibility had been scattered across three different classes, diluting the cohesion of the design, with downstream development and developers paying the price in decreased comprehension and increased complexity.

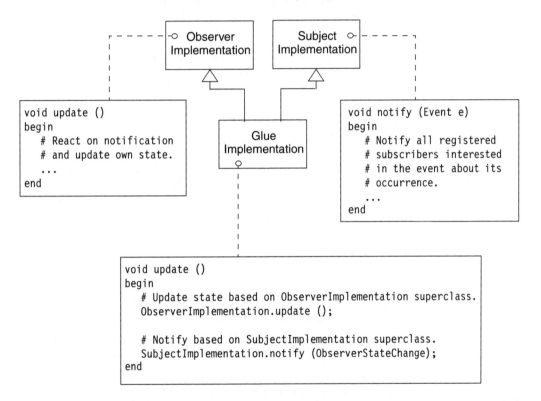

```
void update ()
begin
    # React on notification
    # and update own state.
    ...
end
```

Glue Implementation

```
void notify (Event e)
begin
    # Notify all registered
    # subscribers interested
    # in the event about its
    # occurrence.
    ...
end
```

```
void update ()
begin
    # Update state based on ObserverImplementation superclass.
    ObserverImplementation.update ();

    # Notify based on SubjectImplementation superclass.
    SubjectImplementation.notify (ObserverStateChange);
end
```

A much better solution—and one that the project came up with as a result of design mentoring—is to implement a single class that includes all three roles. This 'integrated' design is much easier to explain and maintain than the 'three class' structure. Moreover, it is still a faithful realization of the OBSERVER pattern, even though it is not an exact reproduction the class diagram in the Gang-of-Four's OBSERVER description [GoF95].

In a State

But of course, the OBSERVER tale is not an isolated case:

> Another development team, recently introduced to UML and Gang-of-Four patterns, found that a number of classes in their system described objects with modal, event-driven behavior. Having initially struggled to represent this vital aspect through sequence diagrams, they recalled the use of statecharts, which greatly simplified the description and communication of the object lifecycles.
>
> The next challenge was to reify such state models in code. Turning to the Gang-of-Four, they came across the STATE pattern. This pattern is the only one in the Gang-of-Four catalog that directly addresses the realization of such stateful behavior, and has a name to match. It is also quite a sophisticated pattern, introducing many new classes into a system and significantly decentralizing the behavior of objects. Following a big up-front design approach, the team chose to implement each object lifecycle they had modeled as a statechart—which ran to quite a few—in terms of the STATE pattern. The result was a class explosion and an increase in the design complexity, with a corresponding decrease in comprehensibility and maintainability.
>
> The indiscriminate use of the STATE pattern arose in part from a misinterpretation of its name—that it was *the* state pattern rather than *a* state pattern—and in part from a desire to pigeonhole all design problems of a particular type with a single solution, namely that all statecharts should be implemented the same way.

A more careful reading of the STATE pattern description reveals that it is better served by its 'also known as' name of OBJECTS FOR STATES— a name that both accurately describes its structure and accommodates the idea of alternative solutions. More profoundly, however, comes the understanding that many design problems are superficially related—for example, the common use of state machines as an abstraction to describe object lifecycles neither requires nor implies a common design approach for all classes so modeled.

No matter how attractive the idea of a one-size-fits-all solution might be, such a supposedly simplifying assumption is simplistic rather than simple. In this case it led to an overall increase in complexity, because a heavyweight pattern was used beyond its scope of applicability.

Sometimes lookup tables or collections of objects are the appropriate solution for managing object lifecycles. At other times the solution can be even simpler, by introducing an extra flag variable or query method. In a few cases, however, the power of the OBJECTS FOR STATES pattern is both appropriate and simplifying.

Beyond Prescription

Part of what makes design *design* is the recognition of alternative competing solutions. Patterns can help make these solutions explicit along with the criteria for their selection—their *forces* and their *consequences*. It is perhaps revealing that one member of the team in the STATE story above expressed disappointment on discovering that there were more than twenty-three patterns available for software development! The hope that the Gang-of-Four had created a potted, packaged, and predigested cure-all was frustrated.

The question remains as to why these and other such episodes take place. Why did so many projects fail to use patterns successfully? Worse yet, why do many projects continue to fail to use patterns successfully despite the wealth of literature and experience gained during the past decade? All these projects hoped, after all, to *benefit* from using patterns. A cynical response would be to point the finger of blame at the whole pattern concept: are patterns really an effective way to capture and communicate design knowledge of any sort? By exploring pattern concepts and examples in detail in this book, we hope to reaffirm that patterns are one of the more effective means for naming, organizing, and reasoning about design knowledge.

A less cynical, but nonetheless pessimistic, response would be to observe that nothing can ever be perfect, therefore mistakes are an inevitable part of any human undertaking. There is a more constructive perspective, however, that both accepts human imperfection and recognizes there is always room for improvement in practice. It appears that many projects that fail to use patterns effectively claim to follow popular pattern definitions explicitly and to the letter, applying the selected patterns as specified in their descriptions. Perhaps there is something missing from or overlooked in the existing definitions of the software pattern concept, or even in the patterns themselves and their content?

0.3   Pattern Definitions and their Interpretations

To seek answers to the previous questions, and to help developers gain a sufficiently complete, realistic, and accurate picture of patterns, it is worth examining some of the more popular pattern definitions, as well as their mainstream interpretations by the software community.

Many recent books on software development include a definition of patterns for software and, if it is not the authors' own, they explicitly discuss or reference a definition coined by someone else. In these books, the common objective of the authors is to introduce the concept of patterns, capturing it as precisely and relevantly as possible for the needs and scope of their work. The following is the definition from *A System of Patterns* [POSA1], the first volume of the *Pattern-Oriented Software Architecture* series:

> A *pattern for software architecture* describes a particular recurring design problem that arises in specific design contexts, and presents a well-proven generic scheme for its solution. The solution scheme is specified by describing its constituent components, their responsibilities and relationships, and the ways in which they collaborate.

Along with this definition, [POSA1] and [Sch95] discuss several properties of patterns for software architecture that we revisit below:

- *Patterns document existing best practices built on tried and tested design experience.* Patterns are not invented or created artificially just to be patterns. Rather they 'distill and provide a means to reuse the design knowledge gained by experienced practitioners,' so that developers familiar with an adequate set of patterns 'can apply them immediately to design problems without having to rediscover them' [GoF95]. If the patterns are implemented appropriately, developers can rely on their effectiveness.

Experience and best practice have traditionally lived in the heads of skilled developers, or they have been encoded, buried deep and reflected within complex system source code. Explicit highlighting of key design strategies and tactics through patterns can help novice developers and new participants ascend the learning curve on a project. It also lets skilled developers share their knowledge more effectively, giving all parties good role models on which to base their work.

- *Patterns identify and specify abstractions that are above the level of single objects, classes, and components.* A particular application component can rarely address a complex problem alone—at least not very effectively or with any semblance of cohesion. The solution parts of most patterns therefore introduce several roles that multiple application components—deployable components, classes, or objects—can take. In addition, these solution parts specify the relationships and collaborations among the roles they introduce. For example, the OBSERVER pattern introduces two main roles, *subject* and *observer*, that cooperate via a push-based change-propagation mechanism to ensure that components can keep their state consistent with one another.

- *Patterns provide a common vocabulary and shared understanding for design concepts.* This vocabulary eases the reuse of architectural knowledge and artifacts, even when reuse of particular algorithms, implementations, interfaces, or detailed designs is not practical or possible. For example, once developers understand the OBSERVER pattern, there is less need for them to have lengthy discussions on how to keep two cooperating components consistent in their system. Instead the dialog can be condensed to something like: 'Well, I introduced OBSERVER here with this object playing the role of the subject and those objects being its observers. Events are sent by callback to observers that registered their interest for these events with the subject, while information about the state of the subject is pulled by the observers from the subject.'

Developers familiar with OBSERVER can readily understand the design in question and draw a sketch similar to the following.

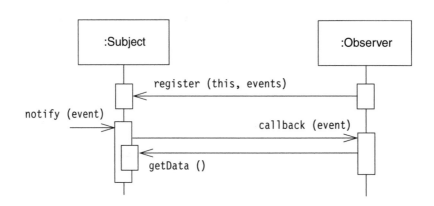

```
void register (Observer subscriber, EventSet events)
begin
    # Register the observer's callback
    # for the event of interest.
    subscribers.add (subscriber, events);
end
```

```
void notify (Event event)
begin
    # For all observers registered for the event
    # notify them via callback.
    for each subscriber in subscribers[event.type]
        subscriber.callback (event);
end
```

```
void callback (Event event)
begin
    # Pull information from the subject
    # and update own state.
    data = subject.getData ();
    myState = ...;
end
```

```
register (this, events)
notify (event)
callback (event)
getData ()
```

As a result, patterns can help to redirect the unproductive pre-occupation with programming language and API zealotry that can often plague a software project. In particular, patterns enable developers from different programming language cultures to share design insights of mutual interest without being distracted by 'language wars.' By way of balance, patterns not only enable communication amongst members from different communities, they also help to refocus the concerns of a particular language community through a recognized body of idiomatic practice. The idioms of C++ are not always useful, benign, or even possible when applied in Java, and vice versa, but they serve to capture knowledge relevant and essential to that community.

Patterns can also help the dialog and transfer of knowledge between different generations of developers and the technologies with which they are most familiar. The code may look different, and the 'acronym soup' may have a different mix, but often there are patterns in common that underpin the old and the new. For example, many patterns that had their origins in the distributed object computing domain, documented, for example, in *Patterns for Concurrent and Networked Objects* [POSA2] and *Server Component Patterns* [VSW02], are still applicable in approaches that have since become popular, such as service-oriented architectures (SOA) [Kaye03] and component models [VSW02]. This transfer of knowledge also occurs with application concepts, not just underlying technology, as evidenced in approaches such as domain-driven design [Evans03].

• *Patterns are a means of documenting software architectures.* With their explicit evaluation of consequences and implementation trade-offs, patterns can be used to track the reasons why specific design choices were selected and others rejected. The practice and path of software development and maintenance can be smoothed and demystified by documenting the intent, structure, and behavior of a piece of software in terms of the patterns found within it [Prec97] [PUS97]. This use of patterns is especially beneficial for product-line architectures [Bosch00] [Coc97]. Developers will struggle to use a product-line architecture correctly and effectively without an understanding of its fundamental structure, control flow, and the mechanisms available for tailoring it toward a specific application, but at the same time they should not be swamped by its implementation details. Similar arguments hold when building an application on top of any software infrastructure, such as communication middleware or GUI frameworks. Pattern-based documentation of an architecture can help to resolve this conflict by allowing developers to focus on key design decisions and their supporting rationale, but avoids getting mired in detail that—although interesting and essential to its creator—does not necessarily help other developers to work with it.

- *Patterns support the construction of software with well-defined properties.* Some patterns define a skeleton of behavior that goes some of the way toward meeting the functional requirements for applications in a particular domain. For example, patterns have been documented for structuring corporate finance and accounting systems [Fow97], telecommunication systems [Ris98], and for improving the capacity of reactive systems [Mes96]. Patterns that have a more architectural focus explicitly address the operational and developmental requirements of software systems, such as resource management [POSA3], security [SFHBS06], performance and scalability [POSA2], and extensibility [GoF95].

- *Patterns capture experience in a form that can be independent of specific project details and constraints, implementation paradigm, and often even programming language.* By abstracting from aspects that can distract from understanding the potential traps and pitfalls in a domain, patterns support developers in the selection of suitable software architectures, designs, and coding principles to address new design challenges in new projects, without wasting time and effort implementing solutions that are known to be inefficient, error-prone, unmaintainable, or simply broken. For example, the patterns documented in the POSA series [POSA1] [POSA2] [POSA3] [POSA4] are described so they can be used to construct almost all types of system: object-oriented or procedural, distributed and concurrent or collocated and sequential, component-based or monolithic, built on top of off-the-shelf middleware or fully hand-crafted.

Other well-known definitions of patterns for software are quite similar to our definition in *A System of Patterns*. For example, the definition given by the Gang-of-Four [GoF95] and those collected from various sources by Brad Appleton [App96] also discuss similar pattern properties. These references capture where we and many others from the pattern community were at the end of the last millennium.

These 'early' definitions served well for introducing patterns to a wide audience, and are still useful today. Developers who participated in projects that applied patterns successfully will probably agree with them and confirm that patterns have the properties we discussed above. Yet these definitions do not seem quite deep enough to ensure a truly shared understanding of patterns. Without wishing to appear overly prescriptive or too formal, there is still too much latitude for misinterpretation and, therefore, misapplication of patterns. In particular, we have observed the following traps and pitfalls repeatedly:

- *Developers may be tempted to recast all their software development activities and artifacts as patterns.* For example, they may document existing algorithms or data structures such as binary searches or linked lists in pattern form. Or, as another example, the so-called 'Java pattern' from *CORBA Design Patterns* [MM97] attempts to recast a discussion of some properties and benefits of the Java platform as a pattern, with the implication that Java is the only solution that can be identified with these properties and benefits. Although this exercise may be intellectually satisfying to the authors, it can be counter-productive if it does not markedly improve key developmental qualities of software development such as communication or comprehensibility, or some operational quality of the software such as efficiency or extensibility.

- *Patterns are not just pieces of neat design.* Developers may be tempted to brand each novel and intricate design—and even each system-specific design decision—as a new pattern of their own invention. Using a pattern form to document these designs is certainly helpful. For example, some of the proposed patterns in *CORBA Design Patterns* [MM97] address general distributed computing techniques, such as the CORBA-CGI GATEWAY, but their definition is very tightly connected to the CORBA context and specification. Other proposed solutions in *CORBA Design Patterns* describe designs that are recurrent but have been shown to be impractical, such as the solution described in the DISTRIBUTED CALLBACK pattern.

Calling such design documentations 'patterns,' however, can give the impression that an application's architecture is based on sound and proven design knowledge, even when it is not. This

impression may in turn prevent other developers from question-
ing the design and implementation decisions made, or from exploring alternatives—patterns are often considered a synonym for quality design, so the design must therefore be good if it is pattern
based, right? Blind trust in any design, whether based explicitly on
patterns or not, is unlikely to ensure that software has the desired
qualities. Solutions therefore require recurrence and generality to
attain the pattern 'brand,' and good patterns are those solutions
that are both recurrent and proven.

- *Developers tend to see patterns as fixed affairs—islands, blueprints,
  or very specific configurations of classes.* Although a formal diagram
  and sample code are often part of a software pattern's description,
  they are not the pattern. As demonstrated by the OBSERVER story
  at the beginning of this chapter, however, the view that the diagram
  is the pattern prevails. This limited view has held many developers
  back from a more reasoned and practical understanding of patterns: adaptation to the specific needs of an application is part of a
  pattern's natural remit. A pattern should be seen as a 'dance of
  interacting parts, pegged down by various sorts of limits' [Bat79].
  Unfortunately, this fluid image is not often conveyed by existing
  pattern definitions.

- *Patterns are not coding guidelines.* Coding guidelines may be put
  together—in part—from patterns focused on code style, but the
  converse is not as faithful a process. Although many coding guidelines are idiomatic, this does not automatically qualify them as patterns. For example, Sun Microsystem's JavaBeans specification
  [Sun97] claimed the consistent use of get and set prefixes for property accessors as 'design patterns.' While these prefixes are 'patterns' in the sense of 'regular-expression pattern matching,' they do
  not solve profound design issues in general design or specifically
  within Java code. There may be pattern here, but it is not the use
  of get and set: it is the use of a consistent naming scheme to establish a protocol in support of a DYNAMIC INVOCATION INTERFACE. The
  chosen protocol was based on get and set prefixes, but could just
  as easily—although perhaps not as intuitively or popularly—have
  been foo and bar suffixes.

- *A limited or misunderstood pattern vocabulary may cause developers to apply the wrong pattern in response to a given problem.* Knowing when a pattern is appropriate for a particular situation requires good judgement: misapplication can yield inappropriate designs and implementations. Similarly, superficial knowledge of a pattern may give developers the impression that they know more about the solution to a problem than they actually do. For example, simply knowing the structure and participants introduced by relatively complex patterns such as PROACTOR and REFLECTION is only a single aspect of effective pattern application. The devil is always in the details, however, and a pattern's essence is reflected in its context and its forces, not just in its structure. The successful realization of a pattern is thus reliant on—and not a replacement for—solid design and implementation skills.

- *Developers may believe that patterns help them to formulate intricate architectures by following a recipe or through mechanical application.* Conscious integration of patterns into software development processes is a human-intensive activity. As with other useful software techniques and tools, the successful application of patterns requires teams with a mix of developers who can draw on both concrete experience in a domain *and* the ability to generalize from myriad implementation details to capture the essential properties of software architectures and components via patterns. Despite the broader geographic net cast by today's 'flat world' of information technology [Fri06], surprisingly few developers today possess both these skills with comparable proficiency.

- *There are software systems whose development can succeed only if its developers explore new ideas.* This need for novelty and exploration is particularly important for systems that 'enter' a new domain that lacks software-based experience. Examples include the first e-commerce applications ever developed and the early software systems for industrial automation. Thinking solely in terms of proven patterns—which, by definition, capture solutions that worked well in the past—might not offer the right toolbox for the new design challenges raised by leading-edge and ground-breaking systems. A narrow, patterns-only focus could therefore actually hinder the success of such projects. Of course, patterns can come into play, but it is likely that they will focus on the support infrastructure, such as patterns for configuration management usage and communication middleware, and on the development process, such as the adoption of an agile process tailored for an R&D lifecycle, rather than patterns for detailed domain-specific design and overall system architecture.

- *Expectations must be managed carefully to prevent patterns from becoming yet another buzzword of ill repute.* Developers and managers often have misconceptions about precisely how and what patterns can contribute to software projects. For example, the use of patterns does not on its own guarantee correct, extensible, and efficient software. Organizations with tight delivery schedules, or those that view software development as a rote uncreative process, often devote inadequate time and developer resources to cultivate the design of their systems or a culture of design. In return, they receive correspondingly limited results when applying patterns, which are—in contrast to their own practice—expressions of *thoughtful* design applied creatively in the appropriate context.

- *The use of patterns cannot be fully tool-based or automated.* Although patterns can contribute significantly to the successful use of generative software technologies, in particular Aspect-Oriented Software Development [KLM+97] and Model-Driven Software Development [Sch06a] [SVC06], their use cannot be fully mechanized [Vö05b]—a hope that both managers and developers often have when talking about patterns and their use in software construction. Both parties often forget that it is humans who are the prime consumers of patterns. By intent, patterns are sketches rather than blueprints. An important part of using a pattern is understanding the problem that it solves, how it solves the problem, and what the trade-offs of the solution are. Only after a problem is *understood* and a suitable pattern for its solution carefully *selected*, can a *specific* implementation of this solution be automated or embodied directly into tools and languages. Put another way: understanding is the bottleneck in software development, not typing source code into a text editor. Automation has an important role to play in development, but not quite in the way that a simplistic automation of patterns would suggest.

The idea that tools can help to recognize patterns in code or models consistently and automatically is also naïve [PK98] [ACGN01] [Pet05]. Some patterns, such as COMPOSITE, certainly have a characteristic look to them, a distinctive signature. Most patterns, however, are more anonymous when stripped of their intent and dynamics: STRATEGY and OBJECTS FOR STATES, for example, share the same class diagram, while in some designs STRATEGY can also be understood as a special case of BRIDGE.

• *Patterns are not components: they are not usable out-of-the-box, commodity items that can just placed into a system in a preplanned way.* Because many software patterns offer a diagram of code components in various roles, there is a temptation to view them as schemas or templates—just fill out the blanks and you are ready to run! The original UML specification is quite clear on its plug-and-play view of patterns [RJB99]:

> A parameterized collaboration that represents a set of parameterized classifiers, relationships, and behavior that can be applied to multiple situations by binding elements from the model (usually classes) to the roles of the pattern. It is a collaboration template.

Although this definition provides patterns with some level of citizenship in the world of UML, it comes at the expense of their freedom. Only by excluding the most essential features of a pattern—the nature of the problem, the rationale for the solution, the consequences of applying the solution—can the pattern concept be shoehorned so tidily into the world of modular parts. In software, parameterization is a useful tool, and it can at times be a convenient metaphor for describing the variability and genericity of patterns. However, metaphor is not identity—'at times' is not 'always' and genericity does not necessarily imply parameterization, since there are other patterns for achieving genericity.

The UML 2 specification moderates the precise (but inaccurate) pattern definition of UML 1 with a broader view that acknowledges a difference in ambition and scope between patterns in the world of UML and software patterns in general:

> A template collaboration that describes the structure of a design pattern. UML patterns are more limited than those used by the design pattern community. In general, design patterns involve many non-structural aspects, such as heuristics for their use and usage trade-offs.

This definition is a step in the right direction, but it is clear that popular methodologies still have a long way to go to reflect a deep understanding of the pattern concept.

- *Pattern-based design is not at odds with—or replaced by—refactoring.* There is a temptation to assume that all identifiable patterns in code must have been applied consciously, that is, put there fully in the knowledge of what pattern was being used and why. Their recurring nature suggests otherwise. Good architects call upon their expertise to produce reasoned designs that are new, yet mature. They will employ patterns, regardless of whether their design thinking is based on subconscious habits or on explicitly documented reasoning.

Refactoring is to software what gardening is to a garden: a continuous process of addition, removal, rearrangement, and reflection. Does a good set of refactorings [FBBOR99] eliminate the need for a pattern vocabulary? After all, refactoring provides a vocabulary for design and a process by which design can be improved, almost unconsciously. What use are patterns if they are not applied directly? Are they simply an expression of *big up-front design*?

To assume that a developer must make an 'either/or' decision between patterns or refactoring is to misunderstand the nature of both patterns and refactoring. Many patterns describe a desired transformation—from problem to solution—but the associated mechanics for performing this transformation are either implied or applicable only when developing new software, while refactorings provide this vehicle for pre-existing code. Sometimes this relationship is quite explicit. For example, the NULL OBJECT pattern describes the 'why' of the idea and the 'how' for green-field design, and the Introduce Null Object refactoring [FBBOR99] describes the 'how' for cultivating brown-field code. The transformation process of a refactoring is often quite specific, mechanical, and code-focused, which allows the automation of many simpler refactorings in modern development environments.

Refactoring describes transformations but does not always describe the resulting structure or its intent. The names of refactorings are always verb phrases, capturing an imperative, whereas pattern names are more often noun phrases, describing a structural solution. For example, although Introduce Null Object clearly contains the resulting design structure in its name, most refactorings tend to be named in terms of programming language features: Extract Method, Extract Class, and Extract Interface result in a method, a class, and an interface respectively, but the notion of an intentional structure is missing. There are many reasons a method, class, or interface may exist, but these structures are not self-describing. The NULL OBJECT pattern, in contrast, describes roles and intention.

When viewed after the fact, a well-factored design is typically pattern-rich. Without recounting the whole story of the system—'And then we had this big class that we split up. And then...'—how else are developers able to talk about the system in richer terms than just its classes and methods? Patterns and refactoring are complementary rather than conflicting [Ker04].

Other software researchers and practitioners report similar misconceptions about the understanding and use of patterns [Vlis98b], and you can probably extend this list with your own observations. The very fact that there are so many misconceptions, misinterpretations, and mistakes, however, suggests that something is often amiss in the popular perception and definitions of the pattern concept. Such misunderstandings inevitably lead to inappropriate application and realization of the patterns themselves. For example, as outlined in the stories from *Section 0.1, Beginnings...*, there are many real-world projects in which developers understand patterns as being specific class diagrams, or fall prey to the 'if your only tool is a hammer then all the world's a nail' syndrome.

0.4 Toward a Deeper Understanding of Patterns

To avoid, or at least minimize, common pattern misconceptions, it seems that some revisiting, discussion, clarification, and revision of the pattern concept is necessary. For example:

• *Current definitions cover only few of the inherent properties of patterns.* These definitions focus typically on the context–problem–solution trichotomy, and often just on problem–solution headlines.

Other pattern properties can find themselves neglected: the role of context, forces, and consequences, the fact that design pattern solutions describe roles for classes rather than complete classes, the genericity of patterns, and so on. Any balanced appreciation of patterns, however, should embrace all such aspects, not just a few.

In addition, as demonstrated nicely by our own definition presented in *Section 0.3, Pattern Definitions and their Interpretations*, the pattern properties that are covered in the definitions are often discussed only briefly and with a strong focus on emphasizing the benefits that can be achieved if patterns are applied correctly and successfully. *How* to apply patterns correctly, and what can happen if they are used incorrectly, is at most superficially addressed. This parsimony, unfortunately, helps neither pattern users nor pattern authors understand the pattern concept itself, or to write patterns with sufficient clarity for general comprehension and use, or to apply patterns productively in their daily work. A sales pitch is not a user guide.

- *Pattern definitions often include inconsistencies.* For example, our pattern definition presented on *page 8* specifies that the solution scheme of a software pattern introduces specific software components. This definition gives the impression that a pattern is actually *composed* of these components. On the following page, however, we emphasized that a pattern introduces roles—not full component specifications—that potentially arbitrary application components can adopt. These inconsistencies lead to misinterpretations, especially if the one-paragraph summary that developers later recall is inaccurate.

- *There are different flavors of the pattern concept.* For example, the pattern concept introduced in the first volume of the *Pattern-Oriented Software Architecture* series [POSA1] and the Gang-of-Four book [GoF95] is engineering-oriented and development-centric. In contrast, Christopher Alexander [Ale79] and Jim Coplien [Cope97] advocate a more holistic, interdisciplinary, and communication-centric approach to patterns. Unfortunately, neither approach serves equally well in addressing *all* the needs of pattern-based software development. For example, some approaches focus on understanding and implementing the details of particular patterns [POSA1], while others concentrate on emphasizing the big picture that pattern languages can provide [Cope97]. There are also off-beat approaches to patterns, such as anti-patterns [BMMM98]. An exploration of the different pattern flavours seems necessary to an understanding of the breadth—not just the depth—of the pattern concept, and to avoiding misconceptions about patterns that follow a particular perspective.

- *Most pattern definitions do not—at least not explicitly—emphasize the many relationships that exist among patterns.* Understanding and using individual patterns as isolated islands without considering their connections to other patterns may help to resolve localized problems, but rarely more. For patterns focused on design, such isolation means that the effect on the big picture is at best limited: large-scale design problems persist, small-scale problems recur without resolution, the architectural vision of a system remains unclear to developers, and acting both globally and effectively with individual patterns becomes hard in the absence of such an all-encompassing vision.

Exploring the types of relationship that can exist between patterns thus not only helps toward a better understanding of the patterns, but also fosters their effective and holistic use in software projects. The pattern compounds, pattern collections, pattern sequences, and pattern languages we describe later in this book offer different ways in which pattern relationships can be used to scale beyond point solutions, to address larger and more sophisticated problem spaces and application domains.

- *Current definitions of the pattern concept often fail to address issues relevant to designing whole software systems using patterns.* The perspective provided by development of a whole system is different than the perspective of parts of a system or individual topics. From a systemic perspective it is hard to address each requirement or aspect of relevance in isolation, because its solution can have an undesirable effect on other properties that must be fulfilled. For example, a design that supports flexibility and changeability requirements often conflicts with requirements for performance and scalability.

Individual patterns cannot resolve this conflict: by definition, a pattern focuses on one specific problem, ignoring its potential relationships with, or impact on, solutions to other problems. Yet being aware of these issues, understanding them, and knowing how to deal with them, is part of effective pattern use. Conceptual support for 'designing with patterns' is needed here, but many current pattern definitions address this topic at best implicitly via case studies, but not explicitly as an integral part of the pattern concept itself.

- *Most definitions of software patterns do not outline the scope of applicability for patterns.* Patterns are no panacea, silver bullets targeting the oft-cited software crisis [Bro86]. Rather, when focused on design or development process, patterns *complement* existing software development techniques and best practices. A solid understanding of what patterns can contribute to software development— and what they cannot—is essential for successful pattern use. It is also important to identify the specific audience for patterns, for example managers versus developers versus testers, and how patterns support—or hinder—the use and adoption of other software development techniques and technologies. This discussion is, unfortunately, missing in most pattern concept definitions.

One way to address the deficiencies of existing pattern definitions is to rewrite and enhance them, to come up with a new and better definition of what patterns are, a definition to end all definitions... for the moment. This is not the goal of this book, however, because we do not think it would be useful to come up with yet another definition. We would prefer to contribute to the ongoing discussion about the characteristics of patterns.

The first part of the book, *Inside Patterns*, therefore reflects on what we have learned over time from using, teaching, reading, discovering, and writing patterns. We start by trying to provide a detailed and consistent picture of what individual patterns are, particularly those that relate to software architecture, and relate the different flavors of pattern concept to one another. Using this picture, the second part of the book, *Between Patterns*, explores the relationships that can exist between patterns and presents various organizational viewpoints on the pattern space. The knowledge of the various pattern relationships gives us the foundation to provide conceptual support for designing with patterns, which we combine in the notion of pattern languages in the third part of the book, *Into Pattern Languages*. Throughout the book we scope the pattern concept with respect to its target audience, applicability, and relationships to other software technologies.

Our explorations of the pattern concept both capture our experiences with patterns over many years and tell a story about patterns and pattern languages, from their finer details to their broader application. This tale will hopefully contribute more to your understanding of patterns than a single formal definition ever could.

I Inside Patterns

Glass mosaic in an old monastery in Latvia
© Mai Skou Nielssen

In the first part of the book we focus on stand-alone patterns, so that we can present and discuss the insights into describing and applying patterns that we have gained over the decade since writing *A System of Patterns* and related pattern works. These insights complement existing discussions and definitions of patterns, helping us to understand patterns at a deeper level that reflects the maturation of the field.

Stand-alone patterns are perhaps the most widespread and most successful flavor of the pattern concept in the software community. Moreover, the majority of all software patterns documented in the body of literature 'stand alone.' To support a better understanding of stand-alone patterns, we therefore investigate this concept in depth, taking three perspectives: concept, implementation, and documentation.

- *Chapter 1, A Solution to a Problem and More*, explores the conceptual aspects of stand-alone patterns. We start with an explanation of the fundamental structure of a pattern and discuss key considerations regarding the quality of its proposed solution. We then address the role and importance of forces, context, and the genericity of a pattern's solution, and end with reflections on the use of diagrams, the naming of patterns, and their maturation over time.

- *Chapter 2, A Million Different Implementations*, explores the tension between the generality of stand-alone design patterns at the conceptual level and the more specific nature of particular pattern implementations. In doing so, we also contrast pattern implementations with generic implementations, reference implementations, and example implementations, and examine the role of design patterns in frameworks, product families and product-line architecture approaches, aspect-oriented software development, model-driven software development, and other software technologies.

- *Chapter 3, Notes on Pattern Form*, presents and discusses forms for describing patterns. A concrete pattern form provides the vehicle for communicating the essence and practicalities of a pattern. A focus on form is therefore as important to pattern readers as it is to pattern writers.

Our explorations of stand-alone patterns, however, are not limited to our own understanding of software patterns. To ensure that our characterization is more complete, faithful, and up-to-date, we also capture, summarize, and relate commonly accepted insights that the software community has gained from the experience and hindsight of applying patterns in many projects for over a decade. Our goal is to paint as complete and coherent a picture as we can of what stand-alone patterns are and are not, to enable their successful use in software projects. The notion of stand-alone patterns is also the foundation for other aspects of the pattern concept—from pattern complements, through pattern compounds, pattern stories, and pattern sequences, to pattern languages.

Although the specific focus of our investigations is on design patterns, most of our considerations, reflections, observations, and statements address stand-alone patterns in general and are not limited to a specific type of pattern.

1 A Solution to a Problem and More

Philosophy, if it cannot answer so many questions as we could wish, has at least the power of asking questions which increase the interest of the world, and show the strangeness and wonder lying just below the surface even in the commonest things of daily life.

Bertrand Russell

In this chapter we take a simple problem–solution pairing and use gradual and reasoned steps to expand and refine it into a description that more obviously qualifies as a pattern description. En route we examine the different facets that a pattern embodies and that its description should contain. Our incremental approach also illustrates the iterative nature of pattern writing. The use of feedback, reflection, growth, and refinement is a normal part of the pattern-writing process, not simply an artifact of how we have chosen to illustrate the facets that comprise a sound pattern description.

1.1   A Solution to a Problem

If asked for a one-sentence characterization of what a pattern is, many pattern-aware software developers might respond with something like:

> 'A pattern is a solution to a problem that arises
> within a specific context.'

This seems a fair summary at first glance. It is certainly not a false one, although it may not cover the whole truth. The truth of the summary is supported by looking around at the common patterns in use today: they provide working, concrete, and adaptable solutions to problems that repeatedly arise in certain situations during software development, from organizational to programming contexts. The summary is also a good fit with most popular pattern definitions.

An Example

A pattern is more, however, than just this soundbite! If it were sufficient, the following would have all that was needed when presenting a pattern:

Context: A client needs to perform actions on an aggregate data structure.

Problem: The client may need to retrieve or update multiple elements in a collection. If the access to the aggregate is expensive, however, accessing it separately for each element over a loop can incur severe performance penalties, such as round-trip time, blocking delay, or context-switching overhead. How can bulk accesses on an aggregate object be performed efficiently and without interruption?

Solution: Define a single method that performs the access on the aggregate repeatedly. Instead of accessing aggregate elements individually and directly from within a loop, the client invokes the method to access multiple elements in a single call.

This description is obviously a solution to a problem that arises within a specific context. But is it, as presented, a pattern in the profound sense in which the term is often applied?

Recurrence and Goodness

It is not simply enough for a solution to a problem to exist to consider a reasoned design for it a pattern. It must recur—which is, after all, the motivation behind the use of the word 'pattern,' as any dictionary will attest. In almost all cases in which the term 'pattern' is used in the context of software design, there is an underlying assumption that we are talking about 'good' patterns—that is, patterns that are complete, balanced, and clearly described, and that help to establish some kind of wholeness and quality in a design. This assumption is so common that the word 'good' is almost always dropped: the word 'pattern' effectively subsumes it.

If a pattern, however, represents a commonly recurring design story— one that varies a little with each retelling—there are not just good stories to tell. Some recurring practices are incomplete, unbalanced, and fail to establish a recognizable wholeness and quality. What they lack in goodness they often make up for in popularity—in spite of usage to the contrary, 'common practice' and 'best practice' are not synonyms [Gab96].

Some patterns have recurrence but not quality. These are 'bad patterns,' a phrasing used by Christopher Alexander in his original framing of patterns [Ale79] and the motivation for identifying 'good patterns.' 'Bad patterns' are dysfunctional, often twisting designs out of shape, leading to a cycle of 'solving the solution,' in which the ingenuity of developers is consumed in fixing the fixes (to the fixes to the fixes...).

In identifying and separating good patterns from dysfunctional patterns or nonpatterns, we first need to distinguish between solution ideas that recur and those that are singular, and so tightly bound to their application that whatever their merits as specific designs, they cannot be considered general patterns. We could say that each recurring solution theme qualifies as a 'candidate pattern.'

We also need more than just the idea of recurrence in a pattern to make it a useful part of our development vocabulary. We need to know that its application is beneficial rather than neutral or malignant—a pattern with no effect or ill effect. Before hastily branding 'dysfunctional' any candidate pattern that fails to contribute successfully to a design, however, we must also be able to distinguish between patterns that are truly dysfunctional and patterns that have simply been misapplied—in other words, dysfunctional applications of otherwise sound patterns. To assess these qualities reasonably we need to render our candidate pattern in some form that makes them visible. A pattern description must be clear and must make it possible to see the qualities of the pattern—a poor pattern description can obscure a good pattern, selling it short, whereas a good 'spin' can mask a poor pattern, overselling it [Cool98].

Looking back at our original example above, we can see that it qualifies as a 'candidate pattern,' but that those additional qualities of interest are still not quite visible in its current form. Until we can be confident of the pattern's viability and the ability of our documentation to convey that, we should consider it a 'proto-pattern.' So what is missing from our proto-pattern description that might confirm its candidacy as a good pattern?

1.2   A Process and a Thing

When analyzing the content of our example proto-pattern, perhaps the most glaring deficiency is the vagueness of its solution part: it describes a process for creating a solution, but does not suggest what concrete solution to create. Although a pattern can be realized a 'million different ways,' [Ale79] this diversity arises from the precise detail of an actual problem and its context, not from the vagueness of a proposed solution structure. A pattern should inform its reader how to build a solution in a way that is loose enough to be general, but tight enough to avoid vagueness and accidental ambiguity.

Many solution implementations are possible for our example proto-pattern: all could be said to follow its solution process, but few could be said to follow the spirit of the pattern's message. For example, one valid implementation would be to define a method in the client that contained the loop. This design would be a simple refactoring within the client code, extracting one method from another, but having no effect whatsoever on the issues highlighted in the problem statement.

Another valid implementation would be to define a single method on the aggregate object and have it return each individual result to the client by callback, in the style of a push notification. Such an implementation, however, would not be very practical, presenting more of a problem than a solution in its costly accumulation of round-trip time. It might follow the letter of the proposed solution, but it would not follow its spirit. For the original problem there are many known (and better) solution paths: it is the job of the pattern description to document its chosen route with accuracy and precision.

The solution part of a good pattern describes both a *process and a thing*: the 'thing' is created by the 'process' [Ale79]. For most software patterns, 'thing' means a particular high-level design outline or description of code detail. There is an important distinction between this understanding of the term 'process' and the idea of 'process' as a full-lifecycle prescription of software development. The popular and traditional notion of software development process targets the development of a whole system, from its inception to its deployment. It is ambitious in scale, general in nature, alone in its application.

An individual pattern, by contrast, is focused on solving a single specific problem. It is unambitious but determined, with well-defined boundaries and a generality that arises from depth rather than breadth. On a project, an individual pattern will enjoy the company of other patterns rather than sit on its own. A pattern might be considered a microprocess—or even nanoprocess—against the backdrop of a full-lifecycle software development process.

An Example (Take 2)

Our proto-pattern's original solution part is missing the concrete 'thing' to build. We can revise that paragraph to arrive at a second version:

> Define a single method that performs access on the aggregate repeatedly. This method is defined as part of the interface of the aggregate object. It is declared to take all the arguments for each execution of the action, for example via an array or a collection, and to return results by similar means. Instead of accessing aggregate elements individually and directly from within a loop, the client invokes the method to access multiple elements in a single call.

This second solution version is much clearer than the original one: we now know *what* concrete solution to build to resolve the given problem, not just *how* to build this solution.

1.3   Best of Breed

Now that our revised solution statement gives us a better idea of what to build, we can more clearly see the mismatch between what is described as a problem and what is proposed as a solution. Although the recommendation is to encapsulate all repeated accesses of an aggregate object in a single method, the problem statement says the following:

> The client may need to retrieve or update multiple elements in a collection. If the access to the aggregate is expensive, however, accessing it separately for each element over a loop can incur severe performance penalties, such as round-trip time, blocking delay, or context-switching overhead. How can bulk accesses on an aggregate object be performed efficiently and without interruption?

This statement does *not* say that there is only one form of access or action on the aggregate object. Rather it refers to bulk accesses in general, of which retrieval and update are obvious and representative examples. If we implement the second solution version, however, we would find that all bulk accesses would be channeled through a single method. We would have to include some additional parameter or parameters to accommodate the variation in the actions that might be performed against the aggregate object. This method would be weakly cohesive, supporting a superset interface for any data that might flow to and from the aggregate, and some kind of selector to indicate which action was required. Such a method would be tedious and error-prone to use and maintain.

SINGLETON is an example of a well-known pattern with a weak solution. Its original intent is to 'ensure a class only has one instance, and provide a global point of access to it' [GoF95]. The solution proposed to resolve this problem is to disallow creation of an instance of a class via its constructor. Instead, the pattern introduces a *globally* accessible method that creates and returns a new instance of the class on demand: if a class-level static reference to a singleton instance is null, a new instance is created and returned, otherwise the reference to the existing singleton instance is returned.

The problem with this solution is the use of a single global access point to an object, which is considered poor practice in modern programming, whether in enterprise or embedded systems, since it tightly couples code that uses the singleton class to a particular context, inappropriately hardwiring the architecture to a set of potentially unstable assumptions. Consequently, a number of issues arise when dealing with SINGLETON, including (but not limited to):

• How to make a SINGLETON thread-safe?

• How to customize SINGLETON behavior?

• How to dispose of or exchange a SINGLETON instance?

• How to unit-test code dependent on a SINGLETON?

The literature, such as [Vlis98b] [BuHe03] [POSA2], that discusses these issues dwarfs the page count of the original pattern description in the Gang-of-Four book! Working around or fine tuning SINGLETON appears to be as popular a sport as introducing it into a system. Deconstructing the SINGLETON pattern, therefore, suggests that it may introduce more problems than it resolves—a fact that Kent Beck summarized nicely [Beck03]: 'How do you provide global variables in languages without global variables? Don't. Your programs will thank you for taking the time to think about design instead.'

In practice a useful pattern should therefore not propose just any solution for the problem it is addressing. Instead, it should present a robust solution that resolves the problem optimally. The solution in a *good* pattern, moreover, needs to have a proven track record. Quality patterns do not represent neat ideas that *might* work, but concepts that have been applied repeatedly and successfully in the past—this recurrence is what makes a pattern a pattern, and the track record is what demonstrates its quality.

The Gang-of-Four puts it this way: 'Patterns distill and provide a means to reuse the design knowledge gained by experienced practitioners' [GoF95]. Brian Foote put it even more succinctly: 'Patterns are an aggressive disregard of originality' [PLoPD3]. Consequently, new ideas must first prove their worth in the line of active duty—often many times—before they can truly be called patterns.

An Example (Take 3)

Another revision of our proto-pattern solution provides us with a third version—which has the quality we expect from a 'good' pattern:

> For a given action, define a single method that performs the action on the aggregate repeatedly. This method is defined as part of the interface of the aggregate object. It is declared to take all the arguments for each execution of the action, for example via an array or a collection, and to return results by similar means. Instead of accessing aggregate elements individually and directly from within a loop, the client invokes the method to access multiple elements in a single call.

> Each method folds repetition into a data structure rather than a loop within the client, so that looping is performed before or after the method call, in preparation or follow-up. Consequently, the cost of access to the aggregate is reduced to a single access, or a few 'chunked' accesses. In distributed systems this 'compression' can significantly improve performance, incur fewer network errors, and save precious bandwidth.

> The trade-off in complexity is that each method performs significantly more housekeeping to set up and work with the results of the call. This solution also requires more intermediate data structures to pass arguments and receive results. The higher the costs for networking, concurrency, and other per-call housekeeping, however, the more affordable this overhead becomes.

This third version better resolves the original problem, avoiding the problems identified for the second version.

1.4   Forces: the Heart of Every Pattern

The previous discussion reveals that the problem addressed by our proto-pattern is not as easy to resolve as it might first appear. The pure problem cannot be considered in isolation. There are also a number of requirements on its solution—for example, that it should be bandwidth-friendly. It is hard—if not impossible—to derive such requirements from the simple problem statement, however. Yet to achieve the desired quality of implementation, the problem's solution needs to address them.

If, on the other hand, such requirements were added to the proto-pattern's problem statement, they would become explicit, and a concrete solution for the problem could deal with them appropriately. The same argument holds for any desired property that the solution should provide. Similarly, there may be some constraints that limit the solution space for the problem, or just some things worth taking into account when resolving it. These requirements, desired properties, constraints, and other facts fundamentally shape every given problem's concrete solution. The pattern community calls these influencing factors *forces*, a term taken from Christopher Alexander's early pattern work [Ale79].

Forces tell us why the problem that a pattern is addressing is actually a problem, why it is subtle or hard, and why it requires an 'intelligent'—perhaps even counter-intuitive—solution. Forces are also the key to understanding why the problem's solution is as it is, as opposed to something else. Finally, forces help prevent misapplications of a pattern in situations for which it is not practical [Bus03a].

For example, much of the confusion about SINGLETON could have been avoided if the original description [GoF95] had listed a force like 'The property of having only one instance of class is a property of the *type* being represented, such as a class that realizes a stateful API to a specific piece of hardware in a system, and not simply an incidental property of an *application* that uses only a single instance of a class.' SINGLETON would still have a place in the pattern space, but not the broad and overbearing dominion it has now—which is a root cause for the trouble this pattern can cause [Ada79].

An Example (Take 4)

To motivate the concrete solution proposed by our proto-pattern, we therefore add the following four forces [Hearsay01] to its description:

An aggregate object shared between clients in a concurrent environment, whether locally multithreaded or distributed, is capable of encapsulating synchronization for individual method calls but not for multiple calls, such as a call repeated by a loop.

The overhead of blocking, synchronization, and thread management must be added to the costs for each access across threads or processes. Similarly, any other per-call housekeeping code, such as authorization, can further reduce performance.

Where an aggregate object is remote from its client, each access incurs further latency and jitter, and decreases available network bandwidth.

Distributed systems are subject to partial failure, in which a client may still be live after a server has died. Remote access during iteration introduces a potential point of failure for each loop execution, which exposes the client to the problem of dealing with the consequences of partial traversal, such as an incomplete snapshot of state or an incompletely applied set of updates.

A quick check reveals that the third version of the solution statement already satisfies the first three forces, either directly or as a by-product of the proposed design. In particular, synchronization is isolated to a single method call rather than across many, the concurrency cost is reduced by replacing multiple calls with a single call, and the remote access cost is reduced by replacing multiple calls with a single call. The fourth force is not yet addressed by this third solution version, however, since the result of a failed call could yield a partial update or an incomplete query. We noticed this deficiency only because we thought hard about the forces and made them explicit. We also noticed that we can afford to make some other consequences more explicit.

These considerations lead to a fourth version of the solution:

For a given action, define a single method that performs the action on the aggregate repeatedly.

This method is defined as part of the interface of the aggregate object. It is declared to take all the arguments for each execution of the action, for example via an array or a collection, and to return results by similar means. Instead of accessing aggregate elements individually and directly from within a loop, the client invokes the method to access multiple elements in a single call.

Each method folds repetition into a data structure rather than a loop within the client, so that looping is performed before or after the method call, in preparation or follow-up. Consequently, the cost of access to the aggregate is reduced to a single access, or a few 'chunked' accesses. In distributed systems this 'compression' can significantly improve performance, incur fewer network errors, and save precious bandwidth.

Each access to the aggregate becomes more expensive but the overall cost for bulk accesses has been reduced. Such accesses can also be synchronized as appropriate within the method call. Each call can be made effectively transactional, either succeeding or failing completely, but never partially.

The trade-off in complexity is that each method performs significantly more housekeeping to set up and work with the results of the call. This solution also requires more intermediate data structures to pass arguments and receive results. The higher the costs for networking, concurrency, and other per-call housekeeping, however, the more affordable this overhead becomes.

Now all four forces are resolved and the resulting solution is stronger. Even though the second and third force were addressed together, it is still important to list them as separate forces: they are different and they are independent. Network bandwidth is the not the same kind of resource or consideration as context switching cost: the communication cost may vary independently from platform processing power. This variability underscores the importance of listing all forces explicitly, even if at first glance they appear superfluous.

Unfortunately it might not always be possible to resolve all forces completely in a solution: forces are likely to contradict and conflict with one another. A particular force may address an aspect that can only be resolved at the expense of the solution's quality in respect to aspects addressed by other forces. For example, efficiency can often be achieved only by giving up flexibility, and vice versa. In such cases a solution must *balance* the forces, so that each is resolved sufficiently, if not completely, to meet the requirements sufficiently.

Dysfunctional, Bad, or Anti?

Having discussed forces, we now are in a position to revisit and clarify some distinctions in terminology. Christopher Alexander favored characterizing recurring problematic approaches as *bad* patterns [Ale79], whereas our emphasis has been to characterize them as *dysfunctional* patterns. You may also have come across the term *anti-patterns*, which also sounds applicable.

The term 'anti-pattern' has quite a sensational ring to it, since it sets up some kind of contrast or conflict. It is not immediately clear, however, what the term entails. In looking at other words that follow the 'anti-' pattern, there are a number of possibilities. For example, in the manner of antibiotics and antidotes, perhaps they are a cure for someone with 'patternitis'—a term often used to describe someone who has become too carried away in their use of patterns.

Perhaps anti-patterns provide a cosmic balance for patterns, canceling them out in some dramatic way, as matter and antimatter do on contact? Perhaps they are simply against patterns, in the manner of many political 'anti-' slogans, or they are a way of bringing them down, in the manner of anti-aircraft devices? Perhaps they precede a deeper understanding of patterns, as antipasto precedes a main course? Perhaps they offer only a disappointing conclusion, an anti-climax? Jim Coplien [Cope95] offers the following clarification:

> *Anti-patterns* are literature written in pattern form to encode practices that don't work or that are destructive. Anti-patterns were independently pioneered by Sam Adams, Andrew Koenig [Koe95], and the writer. Many anti-patterns document the rationalizations used by inexpert decision makers in the Forces section. [...]

> Anti-patterns don't provide a resolution of forces as patterns do, and they are dangerous as teaching tools: good pedagogy builds on positive examples that students can remember, rather than negative examples. Anti-patterns might be good diagnostic tools to understand system problems.

This description was written before the first *Antipatterns* book [BMMM98] popularized the term. In that book the notion of anti-pattern is at times ambiguous: sometimes *anti-pattern* refers to a recurring problem situation—a failing solution—that results from misapplied design practices. At other times *anti-pattern* also appears to include a solution response to these problem situations.

The former definition appears closer to the medical metaphor of diagnoses [Par94] [EGKM+01] [Mar02a] [Mar02b] [Mar03], identifying a problem situation through its symptoms and root causes. The latter approach also appears to fit this metaphor, with a proposed remedy and prognosis, but it also fits the basic pattern concept: the failing solution is the problem and the cure is the solution. In this latter form there appears nothing special—let alone 'anti'—about so-called anti-patterns as solutions to problems. The ambiguity lingers, however, which motivates the need for a clearer, less affected term for discussing recurring, problematic approaches.

The definition provided by Jim Coplien seems both the most useful and the most cautionary. Labeling the problem of unresolved forces with an 'anti' is a little ambivalent and does not properly communicate the problematic nature of such recurring solution attempts. By contrast, the term 'bad patterns' pulls no punches. As a characterization, however, partitioning designs into 'good' and 'bad' can seem a little simplistic or even sententious. This kind of value judgment may be meaningful for an individual, but does not necessarily encourage open and balanced discussion with others.

With patterns we seek to communicate and understand, so drawing on a more neutral vocabulary seems prudent. For this reason, we favor characterizing successful solutions that address the forces in a problem adequately as 'whole' and those that do not as 'dysfunctional' [Hen03a]. The former term entails balance and completeness—whole as opposed to half-done or half-baked—whereas the latter suggests that a design is impaired in some way and may undermine the stability of a larger whole.

1.5   The Context: Part of a Pattern or Not?

Now that the forces supplement the problem statement, and the solution for the problem is adjusted accordingly, we can turn our attention to the context part of the proto-pattern:

> A client needs to perform actions on an aggregate data structure.

This is a fairly general context. It probably gives rise to a number of different problems, not just to the one that the example proto-pattern addresses. In fact, it is so general that little is lost if it is dropped completely.

The context plays an important role in a pattern, however, since it defines the situation to which it applies. The more precisely this situation is described, the less likely it is that developers will use the pattern inappropriately. Ideally, the context should describe only the particular situation that can lead to the problem for which the pattern specifies a solution.

A context that is too broad, in contrast, will run the risk of making a pattern a jack-of-all-trades but a master of none. One example of such a pattern is BRIDGE, whose original intent in [GoF95] is: 'Decouple an abstraction from its implementation so that the two can vary independently.' Many designs can benefit from this level of indirection, ranging from making implementation bindings more flexible to writing C++ code with strong exception-safety guarantees [BuHe03].

Each of the many possible problems addressed by BRIDGE, however, has its own context, such as 'we are creating a component whose implementation must be exchangeable at runtime' or 'we are implementing a C++ application that must be exception-safe.' These differences result in corresponding differences in the forces associated with the problem and also differences in the concrete solutions proposed to resolve them. Remember, a pattern is often cast as a solution to a problem that arises in a specific context—which is the (incomplete) 'definition' for patterns from the beginning of this chapter. Consequently, lacking a precise context, a pattern can become all things to all people, with each having their own different—and often incompatible—view [BuHe03].

An Example (Take 5)

To sharpen the context of our proto-pattern, we merge the first two sentences of its problem statement—which already provides some context information—with the original context, and also add information about the design activity and the corresponding application's usage that lets the problem arise:

> In a distributed system, the client of an aggregate data structure may need to perform bulk actions on the aggregate. For example, the client may need to retrieve all the elements in a collection that have specific properties. If the access to the aggregate is expensive, however, because it is remote from the client, accessing it separately for each element over a loop can incur severe performance penalties.

This context is much more precise in describing the situation in which the problem arises. The context tells us where our proto-pattern may be applicable and, by implication, where it may not be applicable. Based on an understanding of the context, the developer can actively decide *not* to introduce the design. For example, if the aggregate object is not remote from the client, an alternative approach may be preferable, such as one of the solutions that we mentioned before modifying the original solution for the first time (see *page 32*). In this particular case, the proto-pattern's current solution idea for minimizing execution overhead would be like 'shooting mosquitoes with a machine gun.'

Moving information from the problem to the context statement requires rephrasing the remaining part of the problem description so that it becomes meaningful again:

> How can bulk accesses on an aggregate object be performed efficiently and without interruption if access is costly and subject to failure?

As a side effect of removing context information from the problem statement, the 'real' problem shines through more clearly. It is briefer and crisper, and we understand more directly that this is a problem.

Context Generality

Narrowing the generality of the original context has the benefit of being more precise... but it also has a drawback. There may be other situations in which the problem addressed by the example proto-pattern can arise, and where the same solution helps to resolve the problem. Consider, for example, the following context:

> In an application with a custom, in-memory database of complex—as opposed to relational—objects, separate key-based searches for individual objects are possible but potentially a bottleneck when performed repeatedly. However, certain well-defined actions, each of which returns a result, must frequently be performed on all objects in the database that satisfy a specified search criterion.

Knowing that there may be even more such situations gives rise to a challenge: how can we ensure the context's completeness? An overly general context that acts as an umbrella for many possible problem situations may be too vague, leading to inappropriate applications of a pattern. On one hand, too much detail will probably yield an unreadable pattern prefixed by an exhaustive 'laundry list' of specific context statements. On the other, an overly restrictive context may prevent developers from applying a pattern in other situations in which it is also applicable. They may take the pattern only as written and fail to grasp the opportunity for generalization it implies.

One way of coping with this problem is to start with a context that describes the known situations in which a pattern is useful, and to update this context whenever a new appropriate situation is found. The context section would then look and feel similar to the *Applicability* section of the Gang-of-Four pattern description form [GoF95], where the Gang-of-Four listed all the specific situations in which they knew the pattern could be and had been applied.

Another way to resolve this problem is to follow the approach taken in the second volume of the *Pattern-Oriented Software Architecture* series, *Patterns for Concurrent and Networked Objects* [POSA2]. There the focus of the context statements was narrowed to the theme of the book: concurrency and networking. Each pattern's context addressed situations related only to these topics, and the patterns' applicability in other situations was addressed in a separate chapter.

A narrow approach to contexts works well if a collection of patterns is centered around a common theme: the context attached to each pattern is lean, so readers can readily identify applicability in a particular domain. Other situations in which the patterns may help are not stressed, although they are not forgotten. The patterns benefit from being focused, narrowed with respect to context, rather than trying to be all things to all people.

Unfortunately, neither approach truly resolves the context-completeness problem: overlooking a situation in which a pattern is applicable is quite likely. As a result, the overly general contexts in *A System of Patterns* and this section's example proto-pattern, the split contexts in *Patterns for Concurrent and Networked Objects*, and the applicability section of the Gang-of-Four patterns [GoF95] do not work very well. On the other hand, the two latter approaches seem more practical than a general and possibly vague context. It is better to support the appropriate application of a pattern in a few specific situations than to address the possible application of a pattern everywhere—a jack of all trades, but a master of none.

Context Detached

A completely different approach is to consider the context as *not* being a part of an individual pattern at all. We have already shown that multiple contexts are possible for the example proto-pattern, but there is only one problem and one solution statement. Another possible perspective is that contexts are needed only for describing pattern languages, where they are used to specify how the languages integrate their constituent patterns. In other words, the contexts define a network of patterns—the pattern language—but the nodes—the individual patterns—are independent of the network, hence they are context free. Consequently, the context-completeness problem appears not to arise. If there are multiple pattern languages in which a pattern is useful or needed, each will provide its own context for the pattern.

While this extrinsic approach seems tidy, it gives rise to another problem. If a pattern does not characterize the situation in which a problem occurs, how can the pattern be said to honestly characterize the nature of the problem and its scope? Problems are not context-free modular parts that can simply be plugged into any context. Context is not simply glue: there is the implication of fit, not simply adhesion, between context and problem. Thus characterization of a problem implies characterization of the context.

To some extent the question of context is a question of perspective. From the perspective of an individual pattern it is important to know the situations in which it can be applied successfully. The question of how a pattern is integrated with other patterns is useful, but less important. So the context is probably part of a pattern, which, unfortunately, allows the context-completeness problem to arise.

From a pattern language perspective it is necessary to know how the language's constituent patterns connect. It is not necessary to know which other pattern languages also include a particular pattern. The context is therefore only needed to define a specific pattern language, not to properly describe a particular pattern and the many situations to which the pattern applies. Under this characterization, therefore, the context-completeness problem appears to go into remission. This simplification, however, comes at the expense of limiting the scope of applicability of the underlying pattern. This tension and interplay between the general and the specific is an enduring and (appropriately) recurring theme in our exploration of the pattern concept.

This chapter is about stand-alone patterns, not pattern languages, so it takes the patterns-eye view: some or all of the context is part of a pattern. This view also corresponds to the majority of the software patterns, which stand alone and are not yet organized into pattern languages. We will return to the question of context in later chapters that focus on more than stand-alone patterns.

An Example (Take 6)

We can revise the context of our proto-pattern such that it captures and characterizes the known situations in which it applies and which are of interest—in this case systems with an element of multithreading, distribution, or both:

> In a distributed or concurrent system, the client of an aggregate data structure may need to perform bulk actions on the aggregate. For example, the client may need to retrieve all elements in a collection that have specific properties. If the access to the aggregate is expensive, however, because it is remote from the client or

shared between multiple threads, accessing it separately for each
element over a loop can incur severe performance penalties, such
as round-trip time, blocking delay, or context-switching overhead.

Independent of the 'context-completeness question,' the proto-pattern
has improved once again. Developers can get a good picture of the situations in which it may be applied, even if the new context does not
enumerate all possible situations.

1.6 Genericity

With the revised context, problem, and solution sections described
above, the example proto-pattern looks much more like a useful and
beneficial pattern than the version with which we started. We are still
not done, however. Although the solution section is quite specific with
respect to its use of objects and methods, this might not be our intention. In particular, is the essence of the pattern solution being overly
constrained? Is the solution offered at the same level as the problem
to be solved?

Specific problems with object structure should be addressed using the
tools and concepts of object orientation. A problem expressed more
generally, however, should not suddenly be shackled to an object-
oriented frame of reference. Conversely, patterns that deal with programming language specifics in the problem must also articulate their
solutions at that level—anything more general will appear vague and
imprecise. In general, patterns are as independent or dependent on a
particular implementation technology as is necessary to convey their
essence. For example, the problem our proto-pattern addresses can
arise in procedural code, not just in object-oriented code. It is possible
to express the solution for this problem in the context of objects and
methods, plain functions, wire-level protocols, or even overseas parcel
delivery. These alternatives do not violate the solution's core principle.[9]

---

9. Even patterns that seem to depend on a specific implementation paradigm, for example object technology, often do not: PROXY, for example, loses little of its essence by
giving up inheritance, while STRATEGY can be implemented in C by using function
pointers instead of object-level polymorphism.

If the problem addressed by a pattern requires the presence or the use of a specific technology or paradigm, this dependency should be stated explicitly. If not, a conscious decision should be taken as to whether narrowing the description in this way benefits the intended audience. Otherwise the pattern should not depend on the technology or paradigm, to avoid overly constraining its applicability and implementation options.

An Example (Take 7)

Let us assume that our goal was to provide an object-oriented solution for our problem. This aspect can be 'fixed' either by adding another force to the proto-pattern's description, if the use of object technology is a requirement for resolving the problem, or by extending its context, if using object technology is a precondition in our situation. We decide on the latter and change the first and last sentences of the context statement:

> In a distributed or concurrent object system, the client of an aggregate object may need to perform bulk actions on the aggregate. For example, the client may need to retrieve all elements in a collection that have specific properties. If the access to the aggregate is expensive, however, because it is remote from the client or shared between multiple threads, accessing it separately for each element over a loop—whether by index, by key, or by ITERATOR— can incur severe performance penalties, such as round-trip time, blocking delay, or context-switching overhead.

These changes may not be the best way to indicate that object technology should be used to resolve the problem addressed by our example proto-pattern, but at least the assumption is now explicit and the wording more precise. This discussion also leads us to another consideration: the aggregate object's interface. Consider the second sentence of the current solution section:

> Each method is defined as part of the interface of the aggregate object.

What does this imply about the aggregate object? Does it mean that whatever interface is used to declare its capabilities must include a declaration for the new method? Or are other schemes possible? For example, a separate EXPLICIT INTERFACE that offers just the iteration capability can be defined and used as a commodity to specify the same capability in other object types, allowing the uniform treatment of many different aggregate types via a common type.

And what of the aggregate's implementation? The proto-pattern currently has nothing to say on the matter. It may be that the aggregate's class implements the new method directly. It is also feasible, however, that the underlying aggregate mechanism is left untouched and an OBJECT ADAPTER is used instead, adapting the mismatched interfaces of a distribution-friendly model and an in-process implementation.

A generic problem resolution does not necessarily introduce specific classes, components, or subsystems. Instead, it introduces *roles* [RWL96] [Rie98] [RG98] [RBGM00] that particular components of the system must adopt to resolve the original problem well. A role defines a specific responsibility within a system, and includes interaction with other roles.

Although separating the implementations of different roles is recommended, encapsulation in separate, distinct components is neither required nor implied. A single component may take on multiple roles. Roles can be assigned to existing components or they can be expressed in new components. If necessary, developers can introduce role-specific interfaces for components, so that clients see only the roles they need.

Roles are key to the seamless and optimal integration of a pattern into an existing software architecture, and for combining multiple patterns in larger-scale designs. We therefore revise the proto-pattern's solution part once again, producing a new version:

> For a given action, define a single method that performs the action on the aggregate repeatedly.

> Each method is defined as part of the interface of the aggregate object, either directly as part of the EXPLICIT INTERFACE exported for the whole aggregate type, or as part of a narrower, mix-in EXPLICIT INTERFACE that only defines the capability for invoking the repeated action. The method is declared to take all the arguments for each execution of the action, for example via an array or a collection, and to return results by similar means. Instead of accessing aggregate elements individually and directly from within a loop, the client invokes the method to access multiple elements in a

single call. The method may be implemented directly by the aggregate object's underlying class, or indirectly via an OBJECT ADAPTER, leaving the aggregate object's class unaffected.

[...]

Now developers can declare the method for accessing the aggregate as part of an existing interface or in an interface of its own and, similarly, implement the method as part of an existing class or in a class of its own. The roles within the proto-pattern are stable but accommodate variation in implementation.

The solution part of a pattern should therefore state explicitly which particular roles must be implemented in their own components. For all other roles it introduces, a pattern should not prescribe an implementation that unnecessarily restricts the solution's genericity.

The latest solution version still describes how to construct a structure that resolves the original problem. With roles, however, there are many more implementation choices available for the solution. Roles thus contribute significantly to the genericity of a pattern— much more than a strict class approach can ever do. Roles also make it easier to adapt a pattern's core idea to the needs of a concrete application. Unnecessary complexity and indirection levels can be avoided, which leads to simpler, more flexible, and more effective pattern implementations.

1.7 A Diagram Says More than a Thousand Words... or Less

Now that the latest solution version provides more of the qualities we expect from a whole pattern, it is worth spending some time discussing a pattern's solution part more generally. Abstracting from its concrete look-and-feel, the solution part of a software pattern commonly specifies a design structure consisting of roles that are connected through various relationships. The structure is completed by some behavior that 'happens' in this structure.

The solution part of a code-centric pattern typically offers a code fragment in which designated elements of a programming language are arranged in a specific way, together with this code's behavior.

For organizational patterns, the solution part introduces a particular organizational structure, roles in this structure, their responsibilities, and the communication between the roles. Speaking most generally, a pattern is often said to define a spatial configuration of elements that exposes or enables particular dynamics.

To complement the textual description of their solution part, many patterns therefore include diagrams that illustrate and summarize this configuration of elements, the interactions within this configuration, and, if relevant, its evolution over time. These diagrams can help communicate the essence and detail of a pattern. They provide a graphical description of that pattern's 'big picture.' A diagram often says more than a thousand (and twenty-four)[10] words.

Diagrammability and Patterns

It has been suggested that the capability of providing such a diagram is a fundamental property of patterns. However, there are software concepts, such as very specific design and implementation decisions taken for very specific systems, for which it is also possible to provide an illustrating diagram, that are not patterns. A concept in software must fulfill many more properties before it can be called a pattern. The flip side of 'if you can't draw a diagram of it, it isn't a pattern' [Ale79] is that even if you can draw a diagram of it, it is not necessarily a pattern. The ability to draw a diagram may appear necessary for something to be a pattern, but it is certainly not sufficient.

A diagram may therefore be helpful to a pattern's readership, but we should be cautious in stating that diagrammability is a key identifying property of patterns. Humans are versatile and imaginative, which means that in practice it is possible to express any concept in human experience, no matter how abstract, through some form of diagram. It is true that a diagram of a particularly abstract concept may not convey its meaning effectively to all observers, but it is also true that not only is the diagrammability of something not sufficient for patternhood, it fails to distinguish a pattern from anything else that may be conceived, experienced, invented, or otherwise formed.

---

10. Trygve Reenskaug, ROOTS 2001 conference, Norway.

Perhaps a more useful distinction is to emphasize that the concept in question must be a designed artifact, as opposed to something occurring in nature, and that a diagram must be based on the design's spatial configuration. Of course this does not uniquely distinguish patterns from other design concepts, but as a way of thinking about diagramming it is perhaps a more useful path to take.

For example, it is certainly possible to create diagrams that illustrate fundamental design principles like 'separation of concerns' and 'encapsulation,' but such diagrams will tend to be general and abstract, and thus hard to communicate and discuss. When applied in a specific design, however, these principles come to life and are more tangible by developers. For example, our proto-pattern *encapsulates* the iteration over elements of an aggregate object within the data structure that is returned when accessing these elements:

> [...] Instead of accessing aggregate elements individually and directly from within a loop, the client invokes the method to access multiple elements in a single call. [...]

A diagram that illustrates this specific case of encapsulation is easier to understand, communicate, and discuss—and thus of more value in the context of a concrete design than a diagram that illustrates encapsulation in general.

Even the path of showing a concrete design, however, is not without its own pitfalls and pratfalls. The notion of space—and hence 'spatial'—in the aphysical and invisible domain of software is more about metaphor than matter [Hen03b]. It is a subtle but significant distinction, but one that should be kept in mind when carrying ideas from physical engineering and architectural disciplines to aphysical ones, such as software development. With the exception of software artifacts such as user interfaces, spatial concepts in software design derive from constructed visualizations that are the result of choice, as opposed to being a given. Consequently, a different choice of mapping can create a different notion of space. It is possible, therefore, to make a poor design look good through simple cosmetics and a flattering choice of abstractions, and a good design look poor by not paying enough attention to the choice and detail of visualization.

In advocating diagrams for patterns, it may be more useful to consider diagramming a matter of taste, form, and presentation than as something deeper. With this sensibility in mind, we can provide the following diagram for our proto-pattern.

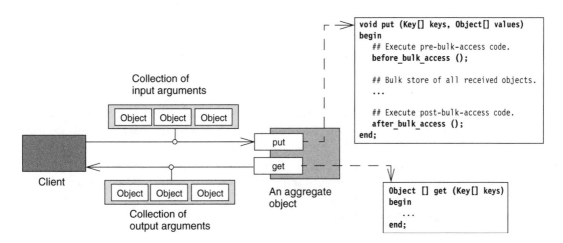

This diagram intentionally does not follow popular modeling notations such as UML [BRJ98]. The reason for this is simple: a formal (UML) structure diagram is too often interpreted as the *one and only* true solution for a given problem. In the context of patterns, however, it is not the only solution! A pattern is generic, it defines roles, not classes, and so there can be many ways to implement it. A formal diagram, on the other hand, can often depict only one particular of the many possible configurations and interactions of these roles, or only one of their many possible evolution paths.

In addition, the more formal a diagram is, the more tempting it is to implement the pattern as specified in the diagram, because it appears to represent a standardized reference solution that is reusable wholesale and without adaptation in every situation to which the pattern is applicable. The OBSERVER story from *Chapter 0* illustrates this misconception nicely. The less formal a pattern diagram is, in contrast, the more developers are forced to think how to implement the pattern in their own systems, or how to specify its implementation in the design notation they use. Thinking is the essence of design, not (rote) automation.

If developers think in roles, however, and interpret any diagram as just an illustration of one of many possible concrete solution structures for resolving a particular problem, the specific notation selected becomes less important. When thinking in roles it may even be beneficial to follow known notations to illustrate the solution, because everybody is familiar with them. In much of the *Pattern-Oriented Software Architecture* series we assume that readers are familiar with the basics of the pattern concept and know that pattern participants denote roles, at least after reading the introduction to patterns in *A System of Patterns* [POSA1].

It was in exercising this matter of choice, therefore, that OMT and UML diagrams were favored over informal sketches [POSA1] [POSA2] [POSA3]. But this choice was made in context, and does not mean the same decision applies in all cases. For example, in *A Pattern Language of Distributed Computing* [POSA4] a less formalized, made-up notation is used to illustrate pattern structure. This 'Bizarro'[11] notation is also used here to illustrate our pattern-in-progress.

1.8   Evocative Names Help Pattern Recollection

To be used successfully, a pattern description must at least provide a clear and sound solution to a recurring problem that is well-presented through prose and pictures, as discussed above. But if we want to use patterns in our designs and implementations effectively, we must also be able to identify and reference each individual pattern quickly and unambiguously. In addition, even if we do not have particular pattern descriptions or their structure diagrams to hand, we still need a way of talking about these patterns and the designs in which they occur. In other words, we must be able to remember a pattern, otherwise it

---

11. The chunky and blocky appearance is reminiscent of the cubic Bizarro world, Htrae, home of Bizarro, a character from DC Comics' Superman series. Bizarro logic is also slightly inverted and different, giving Bizarro modeling a distinctly different feel to UML: where UML documents models different aspects through a multitude of diagrams, Bizarro notation uses only a single diagram that integrates multiple aspects. Where UML is formalized, Bizarro notation is more ad hoc: where UML is a marketable skill, mastery of Bizarro notation confers no career advantage (except on Htrae).

cannot become a word in our design vocabulary. A pattern that cannot be remembered is less likely to be recalled in practice, regardless of its other qualities.

Every pattern therefore needs a name. This name should be evocative [MD97]. Ideally, if someone references a pattern by its name, anyone familiar with it should be able to recall it from that cue alone. This familiarity is not always easy to achieve. Cute and obtuse names that are meaningful only to a handful of people, such as the clique of the pattern writer, are not necessarily meaningful to others. Recalling that a pattern is a vehicle for communication, a poorly named pattern offers poor transportation. Patterns are most memorable if their names conjure up clear images that convey the essence of their solutions to the target audience [MD97].

A Grammatical Classification of Names

Grammatically, two 'types' of names are used commonly in pattern naming:

- Noun-phrase names describe the result created by a pattern. For example, ACTIVE OBJECT and COMMAND PROCESSOR. Noun-phrase names typically describe the solution structure of the pattern, and in some cases may explicitly enumerate the key roles, for example, MODEL-VIEW-CONTROLLER or FORWARDER-RECEIVER.

- Verb-phrase names are imperative, giving an instruction that describes how to achieve a pattern's desired solution state. For example, the ENGAGE CUSTOMERS organizational pattern and the INVOLVE EVERYONE pattern for organizational change are both examples of verb-phrase names, as is DON'T FLIP THE BOZO BIT, which is one of the more colorful cliches of effective software leadership and interpersonal dynamics within groups.

Noun-phrase names are more common than verb-phrase names, and are normally preferred. Noun phrases highlight the structural nature of the solution and can be used most easily as part of an ordinary sentence. In considering patterns as being both 'a process and a thing,' noun-phrase names emphasize the 'thing,' whereas verb-phrase names emphasize the 'process.'

Literal Versus Metaphorical Names

The style of a name is also important. In conjuring up images of a pattern's essence there is a continuum with two contrasting extremes—*literal names* and *metaphorical names*:

- Literal names are direct descriptions of patterns that use terminology in its primary sense, rather than in a metaphorical way. For example, EXPLICIT INTERFACE and ITERATOR are literal names.

- Metaphorical names create associations between a pattern and another concept, such as one from everyday life, with which readers are hopefully familiar. VISITOR, OBSERVER, and BROKER are examples of metaphorical names.

Given the abstract nature of software development, many terms are based on metaphors to begin with—sockets, files, windows, and so on—so from a different point of view, some literal names may be considered metaphorical. Many names are therefore part literal and part metaphorical, for example, RESOURCE LIFECYCLE MANAGER.

Which type of name works best is often subject to personal preference. For example, REPEATING METHOD would be a literal noun-phrase name for our proto-pattern and BOXCAR METHOD a metaphorical noun-phrase name. Both names capture the essence of the pattern's solution equally well. We favored a third name, BATCH METHOD, which has elements of both naming styles. We could have chosen a name that was both literal and a verb phrase, but it is often hard to phrase short and crisp instructions that capture a pattern's essence precisely. For example, EXPRESS EACH FORM OF REPEATED ACCESS AS A LOOP-ENCAPSULATING METHOD is an instruction that captures the fundamental idea of our proto-pattern, but it is far too verbose to be a handy and evocative pattern name. Inconvenience is also not a good property of a transport medium.

1.9 Patterns are Works in Progress

After a long and scenic journey, we have finally arrived at the following description of the proto-pattern:

Batch Method

In a distributed or concurrent object system, the client of an aggregate object may need to perform bulk actions on the aggregate. For example, the client may need to retrieve all elements in a collection that have specific properties. If the access to the aggregate is expensive, however, because it is remote from the client or shared between multiple threads, accessing it separately for each element over a loop—whether by index, by key, or by ITERATOR—can incur severe performance penalties, such as round-trip time, blocking delay, or context-switching overhead.

How can bulk accesses on an aggregate object be performed efficiently and without interruption if access is costly and subject to failure?

Four forces must be considered when resolving this problem:

- An aggregate object shared between clients in a concurrent environment, whether multithreaded locally or distributed across a network, is capable of encapsulating synchronization for individual method calls but not for multiple calls, such as a call repeated by a loop.

- The overhead of blocking, synchronization, and thread management must be added to the costs for each access across threads or processes. Similarly, any other per-call housekeeping code, such as authorization, can further reduce performance.

- Where an aggregate object is remote from its client, each access incurs further latency and jitter and decreases available network bandwidth.

- Distributed systems are subject to partial failure, in which a client may still be live after a server has died. Remote access during iteration introduces a potential point of failure for each loop execution, which exposes the client to the problem of dealing with the consequences of partial traversal, such as an incomplete snapshot of state or an incompletely applied set of updates.

For a given action, therefore, define a single method that performs the action on the aggregate repeatedly.

Each BATCH METHOD is defined as part of the interface of the aggregate object, either directly as part of the EXPLICIT INTERFACE exported for the whole aggregate type, or as part of a narrower, mix-in EXPLICIT INTERFACE that only defines the capability for invoking the repeated action. The BATCH METHOD is declared to take all the arguments for each execution of the action, for example via an array or a collection, and to return results by similar means. Instead of accessing aggregate elements individually and directly from within a loop, the client invokes the BATCH METHOD to access multiple elements in a single call. The BATCH METHOD may be implemented directly by the aggregate object's underlying class, or indirectly via an OBJECT ADAPTER, leaving the aggregate object's class unaffected.

A BATCH METHOD folds repetition into a data structure rather than a loop within the client, so that looping is performed before or after the method call, in preparation or follow-up. Consequently, the cost of access to the aggregate is reduced to a single access, or a few 'chunked' accesses. In distributed systems this 'compression' can significantly improve performance, incur fewer network errors, and save precious bandwidth.

By using a BATCH METHOD, each access to the aggregate becomes more expensive, but the overall cost for bulk accesses has been reduced. Such accesses can also be synchronized as appropriate within the method call. Each call can be made effectively transactional, either succeeding or failing completely, but never partially.

The trade-off in complexity is that a BATCH METHOD performs significantly more housekeeping to set up and work with the results of the call, and requires more intermediate data structures for passing arguments and receiving results. The higher the costs for networking, concurrency, and other per-call housekeeping, however, the more affordable this overhead becomes.

There is a marked difference between this version to the one with which we started: all the features that make up a good pattern description are now present. We have an evocative pattern name, a concrete and precise context, a crisply phrased problem statement, an explicit description of all forces that inform any viable solution, and an appropriate solution that resolves the problem and its forces well.

The latest solution description consists of a specific role-based structure that includes static and dynamic considerations, as appropriate, and a process to create this structure. It is also possible to draw one or more illustrative diagrams. The solution is concrete but also generic: it can be implemented in multiple ways that still preserve its essence and are recognizably the same pattern. Both the original and the final versions meet the 'a pattern is a solution to a problem that arises within a specific context' definition, but there are worlds between them. The latter can be considered a good pattern description, the former cannot.

Just as most useful software evolves over time as it matures, many useful pattern descriptions evolve over time as they mature. This maturity results primarily from the deeper experience gained when applying patterns in new and interesting ways. For example, the ABSTRACT FACTORY pattern evolved from the version in the Gang-of-Four book [GoF95], which allows only object creation, to a version that offers both object creation and object disposal [Hen02b] [Bus03a]. The later versions balance the aspects and forces of object lifetime management better than the original version.

Similarly, the original description of the BROKER pattern in *A System of Patterns* [POSA1] has been revised three times. The first revision was in *Remoting Patterns* [VKZ04], which decomposed the broker role of the original POSA1 version into several smaller, more specialized roles. This version was then revised a second time to use the original POSA pattern format and elaborate the implementation details of the revised structure [KVSJ04]. The third revision of BROKER, which is described in *A Pattern Language for Distributed Computing* [POSA4], extends the second and third version by integrating it with even more patterns that help implement BROKER-based communication middleware. All three revisions reflect a better understanding of the pattern itself, as well as its integration with the growing number of patterns that can be combined into a pattern sequence or language to implement it. But three need not be the number of the counting: as John Vlissides observes, 'The deliberations herein should convince you, in case you need convincing, that a pattern is never, *ever* finished.'

Sisyphus the Pattern Writer

We could try to improve our BATCH METHOD pattern further. For example, we could revise the context to cover even more situations in which the pattern applies, such as dealing with access to local, in-memory complex data structures (a situation that we discussed as an alternative context on *page 44*, but did not integrate into the pattern's context description). The fact that the solution uses object orientation could be expressed as a force rather than as a prerequisite in the pattern's context. We could also extend its description with known uses, such as examples of production software systems that have used this pattern successfully, and comparisons with related patterns, such as ITERATOR.

In other words, improving a pattern is an open-ended process. The pattern community therefore considers every pattern as a *work in progress*, subject to continuous revision, enhancement, refinement, completion, and sometimes even complete rewriting. Only this perspective allows a pattern to evolve and mature, as the various versions of our example pattern demonstrate. Just compare the patterns from the *Pattern-Oriented Software Architecture* series with their early versions published in the PLoPD series to see how they evolved over time.

Unfortunately, considering patterns as works in progress is a time-intensive process that demands a great amount of effort. This is one reason why there are many more pattern users than pattern authors, and why so many patterns do not escape their place of origin. On the other hand, the return on investment of this time and effort is the reward of the feedback that you receive from the software community and your own increased understanding of the patterns.

For example, if you take the time to discover and document useful patterns, developers may choose to employ the patterns you describe into new systems, or they may recognize them in existing systems. Spreading the word on specific good practices raises the level of design. Diving into the patterns to document them can only increase your knowledge, such that casual familiarity with a design solution is replaced by deep understanding.

1.10 A Pattern Tells a Story and Initiates a Dialog

Despite the fact that the 'final' version of our pattern is still a work in progress, the improvement is sufficient—and the length still short enough—that it does not need explicit section headings to guide the reader. The pattern still reads well enough that readers are carried naturally from one logical part to the next. This progression is another property of a good pattern: *it tells a story*—albeit a short one. More precisely, in the context that most interests us, it is a 'successful software engineering story,' to borrow an observation from Erich Gamma.

Bob Hanmer [CoHa97] takes Erich's observation further, describing how the pattern's name is the story's title, the context is the story's setting, the problem statement is its theme, the forces develop a conflict that is hard to resolve, and the solution is the story's catharsis: the new resulting context and the situation with the solution in place is the concluding 'and they all lived happily ever after.' As we will see in the rest of this book, however, there is often the prospect of a sequel.

A pattern, however, does not just tell a story. It also *initiates a dialog* with its readers about how to resolve a particular problem well: by addressing the forces that can influence the problem's solution, by describing different feasible solutions, and finally by discussing the trade-offs of each solution option. A pattern invites its readers to reflect on the problem being presented: its nature, the factors to be considered when resolving it, its various solutions, and which solutions are most feasible within the readers' own context.

On first reading, a pattern encourages people to think first and then to decide and act, explicitly and consciously, rather than blindly follow a set of predefined instructions. They receive guidance, but all activities they perform are under their own control. This difference allows the pattern to become part of the readers' design knowledge: over time experience becomes expertise that is applied intuitively rather than dogmatically.

1.11 A Pattern Celebrates Human Intelligence

Although the seeds of a solution may be found in a careful statement of the problem, the transition and transformation from one to the other is not always trivial or direct. Patterns are not automatic derivations from problem ingredients to fully-baked solutions. Patterns often tackle problems in more lateral ways that can be indirect, unusual, and even counter-intuitive.

In contrast to the implied handle-turning nature of many rigid development methods or model-driven tools, patterns are founded in human ingenuity and experience. Although a pattern's forces constrain the set of possible, viable solutions, these constraints are not so rigid as to ensure only a single outcome that can be captured as an automated transformation. In contrast, the constraints that bind a refactoring are strict and easily formalized: a refactoring alters the structure of code in a limited way so as to preserve its functional behavior.

In our example pattern the avoidance of the common ITERATOR pattern or even a humble subscripting index to perform iteration may be considered odd by many developers accustomed to thinking of these as the ordinary means for expressing iteration over an aggregate object's contents. ITERATOR has become the commonplace means for expressing iteration decoupled from a collection's representation in many mainstream languages, so much so that it has almost gone from being 'pattern' to 'default.'

What interrupts this tidy, uniform view of iteration design is the context of distribution, where the principle of minimizing the number of remote calls disturbs the peace. Little tweaks to the basic ITERATOR model do not work and a quite different solution is needed, one based on another line of reasoning.

1.12 From a Problem–Solution Statement to a Pattern

It is now easier to see that a pattern is much more than just a solution to a problem that arises within a specific context. On the other hand, this does not mean that this context–problem–solution triad is inappropriate for capturing patterns. It is an important form for describing patterns succinctly, as well as a denotation for every pattern's main structural property. It does not, however, specify how to distinguish a true pattern from an 'ordinary' solution to a problem. The context–problem–solution trichotomy is necessary for a specific concept to be a pattern, but it is not sufficient.

In case the intent of this chapter is misread, it is also worth clarifying that just improving a description does not automatically convert any given solution to a problem into a pattern. Patterns cannot be word-smithed into existence. Only if a problem–solution pair *has* the other properties we discussed above can it be considered a good or whole pattern. The original example was just poorly expressed, but all the players were there or waiting in the wings, so stepwise refinement and piecemeal addition was possible. If a specific solution to a problem is lacking any of a true pattern's anatomical necessities, it is probably just *a* solution to a problem, and most probably a specific design and implementation decision for a specific system—but not a pattern.

2 A Million Different Implementations

Don't fight forces, use them.

R. Buckminster Fuller

This chapter explores the tension between the generality of patterns and the more specific nature of particular pattern implementations. In doing so, we examine the role of software patterns in frameworks and the contrast with generic implementations, reference implementations, and examples.

2.1   Does One Size Fit All?

An important conclusion from *Chapter 1* is that a pattern provides a *generic* solution for a recurring problem: a solution that can be implemented in many ways without necessarily being 'twice the same' [Cool98]. We discussed in depth what this means from the perspective of the pattern concept. Specifying what patterns are, however, is just one side of the coin. Developing software with patterns is the other. The following is a code's-eye perspective on the conclusion outlined above:

> Each software pattern implementation must consider requirements that may be unique for the concrete context in which it is applied. Any specific implementation of that pattern may therefore be different from other implementations. Unless the variations in the requirements—and consequently those in the solution—can be constrained, enumerated, and matched, it will not be possible to create these different implementations simply by configuring a common generic implementation. Yet any assumption that the requirement space be bounded and limited would be unrealistic.

> Requirements come from the context of concrete applications. If their variations were constrained and enumerated, the possible variations in the applications and their implementation technologies would be limited. While this is possible—and even suitable for well-defined subsets of application—it is not the general case. By definition, therefore, realizing the best fit for a pattern by configuring a single generic implementation is generally not a viable strategy.

This is quite a strong statement! But can it be justified? To seek an answer, we attempt to take the opposite position. We will propose the hypothesis that it is possible to provide *configurable generic*[12] *implementations* for patterns that cover their whole design space, and try to develop one for a concrete example. Let's see where this hypothesis takes us using the OBSERVER pattern as our case study!

---

12. To clarify, 'generic' here means 'non-specific' and 'general' and should not be confused with the specific (sic) use of the term in the context of *generic programming*, which is an approach to program composition based on extracting commonality of particular algorithm-centred data-structure usage into library components.

Observer: a Quick Recap

The OBSERVER pattern is familiar to many developers. It is widely used in frameworks and is also featured in one of our case studies of pattern misapplication in *Chapter 0*. Here is a brief summary of the pattern to clarify what problem and solution are brought together and which roles are introduced:

> Objects sometimes depend on the state of, or data maintained by, another provider object. If the state of the provider object changes without notice, however, the state of the dependent objects can become inconsistent.

> Therefore, define a change propagation mechanism in which the provider, known as the *subject*, notifies registered dependents, known as *observers*, whenever its state changes, so that the notified observers can perform whatever actions they deem necessary.

The following diagram captures a sketch of a typical OBSERVER implementation:

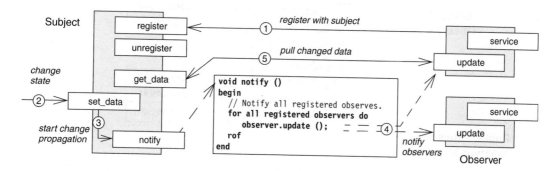

Structural Variation and Roles

The first challenge that arises when trying to develop an all-encompassing generic implementation of a software pattern is that patterns introduce *roles* for components, as opposed to just introducing components, as discussed in *Chapter 1*. Depending on how we arrange OBSERVER'S two main roles—the *subject* and the *observer*—we therefore derive distinct, alternative OBSERVER arrangements. For example, we could assign the role of the subject either to an existing class of the application or to a new class. The same is true for the observer role. In some situations both roles may even be combined within a single class: a class may be an observer in one relationship, and a subject in another.

An observer may receive events from a single subject or from multiple subjects. Similarly, a subject may be observed by a single observer or multiple observers. These relationships can be expressed by implementing the appropriate form of observer registration explicitly in the interface of the subject, and by including or excluding knowledge of the subject in the observer. Alternatively, by implementing OBSERVER using PUBLISHER-SUBSCRIBER middleware, we can decouple the subject completely from its observers. PUBLISHER-SUBSCRIBER middleware can also reside on different computing nodes than the subject(s) and their observer(s), thereby supporting distributed event notification.

The following class diagrams outline a 'classic' OBSERVER structure and an OBSERVER structure using PUBLISHER-SUBSCRIBER middleware.

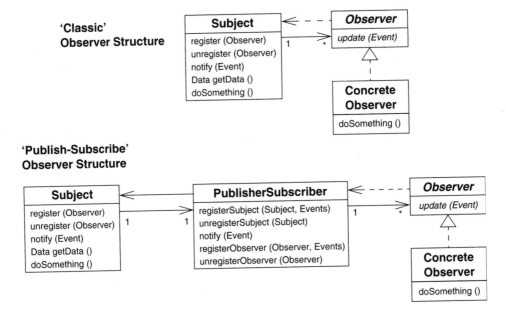

The alternative approaches outlined above result in quite different concrete OBSERVER structures, with different assignments of roles to classes, and also with different types of classes. Even within this relatively narrow range of structural variation, therefore, the goal of a general generic implementation is already moving further away rather than closer. Although a generic implementation is not impossible from this perspective, it certainly appears less trivial.

Behavioral Variation

Variation is not restricted to structural alternatives, however, since the behavioral aspects of OBSERVER can also vary. For example, the implementation of the pattern's state propagation mechanism can follow either the push or the pull model for exchanging any type of state information between the subject and its observers. This state information is either passed with the notification callback (the push model) or the observer must call the subject explicitly following notification (the pull model). Yet another option is to implement state-specific propagation mechanisms, in which specific state information is pushed or pulled rather than any and all state information.

The two sequence diagrams below outline the data pull and data push interaction models for a 'classic' OBSERVER arrangement.

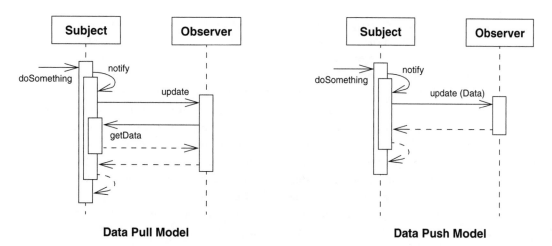

Data Pull Model   **Data Push Model**

Other behavioral variabilities center on support for a range of different quality of service properties. For example, some PUBLISHER-SUBSCRIBER infrastructures forward events to observers in the order they are received, whereas others use the relative importance of the different observers to prioritize the order in which the events are forwarded [HLS97]. Similarly, some implementations of OBSERVER notify all registered observers, whereas others support filtering and correlation operations that only notify specific subsets of observers for specific events [CRW01].

Behavioral aspects can vary independently of the concrete OBSERVER structure and can also be realized differently in different structural variants of the OBSERVER pattern. For example, the event-specific information-pull model is implemented differently in a 'traditional' OBSERVER [GoF95] structure than when implemented using PUBLISHER-SUBSCRIBER middleware. In the former case the subject notifies observers directly, in the latter there is an indirection via a publisher-subscriber infrastructure. Again, the notion of a generic implementation is stretched between truly distinct and competing designs. This tension is particularly acute if the implementation must cover all feasible structural and behavioral variants of OBSERVER *and* be optimized for the particular time and space constraints of specific application domains and runtime platforms.

Internal Variation

Since core implementation aspects can also vary, we are not yet done with the potential variations in a pattern's realization. In the OBSERVER pattern, for example, the subject often uses a collection to maintain references to all registered observer objects. There are many types of collections, such as maps, sets, bags, and sequences. There are also many specific implementation types to choose from, for example hash tables, trees, arrays, and lists. These collection types differ in their interfaces and their performance for specific operations, such as constant versus logarithmic versus linear-time operations. They also differ in their resource usage, such as contiguous memory versus linked nodes, and their organizational principle, such as by positional index versus by key. Which of these collection types is the most suitable cannot be decided meaningfully and independently of the context in which OBSERVER is employed.

Another core implementation aspect that can vary is error handling. What happens if an observer that registers with the subject cannot be inserted into the collection? Perhaps the maximum number of observers is fixed and the limit has already been reached. Perhaps the collection has set—rather than multiset—semantics and already holds that observer. Perhaps the system is running low on memory in a resource-constrained environment. Is the collection responsible for dealing with such situations? Or perhaps the subject? Or is it the party that tries to register the observer? Or is it simply somebody else's problem [Ada82]?

A similar discussion can occur for ITERATORS, which are often used to traverse the observer references maintained in the collection. Should they support referential integrity, so that iterators do not unknowingly refer to elements that are no longer held in the collection? What happens if an observer that is currently referenced by an iterator is unregistered from the subject and considered garbage? As before, a single answer to this question cannot be given sensibly in advance. It is the application- and runtime-specific context surrounding the OBSERVER pattern that finally determines the best path through the possible design options.

This discussion already suggests that any two implementations of a pattern can differ in fundamental ways, even with the three very conservative variations that we have introduced: structure, behavior, and core implementation. Yet the rapidly growing complexity foreshadows quite a challenge for designers of generic implementations and their users.

Language and Platform Variation

So far we have not even mentioned programming language or other technology-specific issues. For example, a generic implementation of OBSERVER for .NET is not directly suitable for other platforms or non-.NET languages. A C# implementation, for example, even when transliterated into another language, is unlikely to be the best or even a good idiomatic fit. Appropriate idioms do not translate well, or even make sense, when taken from C# into C++ or Ruby, and vice versa. In other words, these implementations cannot be universally generic: at best they might aspire to be generic within the context of a given language and a particular runtime platform. The same holds for an implementation of OBSERVER using Aspect-Oriented Programming (AOP) [KLM+97]. The two roles of this pattern, subject and observer, can quite reasonably be considered as cross-cutting concerns in the classes that participate in a concrete OBSERVER arrangement [HaKi02]. The following code fragment outlines an AspectJ realization of the observer protocol [HaKi02]:

```
public abstract aspect ObserverProtocol {
    protected interface Subject {}
    protected interface Observer {}
    private WeakHashMap perSubjectObservers;

    protected List getObservers(Subject s) {
        if(perSubjectObservers == null) {
            perSubjectObservers = new WeakHashMap();
        }
        List observers = (List) perSubjectObservers.get(s);
        if(observers == null) {
            observers = new LinkedList();
            perSubjectObservers.put(s, observers);
        }
        return observers;
    }

    public void addObserver(Subject s, Observer o) {...}
    public void removeObserver(Subject s, Observer o) {...}

    abstract protected pointcut
        subjectChange(Subject s);

    after(Subject s): subjectChange(s) {
        Iterator iter = getObservers(s).iterator();
        while (iter.hasNext()) {
            updateObserver(s, (Observer) iter.next());
        }
    }

    abstract protected void
        updateObserver(Subject s, Observer o);
}
```

Implementing the subject and observer roles as aspects separates the OBSERVER code from application-level code that embodies these roles. This solution, however, is no more generic when compared to a direct realization of OBSERVER, since the corresponding application classes use the 'main' programming language.

The key benefits of an aspect-oriented realization of OBSERVER is that pattern implementation becomes more explicit and visible, so it can be maintained and evolve separately from the application code [HaKi02]. A potential liability, however, is that some of the behavior of domain classes involved in an OBSERVER design is now implicit and less visible.

The relative pros and cons of using an aspect-oriented approach are a design consideration in their own right. Any specific aspect implementation of OBSERVER, however, is subjected to the same considerations about the pattern's core structure, behavior, and internal realization as outlined above, and can implement only one of the many possible pattern variants. For example, the AspectJ code fragment outlined above makes explicit assumptions about what model is used to exchange state information and what data structures are used to maintain information about observers within the subject. Moreover, an AspectJ implementation is necessarily wedded to Java, which is cold comfort to developers programming in other languages.

What about trying to approach the problem of genericity from a metalevel? For example, a model-based generative approach, such as Model-Driven Architecture (MDA) [Fra03] or Model-Driven Software Development (MDSD) [SVC06] [Sch06a] [KLSB03] [GSCK04], that translates some type of metadescription into a configurable implementation targeted for a variety of programming languages and runtime platforms? Some generative technologies, such as Model-Driven Architecture, achieve their generality by addressing only a lowest common denominator of possibilities, rather than by promotion of more context-driven solutions that exhibit the kind of design quality we seek in patterns. Other generative technologies, such as Model-Driven Software Development, promote context-driven solutions, but at the expensive of generality in their domain-specific languages.

Domain- and Environment-Dependent Variation

Variations in a pattern's realization also do not stop at the visible boundaries of a pattern. Each pattern's concrete application context will bring with it many implied demands and hidden assumptions that must be satisfied. In the OBSERVER pattern, for example, developers must decide when to start the change propagation on the subject-side to avoid unnecessary updates or update cascades [GoF95] [SGM02]. A subject could also let a specific period of time elapse after every update before triggering the next. On the observer-side developers must decide whether a change notification should always result in updating data, or if only specific ones start the update, such as every nth notification. An implementation that is suitable for one combination or style of combination of components may be unsuitable for others.

For example, to use the general AspectJ observer protocol outlined above in a concrete application, it is necessary to define what classes take what roles, as well as to refine the abstract pointcut subjectChange and the abstract method updateObserver to the specific context that uses this general protocol, otherwise the aspect-oriented implementation of OBSERVER is incomplete. The following code fragment illustrates such a refinement for a graphical application in which points play the role of subjects and the screen that displays graphics plays the subject [HaKi02]:

```
public aspect CoordinateObserver extends ObserverProtocol {
    declare parents: Point  implements Subject;
    declare parents: Screen implements Observer;

    protected pointcut subjectChange(Subject subject):
        (call(void Point.setX(int)) ||
         call(void Point.setY(int))) && target(subject);

    protected void updateObserver
        (Subject subject, Observer observer) {
        ((Screen) observer).display("Screen updated " +
            "(point subject changed coordinates).");
    }
}
```

To further complicate matters, a pattern implementation may also need to satisfy system-wide requirements, such as real-time constraints, security aspects, or runtime configurability. In addition, the implementation is influenced by other design decisions made earlier in the system's development. For example, the communication between subjects and observers depends on the concurrency, collocation, and component architecture and environment of the system under development. This communication may be expressed differently if subject and observer are located in the same thread of control, in different threads, or even in different address spaces. It might also be necessary to use middleware platforms, such as Java [CI01], .NET [PB01], or CORBA [OMG04a], to broker the communication, or use different types of networks, such as a local area network or a wide area network.

The coordination of such domain- and environment-dependent factors depends on the desired functional, operational, and developmental requirements to which a concrete pattern implementation is exposed. An implementation that fits well for one application may be completely inappropriate for another, Consequently, it is infeasible to provide a generic pattern realization that is equally well suited for all potential application contexts to which a pattern can be exposed.

Hypothesis Revisited

It appears that the challenges discussed in the previous subsections suggest rejection of the hypothesis of configurable generic implementations for patterns. We could, however, take a simpler perspective and accommodate variation along a set of a few carefully selected and narrow axis. For example, we could provide an OBSERVER implementation that supports a single structural and behavioral variant, uses a specific implementation language and platform, and addresses a specific set of operational and environmental concerns. This implementation might allow several error-handling models, could be configured with specific types of collections and iterators in a particular language, and may use a communication middleware platform that conforms to a specific standard.

Even in this restricted case, however, we are limited to collections, error-handling models, and communication middleware that support the interfaces we expect in our implementation—or we must insert an additional layer of adaptation. Moreover, this realization of OBSERVER covers no domain-specific aspects, such as what classes of an application take what roles and under what conditions interactions between roles are executed. Consequently, even a fixed set of different factors is hard to coordinate, regardless of the steps we can take toward a 'more' generic pattern implementation.

Most production software projects are even more complex, since the different factors are unbounded. Limiting the number of axis of variation therefore does not help: each axis is a continuum, a cocktail of implementation technology, application requirements, and personal taste. Yet a truly generic implementation for a pattern must—without exception—consider all axis of variation, and within this multi-dimensional variation space it must consider all feasible combinations of variation options from each axis. A flexible and parameterizable implementation that does not consider these variations and their combinations may well be a sound implementation that captures and expresses a number of particular uses of a pattern. It is not, however, fully generic in the sense of covering *all* the possible variations of the pattern.

As a result of our OBSERVER case study above, therefore, we can conclude that it is infeasible to provide a fully generic implementation for any given pattern. But is this inability actually a weakness of the pattern concept? From a naïve perspective we could argue that it is, but closer analysis reveals that much of the power of patterns stems from the fact that they do *not* prescribe a particular implementation.

It is, however, a strength of patterns that they capture the commonalities that many specific solutions of a single problem share, and also support adapting this common core to new specific situations raised by other applications. A pattern describes a coherent yet infinite *design space*, not a finite set of implementations in that space. It is the application's specific requirements that shape the path to take through—and destination within—the design space embodied by the pattern. It is the responsibility of the pattern, however, to ensure that any specific problem resolution is governed by the advice given in its solution. A pattern's solution is not passively generic, but *generative*.

Despite the insight that any narrowing of a pattern's solution space contradicts the idea of a universally applicable and truly generic pattern implementation, however, it can nevertheless be a very useful activity. Careful scoping and constraint of problem–solution variations is the basis of application frameworks [John97], product-line architectures [Coc97], and other approaches that address commonality and commodity [CHW98]. These approaches have helped to improve software quality and development productivity in many areas of software construction. Using such technologies to realize 'semi-generic' pattern implementations can therefore:

- Support the effective and correct use of patterns and help limit pattern misapplication, and

- Improve developer productivity, particularly when these implementations are written in the language(s) and for the platform(s) and domain(s) on which your projects are based.

In contrast to fully generic implementations, custom, application- or domain-specific pattern implementations—or even the families of implementations that are often found in frameworks and product-line architectures—are often a simpler, elegant, and more effective option. These approaches brings key portions of the design back under developer control, rather than putting them at the tender mercy of someone else's vision of all that a pattern can be.

The key to success in providing predefined, partly generic pattern implementations is finding the right balance between guided support and freedom to address the variabilities in a given application domain. In some areas of software development, such as embedded system design, it may be possible to provide quite rigid architectures with only few configurable aspects. In other areas, almost *any* predefined realization of patterns would hinder their productive and successful use on concrete projects, such as in the area of software development organizations and software development processes [CoHa04]. The following considerations, therefore, apply largely to design patterns only—which, nevertheless, are the predominant type of patterns documented and applied in software projects today.

2.2   Patterns and Frameworks

Despite the fact that a universally applicable, generic pattern implementation is a mirage, there are already common implementations of patterns that are widely available and successfully used. Examples include the Java AWT and Swing libraries [RBV99], Boost [Boost], and ACE [SH02] [SH03]. Nevertheless, these libraries do not intend to offer fully generic implementations of patterns. Instead, they are frameworks[13] that provide a predefined architecture and partial implementation for a family of applications in particular domains. Some frameworks may have specific properties that allow their reuse in

---

13. Unless otherwise qualified, we use the term *framework* in the general sense—defined by Carolyn Morris as 'a skeleton on which a model of work is built'—as opposed to the common but more specific usage of a group of inter-operating classes to be subclassed in the context of a specific application [John97].

unanticipated contexts for new purposes. Step outside this scope, however, and the specific fitness for purpose of any framework becomes apparent. This measure of fit is as true for classic object-oriented application frameworks [FJS99b] as it is for more generative frameworks that underpin product-line architectures [DLS05].

For example, Swing supports the construction of systems with a graphical user interface in Java. ACE supports the construction of networked and concurrent applications in C++. The design of these frameworks is consciously guided by many patterns, such as those documented by the Gang-of-Four [GoF95] and the POSA series [POSA1] [POSA2] [POSA3] [POSA4], but they are implemented in a specific context, for a specific purpose, and with specific constraints in mind. When these constraints are met, the framework can be exceedingly useful in practice.

For some systems, however, the patterns found in a framework may be right, but their implementation is inappropriate. For example, the patterns embodied in C++ by the ACE framework may be of little direct use in a Smalltalk or Ruby application. A willful attempt to use the framework beyond its applicability will lead to workarounds that reduce rather than increase the quality of the software [SB03]. Instead of having the architecture driven by the specific patterns, the developer must compensate for the framework's specific implementation. For example, the Reactor framework in ACE [SH03] is an implementation of the REACTOR pattern that demultiplexes and dispatches general I/O, timer, and networking signal events to application-defined components that process these events.

The following diagram and table outline the participants in the ACE REACTOR framework:

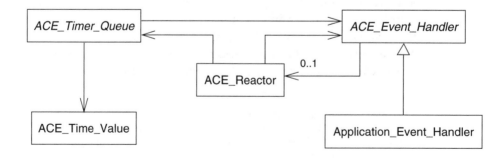

Pattern	Description
ACE_Time_Value	Provides a portable, normalized representation of time and duration that uses C++ operator overloading to simplify time-related arithmetic and relational operations.
ACE_Event_Handler	An abstract class whose interface defines the hook methods that are the target of the ACE_Reactor callbacks. Most application event handlers developed with ACE are descendants of ACE_Event_Handler.
ACE_Timer_Queue	An abstract class defining the capabilities and interface for a timer queue. ACE contains a variety of classes derived from ACE_Timer_Queue that provide flexible support for different timing requirements: ACE_Timer_Heap, ACE_Timer_Hash, ACE_Timer_Wheel, ACE_Timer_List.
ACE_Reactor	Provides the interface for managing event handler registrations and executing the event loop that drives event detection, demultiplexing, and dispatching in the ACE_Reactor framework. ACE contains a variety of concrete ACE_Reactor implementations: ACE_Select_Reactor, ACE_TP_Reactor, ACE_WFMO_Reactor.

The ACE REACTOR framework implementation, however, cannot easily or efficiently dispatch special-purpose events generated by a GUI to their corresponding user interface element, which is another context in which the REACTOR pattern [POSA2] applies.

Our point here, of course, is not that the ACE Reactor framework is insufficiently general, it is that it is sufficiently general within a well-defined context of application. It works well as the basis for platform-independent, object-oriented network applications written in C++. Instead, we are underscoring the fact that the REACTOR *pattern* captures a broader and deeper concept than any given *implementation*, as evidenced by its integration into many other frameworks, such as Interviews [LC87], the Xt toolkit [NOF92], and Java's Selector [Lea00].

Commodity and Context

Frameworks represent commodities that developers can apply to prevent reinventing of the wheel—and all the questions that go with it, such as size, shape, color, and texture—in well-defined contexts. These contexts are rarely arbitrary, however, and as with the discussions in *Section 1.5, The Context: Part of a Pattern or Not?*, it is important that there is a good fit between a solution and the context in which it is used. This context may sometimes be a good fit, even if it is not the framework author's intended context. In other words, frameworks may be reusable in the sense of the common use of the word 'reuse,' which implies use and adaptation in a different context and for a different purpose [JGJ97].

It is inevitable—even desirable—that the design of a comprehensive framework will contain a rich set of patterns [Gam95]. In fact, few frameworks developed since the mid-1990s are *not* heavily guided by patterns, since the synergy is so pervasive! A framework's use of patterns, however, should be a means to an end and not vice versa. The framework's purpose is supported by the patterns, whereas a framework that is no more than a patterns wholesaler is, in the deepest sense, meaningless: it is free of semantics—a solution in search of a problem.

A Tale of Two Frameworks

By way of counter-example, consider the purpose of the `Observable` superclass and `Observer` interface in the JDK's `java.util` package. The `Observable` superclass holds a simple, flag-and-array-based implementation of notification that a subject's type is expected to use and inherit. The interface to the corresponding `Observer` is (un)suitably vague: it is weakly typed with a single `update` method taking a reference to an `Observable`, the source of the notification, and an `Object`, which is supposed to represent something about the notification. This simple, even simplistic, sketch of a notification collaboration is not used anywhere in Java's own core libraries, which is a telling observation.

Although Java has a statically checked type system, the protocol between any specific observer and subject that choose to use the `Observer` class and `Observable` interface is outside the type system. The types of notification and their associated event information are buried in the implementation, hidden in a cascade of runtime type checks. Of course, developers can certainly choose to use Observer and Observable as provided and realize an OBSERVER implementation in their code. The issue, however, is not whether or not a particular approach can be made to work—we are talking about the ingenuity of developers and the resources of a universal computing machine, so anything is in principle possible. Instead, the issue is whether or not a particular approach is effective and efficient, which is a question of quality, not possibility.

The example below shows the problems with Observable and Observer:

Assume we model a source of values that can be observed and never goes below zero and also has an upper limit. On reaching or going below zero, the value is set to zero and observers are notified and on exceeding the upper limit observers are also notified. Using Observer and Observable, the value source appears as follows, omitting import statements and method and field detail:

```
public class ValueSource extends Observable {
    public ValueSource(int limit) ...
    public int getValue() ...
    public int getLimit() ...
    public void increaseValue(int amount) ...
    public void decreaseValue(int amount) ...
}
```

By virtue of inheritance, class ValueSource also acquires the complete interface and implementation of Observable. The Observable provides a flag-based approach to managing notification, requiring the ValueSource author to set a flag, via a method, before announcing an update.

By default Observable does not necessarily reflect how a ValueSource behaves, because it allows both registration and deregistration of arbitrary observers, without any checking of whether the registered observers understand how to observe a ValueSource. Detection of this problem can be deferred until notification, or extra code for registration can be introduced by overriding the registration method.

However, although overriding can change the implementation, there is no suitable way to feed back to the caller the fact that an observer has already been registered, so a second registration will be ignored. There is no way to change the return value to return a success or failure indication, and throwing an exception is both in violation of the method's contract and too severe a response.

The notification protocol is captured informally via two empty classes:

```
public class ValueExceededLimit {}
public class ValueAtZero {}
```

Imagine that an example observer can potentially observe both a ValueSource and SomeOtherSource, the code would be as follows:

```
public class ExampleObserver implements Observer {
    ...
    public void update(Observable subject, Object event) {
        if(subject instanceof ValueSource) {
            ValueSource valueSource = (ValueSource) subject;

            if(event instanceof ValueExceededLimit) {
                // handle notification of
                // value exceeding limit
            }
            else if(event instanceof ValueAtZero) {
                // handle notification of value at zero
            }
            else {
                // handle error for unknown notification
            }
        }
        else if(subject instanceof SomeOtherSource) {
            // handle notification protocol
            // for SomeOtherSource
        }
        else {
            // handle error for unknown type of subject
        }
    }
    ...
}
```

As this example shows nicely, an OBSERVER implementation based on Observer and Observable will contain numerous casts and instanceof runtime checks embedded in an ever-growing if…else…if arrangement. What such an implementation lacks in grace it more than makes up for in unmaintainability! A more comprehensible and efficient design for both programmers and compilers would reveal these types in the declared interfaces of the collaborating types.

In contrast, the EventListener model, also found in the JDK, is more open, accommodating of specifics, and used extensively in the Java libraries whenever such notification capability is required. It allows notification to define both the type of notification and the information provided with such a notification. Yet EventListener is not some generic implementation for notification: it is no more than a marker interface used to indicate a notification relationship that follows the conventions of a particular style of OBSERVER implementation.

Specific relationships are elaborated clearly and separately in the EventListener model. For example, the difference between a Window-Listener and a MenuListener is as clear from their names as it is from the specific types of notification supported in their respective interfaces: windowActivated and windowClosed versus menuSelected and menuCanceled. The following code illustrates the clarity of the EventListener model by revising the ValueSource example from above:

For the second version of class ValueSource, following the EventListener model, a protocol rather than a library class is used:

```
public class ValueSource {
    public ValueSource(int limit) ...
    public boolean addValueListener(
        ValueListener observer) ...
    public boolean removeValueListener
        (ValueListener observer) ...
    public int getValue() ...
    public int getLimit() ...
    public void increaseValue(int amount) ...
    public void decreaseValue(int amount) ...
}
```

The code above is similar in appearance to the corresponding code in the first take of the example, except that the programmer of ValueSource now has to manage the registration step. This step, however, is just two one-line methods and the addition of a collection. The key advantage of this approach is that the programmer now has full control of the registration interface and behavior and the registration is type checked. The advantage arises with the visibility of the notification protocol, which is more obviously explicit and cohesive:

```
public interface ValueListener {
    void valueExceededLimit(ValueSource subject);
    void valueAtZero(ValueSource subject);
}
```

The major difference to the first part of the example is in handling the notification, however:

```
public class ExampleValueListener
        implements ValueListener, SomeOtherListener {
    public void valueExceededLimit(ValueSource subject) {
        // handle notification of value exceeding limit
    }
    public void valueAtZero(ValueSource subject) {
        // handle notification of value at zero
    }
    ...
    // methods for handling notification protocol
    // for SomeOtherSource
}
```

In contrast to the ExampleObserver code in the first discussion of the example, the code for ExampleValueListener exposes a clear visibility of relationships, no type switching, and no surprising runtime errors. Where the first approach tried to reduce the amount of code required for a subject, the second approach successfully tackles the real source of complexity by reducing and simplifying the code required to fulfill the observer role.

The differences in purpose between one context and another lead inevitably to the differences in implementation. How can a framework be both good and universal? A good framework is therefore by definition not a universally generic implementation, and any attempt at such a generic implementation is, from experience, not likely to be much good. Instead, it will resemble a pastiche of a good design idea rather than a good design in its own right.

2.3   Patterns and Formalisms

Similar issues are raised—and a correspondingly similar discussion held—on formalizing patterns. It has been argued that a plain-text description of a pattern illustrated with some diagrams is not precise enough to ensure a correct implementation.[14] The term 'blueprint' is often used in connection with the question of precision and correctness, but this can also be misleading [Bry02]:

> *Blueprint* as a metaphor for a design or plan is much overworked. If the temptation to use it is irresistible, at least remember that a blueprint is a completed plan, not a preliminary one.

A pattern is not a single destination with every detail finalized, ready to wear or ready for software. A pattern defines a space, not a point, a continuum of solutions, not a singularity. It should be seen as a sketch and an inspiration rather than a blueprint or a requirement. Patterns define relationships between requirements and solutions. Without a good understanding of motivation, context, and problem forces, the solution aspect of a pattern makes little sense.

Constrained Versus Unconstrained Genericity

The variety of options and the intimate dependency on application-specific requirements and constraints suggests that few aspects of a pattern can be specified formally without loss of intent and genericity. Such lossy specifications tend to describe no more than a few examples from all possible pattern implementations, and sometimes no more than one. Although the specification might be reasonable and concrete, the result is a useful generative design—in the sense of *generative programming* [CzEi02]—but not a pattern.

Good generative programming comes from careful scoping of problems and finite enumeration of design variations. Coverage of a software family is provided without duplication of code or effort by capturing a description of the problem and solution space that intentionally excludes features not related to the application. Although the resulting architecture can be quite useful and open to change, it cannot claim to meet the needs of any arbitrary application that wants to use the specified patterns.

---

14. Formalizing patterns is a popular sport, particularly in academia. Many diverse approaches have been developed, including—but not limited to—the following references: [Hed97] [LBG97] [MK97] [LK98] [Mik98] [BGJ99] [EGHY99] [CH00] [XBHJ00a] [XBHJ00b].

On the other hand, if many important parts of the solution are left unspecified because it is impossible to specify them generically, developers who want to use such specifications must define all the missing aspects on their own. Like code generators that just spit out class names, operation signatures, and matching curly braces, this approach roundly misses the point of both patterns and formalisms that aspire to genericity. Typing speed is not the bottleneck in software development—understanding is. A generic solution that offers little more than a code skeleton peppered with 'TO DO' comments—omitting, conveniently enough, all the subtle and intricate bits—is not a design solution for any reasonable definition of the words *design* and *solution.*

Moreover, developers also have to learn the formalism, and must deal with specifications that are often longer than the complete code they will finally produce. Without integrated support from other tools and development methods, such as the artifacts and processes needed to create, validate, and evolve product-line architectures, a 'half-baked' formalism may actually be more of a burden than a benefit. The role of formalism in software development depends on multiple factors and specific situations, such as safety-critical systems that require certifiable properties, or mature domains whose solutions are highly constrained and repetitive and thus lend themselves to automated code generation. That a specific situation warrants such an approach, however, is not an indicator that any particular formalism is appropriate as a general model for capturing *all* designs, particularly given the kind of generality on which patterns focus.

A formal description that claims to be *the* definitive description of a pattern simply cannot be: it must always be restricted to a subset of possibilities. Like proof by induction, it is always trivial to take a 'complete' description and add another case. The complexity of such totality is likely to present a developer with more of a problem than a solution.

Consequently, the genericity of a pattern's solution conflicts with the necessary level of detail required by formal approaches. Note that this does *not* mean that it is useless to document *specific* pattern implementations formally. For example, formal techniques such as domain-specific modeling languages [GTK+07], in conjunction with preconditions, postconditions, and invariants embodied in *design by contract* [Mey97] and declarative constraint languages [WaKl98], can help communicate the implementation of object-oriented patterns precisely within a particular application or product-line. Similarly, UML [OMG03] stereotypes and parameterized collaborations can be used to tag specific classes to illustrate their role or suggest common arrangements [BGJ99].

The following diagram illustrates a concrete OBSERVER arrangement using UML stereotypes. In this arrangement, instances of ClassA are observed by instances of a ClassB, which are observed by instances of ClassC.

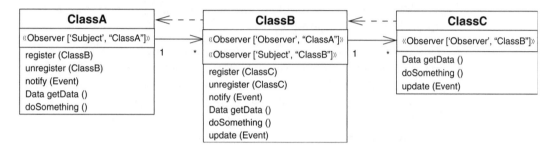

Although formal representations of specific pattern implementations support their understanding, they cannot, however, sensibly be called reference specifications. Similarly, any formal description of a specific pattern implementation is quite different than trying to capture all possible pattern implementations in a formal cage.

2.4   A Million and One... and then Some

Looking back to our hypothesis, the experiments we applied to evaluate it, and our other explorations in this chapter, we can see that the vision of generic implementations for patterns is simply a myth—not even a theoretical possibility—and in practice a time-wasting distraction. Patterns are neither templates nor blueprints, although they are certainly useful for guiding the creation of templates and blueprints. Christopher Alexander recognizes this explicitly in his original articulation of patterns [AIS77]:

> Each pattern describes a problem which occurs over and over again in our environment, and then describes the core of the solution to that problem, in such a way that you can use this solution a million times over, without ever doing it twice the same.

In other words, a good pattern implementation for a specific application or kind of application may find itself unusable outside this intended context or similar contexts. The fine tuning that makes the pattern such a good solution can also exclude it from being used arbitrarily or even reasonably in other situations that are dominated by different forces [Cool98].

This restraint does not mean that we cannot find generality to capture in the form of concrete reuse technologies such as frameworks, product-line architectures, and generative tools. It does mean, however, that the viability and value of these technologies comes explicitly and precisely from bounding the types of variation and application considered. A good framework or model-driven tool is clearly more general than a highly specific handcrafted implementation intended for single use. The value of frameworks and tools, however, stems not from attempting universal coverage of all possibilities, but instead from capturing common structure, behavior, and control flow within particular domains.

Of Reference Implementations and Example Implementations

We have seen that framework implementations may provide mechanisms that embody particular patterns, and save developers from handcrafting their own versions in the context of using the frameworks. The misconception we are trying to clarify comes from mistaking the framework *implementation* of a pattern as *the* pattern. It is an embodiment of the pattern in the trivial sense that it implements the pattern, but it is neither a reference implementation nor a generic implementation of the pattern.

In software development, a reference implementation is often a realization of a particular standard that not only demonstrates proof of concept, but also represents a 'gold standard' against which other implementations are measured. An implementation that diverges in significant respects—namely those that have been standardized—is considered erroneous. While this approach is valuable for standards, it is clearly at odds with the pattern concept, although it might be grist for the mill by the 'design pattern police' found in some corporate architecture teams. Patterns are not standards in the sense of the POSIX, Java, CORBA, and XML standards, so the concept of a reference implementation has little meaning. At best it is misleading, at worst it is quite harmful by mistaking a particular instance of a pattern for the whole pattern.

For example, ACE offers half a dozen frameworks inspired by many POSA1 and POSA2 patterns, such as PIPES AND FILTERS, REACTOR, PROACTOR, ACCEPTOR-CONNECTOR, COMPONENT CONFIGURATOR, and AC-TIVE OBJECT. These frameworks, however, are *example* implementations, not *reference* implementations, of these patterns. It is in these example implementations of patterns that we find both the diversity and the concreteness for which we are searching. Patterns are based on recurrence, so examples help to locate actual points in the design space covered by a pattern.

Example implementations can also teach us a great deal about patterns and best practices of software development. Indeed, some example implementations, such as the Lexi drawing editor in the [GoF95] book, are used only for teaching and not for production. In teaching a particular design pattern, it makes sense to simplify the presentation and excise details that would distract from the essential idea of the pattern. For this reason, the Gang-of-Four's example implementation of OBSERVER is necessarily simplistic, but by intent, not by omission. If it were more comprehensive it would, ironically, be less comprehensible!

3 Notes on Pattern Form

Words differently arranged have different meanings, and meanings differently arranged have a different effect.

Blaise Pascal

This chapter examines the written form of patterns, revisiting some of the concepts examined in *Chapter 1, A Solution to a Problem and More*. This pattern form acts as the vehicle through which a pattern description communicates the essence and practicalities of the pattern. A focus on form is therefore as important to pattern readers as it is to pattern writers.

3.1 Style and Substance

Now that we have a more precise idea of the essential role and content of patterns, we can turn our attention toward their effective presentation. Even though a pattern can be considered independently of its presentation—the presentation is a vehicle for communicating a pattern—presentation is far from just a secondary detail. In fact, the presentation of patterns is considered as important to the whole idea as the content. It is not a question of style versus substance: the intimacy between communication and content is such that the style is part of the substance—there is no contradiction or conflict between the two.

One of the original aims of the pattern community was to spread the word about good practices in software development. From a practical perspective, good practice poorly communicated is the same as no practice at all: it might as well not exist, and is as mute and unnoticed as any practice communicated poorly. Worse, good practices communicated poorly will lose out to poor practices communicated clearly. In his essay 'Writing Broadside,' Dick Gabriel [Gab96] conveys this point when he cites Thucydides [Thu81], who—over two millennia ago—wrote:

> 'A man who has the knowledge but lacks the power to clearly
> express it is no better off than if he never had any ideas at all.'

An appropriate presentation is therefore essential to communicate a pattern successfully, and for the success of a pattern its proper communication is essential. A pattern's audience is ultimately always human. Although a developer may support application of a software pattern solution through libraries and generators, it is the developer and not the technology that is aware of the pattern. A pattern is more than just a solution structure, so its audience must also have a sense of the context, the forces, and the consequences that are associated with a solution [Cool97].

A pattern can be communicated face-to-face through conversation, whiteboards, sketches on envelopes, or any other medium that comes to hand. However, the opportunities for such rich dialog are highly localized. Thus the more common form of communication for patterns is through writing. In contrast to a dialog with a pattern expert, however, communicating a pattern via writing is fundamentally narrative rather than interactive.

In conversation with pattern authors or proponents, would-be pattern users have the opportunity to question and clarify anything doubtful or unclear. They can also probe details, talk through specific examples, and exchange other thoughts. Through the medium of writing, authors are granted greater precision and control over presentation, but they lose any voice beyond pattern text to assist readers with implementation details, questions of applicability, or clarification of the problem. The dialog gets lost: the audience loses the ability to engage and pattern authors lose the ability to respond. This challenge is one to be overcome in writing a pattern: there still needs to be a sense of dialog.

The narrative of a pattern's documentation must therefore not only express the pattern faithfully and unambiguously, it should also capture some scope of the lost dialog, rather than adopting the stiff character of a monologue. Indeed, if the choice is between a precise but dry account that presents *at* the reader and a slightly less thorough treatment that draws the reader in, pattern authors should favor engagement over disengagement.

An Example Revisited

In *Chapter 1* we used the task of documenting a pattern to explore the pattern concept, from context to consequences, as well as to make observations on the form of presentation. The emphasis of this chapter is different: it focuses more on the form of presentation of a pattern than on the anatomy of the pattern concept itself.

As a reminder, here is the pattern description we had at the start:

Context: A client needs to perform actions on an aggregate data structure.

Problem: The client may need to retrieve or update multiple elements in a collection. If the access to the aggregate is expensive, however, accessing it separately for each element over a loop can incur severe performance penalties, such as round-trip time, blocking delay, or context-switching overhead. How can bulk accesses on an aggregate object be performed efficiently and without interruption?

Solution: Define a single method that performs the access on the aggregate repeatedly. Instead of accessing aggregate elements individually and directly from within a loop, the client invokes the method to access multiple elements in a single call.

After many refinements and reflections, here is the description we reached at the end:

Batch Method

In a distributed or concurrent object system, the client of an aggregate object may need to perform bulk actions on the aggregate. For example, the client may need to retrieve all elements in a collection that match specific properties. If the access to the aggregate is expensive, however, because it is remote from the client or shared between multiple threads, accessing it separately for each element over a loop—whether by index, by key, or by ITERATOR—can incur severe performance penalties, such as round-trip time, blocking delay, or context-switching overhead.

How can bulk accesses on an aggregate object be performed efficiently and without interruption if access is costly and subject to failure?

Four forces must be considered when resolving this problem:

- An aggregate object shared between clients in a concurrent environment, whether locally multithreaded or distributed, is capable of encapsulating synchronization for individual method calls but not for multiple calls, such as a call repeated by a loop.

- The overhead of blocking, synchronization, and thread management must be added to the costs for each access across threads or processes. Similarly, any other per-call housekeeping code, such as authorization, can further reduce performance.

- Where an aggregate object is remote from its client, each access incurs further latency and jitter, and decreases available network bandwidth.

- Distributed systems are subject to partial failure, in which a client may still be live after a server has gone down. Remote access during iteration introduces a potential point of failure for each loop execution, which exposes the client to the problem of dealing with the consequences of partial traversal, such as an incomplete snapshot of state or an incompletely applied set of updates.

For a given action, therefore, define a single method that performs the action on the aggregate repeatedly.

Each BATCH METHOD is defined as part of the interface of the aggregate object, either directly as part of the EXPLICIT INTERFACE exported for the whole aggregate type, or as part of a narrower, mix-in EXPLICIT INTERFACE that only defines the capability for invoking the repeated action. The BATCH METHOD is declared to take all the arguments for each execution of the action, for example via an array or a collection, and to return results by similar means. Instead of accessing aggregate elements individually and directly from within a loop, the client invokes the BATCH METHOD to access multiple elements in a single call. The BATCH METHOD may be implemented directly by the aggregate object's underlying class, or indirectly via an OBJECT ADAPTER, leaving the aggregate object's class unaffected.

A BATCH METHOD folds repetition into a data structure rather than a loop within the client, so that looping is performed before or after the method call, in preparation or follow-up. Consequently, the cost of access to the aggregate is reduced to a single access, or a few 'chunked' accesses. In distributed systems this 'compression' can significantly improve performance, incur fewer network errors, and save precious bandwidth.

By using a BATCH METHOD, each access to the aggregate becomes more expensive, but the overall cost for bulk accesses has been reduced. Such accesses can also be synchronized as appropriate within the method call. Each call can be made effectively transactional, either succeeding or failing completely, but never partially.

The trade-off in complexity is that a BATCH METHOD performs significantly more housekeeping to set up and work with the results of the call, and requires more intermediate data structures to pass arguments and receive results. The higher the costs for networking, concurrency, and other per-call housekeeping, however, the more affordable this overhead becomes.

Note the progression of the description and how it draws in all the aspects we consider important in characterizing a pattern: its name, the context in which the problem arises, a summary of the problem, the forces that go to make up the problem, a summary of the proposed solution, a more detailed elaboration of the solution, and consideration of the consequences of introducing the solution.

There are also other matters of style that support the pattern's presentation, such as the emphasis used for pattern names, the bulleted list of forces, and the use of a question to summarize the problem. These matters of style also relate to choices that are questions of form: change the form and the description will change in a way that affects its readability—how it is best read, for what purpose, and by whom.

3.2   The Function of Form

A pattern as a piece of writing is a creation of its author. Each pattern description will be individual, but not entirely free of convention. The vehicle that carries a pattern is its *form*, which guides its overall appearance, structure, and prose style. Yet, like the search for the ultimate programming language, the one 'true' indentation style, and other such holy-grail pursuits popular with software developers, the quixotic quest for the ultimate pattern form is also destined to remain elusive.

The variation in personal aesthetics and types of patterns ensures that one form cannot satisfy all needs. Rather than suggesting the Dada-esque abandonment of form, however, all these factors underscore the importance of a pattern's form. In addition to individual preferences, form must serve some function: the aesthetic sense of the author is combined with the technical message of the content and the clarity of communication for the chosen audience. Like forces within a pattern, these concerns must be balanced.

Questions of Form

Pattern authors need to ensure the appropriate breadth and depth of technical content, and frame that is suitable for the intended audience(s) of their patterns. What is the context of the pattern? What forces are at work? What are the consequences, both good and bad, of the pattern? Is the reader expecting a high-level sketch or a detailed pyrotechnic display of curly braces, replete with API detail? Is the reader an experienced architect in search of a highly specific solution or a novice programmer looking for guidance in general techniques? What is the ideal example to illustrate the pattern? Is the pattern part of a larger collection within which it should be consistent?

It may appear that having a single form for all pattern authors to conform with would remove many of these questions, freeing authors from this burden of free will. As with the problem of generic implementations discussed in *Chapter 2*, however, a single reference form would become unwieldy and incomprehensible. It would need a meta-model bristling with optionality. Writing a pattern would quite literally become a matter of filling out a form—and would be just as exciting to read or write. Instead, the healthy diversity of pattern forms allows authors to exercise their own judgment with presentation form, while retaining some common ground and familiarity with other patterns in the literature.

The diversity of available forms, however, leaves pattern authors with a decision to make. For patterns collected together in a catalog or language, consistency of form is a factor that influences authors and readers more than the needs of the individual pattern. Taken individually, some patterns may be best served by different forms: short and narrative versus long and structured. Taken together, the use of multiple forms in a pattern catalog or language can look messy, making comparison, continuity, or connection between patterns harder than necessary. Inconsistency of form suggests that authors are indecisive and unclear rather than selective and direct.

3.3 Elements of Form

If we look to a pattern to tell us about a design, development role, or business practice, and expect it to engage us in a dialog over its merits and scope, the form of the pattern must reflect our interests and concerns. Where is the emphasis of a given pattern description? Is the pattern better communicated through a soft and narrative style free of fixed and explicit section headings, or through a more structured form? How easy is it for the reader to recognize the solution in their own work or apply it in new work immediately?

Working forwards through the natural flow of a pattern, we first encounter the pattern's name: BATCH METHOD in the case of our example pattern. The role of a pattern as an element of design vocabulary cannot easily be fulfilled if its name is long and unwieldy or obscure and cute. A long name may be accurate and precise, but inconvenient. An obscure or cute name may be memorable and metaphorical, but uninformative. Unless readers share in the connection between the metaphor and the pattern, it will be memorable for its obscurity rather than for its insight.

A pattern is not a general-purpose rule or universal principle, so the context in which the pattern can be applied should be clearly stated. The context situates a pattern in the world of design, management, business, or wherever the domain of interest for a pattern lies, outlining where it does and does not apply. The use of patterns as context-free rules leads to their misapplication. Despite the universal nature of computation, architectural knowledge acquired in one domain does not automatically and blindly transfer to another. For example, patterns that address problems of design in a local address space with sequential control flow rarely translate efficiently or correctly to distributed systems with inherent concurrency. In the case of our BATCH METHOD description, we situate it with respect to distribution and concurrency, with some preview of the problem being addressed.

If forces are the heart of a pattern, that importance should be reflected in the pattern form. A reader should not have to deconstruct and dissect a pattern to discover the nature of the problem it solves. A concise, up-front summary of the problem ensures that careful readers have a useful overview of what they are about to read and casual readers have a complete enough picture not to be misled. Having presented the context and general motivation, our BATCH METHOD description presents its design problem as a question.

There are many ways to list forces in a pattern, ranging from categorized bulleted lists to free-form prose. The four forces for our BATCH METHOD example are each in a distinct paragraph and bulleted to make each one clear as a force. Other prose styles emphasize the conflict between different forces, presenting first one assumption or desired outcome, and then contrasting it with another that is in conflict, often introduced with a 'but' or 'however.'

A brief statement of the solution ensures that readers are left in no doubt as to the general structure of the solution, although they will have to read on to discover its detail. A reader should not be left with the dangling question, 'Which bit of all of the solution detail was the pattern?' It should be easy to identify the essence that solved the problem versus the supporting, connecting, and explanatory detail. For our description of BATCH METHOD, the solution statement immediately follows the listing of the forces. It is direct rather than indirect: rather than discussing what the solution will offer, it describes the essence of the solution concisely. The solution statement reads as a direct response to the question posed by the problem summary. In other forms, where the problem is presented as a statement, the solution statement often begins with a customary 'Therefore.'

Following the solution statement, a pattern description can provide a more detailed presentation of what is involved in realizing the pattern. This presentation can be a mix of prose, diagrams, code, and so on. The solution description can be further structured to offer a similar form for patterns in a catalog that deals with the same kind of domain, such as OO design. For example, the solution of an OO design pattern may begin with a simple solution statement followed by one or two paragraphs of detailed prose, which may be followed by a class diagram and a sequence diagram, which may in turn be followed by an illustrative code fragment, and concluded with a bulleted section describing common variations. An organizational pattern, by contrast, may begin in a similar way, but its diagrams may adopt an informal notation to illustrate the division of responsibilities and interaction of human or departmental roles.

The form and depth of a pattern's solution depends heavily on the type of the pattern and its audience. At the very least, the reader should have a good grasp of the key principles and elements of a pattern. Ideally they should also have a sense of the process behind the pattern, not just the thing it produces: how to apply the pattern in practice.

Reinforcing the observations of *Chapter 1*, no decision is free of consequences, good or bad. A pattern that does not make clear the resulting context of its solution can raise more questions than answers in the mind of designers. A pattern that claims only benefits and no liabilities is more like design by advertising than by engineering. Like a 'get rich quick' scam, a good-news-only billing offers an open invitation to misuse and disappointment. Therefore a pattern description should make explicit both the pros and cons of applying the pattern, so that the reader is in a position to weigh up the liabilities against the benefits in their own situation.

The empirical nature of patterns suggests that they should be grounded in real examples. Many pattern forms choose to present an example, either in an explicit section, or as a running example interwoven with the narrative flow of the pattern from the problem through to its consequences.

The empirical viewpoint also raises another question of form, one concerning identifiable quality. The common practice in identifying and documenting patterns is to focus on proven practice, but sometimes we may wish to contrast a good pattern with a poor one. It is important that the reader is clear which pattern is which, for example by explicitly tagging the unsound patterns 'dysfunctional' [Hen03a]. Even with patterns we regard as sound, not all patterns can necessarily be considered equal, and we may wish to indicate explicitly our level of confidence in a pattern. The form used by Christopher Alexander uses a simple rating for each pattern [AIS77]. This style is used by a number of pattern authors, and is one that we adopted in *A Pattern Language for Distributed Computing* [POSA4]:

> The form begins with the name of the pattern, which is labeled with either no stars, one star, or two stars. The number of stars denote our level of confidence in the pattern's maturity. Two stars mean that we are confident that the pattern addresses a genuine problem in its respective problem area and that it is essential to implement the proposed solution in one of its possible variants to resolve the problem effectively. One star means that we think that the pattern addresses a genuine problem and that its solution is a good one, but know that pattern needs to mature. No stars means that we observed the problem addressed by the pattern every now and then, and also found its proposed solution to be useful, but

the pattern needs significant revision to reach the quality of a one-star or two-star pattern. A no star pattern description may also indicate there are alternative, better patterns to take its place.

The star rating is not necessarily an absolute rating of a pattern: it should be considered relative to the context in which it is presented for use. For example, in POSA4 the BLACKBOARD pattern had no stars: in the general context of distributed computing, this makes sense, but in the context of a collection of patterns focused on non-deterministic problem solving it would receive a higher star rating. Similarly, the REFLECTION pattern was marked with a single star, but had its context been a collection of patterns for building software tools, it would have received two stars.

The following diagram summarizes the essential elements of pattern form and their purpose:

```
Pattern
    |
    |---- Identification
    |          |___ Name and classification for identifying the pattern
    |---- Context
    |          |___ Situation giving rise to a problem
    |---- Problem
    |          |___ Set of forces repeatedly arising in the context
    |---- Solution
    |          |___ Configuration to balance the forces
    |___ Consequences
               |___ Consequences arising from application of the pattern
```

3.4   Details, Details

Although any pattern description should address the essential elements of pattern form outlined above, additional detail is often appropriate to provide meaningful guidance on where a pattern applies and how to apply it. The level of detail at which a pattern description is written can vary considerably depending on the situation. Should the pattern description be a brief sketch or a detailed exploration? Should there be diagrams? If so, what kind and how many? What is the relevance of code, case studies, or examples? The appropriate answers depend on the type of pattern and the target audience.

In some situations a short form can be too much of a tease, hinting at a good design but withholding essential details. In other situations, however, a short form may be ideal. The author may understand the value of brevity; conciseness and accuracy may be precisely what the reader needs to think about their system. Similarly, in some situations a high level of detail in a pattern description can be a distraction, offering a level of precision that may be misleading and open to literal interpretation. In other situations, it may be just what the reader needs to apply the pattern confidently and correctly.

A pattern presents a slice of the design space, which means that it cannot—or should not—cover all of the incidental concerns or questions that may arise. Patterns touch on other patterns and, rather than repeat the content or concepts of other patterns, a pattern's solution or context may refer to other patterns to help set the scene for the reader, or suggest further reading and implementation details.

Leading by Example

Examples in a pattern description determine the audience for that pattern. No matter what the level and style of the rest of the pattern description, the example defines the entry level. A pattern description targeted at novices should therefore avoid industrial-strength examples. A detailed and gritty example may convince an expert, but in a pattern description intended for novices it is not the experts that need convincing. Even expert readers may be distracted if an example is dominated by accidental complexity and incidental detail that has no direct relation to the core pattern.

Although some short pattern descriptions contain no example, many patterns include some kind of example. If one of the constraints on a pattern description is its length—for example, a pattern per page— dropping the discussion of an example would make space for deeper discussion of forces and solution details. There are also different expectations depending on the type of pattern: a code-centric pattern can obviously benefit from the concretion of the problem and solution in compileable form, but an organizational pattern that uses a made-up example involving Alice, Bob, and Charlie in some situation may look a little too contrived. In the former case an example would offer the reader an obvious source of clarification, but the absence of an example might leave them guessing. In the latter case an example might be a distraction from the message of the pattern and, if omitted, would probably not be missed.

Some patterns even include more than one example [Hen01a], and with good reason. A common mistake in reading and applying a pattern is to assume that the example *is* the pattern, or that the pattern can only be applied in software related directly to the example. This is a problem that is more likely to occur with design-focused patterns than patterns relating people and process.

The variations in the design space covered by a pattern may also be far broader than can be reasonably presented in a single example. Two or more examples offer an additional point of triangulation: a binocular rather than monocular view of the problem–solution space. Similarly, offering a counter-example—a common example of how a pattern is misapplied—can also help to clarify a pattern's boundaries.

We highlighted the role of examples in learning about a pattern in *Section 2.4, A Million and One… and then Some.* There are two types of examples on which a pattern description can draw: field examples, which represent known uses of a pattern, and teaching examples, which are created solely for exposition. Of course a pattern description does not necessarily have to make a choice: it can contain both types of examples, citing and summarizing field examples and elaborating teaching examples. It is also not the case that these two types of example are necessarily distinct. Some field examples, for instance, are sufficiently compact and direct that they can be used directly for teaching. For example, the experience reports and known uses of introducing new ideas into organizations in *Fearless Change: Patterns for Introducing New Ideas* [MaRi04] are sufficiently brief and complete to include in their entirety.

For code-related patterns, completeness can lead to overwhelming detail, so shorter examples are often more appropriate. This brevity does not mean, however, that the examples are just constructed for the purpose of illustration: many code examples in POSA2 are distillations of code found in ACE [SH02] [SH03], reduced and focused for the purpose of teaching, but still retaining their roots in the field.

Picture This

Diagrams are perhaps one of the elements of form that are most ritualized, and most often misapplied. The question of diagrams and diagrammability was covered in detail in *Section 1.7, A Diagram Says More than a Thousand Words... or Less.* We revisit this question briefly here, however, now that we are focusing on matters of pattern form rather than the pattern concept.

A class diagram may make sense for a design that is focused on the static relationship between classes in a design. It is less helpful, however, when the design is characterized by a dynamic choreography, an interplay of objects, across a simple model. Of course, if a solution has nothing to do with objects, an object-oriented notation may be irrelevant and an alternative notation aligned with the concepts presented should be used.

A recognized notation, such as UML, can frame a design in terms familiar to readers. Conversely, a notation that is under the control of the author and specifically matched to the solution may be preferable (see *page 54* for a brief discussion of our 'Bizarro' notation). Where a sketch of a solution is needed, UML can be inappropriately precise, and therefore misleading.

Where some degree of precision is appropriate, a formalized diagram can be of great value to many readers. As we discussed in *Chapter 2*, it is important to remember that such diagrams are a representative example of the pattern, not the pattern itself. In discussing a particular application of the COMPOSITE pattern, John Vlissides makes a similar observation [Vlis98b]:

> The pattern's Structure section presents a modified OMT diagram of the canonical COMPOSITE class structure. By *canonical* I mean simply that it represents the most common arrangement of classes that we (Gang-of-Four) have observed. It can't represent the *definitive* set of classes and relationships, because the interfaces may vary when we consider certain design or implementation-driven trade-offs.

Recalling some of the common pitfalls of pattern application discussed in *Chapter 0*: a pattern is *not* the diagram, the whole diagram, and nothing but the diagram.

<code>...</code>

Whether code is appropriate or not in a pattern description depends on whether the pattern is related to programming, as opposed to, say, organizational structure. A pattern concerning C++ practices whose description does not present any C++ code will be less convincing than one that does. The code qualifies as a strong part of the substance of the pattern and thus of the presentation of the pattern.

On the other hand, there is such a thing as too much detail: some pattern descriptions become lost in a fog of code. Simplification or omission of incidental details of production code in a complex middleware pattern is more likely to benefit readers than annoy them. If brevity is the soul of a particular pattern description, excluding code can be the more appropriate choice, even if the pattern is code-centric. Even in these cases, however, including even a simple fragment or sketch often lends some additional weight and validity to the pattern. For example, the BATCH METHOD description could be illustrated with code fragments for the interface of a concrete example of the pattern, such as a remote directory.

```
interface RemoteDictionary ...
{
    Object[] get(Object[] keys);
    void put(Object[] keys, Object[] values);
    ...
}
```

Authors who write code-centric patterns should also remember that the quality of their code examples will also be part of what the pattern is judged on. Otherwise sound patterns have been ignored because the quality of the code did not match the expectations of readers. Some documented patterns have actually been dismissed because careful readers noticed that the code presented actually exposed deficiencies in the patterns.

3.5   Aerial View

To offer an accessible summary in the face of perhaps overwhelming detail, many patterns are preceded by a *thumbnail*, which is similar to a prologue to a play or an overture to an opera. A thumbnail is a reduced view of the pattern as a whole, normally comprising a problem statement—perhaps a question—followed by a solution statement. There may also be a suggestive sketch of the structure. These thumbnails are sometimes also known as *patlets*.

From Pyramid to Patlet

Pattern sections are sometimes written in the style of an inverted pyramid, so that the most significant information is presented first, briefly, with the detail following. This approach—also known as 'newspaper style' due to its common use in newspapers—provides readers with a quick summary of a story just by browsing its opening paragraph. The problem and solution parts of a thumbnail are often direct quotes from the problem and solution statements of the full pattern description. For example, here is a thumbnail of BATCH METHOD in this style:

> How can bulk accesses on an aggregate object be performed efficiently and without interruption if access is costly and subject to failure? For a given action, define a single method that performs the action on the aggregate repeatedly.

Sometimes the problem and solution part are made explicit, making the thumbnail more obviously like a scaled down form of a more complete pattern description:

> **Problem:** How can bulk accesses on an aggregate object be performed efficiently and without interruption if access is costly and subject to failure?
>
> **Solution:** For a given action, define a single method that performs the action on the aggregate repeatedly.

The word 'therefore' features prominently in many pattern forms, from Alexander to POSA4, as a way of introducing the solution section. By phrasing the problem clause of a thumbnail as a statement rather than a question, 'therefore' can play a similar dividing role in the thumbnail:

> Access on an aggregate object is costly and subject to failure, but bulk accesses on the aggregate object need to be performed efficiently and without interruption. Therefore, for a given action, define a single method that performs the action on the aggregate repeatedly.

Pattern Sketches

The thumbnail form can also be used when initially sketching out a pattern or group of patterns. Although the omission of context, forces, consequences, and other details means that we are not presented with all the aspects of a pattern that we consider essential, the inclusion of the problem–solution pairing offers a description that is still in some sense complete, capturing the basic thrust of the pattern and inviting further elaboration. An example of this initial sketching technique can be seen in *Web 2.0 Design Patterns* [ORei05]. Here is the description of the SOFTWARE ABOVE THE LEVEL OF A SINGLE DEVICE pattern taken from that collection:

> The PC is no longer the only access device for internet applications, and applications that are limited to a single device are less valuable than those that are connected. *Therefore*: Design your application from the get-go to integrate services across handheld devices, PCs, and internet servers.

Another example of the different roles short forms can play is illustrated in the following compact presentation of the NULL OBJECT pattern:

if

- An object reference may be optionally null and
- This reference must be checked before every use and
- The result of a null check is to do nothing or assign a suitable default value

then

- Provide a class derived from the object reference's type and
- Implement all its methods to do nothing or provide default results and
- Use an instance of this class whenever the object reference would have been null

This rule-based description is used as the thumbnail in a more complete write-up of NULL OBJECT [Hen02a], but was originally drawn up for use in a conference slide presentation [Hen97]. The context in which a pattern description is presented influences the form and amount of detail that are suitable. In this particular case, the constraints for presenting patterns on slides encourages a patlet-like approach comprising a concise but precise textual description and a simple diagram.

In addition to individual pattern presentation [Hen97] or thumbnailing [Wake95] [Hen02a], the rule-based form has also been used for summarizing patterns in larger collections. For example, here is the summary of the BUILD PROTOTYPES pattern [CoHa04]:

> *If* early requirements are difficult to validate without testing, *Then:* build a prototype whose purpose is to help clarify requirements and assess risk.

It is also possible to vary the rule-based form with a 'therefore,' as this summary of ARCHITECT ALSO IMPLEMENTS shows [CoHa04]:

> *If* an architect is in an ivory tower, he or she is out of touch with reality, yet someone needs to reconcile the high-level overview with practice. *Therefore*, ensure that the architect is materially involved in day-to-day implementation.

The rule-based form offers a clear separation between problem situation and proposed solution, with the ability to accommodate additional detail in a simple, structured form. For example, here is another summary of BATCH METHOD in this style:

> **If** individual method access on an aggregate object is costly and subject to failure **and** repeated accesses on the aggregate object need to be performed efficiently and without interruption,
>
> **Then** for a given repeated access, define a single method that performs the action on the aggregate repeatedly **and** call the batch method with any parameters passed or results collected in a collection.

Summary of Intent

Another approach to summarizing a pattern is to briefly document its intent—that is, the purpose of the pattern. In documenting intent, the focus is on the problem rather than the solution. The following intent is given for the ITERATOR pattern [GoF95]:

> Provide a way to access elements of an aggregate object sequentially without exposing its underlying representation.

A benefit of this approach is that it makes it easier to spot patterns with similar aims, a topic we explore in more detail in *Chapter 5, Pattern Complements*. For example, BATCH METHOD can be said to satisfy the same intent as ITERATOR. At the same time, a potential liability of this approach is precisely that it can fail to differentiate between patterns that at one level have similar aims, but at another offer quite distinct trade-offs. It can be argued that the summary form of a pattern should help to distinguish one pattern from another. In this case, some fine-tuning and refocusing to include more of the problem context more clearly identifies the intent of BATCH METHOD:

> Provide an efficient way to access elements of an aggregate object in a distributed environment.

Pattern Abstracts

It is also possible to provide a more conventional abstract of a pattern that embraces its motivation and its solution. This approach is used in all the *Pattern-Oriented Software Architecture* volumes: in [POSA1], [POSA2], and [POSA3] the abstract form is used in a visually distinct frame at the start of each pattern, while in [POSA4] the abstract form is used in the introductory material ahead of each grouping of patterns. In this volume the abstract form is used in the *Referenced Patterns* appendix. Here is the abstract form of BATCH METHOD presented in [POSA4]:

> The BATCH METHOD pattern folds together repeated accesses to the elements of an aggregate object to reduce the costs of multiple individual accesses.

Interestingly, many of the statements of intent presented by the Gang-of-Four go further than just stating intent, and are closer to the abstracts found in POSA. For example, here is the 'intent' of the TEMPLATE METHOD pattern [GoF95]:

> Define the skeleton of an algorithm in an operation, deferring some steps to subclasses. Template Method lets subclasses redefine certain steps of an algorithm without changing the algorithm's structure.

There is a description of both the solution structure and motivation for applying the pattern, which goes further than just intent. The issue here is with the terminology ('intent') rather than with the utility of such a description, which has obvious value.

3.6   Different Pattern Forms

A wealth of different forms is available for documenting patterns from which we can choose: the very structured and detailed Gang-of-Four and POSA forms [GoF95] [POSA1], the short and essence-focused form introduced by Jim Coplien [Cope95], Ward Cunningham's more narrative 'Portland' form [Cun95], the form used by Christopher Alexander [AIS77], and even unusual forms, such as the one developed by

Alistair Cockburn, which introduces aspects like the 'overdose' effect of a pattern [Coc97], reminiscent of the medical diagnostic metaphor discussed in *Chapter 1*.

Metamorphosis

The BATCH METHOD pattern description arrived at by the end of *Chapter 1*, can, for example, be transformed easily into the Coplien form by adding the appropriate headings to each part and rearranging as necessary:

Name: BATCH METHOD

Problem: How can bulk accesses on an aggregate object be performed efficiently and without interruption if access is costly and prone to failure?

Context: In a distributed or concurrent object system, the client of an aggregate object may need to perform bulk actions on the aggregate. For example, the client may need to retrieve all elements in a collection that match specific properties. However, if the access to the aggregate is expensive, because it is remote from the client or shared between multiple threads, accessing it separately for each element over a loop—whether by index, by key, or by iterator—can incur severe performance penalties, such as round-trip time, blocking delay, or context-switching overhead.

Forces:

- An aggregate object shared between clients in a concurrent environment, whether locally multithreaded or distributed, is capable of encapsulating synchronization for individual method calls but not for multiple calls, such as a call repeated by a loop.

- The overhead of blocking, synchronization, and thread management must be added to the costs for each access across threads or processes. Similarly, any other per-call housekeeping code, such as authorization, can further reduce performance.

- Where an aggregate object is remote from its client, each access incurs further latency and jitter and decreases available network bandwidth.

- Distributed systems are open to partial failure, where a client may still be live after a server has gone down. Remote access during iteration introduces a potential point of failure for each loop execution, which exposes the client to the problem of dealing with the consequences of partial traversal, such as an incomplete snapshot of state or an incompletely applied set of updates.

Solution: For a given action, define a single method that performs the action on the aggregate repeatedly.

Each BATCH METHOD is defined as part of the interface of the aggregate object, either directly as part of the EXPLICIT INTERFACE exported for the whole aggregate type, or as part of a narrower, mix-in EXPLICIT INTERFACE that only defines the capability for invoking the repeated action. The BATCH METHOD is declared to take all the arguments for each execution of the action, for example via an array or a collection, and to return results by similar means. Instead of accessing aggregate elements individually and directly from within a loop, the client invokes the BATCH METHOD to access multiple elements in a single call. The BATCH METHOD may be implemented directly by the aggregate object's underlying class, or indirectly via an OBJECT ADAPTER, leaving the aggregate object's class unaffected.

Rationale: A BATCH METHOD folds repetition into a data structure rather than a loop within the client, so that looping is performed before or after the method call, in preparation or follow-up. Consequently, the cost of access to the aggregate is reduced to a single access or a few 'chunked' accesses. Specifically in distributed systems, this 'compression' can improve performance significantly, incur fewer network errors, and save precious bandwidth.

Resulting Context: By using a BATCH METHOD, each access to the aggregate becomes more expensive, but the overall cost for bulk accesses has been reduced. Such accesses can also be synchronized as appropriate within the method call. Each call can be made effectively transactional, either succeeding or failing completely, but never partially.

The trade-off in complexity is that a BATCH METHOD performs significantly more housekeeping to set up and work with the results of the call, and requires more intermediate data structures to pass arguments and receive results. The higher the costs for networking, concurrency, and other per-call housekeeping, however, the more affordable this overhead becomes.

It could also be converted to the POSA form by adding the missing sections, diagrams, graphics, and CRC cards. Or it could stay as is, just as plain, ordered prose. Each of these forms documents a pattern.

In some cases, as in the example just shown, moving between pattern forms can be a simple transliteration, but more often the form elements and styles are sufficiently misaligned that a more studied translation is required. A pattern expressed in a form that lists forces as bullet points needs more than copying and pasting to come alive in a form that is more narrative. A pattern that is expressed in a form that does not identify forces explicitly, such as the Gang-of-Four form, demands more than just rephrasing to succeed in a form that informs the reader of the forces. Patterns written in short, high-level form need further detail and more work to fill a longer, more precise form. Patterns written in longer forms need good editing and summary to fit comfortably into shorter forms.

As an example of the last point, all of the patterns in *Patterns for Concurrent and Networked Objects* [POSA2] were included in *A Pattern Language for Distributed Computing* [POSA4]. Although both books are approximately the same length, POSA2 contains descriptions of seventeen patterns and POSA4 contains 114 patterns. The pattern descriptions in POSA2 are typically twenty to thirty pages in length—which includes code, diagrams, tables, and detailed consideration of implementation options—whereas most of the descriptions in POSA4 are two pages long, with a few of three pages.

The different emphasis of these two works is essentially that of forest versus trees: POSA4 offers a broader connected view of its patterns, where POSA2 offers a close-up, detailed view—hence the difference in length and depth. In bringing the POSA2 patterns into POSA4, however, reducing their length by an order of magnitude is more than just a simple matter of dropping obvious details such as code and diagrams. The resulting description must still stand—and be read—as an honest and whole representation of the pattern.

There are examples where we can move easily from one form to another, as we just demonstrated with revising BATCH METHOD into Coplien form. These examples, however, are the exception rather than the rule. In most cases moving from one form to another is largely a matter of rewriting and remining the pattern, which is a profoundly creative activity.

There is little about moving between forms that is automatic. Although readers will recognize the commonality between two forms of the same pattern, the regularity that is present does not afford useful automation. The idea of a pattern markup language that uses a simple schema transformation to present patterns in different forms is somewhat fanciful. Only the most trivial extractions are open to this approach, such as the extraction of the first (or last) sentence of the problem statement and the first sentence of the solution statement to form a pattern thumbnail.

Choices, Choices

The form most appropriate for describing a particular pattern is not something that can be easily defined through objective rules. At best we can evaluate recommendations and considerations, but subjectivity tempered by experience plays the dominant role. The form depends very much on the intent that pattern authors have in mind with the description, and also the target audience they want to address. At the risk of over-generalization, we summarize some heuristics below that can help pattern writers decide which form to use for their pattern descriptions.

A pattern description whose goal is to present a pattern's essence or raise awareness of a problem and summarize a way out—and whose audience is managers or project leaders—is often best served by a short form, such as the Coplien form, than a form that discusses a pattern's implementation in depth. The description of the BATCH METHOD pattern we developed in *Chapter 1*, and revisited in this chapter, is also a good candidate for this kind of pattern form.

Short forms tend to emphasize the essential, stable character of a pattern better than longer forms. Implementation details of general patterns may become dated as new programming paradigms, languages, and features emerge. In contrast, the core essence of a good pattern is often timeless, although not necessarily static. More pragmatically, short and essence-focused forms are helpful for browsing the existing pattern space to find patterns that can help to resolve a particular problem. Of course, a thumbnail of a larger pattern description—which we can consider a very short form—can play this role.

A short form is often insufficient, however, if a pattern author wants to guide developers in *implementing* a pattern using a programming language. In this case we need a description of a pattern's structure and dynamics, implementation guidelines, and concrete examples. In other words, we need to capture both the essence *and* the details of a pattern for this audience.

The description form we defined and used in the first three volumes of the *Pattern-Oriented Software Architecture* series was intended to meet these needs [POSA1] [POSA2] [POSA3]: it allowed us to draw the 'big picture' of a pattern, detail its concrete structure and dynamics, and guide its implementation. Readers who want to grasp the key ideas behind a specific pattern only need to read its Context, Problem, and Solution sections. These three sections describe a pattern's core—all other sections provide additional information. The Structure, Dynamics, and Consequences sections give an overview of a pattern's look and feel. The Example, Implementation, Example Resolved, Variants, Known Uses, and See Also sections provide the details for applying and implementing the pattern in production applications.

Yet overall pattern form is not the only aspect of a pattern that affects its successful communication. A pattern description that is hard to read, passive to the point of comatose, formal, and aloof is likely to disengage the reader. A pattern that introduces complex issues too early, or one that uses an example whose incidental details distract the reader and dominate the pattern, or a pattern that cannot be understood without deep subject matter expertise, will not attract a broad audience. A pattern description should be precise, informative, and fun to read—a story should be told.

3.7   Style and Substance (Redux)

The form used for a pattern description matters a great deal to both pattern authors and readers. It defines a vehicle for presentation, along with the perspective and bias that can bring. Thus, although in one sense the choice of form can be considered arbitrary, in another sense it is anything but: the essence of a good pattern can be considered independent of any description of it, but the description frames how the pattern will be perceived.

Lest we become *too* absorbed in the question of form, however, recall what we said in *Section 1.12, From a Problem–Solution Statement to a Pattern*:

> It is also worth clarifying—in case the intent of this chapter is misread—that just improving a description does not automatically convert any given solution to a problem into a pattern. Patterns cannot be wordsmithed into existence. Only if a problem–solution pair *has* the other properties we discussed above can it be considered a good or whole pattern.

The same observation is equally true of this chapter and its content. Form matters—a lot—but it exists to bring out the qualities in a pattern, not to substitute for them. Without meeting the following conditions, we may have nothing more than a good description of a hollow pattern [Ale79]:

> So we say that a pattern is good whenever we can show that it meets the following two empirical conditions:
>
> 1. *The problem is real.* This means that we can express the problem as a conflict among forces that really do occur within the stated context, and cannot normally be resolved within that context. This is an empirical question.
>
> 2. *The configuration solves the problem.* This means that when the stated arrangement of parts is present in the stated context, the conflict can be resolved, without any side effects. This is an empirical question.

In short, pattern form matters most when pattern content actually describes something of substance! We therefore aspire to combine the appropriate form, good description, and a whole pattern.

II Between Patterns

"World's End" at Oslo Fjord in Norway
© Mai Skou Nielssen

In the second part of the book we move outside the space of the individual pattern to explore the relationships between patterns. Patterns are fond of company: sometimes with one pattern as an alternative to another, sometimes with one pattern as an adjunct to another, sometimes with a number of patterns bound together as a tightly-knit group. Patterns organized as a sequence, applied one after another in a narrative flow, can add an active voice to the use of patterns in design. Last but not least, there is the general issue of organizing many patterns together as pattern collections.

No pattern is an island—they are fond of company and the space between them is full of 'life.' The manifold relationships that can exist between patterns help to realize, reinforce, strengthen, and extend the power of an individual pattern beyond its specific focus or location in a concrete pattern arrangement or software design. In this part of the book we therefore investigate the various types of relationships between patterns, and discuss how these relationships support the effective and productive use of patterns in concrete software projects.

- *Chapter 4, Pattern Islands?*, presents a simple yet expressive design experiment that motivates how the relationships between patterns can help to create pattern-based designs that are of higher quality and *wholeness* than designs created with patterns applied in isolation.

- *Chapter 5, Pattern Complements*, looks at how one pattern can complete the design of another. It also explores how two or more patterns can make a design process more complete by offering contrast and competition between them. Sometimes the two views of complements—structure and process, co-operative and competitive—fall together when competing patterns are combined.

- *Chapter 6, Pattern Compounds*, discusses how a group of patterns can cling together in a tightly connected arrangement that forms a pattern in its own right. Such a compound organization of patterns helps to address problems that reside at a coarser granularity and scope than the problems addressed by each of the arrangement's constituent patterns.

- *Chapter 7, Pattern Sequences*, explores how patterns can support the design *process* of a specific piece of software. Pattern stories offer a presentation form that describes how patterns have been (or might be) applied concretely to construct a given system or feature. Pattern sequences generalize this narrative into something more fundamental, distilling the actual sequence of patterns applied so that the same sequence can be considered elsewhere.

- *Chapter 8, Pattern Collections*, looks at pattern collections and catalogs, which act as repositories of patterns. We look at the different schemes available for organizing collections. In doing so, we discuss problem frames as a technique for exploring the context and problems in which patterns may be applied. We also present a semiotic perspective on pattern structure and relationships.

It is important to note that the concepts presented in this part of the book are of differing maturity and have differing acceptance in the software pattern community. Some concepts, such as pattern complements and pattern compounds, are well understood, elaborated, and established. Other concepts, such as pattern stories and pattern sequences, are not yet completely explored and accepted, although in practice their use has often been implicit. Similarly, while pattern catalogs and collections are a popular and widely accepted form of organizing patterns, the problem frame and semiotic perspectives are more recent approaches in this field, and thus are not yet widespread in the pattern community.

Our goal is to provide as complete and up-to-date an exploration of the relationships between patterns as we can. We therefore present and discuss *all* of the above concepts in this part of the book, regardless of whether they are novel or mature, or advocated and used by few or many. We also believe that each of the concepts discussed has its specific and unique value and that all concepts integrate well with one another, reinforcing and strengthening their individual properties rather than conflicting. The picture of the space between patterns would therefore be incomplete if any of the concepts we discuss were missing.

As with Part I, *Inside Patterns*, all our considerations, reflections, observations, and statements are not bound to a specific type of pattern, even though our examples focus solely on design patterns.

4 Pattern Islands?

Is it best to consider patterns as distinct islands of design, or as more naturally a part of an interwoven whole? In popular literature and usage they are often considered and applied separately. In this chapter we explore the consequences of taking this perspective to its logical conclusion with a simple design experiment. This experiment further reinforces the notion that design patterns define roles for structural parts, rather than just structural parts.

4.1   Patterns Connect

Many pattern authors and experienced pattern users profess that patterns rarely exist in isolation. Each pattern generally has relationships to other patterns. The interdependencies between these relationships become more apparent when patterns are applied consciously or mined from production software systems.

The Gang-of-Four book [GoF95], for example, includes a map that illustrates the dependencies among its twenty-three patterns. More detailed information about these dependencies is presented in the Related Patterns sections of the corresponding pattern descriptions. In *A System of Patterns* [POSA1] we also discussed the fact that a pattern may refine other patterns, may be a variant of another pattern, or may combine with other patterns. Every pattern included in the *Pattern-Oriented Software Architecture* series, regardless of which volume, explains which other patterns are related to it in one or more of the ways outlined above.

Our latest and most up-to-date coverage of the relationships between patterns is documented in *A Pattern Language for Distributed Computing* [POSA4]. Each of the 114 patterns described in POSA4 references other patterns we find useful for their use or realization in the context of building distributed software systems. For example, the description of the MODEL-VIEW-CONTROLLER pattern references twelve patterns: DOMAIN OBJECT, TEMPLATE VIEW, TRANSFORM VIEW, PAGE CONTROLLER, FRONT CONTROLLER, COMMAND, COMMAND PROCESSOR, APPLICATION CONTROLLER, CHAIN OF RESPONSIBILITY, WRAPPER FACADE, DATA TRANSFER OBJECT, and OBSERVER. In POSA4 we also address a form of relationship that we did not discuss in POSA1: a pattern can be a (competing) alternative to another pattern.

The types of relationships and interdependencies that can exist between patterns are widely discussed in the pattern literature and also in this and the following two chapters. This section therefore focuses on *why* the relationships and interdependencies between patterns are important for their effective comprehension and application.

4.2 A Design Experiment: Patterns as Islands

To illustrate why relationships between patterns are important, we will conduct a simple design experiment aimed at developing an extensible request-handling framework that helps to transform service requests from clients into concrete method invocations on an application. In this experiment, we will assume that no relationship between any two documented patterns exists, and that no integration is allowed between their implementations. In other words, we treat every pattern as an island, a self-contained whole whose roles do not mix with those of other patterns.

The first design problem we must resolve when developing the request-handling framework is to 'objectify' the requests issued by clients, who may be human users or other computing systems. The COMMAND pattern addresses this design problem, so we apply it to create our initial design. An abstract class, Command, declares a set of abstract methods to execute client requests. A set of ConcreteCommand classes derives from the Command class to implement the *concrete commands* that applications handle, as shown in the following diagram.

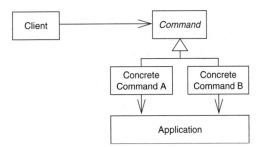

When clients issue a specific request they instantiate a corresponding ConcreteCommand object and invoke it through one of the methods inherited from the abstract Command class. The ConcreteCommand object then performs the requested operations on the application and returns the results, if any, to the client.

Since multiple clients can issue command objects independently, it is useful to coordinate the general command handling within a central component. The COMMAND PROCESSOR pattern provides such a structure. Clients pass concrete commands they create to a special *command processor* component for further handling and execution.

Integrating the COMMAND PROCESSOR pattern with the existing architecture is straightforward and introduces no appreciable accidental complexity: a CommandProcessor class is inserted between the clients and the Command class, as shown below.

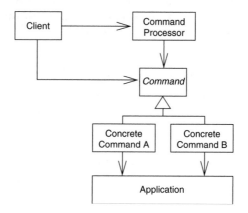

Many systems also support undoing the actions performed in response to requests. Implementing such a rollback mechanism may require taking a whole or partial snapshot of the application's state before executing a request, and restoring this state when users undo the request later. The MEMENTO pattern specifies such a mechanism via the *memento*, which maintain copies of the state of another component termed the *originator*. A *caretaker* component creates a memento, holds it over time, and, if necessary, passes it back to the originator. One of the common motivating examples for the MEMENTO pattern is an undo mechanism [GoF95], which is exactly what we want to design.

Conceptually, concrete commands are caretakers that create mementos before executing a request, maintain these mementos while the concrete command can be rolled back, and pass the memento back to the application when a concrete command's undo operation is invoked. The memento is a new component in our design whose instances capture the current state of the application, which plays the role of the originator.

We will not supplement the concrete command role with the caretaker role, however, because the purpose of our experiment is to treat patterns and their roles in strict isolation. Instead we introduce a separate `Caretaker` class and connect it to the `Command` class, so that every `ConcreteCommand` object can use an instance of this class to create, maintain, and restore an instance of a class `Memento`. A direct consequence of this strict separation of pattern responsibilities is that the resulting design looks a little awkward and introduces unnecessary structural and logical complexity in the area of undoing concrete commands—as shown in the following diagram.

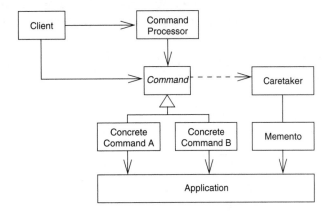

A further requirement for our framework is to define a mechanism for logging requests. Developers that use the framework might want to log requests differently: some will log every request, others just particular types of requests, and others might not log any requests at all. Another design problem we must resolve, therefore, is satisfying the logging needs of different users in a flexible and efficient manner.

A candidate pattern for resolving this problem is STRATEGY, which supports the encapsulation and exchange of algorithms that can vary in a system to enable 'pluggable' behavior. The integration of STRATEGY into our design, however, leads to another minor clash. Ideally the `CommandProcessor` should provide or call the logging service. Since we are disallowing the integration of roles from different patterns within the same component, however, the logging service's invariant parts must be implemented separately from our `CommandProcessor`, in the STRATEGY pattern's context component.

STRATEGY is therefore applied as follows: the CommandProcessor passes the ConcreteCommand objects it receives to a LoggingContext object that plays the *context* role in STRATEGY. This object implements the invariant parts of the logging service and delegates the computation of customer-specific logging aspects to a ConcreteLoggingStrategy object, which plays the role of a *concrete strategy* in the STRATEGY pattern. An abstract class Logging offers a common protocol for all ConcreteLoggingStrategy classes, so that they can be exchanged without modifying LoggingContext. This design is not the most elegant application of STRATEGY and introduces unnecessary structural and logical complexity, as does our design for undoing concrete commands, but it satisfies our rule on keeping patterns apart.

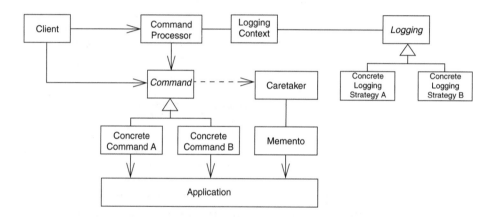

The final step in our design experiment is to support compound commands. A ConcreteCommand object may be an aggregate of other ConcreteCommand objects that are executed in a particular order. The design pattern that provides this structure is COMPOSITE, where compound commands can be represented as *composite* objects and 'atomic' commands as *leaf* objects. Since we are disallowing pattern role integration, however, adding COMPOSITE to the design is not as straightforward as we would like—indeed, it becomes a bit of a hack.

One possible integration of COMPOSITE into our design is to let clients instantiate Component objects, which may be instances of either Composite or Leaf, according to the COMPOSITE pattern. Leaf objects include a reference to the Command class and can thus represent any specific `ConcreteCommand`. `Composite` objects in turn can aggregate several `Leaf` objects and therefore several `ConcreteCommand` objects, which then form the compound command.

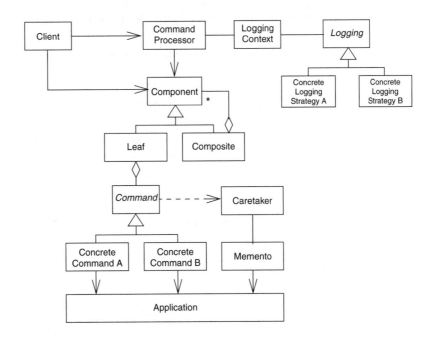

The final architecture of our request-handling framework shown in the diagram above includes five patterns. Although each pattern resolves a particular problem well, the design as a whole does not reflect the expected qualities of these individual parts. The design is gratuitously complex and does not function as a whole: it is hard to understand, maintain, and extend. Furthermore, its performance may suffer due to the number of components involved in executing each request.

The primary metrics this design will score highly on are 'lines-of-code' and 'number-of-classes,' neither of which is a measure of quality. Quality and quantity should not be confused with one another, although they often are.

There is another aspect that might perhaps please some consumers of this design: if patterns are considered to be modular parts, such a modular structure is easy to document. The application of each pattern is quite divorced and quite distinct from the other patterns, lending itself to an apparently simple diagram to show the patterns used.

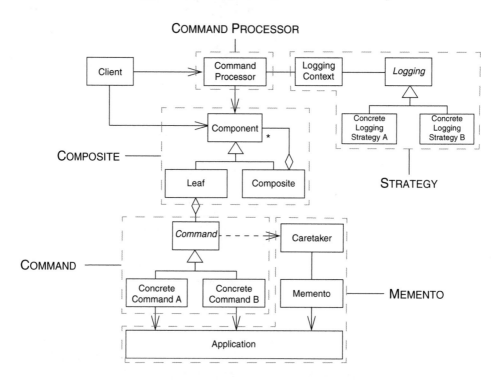

However, this is not so much simple as simplistic. As our previous deliberations have shown—see, for example, *Chapter 2*—patterns are not components to be snapped together like children's constructor toys.

The lesson of this experiment is that overly complicated designs can occur when developers apply patterns naively, without appreciating how they interrelate.

4.3   A Second Design Experiment: Interwoven Patterns

If we remove the constraint that roles introduced by patterns cannot cohabit the same component, the architecture of our request-handling framework will look, feel, and evolve quite differently and smoothly. For example, we can assign the caretaker role introduced by the MEMENTO pattern to the Command class. The ConcreteCommand classes that execute requests therefore also handle Mementos. This simplification removes the need for a separate Caretaker class to maintain Mementos on behalf of ConcreteCommand objects, which only introduced structural complexity and performance overhead. The abstract Command class can also be implemented as an EXPLICIT INTERFACE, which supports an even looser coupling between clients that issue requests and the ConcreteCommand implementations that objectify those requests.

In addition, it is possible to make the CommandProcessor class play the role of the context component introduced by STRATEGY, which eliminates the need for a separate LoggingContext object, since CommandProcessor can implement the call to a particular logging strategy. If no logging is required, we can configure a NullLogging strategy with the CommandProcessor, according to the NULL OBJECT pattern. This integration of the COMMAND PROCESSOR with the STRATEGY pattern removes another class from the original design.

Our request-handling framework's architecture can be refactored further by combining COMMAND with COMPOSITE. The compound command design becomes much less tortured if the Command class from the COMMAND pattern also implements the role of the COMPOSITE pattern's component participant, the ConcreteCommand classes are also considered as leaves, and a CompositeCommand class is added to this structure.

As a result of these refactorings, we arrive at the following structure:

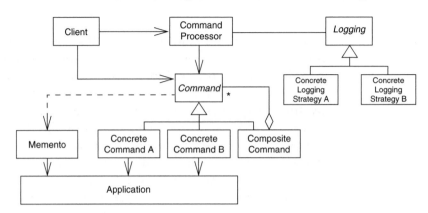

This new request-handling framework architecture is much easier to understand and maintain than the Frankenstein's monster we constructed in the first experiment. It is more economic in its expression—whether counted in terms of classes or lines of code—and is also likely to be more economic in its use of CPU and memory. If performance is important, this design will be easier to optimize than the first experiment's design by virtue of its economy—'Remember that there is no code faster than no code' [Tal94].

The economy in design is arrived at by taking advantage of the relationships that exist between the roles of the five constituent patterns. For example, COMPOSITE and MEMENTO complete COMMAND, and COMMAND and STRATEGY complete COMMAND PROCESSOR. Some refactored components now also play roles in several patterns, so the new design has a higher *pattern density* than its predecessor. For example, the Command class embodies the command role of the COMMAND and COMMAND PROCESSOR patterns, the component role of the COMPOSITE pattern, and the caretaker role of the MEMENTO pattern. Similarly, the CommandProcessor is involved in the implementation of COMMAND PROCESSOR and STRATEGY.

Of course, in rejecting a modular view of pattern application, along with the accidental complexity that comes with it, there is the question of documenting and diagramming pattern use in a design. Classes are no longer hierarchically organized with respect to patterns, 'belonging' mutually exclusively to one pattern or another. Diagramming pattern usage as we did before is likely to make a mess of the diagram because of the number of overlapping areas. Instead we must look to a different approach, one based more on annotation than on delineation. The diagram below uses the notation *pattern:role annotation*, as defined by Erich Gamma in the mid 1990s [Vlis98b].

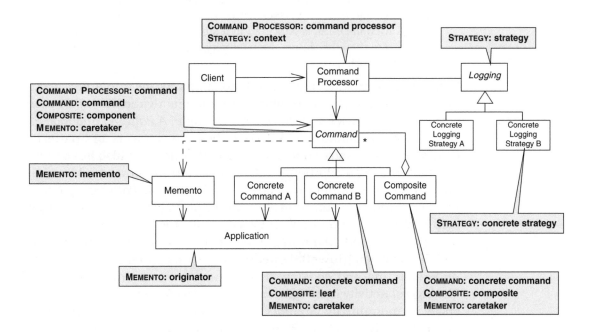

4.4 Pattern Density

Analysis of 'good' software architectures tends to reveal a high density of tightly integrated patterns. Closer examination suggests that it is actually this pattern density that supports the developmental properties of these architectures—a good architecture encapsulates change [Cope98] and is both reasoned and reasonable. From a pattern perspective, creating such architectures is possible only if patterns expose manifold relationships between themselves. They need to complement and complete one another and combine into larger structures in many different ways. In other words, relationships between patterns cannot reasonably be ignored in successful architectures. However, achieving higher pattern density is not simply a matter of arbitrarily throwing together as many patterns as possible in as few classes as possible [Vlis98b]:

> Density has its pluses and minuses. Having multiple patterns dwell in relatively few classes lends a certain profundity to a design; much meaning is captured in a small space, not unlike good poetry. On the other hand, such density can be reminiscent of less inspired efforts.

Capturing these inter-pattern relationships as meaningfully, accurately, and precisely as possible is a strong motivation behind much of the ongoing work on patterns. For example, *A Pattern Language for Distributed Computing* [POSA4], describes and connects 114 patterns to support the construction of distributed systems. It also links these 114 patterns to an additional 180 or so patterns documented in other pattern sources. Similarly, Martin Fowler's book *Patterns of Enterprise Application Architecture* [Fow02] connects fifty-one patterns that help the construction of Web-based, multi-tier enterprise information systems, and *Enterprise Integration Patterns* by Gregor Hohpe and Bobby Woolf [HoWo03] integrates sixty-six patterns that help the understanding and construction of quality messaging middleware. The biggest activity in integrating the patterns from the known pattern space is undoubtedly Grady Booch's *Handbook of Software Architecture* project [Booch], which, at the time of writing, addresses over a thousand patterns documented to date in the domain of software development.

All these works focus primarily on synthesis and connection, rather than on documenting new patterns. Their goal is to understand patterns as connected nodes in a larger network of relationships, rather than as individual islands awaiting arbitrary discovery by some seafaring software explorer. As we demonstrated in our two design experiments, a set of disjointly applied patterns may have twice the number of classes but only half the value of a more intimately connected set.

It All Comes Down to Roles and Relationships!

The main property of patterns that allows us to take advantage of their relationship potential is simple: patterns introduce roles and responsibilities for components, but not necessarily new specific components. These roles can be combined and integrated in many ways without ever quite being the same, and without violating the essence of the patterns that participate in such an integrated structure [Cool97] [Cool98].

A statement we made before, and which is supported by our experiments, is that patterns are not simply components of the same order as classes or packages, with strict modular boundaries that enable brick-like composition. Only when integrating the roles introduced by each pattern can developers consciously and effectively use patterns in their designs. A self-conscious approach that keeps patterns separated is likely to produce overly complex architectures. Explicit use of patterns then becomes more of a hindrance than a help, even if each application appears to resolves its own problem well.

Although some details of the first design experiment were contrived for this chapter, the example is representative of how patterns have been (mis)applied in some systems—for example, the OBSERVER story from *Chapter 0*. The project in that story had problems because the development team considered patterns as islands, as we did in our first design experiment, and not as sets of combinable and composable roles, as we did in our second experiment. Patterns map out potentially overlapping regions of design space rather than untouchable, modular class diagrams.

Conversely, roles alone are insufficient for successful pattern use. We also need guidelines that specify which role combinations are actually useful. Without these guidelines, inexperienced pattern users are likely to integrate too many, too few, or simply the wrong roles in response to a particular problem. The pattern relationships provide some of these missing guidelines.

Regarding the implementation and practical use of patterns, it is this mutual complement of pattern roles and relationships that provides patterns with much of their potency. Similarly, it is this possibility of building on the results of previous patterns—adding new elements with new roles but also adding new roles to existing elements—that makes a conscious pattern-driven approach to software architecture like a constructive dialog.

5   Pattern Complements

Nothing is more dangerous than an idea,
when you have but one idea.

Émile-Auguste Chartier

A *complement* is something that makes another thing complete in some way. In this chapter we look at how this notion can apply to patterns. First, we see how two or more patterns can enrich a design process by offering contrast and competition between alternative solutions to similar problems. Next, we look at how one pattern can complete the design of another. Last, we see how these two views of complements—process and structure, competitive and cooperative— are not necessarily so very different, by illustrating how competing patterns can cooperate and be combined.

5.1   More than One Solution to a Problem

There is a common perception among many developers that certain types of problems are resolved by only a single pattern [BuHe03] [Bus03a]. This perception is sometimes reinforced in the naming of particular patterns. For example, collection iteration problems can be addressed by ITERATOR, object adaptation problems are addressed by ADAPTER, stateful object lifecycle problems are addressed by OBJECTS FOR STATES, and so on, as we also discussed in *Section 0.2, A Story of Success... with Some Exceptions.*

The idea that one problem maps to one solution acts as a security blanket for some pattern users, since it seems to make life simpler. In particular, the lack of choice and variation is seen as a strength rather than a weakness, since it eliminates design choice and with it the need for any design dialog. Were design such a simple process, however, it is unlikely that skill and judgment would be in such scarce supply or valued so highly. Such a narrow view is simplistic and is a common pitfall in applying patterns.

The lack of diversity in a design vocabulary is an issue to resolve rather than a state to reach. In contrast to the aspirations of an attendee at a tutorial led by one of the authors, 'freedom from thinking' is *not* one of the goals of the patterns community, and anyone expecting patterns to provide them with such a salve will be sorely disappointed! Patterns are intended to provide a vehicle for—not release from—reasoning about design. In constraining certain degrees of freedom, patterns do not eliminate choice, they make the choices clearer by capturing design impact and trade-offs explicitly.

Many different kinds and levels of thinking are involved in tackling design problems and developing software. Developers are often distracted by nitty-gritty details when such details are not related to the broader problem they are trying to solve. Alternatively, they too often rely on particular solutions through habit, without critical consideration of whether the solution is appropriate or effective. What patterns offer is *focus*.

Taking a Broader View

We often hear stories of how a solution was made more complex than necessary by the application of a specific pattern [Bus03a] [Bus03b]. The blame is often laid at the door of patterns in general. A quick review of the design, however, often reveals that the root of the problem was something simpler:

- *The wrong pattern was applied.* For example, the problem looked as if it needed a plain ITERATOR for element access, but in the context of distribution a BATCH METHOD would have been the better option.

- *An ingredient was missing.* For example, a COMMAND class hierarchy was the right design, but without a COMMAND PROCESSOR it was inevitable that the code would become mired in minor details and clever tricks.

With these caveats in mind, we consider the notion of *pattern complements*, which have two aspects:

- *Complementarity with respect to competition.* One pattern may complement another because it provides an alternative solution to the same or a similar problem, and thus is complementary in terms of the design decision that can be taken.

- *Complementarity with respect to structural completeness.* One pattern may complement another because it completes a design, acting as a natural pairing to the other in a given design.

These ideas seem distinct enough at first sight, such that they could always be treated separately. The notion of complementarity, however, runs deeper than with just the patterns—as in other walks of life, competition and cooperation are often not such strange bedfellows.

5.2   Patterns in Competition

Designs may differ with respect to the concrete arrangement of roles and implementation details of a given pattern, allowing the resolution of a particular problem in many different ways, as discussed in *Chapter 2*. Designs may also differ in the choice of the pattern itself, since some problems may also be addressed by more than one pattern. For example, STRATEGY and TEMPLATE METHOD are candidates for use in designs that need to fix the steps in an algorithm while allowing the implementation of the steps to vary. Although these two patterns share a very abstract solution principle, their actual solution structures are sufficiently different that they cannot be considered the same pattern. STRATEGY and TEMPLATE METHOD draw on distinct design ideas to give each one its individual character.

Matters of State

Another contrasting example in this context comes from the OBJECTS FOR STATES (a.k.a. STATE) and COLLECTIONS FOR STATES patterns. Both patterns address the problem that an object's concrete behavior can depend on its current modal state. Both patterns also include the same abstract solution principle for this problem: separating state from behavior. Yet one pattern, OBJECTS FOR STATES, encapsulates the consequences of this solution principle, while the other pattern, COLLECTIONS FOR STATES, explicitly exposes it to clients of the state-dependent object.

The following is a summary of the problem and the solution, plus sketch, for OBJECTS FOR STATES [POSA4]:

> The behavior of an object may be modal, where the mode depends on its current state. Hardwiring the corresponding multi-part conditional code within the object's implementation, however, can frustrate its comprehensibility and future development.

Therefore:

Encapsulate the state-dependent behavior of the object into a hierarchy of state classes, with one class per different modal state. Use an instance of the appropriate class to handle the state-dependent behavior of the object, forwarding method calls.

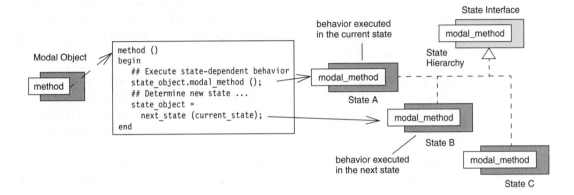

The following is a thumbnail summary of problem and solution, plus sketch, for COLLECTIONS FOR STATES [POSA4]:

Objects whose behavior depends on their current state may be modeled as individual state machines. Sometimes, however, their clients view the behavior of these objects as modal, whereas the objects themselves are independent of any client-specific state model.

Therefore:

Within the client, represent each state of interest by a separate collection that refers to all objects in that state.

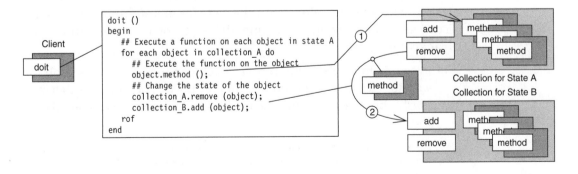

Thus OBJECTS FOR STATES introduces state objects, one for each state, with which another object—the context object—can associate. A particular state object implements the behavior of the context object in the presence of the state it represents. All state objects are maintained by the context object, and state changes are performed transparently for its clients. In contrast, the COLLECTIONS FOR STATES pattern turns this solution principle inside out. Rather then letting the state-dependent object maintain its own state, its clients adopt a managerial role and perform this task, so that the object itself may be unaware of the state in which it is in.

Does this latter approach of extrinsic representation of a concept sound like breaking good and proven object-oriented encapsulation principles? If so, then consider the design of a request-handling framework based on the COMMAND pattern that must support an undo–redo mechanism. In this design command objects are state-dependent. In a do/redo state they execute the request they represent, and in an undo state they cancel this request.[15] Obviously we could apply the OBJECTS FOR STATES pattern in this situation. This design would introduce two state objects for every command object, one for its do-related behavior, and one for its undo-related behavior. Every command object would maintain its two state objects by itself: the command execution mechanism just executes these commands and they 'do the right thing' [Hearsay02] automatically.

Although this solution may look 'good' at first sight—after all, it makes a point of using a well-known pattern—closer examination reveals that the design is overly complex. It creates a sea of objects and substantial overhead for state maintenance, which makes this solution far from 'good' by any reasonable reckoning! For every command (and large-scale systems have many of these) two separate state objects are introduced, along with the code for maintaining the state objects and the code for changing the state of the command object transparently.

If the set of states were different for each command, there is probably no way to avoid the overhead outlined above. The states for do/redo and undo, however, are identical. Although using a Boolean flag to

---

15. For simplicity in this example we assume that all command objects can be undone, a situation that is usually not present in production applications [POSA1].

represent the state is not a 'politically correct' object-oriented design pattern, it might be simpler. That said, the flag-based solution is still not exemplary, even though it represents some improvement on the OBJECTS FOR STATES solution.

Effective command-handling mechanisms, such as the one described by the COMMAND PROCESSOR pattern, follow another strategy for handling command states. Command objects offer two methods, do and undo, which implement their corresponding do-related and undo-related behavior, rather than two state objects. This design saves the state objects and the state object maintenance code. The responsibility for differentiating states has shifted to the command processor object.

This command processor object can introduce two stacks, one for maintaining command objects that are in the undo state, and one for maintaining command objects that are in the redo state. A command object is initially in the do state when it is created. Once a command object is executed, its state changes from do to undo, and the command processor pushes it onto the undo stack.

If the undo function is selected, the topmost command object is popped from the undo stack and its undo method is invoked. When the undo method finishes, the command object's state changes from undo to redo, and it is pushed onto the undo stack. If the redo method is selected, the command processor handles the topmost command on the undo stack analogously. To let the command processor execute this behavior transparently, we could also implement a do method for every stack that encapsulates this behavior, similar to the do method of a command object.

The following diagram shows the structure and behavior described above.

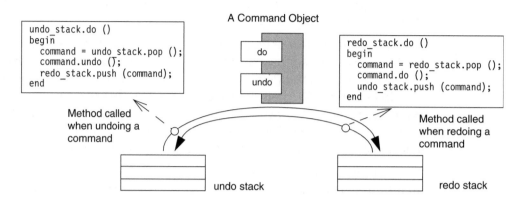

Although the command processor now maintains the state of command objects explicitly, command execution is simpler and more straightforward to implement than when the command objects themselves were maintaining their own state, whether with flags or with OBJECTS FOR STATES. Moreover, this new design avoids many of the overheads and intricacies that the original design introduced. Does this still sound strange? Hopefully not: it is a well-proven, object-oriented request-handling strategy based on COLLECTIONS FOR STATES.

There are many examples for which the extrinsic state model of COLLECTIONS FOR STATES offers a simpler solution or an optimization over other approaches. For example, the collection overhead sometimes associated with AUTOMATED GARBAGE COLLECTION can be reduced by implementing a generational garbage collector, in which objects are organized in different 'generations,' separating young objects from older objects. The majority of newly allocated objects are statistically likely to have short lifetimes, so separating them from older objects optimizes collection through the use of collections.

Operating system task scheduling is another example for which the extrinsic state model of COLLECTIONS FOR STATES offers a simpler solution or an optimization over other approaches. Each task, such as a process or a thread, can be in one of a number of states, such as ready-to-run or blocked-on-I/O. A scheduler that needs to determine the next task to run could scan through the task list, which takes linear time, or it could organize tasks with respect to their states. In this case, a ready-to-run queue would hold all the candidate tasks that are ready to run. The cost associated with finding the next task to run in this design is constant rather than linear time.

You may recall that in *Chapter 0* one of the stories of pattern misapplication concerned the OBJECTS FOR STATES pattern. It was the belief that all stateful lifecycle problems were solved by this one pattern that drove the developers to apply it in cases where it introduced a great deal of accidental complexity, rather than producing a suitable design. A narrow pattern vocabulary had obscured the opportunity for other candidate solutions.

Pattern Pairs, Triples, and More

The pattern literature contains many more such pattern pairs, in which two patterns address essentially the same problem. For example, both the ACTIVE OBJECT and MONITOR OBJECT patterns coordinate access to a shared object in a concurrent program:

> The ACTIVE OBJECT pattern decouples service requests from service execution to enhance concurrency and simplify synchronized access to objects that reside in their own threads of control.

> The MONITOR OBJECT pattern synchronizes concurrent method execution to ensure that only one method at a time runs within an object. It also allows an object's methods to schedule their execution sequences cooperatively.

Both patterns suggest synchronizing the requests so that objects receive them from their clients in different threads, but each is associated with a quite different expression of this principle, and each has different capabilities and overheads. An ACTIVE OBJECT is associated with a thread of its own—hence it is 'active'—and executes method requests asynchronously with respect to the caller of each method. In contrast, each method invocation on a MONITOR OBJECT executes its methods synchronously by borrowing the thread of its caller. Both patterns address the problem of synchronization with respect to objects, but have different pros and cons with respect to properties like flexibility of method execution and runtime overhead.

HALF-SYNC/HALF-ASYNC and LEADER/FOLLOWERS offer another example of a pattern pair in a network server program that processes user requests concurrently:

> The HALF-SYNC/HALF-ASYNC pattern decouples asynchronous and synchronous service processing in concurrent systems, to simplify programming without unduly reducing performance. The pattern introduces two intercommunicating layers, one for asynchronous and one for synchronous service processing.

> The LEADER/FOLLOWERS pattern provides an efficient concurrency model in which multiple threads take turns sharing a set of event sources in order to detect, demultiplex, dispatch, and process service requests that occur on the event sources.

Both patterns can be used to implement thread pools, but again each is associated with a quite different expression of this principle and each has different capabilities and overheads. A HALF-SYNC/HALF-ASYNC design uses a synchronized queue to coordinate the interactions between the threads in the sync layer, which can block, and the thread or interrupt handler in the async layer, which cannot block. In contrast, a LEADER/FOLLOWERS omits the synchronized queue and only has a single layer of threads. Both patterns support thread pools, but have different pros and cons with respect to properties like order of event processing, predictability, and ease of implementation.

In the face of this diversity a question lurks: which pattern to select if several address a similar problem? Selecting a pattern at random is neither a reasoned nor effective approach. The choice matters, therefore, but we need more information to make an informed choice. The key to selecting the 'right' pattern is to consider the context, the forces, and the consequences of the competing patterns, and thus the context and the forces in the design situation itself.

Competing patterns need not just occur in pairs. In the Gang-of-Four catalog, BUILDER, ABSTRACT FACTORY, and PROTOTYPE all vie for the designer's attention as creational patterns at a similar level. Similarly, OBJECTS FOR STATES and COLLECTIONS FOR STATES are further complemented by METHODS FOR STATES. The four patterns in the *Executing Around Sequences* collection [Hen01a] for handling exception safety in C++ are also in competition with one another, but are clearly differentiated in their structures and consequences.

Iterative Development

Following on from its evolution in the previous chapter, we can see that BATCH METHOD—as described in *Chapter 1*—contrasts and competes with the classic ITERATOR pattern as a candidate solution for collection traversal. One of its determinant forces is the cost of accessing an individual element. Repeatedly querying or updating a collection remotely across a network one element at a time is likely to be far more costly than folding the repetition into a single method. The flip side of this approach, of course, is that BATCH METHOD requires more loops to be written than a single-access ITERATOR: for example, a loop before the call in the client to prepare the call, a loop in the server to execute through the batch of items, and a loop in the client to deal with the results.

There is another iteration pattern, ENUMERATION METHOD, whose solution characteristic—the inversion of control flow—might be considered unusual by developers whose programming background is in traditional procedural languages or the 'curly-brace' family of OO-supporting languages. As with a BATCH METHOD, an ENUMERATION METHOD encapsulates the loop mechanism within a method on the aggregate object.

The following C-like pseudocode fragment illustrates a traversal of a collection based on ITERATOR:

```
total = 0
iterator = collection.iterateFromStart()
while(!iterator.atEnd())
{
      total += iterator.currentValue()
      iterator.moveNext()
}
```

The control flow is under the control of the collection user, but this also means that they must manage it. For ENUMERATION METHOD, the structure is inverted:

```
total = 0
collection.forEachElement(
      function(currentValue) { total += currentValue })
```

Unlike BATCH METHOD, which focuses on a single task with inputs and results, an ENUMERATION METHOD takes a COMMAND object or equivalent that is executed as the body of the loop. The COMMAND object is reactive and responds to the ENUMERATION METHOD calling it for each appropriate element in the aggregate. Programmers therefore have neither the means to modify the control flow of an application service nor any direct knowledge about how it is implemented. This inversion is often referred to as the 'Hollywood Principle'—as in 'Don't call us, we'll call you' [Vlis98b]. The Hollywood Principle differs from much classic procedural programming and procedurally influenced object-oriented programming, and is more reminiscent of functional programming.

Here are three patterns summarized together:

> The ITERATOR pattern provides a way to access the elements of an aggregate component sequentially without exposing its underlying representation. A separate, controllable iterator object is used to traverse the aggregate.

> The ENUMERATION METHOD pattern encapsulates iteration over an aggregate component to execute an action on each element of the component into a method on the aggregate. The action is passed in as an object by the caller.

> The BATCH METHOD pattern folds together repeated accesses to the elements of an aggregate object to reduce the costs of multiple individual accesses.

For complex aggregate data structures, an ENUMERATION METHOD is often easier to use. Iteration can be combined with the VISITOR pattern, converting the act of traversal into a simple series of type-differentiated callbacks. Testing is greatly simplified through the use of MOCK OBJECTS, which can be used to test for expected callbacks. Finally, the looping mechanism and policy is fully encapsulated, including details of synchronization and error handling.

Of course, the event-driven programming style is not a perfect match for all problems and all programming languages. But ENUMERATION METHOD serves to reinforce the notion that sometimes the most popular solution—which is sometimes (mis)taken as the most 'intuitive' solution—is not necessarily the most effective one. Familiarity often breeds a notion of intuition, but often the immediacy or obviousness of a solution is more down to a developer's background and experience than to any innate property of the solution itself.

For example, the notion of ITERATORS was missing completely from the early Eiffel libraries [Mey88], leading to overly stateful solutions that required workarounds. The initial Eiffel solution required each collection to hold a cursor to maintain some notion of current position. Moreover, a marker had to be placed to note a cursor position if nested iteration was required.

The concept of ITERATOR objects traversing collection objects is considered 'intuitive' by C++, C#, and Java programmers. In these programming cultures ENUMERATION METHOD is the 'counter-intuitive' approach. The ITERATOR approach is a fine fit for most problems and follows the styles of these languages and their libraries. Knowledge of ENUMERATION METHOD, however, can offer developers greater insight into other problems that would be slightly more awkward, requiring more complex implementation, if rendered in ITERATOR form. For example, tree traversal is trivial with recursion, which is a perfect fit for an ENUMERATION METHOD, but trickier with ITERATOR, which requires additional state to support backtracking.

On the other hand, ENUMERATION METHOD is the common solution in Smalltalk and Ruby, but ITERATOR is not regarded as 'intuitive.' The use of ENUMERATION METHOD is also greatly simplified in these languages because blocks of code can be treated as objects—known as closures. Passing a COMMAND object to an ENUMERATION METHOD is therefore as simple as passing a block of code.

Passing blocks of code is not available as part of C++. In Java, inner classes represent a related concept, but they are still syntactically too heavy to allow ENUMERATION METHOD an equal footing with ITERATOR. In C# 2.0, the lighter-weight feature of anonymous methods offers a more viable alternative. C# 2.0, however, also introduced an alternative technique for expressing ITERATOR logic in the form of iterator methods, which is more attractive for many applications.

The following UML class diagrams show the complementary solutions, and hence the differences in structure, roles, and responsibilities between the ENUMERATION METHOD and ITERATOR patterns.

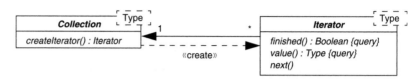

A typical Iterator configuration

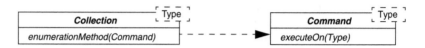

A typical Enumeration Method configuration

There is perhaps one point about naming that deserves clarification: a careful reading of the GoF book suggests that ENUMERATION METHOD is indeed documented within it as a solution. The bulk of their description of ITERATOR is focused solely on what is considered as the classic ITERATOR pattern: a separate object, the ITERATOR, traverses a collection. This form is also listed as EXTERNAL ITERATOR. Its complement, INTERNAL ITERATOR, is what we have referred to as ENUMERATION METHOD.

As discussed above, however, the two forms are not even remotely similar: they are not minor variations of one pattern that is named ITERATOR. Instead, they are two separate patterns with quite distinct solution structures and trade-offs. We have therefore chosen to identify the name ITERATOR with its common use, recognizing that EXTERNAL ITERATOR is a name that is used rarely, if at all, by developers. To avoid adding to the confusion that INTERNAL ITERATOR and EXTERNAL ITERATOR might be simply variants of one another, we have favored the use of ENUMERATION METHOD, which is the name given to this pattern by Kent Beck, who was the first to document the pattern properly on its own terms [Beck96].

Adaptive Development

Another example of two patterns hiding within a single pattern description is the case of OBJECT ADAPTER and CLASS ADAPTER, which are both contained within the description of ADAPTER [GoF95]. The intent of ADAPTER is given as follows:

> Convert the interface of a class into another interface that clients expect. Adapter lets classes work together that couldn't otherwise because of incompatible interfaces.

Against this intent, however, a deconstruction of the pattern description reveals two distinct patterns: OBJECT ADAPTER and CLASS ADAPTER. These are not merely variations on a solution structure: they are based on fundamentally different solution mechanisms, subject to different implementation constraints, and targeted at different problems. Although they share a common intent, their complementary nature is reinforced by a dual narrative that runs through the pattern description.

The following summaries help to both highlight the commonality and outline the basic difference between the two patterns:

> The OBJECT ADAPTER pattern converts the interface of a class into another interface that clients expect. Adaptation lets classes work together that could not otherwise because of incompatible interfaces. The use of an object relationship to express wrapping ensures that the adaptation is encapsulated via forwarding through an additional level of indirection.

> The CLASS ADAPTER pattern converts the interface of a class into another interface that clients expect. Adaptation lets classes work together that could not otherwise because of incompatible interfaces. Class adapters are realized by subclassing both the adapter interface and the adaptee implementation to yield a single object— which avoids an additional level of indirection.

These two patterns can be considered complementary and in competition because they address a common intent with distinct solution structures. The following diagram illustrates the difference in structure:

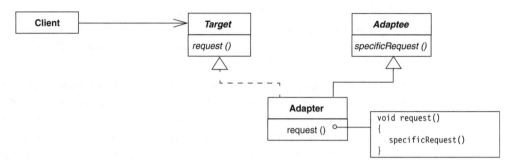

A typical Class Adapter configuration

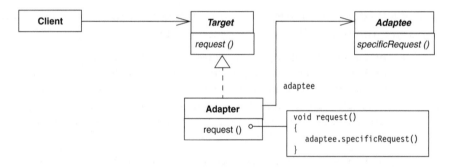

A typical Object Adapter configuration

It is a design decision as to whether a fully encapsulated approach based on forwarding through an object relationship is more appropriate than a more tightly coupled solution based on inheritance. The inheritance solution has the advantage that adaptee methods can be overridden in the adapter, that protected features are visible within the adapter, and that, when instantiated, only a single object is created. It is a more invasive affair, however, and can intrude on other inheritance relationships. From a layered and encapsulated perspective, OB-JECT ADAPTER is considered the stronger and more stable design.

Some of the trade-offs between the two patterns are programming-language dependent:

- C++ allows inheritance to be non-public, whereas the parentage of a Java or C# class is always public knowledge. Thus CLASS ADAPTER is necessarily a visible form of tight coupling in Java and C#, whereas it can be made a bit more discreet in C++.

- C++ and C# can embed objects within objects, so that even when two objects are created, that need not imply two heap allocations, while forwarding involves only an offset, not a true level of indirection. Thus OBJECT ADAPTER can be cheap in terms of memory, although in C# this applies only to cases in which the adaptee is a struct type.

- C++ supports arbitrary multiple inheritance, whereas Java and C# are constrained to single subclassing with multiple interface support. If inheritance is used for adaptation in C# or Java, no other subclassing is possible, so you need to make sure that you 'don't burn your base class' [Gun04].

These language-specific issues can be considered tiebreakers that are worth considering in specific cases. When all the pros and cons are weighed up, CLASS ADAPTER tends to be the special case: it is intrusive and often overly subtle in implementation or interpretation. It is best kept in the toolbox for those occasions when the designer's hand is forced: an adaptee's protected feature must be accessed in the adapter, an adaptee's method must be overridden in the adapter, or an adapter's identity must be the same as the adaptee's. Even with this bias toward OBJECT ADAPTER, however, the complementary nature of the two patterns means that in any given adaptation situation they are both potential candidates.

Following Conway's Law

In 1968 Melvin Conway published an observation that related the architecture of a system to the organization that created it [Con68]:

> Any organization that designs a system (defined more broadly here than just information systems) will inevitably produce a design whose structure is a copy of the organization's communication structure.

This observation has become known as *Conway's Law* [Ray91]:

> The rule that the organization of the software and the organization of the software team will be congruent; originally stated as 'If you have four groups working on a compiler, you'll get a 4-pass compiler.'

In referring to this as a 'law,' the appeal is to a force that will shape a system, much as a physical law, rather than as a rule that should be followed, as with the laws of a community or a state. In this sense it is not a law that can be broken—the force is always there—only one that can be counterbalanced by other forces. As a force, Conway's Law can be considered a specialization or specific application of homomorphism [Con68]:

> This kind of a structure-preserving relationship between two sets of things is called a homomorphism. Speaking as a mathematician might, we would say that there is a homomorphism from the linear graph of a system to the linear graph of its design organization.

But do we want our architecture to necessarily look like a copy of our organization? This sounds more like a problem than a rule to obey unquestioningly. And where there are problems, there are forces that characterize the problem. The homomorphism quoted as Conway's Law is one such force. It is possible to relate other conflicting forces in this problem, as described in the lessons learnt from a workshop on Conway's Law [HvKe05]:

> Informal communication is important in developing software. If a barrier to informal communication is created (e.g. outsourcing or off-shoring) it is necessary to compensate for this barrier. Failure to do so will affect the architecture. [...]

> We are not powerless; we can intervene and change the system concept. Removing barriers requires an active intervention. [...]

> If we do not choose to actively break homomorphism it will take control of the architecture, so we must actively choose to design systems that break homomorphism.

> The problem is: homomorphism is a very strong force but it does not result in good solutions because it overwhelms other forces.

Having characterized a problem and its forces, it is inevitable that we should ask about solutions. The following pattern offers one such solution [CoHa04]:

> If the parts of an organization (e.g. teams, departments, or subdivisions) do not closely reflect the essential parts of the product, or if the relationships between organizations do not reflect the relationships between product parts, then the project will be in trouble. [...]
>
> Therefore:
>
> Make sure the organization is compatible with the product architecture. At this point in the [pattern] language, it is more likely that the architecture should drive the organization than vice versa.
>
> An organization will have periodic reviews of the architecture and potentially of project strategies [...]. At each of these meetings (if indeed they are separate) care should be take to align the structure of the architecture with the structure of the organization by making piecemeal changes to one or the other.

Perhaps a little confusingly, this pattern is itself also known as CONWAY'S LAW. Had it been named after the proposed solution rather than one of its defining forces, it would perhaps have been more accurately named ALIGN ARCHITECTURE AND ORGANIZATION.

Closer inspection, however, reveals that behind the general vision of bringing architecture and organization into alignment, there are two quite distinct propositions:

- Align the structure of the organization with the structure of the architecture.

- Align the structure of the architecture with the structure of the organization.

Although the end result is in essence the same—alignment between the two—the character of these two solution approaches is quite different, and each draws on quite different implementations and skills. The former solution is based on organizational restructuring and the latter is based on software restructuring. The bias of the pattern is given toward the former, but it also accommodates the latter, which is often more achievable politically or economically, and may sometimes also be more appropriate technically.

There is further support for this deconstruction of two distinct patterns. An earlier publication of the CONWAY'S LAW pattern associated it with two aliases [Cope95]: ORGANIZATION FOLLOWS ARCHITECTURE and ARCHITECTURE FOLLOWS ORGANIZATION. These two names quite specifically identify two complementary patterns that offer alternative solutions to the same dominant, underlying problem force, Conway's Law.

Design Dialog with Style

When more than one pattern presents itself as a candidate for addressing a particular design situation, no matter how large or small, we are drawn into a design dialog. In this dialog the pros and cons of a given design can be weighed explicitly, the merits and demerits debated, and a decision reached with a fuller appreciation of the design context and consequences. The design dialog that might begin with a single, stand-alone pattern may now spill over into the consideration of others.

In addition to all of the other considerations we might cite when favoring one pattern over another, there is a further thought: the selection defines the style of a particular design. That style may be dictated strongly by the language and programming culture, it may a characteristic of a particular framework, or it may be specific to a part of a particular system. Sometimes the adoption of one pattern over another is not so much about resolving a problem as about following a vernacular form. Effective design therefore includes subjective and cultural elements that are neither derivable from first principles nor automatable.

At some level the style becomes the substance. For example, Christopher Alexander made many observations about how a collection of one set of patterns helps to define a particular architectural style for buildings that is distinct from other styles drawn from different collections [Ale79]. Similarly, we have seen that the default use of ITERATOR versus the default use ENUMERATION METHOD is primarily a characteristic of different programming languages.

This question of idiomatic style being expressed through design choice is also found in the idiomatic use of pointers and SMART POINTERS to express ITERATORS in C++. As an abstraction of position and traversal, this presentation of an ITERATOR was not obvious until the advent of the Standard Template Library (STL) [StLe95], whereupon the notion seemed like an intuitive opportunity repeatedly missed in the previous decade of C++'s evolution. In C++ this expression gives rise not only to a useful library, but also to a different school of program composition: generic programming [Aus99].

Of course style is not always related to just language, and the question of style is not always a purely subjective choice. In the 1980s and early 1990s there was a stronger emphasis on the use of inheritance as a mechanism for reuse. As a result the CLASS ADAPTER was a common characteristic of many object-oriented systems developed in this era, which at the time were considered good.

A different school of design has gained ground since then, favoring forwarding (sometimes called 'delegation') over inheritance. The Gang-of-Four helped to promote this style with many documented design patterns that focused on object relationships and interfaces rather than a subclassing-heavy approach. In this more loosely coupled school of design OBJECT ADAPTER is favored over CLASS ADAPTER. Of course, choosing between two different schools of design is not simply a lifestyle choice: the greater complexity of inheritance-based solutions is reported both casually and more formally [Hat98].

5.3 Patterns in Cooperation

Competition is not the only close interaction that can occur between groups of patterns. In some designs we find that one pattern may complement another with respect to completeness and, often, symmetry. It is not that the second pattern is necessarily always required, but that it often helps and its presence is less surprising than its absence.

For example, where a FACTORY METHOD introduces a role with the responsibility of creation, a DISPOSAL METHOD plays the opposite role. Where resource management is a concern—whether it is memory in C++ or a higher-level resource in Java—the introduction of a DISPOSAL METHOD answers the question of how an encapsulated act of creation is concluded. A DISPOSAL METHOD makes clear that resources are borrowed rather than truly acquired, and acts as the natural foil and counterbalance for a FACTORY METHOD. Consequently, concrete factories in an ABSTRACT FACTORY or BUILDER arrangement provide both FACTORY METHODS and DISPOSAL METHODS, as illustrated for BUILDER in the diagram below.

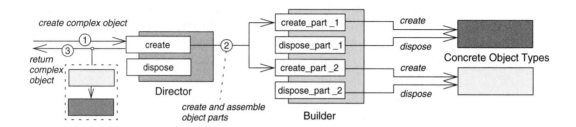

COMMAND PROCESSOR and COMMAND offer us an example that is based on containment rather than a mirror-like symmetry. With respect to the COMMAND pattern, a COMMAND PROCESSOR can often make a design more whole, giving it nameable qualities that would be missing if only the role of the COMMAND hierarchy were elaborated. A COMMAND PROCESSOR is not a mandatory part of COMMAND's elaboration, but in designs in which it is used effectively, it clearly brings a certain completeness and balance to the code.

The diagram below illustrates such a combined arrangement.

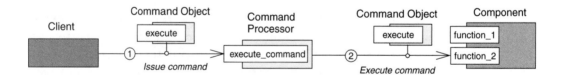

This notion of complementarity can be considered a strong form of the notion of pattern usage or inclusion, in which one pattern is used or included by another. What makes a complement stronger in this sense is that it is based on a more fundamental match between the patterns involved: they could be drawn out as mirror images or dovetailed parts.

An Example of Value

Objects that represent values are often held by reference and shared across multiple contexts, such as different threads. The IMMUTABLE VALUE pattern addresses the issues that arise from aliasing in reference-based languages and frameworks, including thread safety and transparency. IMMUTABLE VALUE's design insight is that where objects are being shared, so that one user can make changes to the object that are then detected by another user, it is not sharing that is the problem to be solved: it is change. Two objects holding the same value should appear to hold the same value, a guarantee that can be preserved by removing any methods that could change the value object's state. The conflicting forces are therefore resolved by removing features that are considered typical of an object interface, making the resulting design simpler to work with.

The summary above, however, is not necessarily the end of the design dialog. When a value remains unchanged after it has been initialized there is little more to tell. But when a change of value is needed, this immutability becomes a conflicting force in its own right.

With an IMMUTABLE VALUE any change of value must be effected either by referring to another existing IMMUTABLE VALUE instance or by creating a new one. In the case of any complex calculation, a number of temporary objects are likely to be created and discarded in the process of attaining the final result. These creations and destructions could be considered wasteful, incurring an unnecessary performance overhead.

To complete the picture we can introduce a MUTABLE COMPANION, a class whose instances are modifiable. Although not directly substitutable for its corresponding IMMUTABLE VALUE type, a MUTABLE COMPANION can be used for manipulations that would require accumulated or frequent change. The MUTABLE COMPANION can be considered a specialized form of BUILDER, which also includes the role of a FACTORY METHOD to produce IMMUTABLE VALUEs, essentially snapshots of its current state. The following diagram illustrates the arrangement.

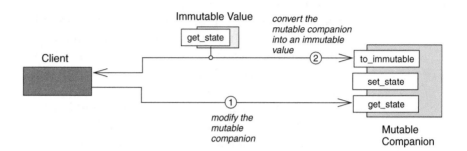

Although a MUTABLE COMPANION is completed with a FACTORY METHOD, this usage relationship of one pattern by another is at the level of detail. This relationship is in contrast to the kind of completion that goes on between IMMUTABLE VALUE and MUTABLE COMPANION. Here the completion is with respect to being a design counterpart rather than a design part.

Design Completion

Some applications of patterns move a design forward, accommodating new features and new possibilities. Other applications of patterns can be considered to 'complete' a design. This completion is not so much a case of moving a design forward to a distinct and new set of capabilities, but instead is a rounding out of an existing design, following it through to its logical conclusion.

Whereas patterns in competition inspire a design dialog based on alternatives, patterns in cooperation rely on a different sense of complements in design, that of *completion*. This completion is not necessarily the use of one pattern by another, but of a more optional use of one pattern by another that makes a design complete in some contexts. There is a tight binding that suggests that two (or more) patterns form integral parts of a larger whole, a balanced arrangement: FACTORY METHOD and DISPOSAL METHOD, IMMUTABLE VALUE and MUTABLE COMPANION, COMMAND and COMMAND PROCESSOR.

5.4   Patterns in Combination

We started looking at pattern complements by stating that certain pattern groupings cannot be classified simply as either competitive versus cooperative or contradictory versus correlated. It is true that in many cases there really is an exclusive-or relationship between the application of one pattern and another. It is also true that some patterns often go together—but it is not true that these form two disjoint groups. Sometimes they overlap, leading to a more yin-and-yang perspective of complementarity.

Returning to the question of OBJECTS FOR STATES versus COLLECTIONS FOR STATES, it is clear that one or other of these designs may be appropriate in a given situation. For example, OBJECTS FOR STATES is suitable for scenarios with a few objects that are acted on individually, with many states and an involved lifecycle. Conversely, COLLECTIONS FOR STATES is suitable for scenarios with many objects that are acted on collectively, with few states in a simple lifecycle. This characterization is a simplified view of the criteria needed to decide between them, but it is sufficient for us to deal with next question: what about a situation in which there are many objects with modal behavior, some states are of interest to manager objects, but others are of interest only locally and individually? It is possible to implement the whole solution using OBJECTS FOR STATES. On the other hand, COLLECTIONS FOR STATES affords an optimization in the case of dealing with those states where collective classification and action is needed. In this design, objects have their state represented and managed both intrinsically *and* extrinsically. These opposing patterns are found working in combination rather than in exclusive competition.

In the context of Conway's Law, we saw that the CONWAY'S LAW (or ALIGN ARCHITECTURE AND ORGANIZATION) pattern included two competing patterns: ORGANIZATION FOLLOWS ARCHITECTURE and ARCHITECTURE FOLLOWS ORGANIZATION. Although these two patterns offer distinct solution approaches, there is no reason why they should be seen as contradictory. The wording of the CONWAY'S LAW pattern makes it clear that these two complementary solution approaches can be combined: 'align the structure of the architecture with the structure of the organization by making piecemeal changes to one and/or the other.'

Further Iterative Development

We can see a similar unification of opposites when we consider the obvious alternatives of ITERATOR and ENUMERATION METHOD. These patterns offer two very different models of traversal, the primary distinction being in the direction of control flow and ownership of the loop. Although a collection could feasibly offer both alternatives in its interface, this would be a maximalist approach to design that would have the effect of appearing inconsistent and indecisive rather than general and accommodating.

Depending on the context, therefore, it makes sense to offer either IT-ERATOR or ENUMERATION METHOD as public features, but not both. Where an ENUMERATION METHOD is offered, however, it is quite possible that its internal implementation may be in terms of an ITERATOR over an internal collection used for representation. In such a design one might almost view the ENUMERATION METHOD as an adaptor that wraps an underlying pull personality with a pushing callback personality.

For example, the following pseudocode illustrates the implementation of an ENUMERATION METHOD for a structured sequence in terms of an ITERATOR used on an underlying list:

```
class Queue
{
    public push(element) {...}
    public pop() {...}
    public forEachElement(callback)
    {
        iterator = list.iterateFromStart()
        while(!iterator.atEnd())
        {
            callback(iterator.currentValue())
            iterator.moveNext()
        }
    }
    ...
    private elements = new List()
}
```

Another iteration example that more visibly brings competitors into cooperation is traversal of collections in a distributed environment in which round-trip latency is relatively high. A simple ITERATOR may be too fine-grained, in that a simple ITERATOR call repeatedly incurs the round-trip cost of remote communication. A BATCH METHOD, however, may be too coarse-grained, in that a single BATCH METHOD call could incur too much overhead when dealing with access to large numbers of elements.

The overhead of BATCH METHOD stems from a called method spending proportionally longer preparing the result. Moreover, although the round-trip cost is incurred only once, there is a large transmission cost—and therefore a significant delay—in receiving the batch response. The caller remains blocked for a long time before receiving the data. In the event of network or server failure or delay, the caller will receive nothing but an exception, and even that event might be further delayed with respect to timeouts.

This design situation does not highlight any flaws or inadequacies in either the ITERATOR or the BATCH METHOD patterns. It does, however, demonstrate limitations in employing either of them as a stand-alone solution in this particular scenario. In this case there is a path to a solution through synthesis: use both patterns.

We start with the core idea of an ITERATOR, which represents a position in a sequence of elements that can be moved for traversal of the elements. We follow with the core idea of a BATCH METHOD, which represents a single service to pull across multiple elements. We now combine these two core ideas by retaining the notion of an ITERATOR as a position in a stream of elements, but refine its interface by defining traversal in terms of a BATCH METHOD. The diagram below illustrates such a configuration.

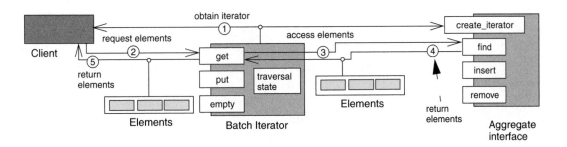

The refined solution, therefore, traverses a collection by taking large steps through the sequence of elements rather than single-stepping through them or trying to cover them all in a single stride. The granularity of the ITERATOR is now coarse, but the notion of an ITERATOR to control traversal has been retained. A BATCH METHOD exists, but on the ITERATOR object rather than the target collection object. The BATCH METHOD focuses on pulling across sub-sequences instead of full sequences, while the ITERATOR can be seen as holding the 'progress-so-far' marker. This design resolves a specific problem in the context of distributed computing more thoroughly by combining quite distinct solutions to related problems.

Further Adaptive Development

Consider another example, that of adaptation in Java. Given a class that has an implementation we would like to reuse, but whose interface does not match our framework, our gut instinct might be to use OBJECT ADAPTER, in which the adapter class holds an instance of the adaptee that receives the calls that it forwards. This design is fine, unless it turns out that we need to override one or more methods of the adaptee or access protected features.

One possible solution is to apply CLASS ADAPTER. There are two drawbacks, however:

- It makes the adaptation, and therefore all of the adaptee, a public feature of the adapter class.

- If the adapter is already subclassing another class to participate in a framework, there is no way to also subclass the adaptee class.

Dead end? Or just a sharp turn? To decide, we start with the idea that CLASS ADAPTER at least allows us to get our hands on the functionality we need, and thus adapt it according to our need. So far so good: we have an adapted class. This adapted class, however, does not support the right interface, and is already inheriting from our original adaptee class. How can we adapt a class that has the wrong interface and already has its single inheritance slot used up? We can use OBJECT ADAPTER to further wrap our adapted class, so that our adapted class now plays the role of adaptee.

One final refinement would be to nest the CLASS ADAPTER within the scope of the OBJECT ADAPTER as an inner class. Here is a Java sketch that illustrates the overall approach:

```java
class ObjectAdapter extends FrameworkSuperClass
{
    public void method()
    {
        ... // forward to appropriate adaptee method
    }
    ...
    private class ClassAdapter extends SuperClassToReuse
    {
        public void methodToOverride()
        {
            ... // access superclass protected features
        }
    }
    private ClassAdapter adaptee = new ClassAdapter();
}
```

The result is that we have combined both OBJECT ADAPTER and CLASS ADAPTER within our code, to address an adaptation problem in two complementary steps that neither pattern was fully capable of addressing on its own.

5.5   Complementary: Competing, Completing, Combining

This chapter makes it clear that we have moved beyond the consideration of patterns as stand-alone pieces of design. A natural tension exists between some patterns, a tension that arises from significant similarities and valuable differences. In such cases we have a view of a design process step that needs to address competitive alternatives, which draws us more deeply into a design situation. To make an informed choice, however, we need to understand the choices and their consequences [Cool02].

In other cases we see that two solutions sit comfortably side by side, with each solution addressing different aspects of a larger problem. Moreover, we can see that the competing and cooperating view of complementarity are not necessarily in competition. Sometimes, when there are two sides of a design story to be told, both can be told, thereby deepening the design dialog and extending what is possible in a design.

6 Pattern Compounds

All know that the drop merges into the ocean
but few know that the ocean merges into the drop.

Kabir, weaver, mystic, and poet

This chapter examines pattern compounds, which are patterns of design that are recurrent and, on closer inspection, have elements of design within them that are also recurrent—patterns! Design often embraces many different levels, so it is not surprising that we can see this reflected in the grouping and separation of patterns. A named pattern provides a description and a way to communicate design, whatever the granularity of the concepts it covers.

6.1   Recurring Pattern Arrangements

Many patterns are grouped together at one apparent level of detail, yet when you examine them closely, you can see other patterns contained within them. For example, COMMAND can be seen within ENUMERATION METHOD. At other times we can see the common, coincident application of two or more patterns, such as a COMMAND implemented as a COMPOSITE, that can be named naturally and almost without thought as a single entity, such as COMPOSITE COMMAND. By analogy with language, where a compound word is a word made up of two or more existing words, we can consider them as examples of *compound patterns* or *pattern compounds*. The analogy with chemical compounds, which are made up of constituent elements, offers another coherent perspective on the idea.

Pattern compounds were originally named *composite patterns* [Rie98], but in the pattern space there is obvious scope for confusion with the more singular COMPOSITE pattern—consider the subtle distinction between 'This design is based on the COMPOSITE pattern' versus 'This design is based on a composite pattern' when spoken aloud. The term *compound pattern* [Vlis98c] is now more commonly used than *composite pattern*. We offer a slight shift in emphasis by referring to them as *pattern compounds*, a shift that, among other qualities, offers a more obvious alignment with concepts we encounter in this and subsequent chapters: pattern stories, pattern sequences, pattern collections, and pattern languages.

6.2   From Elements to Compounds

We can define a pattern compound as a named, commonly recurring, cohesive combination of other patterns. It is a mutually supportive community of patterns that define a tangibly larger design fragment than what might be considered, by implication, a pattern element. The constituent patterns commonly appear together to resolve a particular problem in a given context, hence a pattern compound is itself a pattern with identity, rather than a unique application of patterns, but the constituent patterns also have high visibility.

This notion of a single whole pattern with visible constituent patterns is made explicit in the opening description of the BUREAUCRACY pattern [Rie98]:

> The BUREAUCRACY pattern is a recurring design theme used to implement hierarchical object or component structures which allow interaction with every level of the hierarchy and maintain their inner consistency themselves. It is a composite pattern that is based on the COMPOSITE, MEDIATOR, CHAIN OF RESPONSIBILITY, and OBSERVER patterns.

Because a pattern compound captures one particular configuration, it does not necessarily have more genericity than a pattern that has not been considered in terms of compoundness. Despite being able to view a pattern compound's parts from multiple pattern perspectives, there are relatively few choices regarding the arrangement and use of its constituent parts, since the roles are clearly laid out. Conversely, this very stability allows the capture and concrete discussion of the compound's cohesive whole in terms that we have already explored for stand-alone patterns. It is this nameability and familiarity that can make a pattern compound perspective useful in development.

Pluggable Factories

The ABSTRACT FACTORY pattern is commonly used to capture the creation of families of related objects, known as products. A factory presents an interface of FACTORY METHODS for creating product objects and, optionally, disposing of them using DISPOSAL METHODS. A concrete factory class fulfills the interface by creating specific concrete products, so that concrete factories differ in the product types that are used for creation. However, although the binding between the user of a factory and a specific concrete factory is based on runtime polymorphism and is thus fairly loose, each concrete factory is hardwired to a specific set of products. What if an application needs more flexibility than is offered from the available set of factory types?

One approach would be to provide more concrete factory types, enumerating more of the possible creation combinations explicitly. The downside of this approach, however, is that there will be a lot of extra code due to a by-product of 'speculative generality' [FBBOR99]. Moreover, much of the code across the classes is likely to be duplicated, many of the classes will remain unused, yet some of the possible options will still be unavailable. Hurling a multitude of concrete factory types at the problem is unlikely to address the problem in an optimal fashion, so it is worth taking a step back to reconsider the issues and possible solutions.

As it happens, taking a step back is precisely the approach that the PLUGGABLE FACTORY [Vlis98c] [Vlis99] pattern compound recommends: add a level of indirection. Provide a factory type and parameterize it with exemplars of each of the product types. These product types act as plug-in PROTOTYPEs that are cloned whenever one of the factory's creation methods is invoked. This design avoids the explosion of types that many concrete realizations of ABSTRACT FACTORY would yield, so all the abstractness and variation is expressed through the products, which are simply plugged in. PLUGGABLE FACTORY can be viewed as a compound of ABSTRACT FACTORY and PROTOTYPE, although it can in practice be further generalized using STRATEGY instead of PROTOTYPE for pluggability. A STRATEGY would offer a single FACTORY METHOD for creating a type, or it could be expressed as a function pointer in C++ or a delegate in C#.

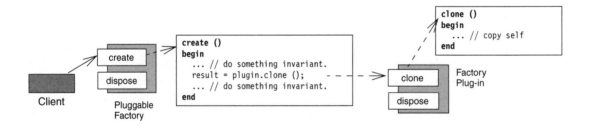

Two Views of Composite Command

A pattern compound must be composed of at least two patterns. It can be viewed and described in terms of its constituent patterns. At the same time, it must also represent a reasonable, whole, and recurring design fragment, one that is a generic and stable configuration and can be described on its own terms as a pattern without reference to its supporting patterns. Both views are valid, but which one offers the most effective documentation for a pattern compound?

Consider the case mentioned before of the relatively common use of COMPOSITE in support of COMMAND, in which a COMMAND is implemented as a COMPOSITE—as opposed to implementing a COMPOSITE as a COMMAND, which is a different proposition altogether. This combination of COMMAND and COMPOSITE is variously and informally referred to as a COMPOSITE COMMAND, MACRO COMMAND, COMMAND SEQUENCE, and so on. This recurrence and its two identifiable sets of roles suggests that it is a pattern compound [VlHe99]. The following pattern description illustrates how we can present it as a pattern in its own right, without reference to the constituent patterns and their roles:

Composite Command

There is a need to execute requests, typically method calls on objects, independently of the point at which the requests are selected for later execution. Not only is request execution decoupled from selection, some requests need to be grouped together and executed as one. For example, executing a group of requests as an uninterrupted sequence in the presence of multiple threads. The distinction between single and multiple request execution needs to be as transparent and simple as possible for all the roles involved in the request initiation and execution.

Therefore, encapsulate requests as objects, hiding the difference between single requests and multiple requests behind a common interface.

A creator defines the requests that are then handed to an executor, which handles and executes the requests. The creator of request objects can choose whether the executor of the requests handles requests individually or as a group. The difference between single requests and a grouping of multiple requests is transparent to the executor. The creator is free to extend the set of requests as they see fit; the executor is decoupled from the creator's decisions.

The consistency of the common interface means not only that multiple requests can be treated uniformly as single requests, but also that existing single requests and multiple requests can be used inside new multiple requests.

Alternatively we can expose the patterns that we see inside:

Composite Command

There is a need to execute requests, typically method calls on objects, independently of the point at which the requests are selected for later execution. Not only is request execution decoupled from selection, some requests need to be grouped together and executed as one. For example, executing a group of requests as an uninterrupted sequence in the presence of multiple threads. The distinction between single and multiple request execution needs to be as transparent and simple as possible for all the roles involved in the request initiation and execution.

Therefore, express requests as COMMAND objects and group multiple COMMANDS together in a COMPOSITE, thereby objectifying requests and treating single and multiple requests uniformly.

The first description is self-contained and precise, but relatively long in its solution detail. By contrast, the second description shares the same goals and problem statement, but expresses its solution structure briefly and directly in terms of existing pattern vocabulary. For a reader familiar with the constituent patterns, the second description is superior to the first, while for others the first description offers a more appropriate level of depth.

Notes on Pattern Compound Form

To answer the opening question of the previous subsection, the choice of how to document a pattern compound depends largely on the target readership and the amount of detail required by the pattern. With respect to the constituent patterns, there are essentially three approaches:

• *Document the pattern compound on its own terms, without reference to its constituent patterns.* This approach is useful for relatively simple compounds, in which the effort required to document its constituent elements is minimal. For compounds with a larger number of roles, however, the amount of implementation detail may be overwhelming if they are all described without reference to the constituent patterns.

- *Document the pattern compound by reference to its constituent patterns.* This approach is likely to scale better for more intricate compounds, keeping the description brief, but it relies on the reader to be familiar with the other patterns or to have their sources close to hand. Clearly, this approach works better for pattern compounds consisting of common patterns, such as those in the Gang-of-Four or POSA books, rather than less widely known patterns.

- *Document both the pattern compound and its constituent patterns.* This approach treats the documentation of a compound as a collection of patterns and then as a specific role combination of the collection. This approach requires more effort from the author, and in one sense is the longest form. It offers more options to readers, however: the option of detail should they need it, or the option to skip it otherwise. It also brings the compound together in a brief description that builds on its constituents.

The third case is essentially a variation of the second. It can be argued that the second approach is the one to favor, especially for pattern compounds based on well-known constituent patterns [Vlis98c]:

> If there's any leverage to be had in a compound, it must build on constituent patterns. There's no point recapitulating those patterns in the compound, because the reader can always consult them directly. A compound would also get very big, very fast if it subsumed its constituents. So it's not just permissible but essential that a compound defer to other patterns. It must add value, too. The cardinal rule for compound pattern readers and writers alike is to focus on the synergies between patterns.

Not all constituent patterns, however, are necessarily well known. We therefore need to consider how self-contained a pattern compound's description should be. If the third option looks appropriate for a particular compound, we do not necessarily need to document everything about its constituent patterns. Instead, we can focus on the aspects of the constituent patterns that are most relevant to the pattern compound. Thus we are using the context of the pattern compound to narrow how much of the solution space we need to describe for each constituent pattern. For example, if we were to document the COMMAND and COMPOSITE patterns in the context of COMPOSITE COMMAND, we would not need to include motivating examples or discussion of issues that were unrelated to the context of COMPOSITE COMMAND.

Most other considerations of pattern form apply equally well to pattern compounds as they do to stand-alone patterns, so most of the discussion we offered in *Chapter 3* still holds. There are, however, two further topics with additional considerations: naming and diagramming.

In terms of naming, we can see that we can name the whole, perhaps using a metaphor, as is the case with BUREAUCRACY. More prosaically we could name the compound after a hyphenated list of its constituents, which may lose in readability what it gains in precision. We could also look for a name that retains the essence of the constituents but is somewhat briefer. For example, COMMAND–COMPOSITE would be a direct rendition, but COMPOSITE COMMAND retains both names arranged in a more natural and readable phrasing, with adjective preceding noun. Sometimes a little more effort is needed to find such a name [Vlis98c]:

> Synergy starts with the compound pattern's name. You can always form it by stringing together the names of the constituents, but there's not much value-add in that—where's the synergy? Such a name will be unwieldy to boot when there are more than a couple of constituents. PROTOTYPE–ABSTRACT FACTORY is a glowing example.

> A good name is as critical to compounds as it is to any other patterns: it should be short, evocative, memorable. It'll be something you can use in conversation without hesitation and without getting tongue-tied.

> 'Pluggable' is fitting here because it connotes dynamic reconfigurability, which as we'll see is highly appropriate. And we're still talking about a factory in the Abstract Factory sense. What is no longer relevant to this compound is the factory's 'abstractness' or how pluggability is achieved (using Prototype in this case). The Abstract and Prototype monikers are thus safely dropped, leaving 'Pluggable Factory.'

When diagramming a pattern compound, a diagram can simply represent the overall structure and theme of a compound, or it can go further and make the contributions from its constituent patterns more explicit. For example, the 'pattern:role' annotation used in *Section 4.3, A Second Design Experiment: Interwoven Patterns*, can be used to highlight the various patterns and their roles that make up the BUREAUCRACY pattern.

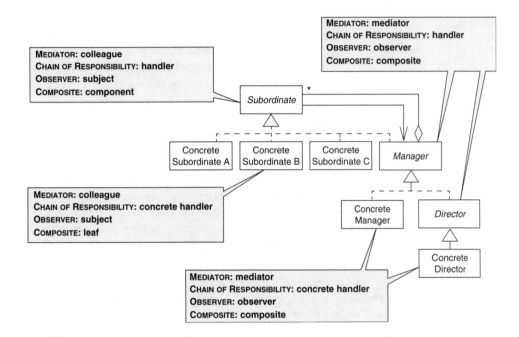

6.3 From Complements to Compounds

Chapter 5 examined the notion that patterns can often exist in competition to one another or in cooperation with one another. *Section 5.4, Patterns in Combination,* demonstrated how patterns that appeared as distinct alternatives to a similar problem could also often be used in combination. What was not mentioned was that many of these examples are not simply one-offs: they have recurrence.

Reiterate

Returning to the iteration example in *Section 5.4, Patterns in Combination*, the combination of Iterator and Batch Method is sufficiently common that we can treat is a single piece of design vocabulary, a Batch Iterator. Here is a summary of the compound:

Batch Iterator

In a distributed environment, it is costly to use a single-stepping Iterator to access the elements of a remote aggregate object sequentially. However, for large numbers of elements, a Batch Method will also be costly. In the former case the cumulative round-trip time will overshadow the time taken for client and server computation. In the latter case, the cost of a single bulk transfer will cause the client and server to block.

Therefore, define an Iterator that uses a Batch Method to take long strides through the sequence of elements. The client and server can remain responsive while the effect of the round-trip cost can be moderated.

This design, as a single identifiable idea, can be seen in many middleware frameworks, including the technically (and politically) different CORBA and COM.

The following describes the motivation and style of Batch Iterator in COM [Box97]:

To address the problems related to passing large arrays as method parameters, COM has a standard interface design idiom that allows the receiver of the data to perform flow control of the array elements explicitly. This idiom is based on passing a special COM interface pointer in lieu of actual arrays. This special interface is called an enumerator and allows the receiver to pull elements from the sender at a rate that is appropriate for the receiver.

The following Microsoft IDL fragment presents the standard interface for iterating over the connections held by a connection point:

```
interface IEnumConnections : IUnknown
{
    ...
    HRESULT Next(
        [in] ULONG cConnections,
        [out, size_is(cConnections), length_is(*lpcFetched)]
            CONNECTDATA * rgcd,
        [out] ULONG * lpcFetched);
    HRESULT Skip([in] ULONG cConnections);
    ...
}
```

The following OMG IDL fragment presents the standard interface for iterating over name bindings in the OMG Naming Service:

```
typedef sequence<Binding> BindingList;

interface BindingIterator
{
    boolean next_n(
        in unsigned long how_many,
        out BindingList bl);
    ...
};
```

Both these examples of BATCH ITERATORs include a BATCH METHOD for retrieving multiple values. The COM ITERATOR also includes a BATCH METHOD for *not* retrieving values—skipping values without marshaling, sending, and unmarshaling them.

Adaptations

Staying with the theme of alternative solutions, we noted in *Section 5.2, Patterns in Competition,* that it is more effective to consider the Gang-of-Four ADAPTER pattern in terms of (at least) two distinct patterns—OBJECT ADAPTER and CLASS ADAPTER—than as a single pattern. Although the theme and general intent is common between them, the two proposed solution alternatives are so divergent in their applicability, structures, and consequences that it is not possible to describe them together simply and uniformly.

In a design situation in which the intimacy afforded by CLASS ADAPTER and the encapsulation offered by OBJECT ADAPTER are both required, *Section 5.4, Patterns in Combination* outlined a solution using both.

The CLASS ADAPTER adapts the original adaptee, overriding methods or accessing protected features as necessary. The resulting class is then itself wrapped by an OBJECT ADAPTER, so that the class playing the role of the adapter in the previous pattern is now playing the role of the adaptee.

This combination is a known technique, particularly in Java code, and can therefore be considered a pattern compound. We can dub this two-level solution a WRAPPED CLASS ADAPTER. The mechanism of inner classes in Java improves the mixing of adaptee and adapter roles from the two competing patterns.

Although not complementary, OBJECT ADAPTER and ITERATOR are combined as a single unit with sufficient frequency that a pattern compound can be said to exist involving the two of them. We can refer to this as an ADAPTED ITERATOR. In the C++ STL there are ADAPTED ITERATORs that express, explicitly and in their core, both the notion of iteration through an ITERATOR and adaptation of one interface to another through an OBJECT ADAPTER. For example, a reverse_iterator wraps a bidirectional iterator so that iteration forward becomes iteration backward and vice versa.

Returning to BATCH ITERATOR, the same ADAPTED ITERATOR design recurs when trying to present the programmer with a fairly normal and simple looking ITERATOR, rather than a BATCH ITERATOR that requires extra management. An ADAPTED ITERATOR handles the additional state and looping resulting from any BATCH METHOD call, but still internally retains the long stride of the BATCH ITERATOR in stepping across the target result set. The ADAPTED ITERATOR also handles the caching and iteration through the cache of each call to the BATCH ITERATOR's BATCH METHOD.

6.4   Element or Compound?

We have seen a number of familiar patterns play a part in 'larger' pattern compounds that can also be seen as patterns. So, the question naturally arises: do patterns fall strictly into one camp or another? Are they either elements or compounds?

On one hand, the general notion of usage or inclusion of one pattern by another suggests that, in principle, we can consider most patterns as pattern compounds, with each pattern drawing on others to realize its full expression. So, the distinction is potentially arbitrary or not even useful at all.

On the other hand, it does not necessarily help to consider all or most patterns as pattern compounds. The term is normally reserved for a more specific granularity, one that is coarser than the level of a given collection of patterns under consideration. For example, if we want to focus on iteration, then considering ITERATOR, ENUMERATION METHOD, and BATCH METHOD as the basic elements means that we consider BATCH ITERATOR a compound and ignore the compound nature of ENUMERATION METHOD with respect to its use of COMMAND. The distinction is therefore relative to a baseline of interest: below that level, fine-grained pattern structure is not necessarily considered in terms of other patterns, while above that level recurring groups of patterns may be considered compound.

Composite Interpretations

Taking COMPOSITE as a 'pattern element,' we can find that BUREAUCRACY, COMPOSITE COMMAND, and INTERPRETER can be considered pattern compounds with respect to it. The first, BUREAUCRACY, has been explicitly documented and published as such, and was one of the motivating examples for the concept of compounds [Rie98].

The second pattern compound, COMPOSITE COMMAND, was seen originally as a convenient application of COMPOSITE in the context of a COMMAND [GoF95]. Its recurrence and nameability, however, highlight that it is more than just an example [VlHe99], and we took the step of documenting it.

The third compound, INTERPRETER, was documented originally as a general-purpose pattern element [GoF95], but on closer inspection it has fine-grained structure that can be described in pattern terms and is somewhat narrower and more specialized in its context and use.

Rather than being a general OO framework pattern, INTERPRETER is a domain-specific pattern that builds on other more primitive and readily identifiable constituents to realize a simple programming-language grammar as an executable whole. Specifically, the goal of

INTERPRETER is to execute a simple scriptable language. A script is therefore treated as an object that both reflects the syntactic structure of the script and allows its execution.

The reification of action in object form is the very essence of the COMMAND pattern. To execute a script, an environment is needed that carries the state of execution, a requirement that is met by the CONTEXT OBJECT pattern. A typical language grammar contains recursive whole–part structures, which inevitably lead to COMPOSITE structures. Indeed, the Gang-of-Four description of INTERPRETER relies heavily on sharing its implementation description with that of COMPOSITE. The simplest whole–part relationship is that of the script to its top-level statements.

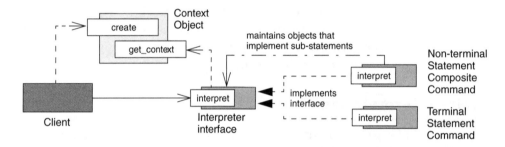

INTERPRETER can therefore be considered a compound of COMMAND, CONTEXT OBJECT, and COMPOSITE. It is also common to associate VISITOR and ENUMERATION METHOD with an INTERPRETER implementation for traversal. These are optional complements, however, rather than mandatory parts of the whole.

Inside Model-View-Controller

POSA1, and many works since, classify MODEL-VIEW-CONTROLLER (MVC) as a single pattern. It is also common, however, to analyze MODEL-VIEW-CONTROLLER in terms of its constituent patterns. These two views are not in conflict. The following deconstruction—which uses the *composite* rather than the *compound* terminology—reaches this conclusion [Rie97]:

> A developer versed in software design patterns might explain the Model-View-Controller paradigm (MVC) for designing interactive software systems like this: '(a) MVC helps you design applications

with graphical user interfaces. Its core are three collaborating objects: a Model object which represents an instance of a domain concept, a View object which realizes a specific user interface representation of the Model, and a Controller object which handles user input in order to work with the Model. (b) These objects interact according to the Observer, Strategy and Composite pattern: a View observes a Model—thus the View is an Observer of the Model which is its Subject. A View does not handle user input but leaves this to the Controller—thus the Controller is a Strategy for handling user input. Moreover, Views can have Subviews which represent smaller parts of the user interface and which can have Subviews themselves—thus the View is a Component in the Composite pattern and different Views can be either Leafs or Composites.'

From MVC's overall point of view (described in (a) above), the use of each of the design patterns (described in (b) above) is of a tactical nature: every pattern is used to solve a specific problem at hand. Taken together and directed towards the goal of designing a reusable and flexible user interface architecture, the patterns achieve a synergy which constitutes a whole that is larger than just the sum of some patterns. *MVC is a composite design pattern.*

The Gang-of-Four do not list MODEL-VIEW-CONTROLLER as a pattern, favoring instead a Smalltalk-specific view of the patterns. They do, however, reach a similar conclusion in terms of its decomposition [GoF95]: OBSERVER for notification, COMPOSITE for nesting of views, STRATEGY for parameterizing controller behavior—with an option on FACTORY METHOD for specifying a default controller class for a system, and the possibility of DECORATOR for adding features to a view.

POSA1 defines MODEL-VIEW-CONTROLLER as both a pattern and with respect to its internal pattern content, but offers a different decomposition that draws on a slightly broader pattern vocabulary: OBSERVER, COMMAND PROCESSOR, FACTORY METHOD, VIEW HANDLER, COMPOSITE, CHAIN OF RESPONSIBILITY, and BRIDGE.

These various and varied perspectives appear to support the idea that it is useful to consider MODEL-VIEW-CONTROLLER both as a single design element and in terms of its fine-grained structure, regardless of whether or not the notion of pattern compound is acknowledged explicitly.

6.5   Compound Analysis and Synthesis

It is not uncommon to see recurrence at different levels of any kind of system. For example, systems are composed of subsystems, each of which can be viewed as a whole or decomposed into constituent parts (each of which may in turn decompose further). This recursive whole–part nature can be seen as a universal theme in the realm of design. We view systems recursively in this way because the whole is more than the sum of its parts, otherwise we would not need to support multiple perspectives.

Viewing wholeness for its own sake may relate to genuine emergence, or it may be an artifact of how we are able to consider and understand structures. Certainly with pattern compounds we can see both emergence and comprehension as being greater than the sum of the parts, hence our desire to name and focus on multiple levels. Such 'patterns of patterns' represent a more second-order—and hence deeper—style of thinking about our patterns and recurrence.

Non-Design Pattern Compounds?

We note that all of the examples we have seen, which either have been documented as pattern compounds or can be viewed easily as compounds, are design examples. There are a number of possible reasons for the apparent lack of non-design examples:

- We have yet to see them or have them pointed out to us.

- The different traditions of design and non-design patterns, such as organizational and pedagogical patterns, are biased toward different pattern styles and presentations. For example, the oft-cited classic work in the world of software design patterns is *Design Patterns* [GoF95], which favors a view of patterns based on stand-alone patterns. By contrast, key works in development process patterns, such as *A Generative Development-Process Pattern Language* [Cope95], have favored collections of patterns, typically structured as pattern languages. Viewed as complete patterns in their own right, the idea of pattern compounds is more likely to find a sympathetic viewpoint in a tradition that places value in stand-alone patterns.

- The strongly structural nature of pattern compounds and their fixed arrangement of roles is perhaps less suitable for patterns that focus on people and practices. Although relationships between human roles and responsibilities can be presented using a spatial metaphor, such a presentation does not represent the same kind of structure as found in designed artifacts—to treat it as such would be a dehumanizing simplification that ignores the fluid nature of people and their relationships. This looseness may make the stable nature of pattern compounds less suitable as a mechanism for grouping patterns.

None of this is to say, of course, that we do not find interplay between, or recurrence of, groups of non-design patterns. Far from it: we see this all the time; it is very much a defining theme for patterns that relate people and practices. For example, the advice to ALIGN ARCHITECTURE AND ORGANIZATION draws on a balance between ORGANIZATION FOLLOWS ARCHITECTURE and ARCHITECTURE FOLLOWS ORGANIZATION. The interplay in this example, however, does not follow the notion of a fixed arrangement of roles: whether to favor one approach over another, or to mix the two (and how to mix them), is more strongly feedback driven than we would find in a pattern compound.

In documenting groupings of non-design patterns, we have found that other approaches, such as pattern collections, pattern sequences, and pattern languages, are more likely to capture the appropriate space of variation, recurrence, and feedback than pattern compounds.

Design Pattern Compounds

In design, what constitutes a pattern compound—as opposed to a more primitive pattern element—can vary, being defined more by utility than some inherent quality of a pattern. Pattern compounds are therefore not so much a special kind of pattern as they are a perspective for viewing a group of patterns. For example, in identifying a number of pattern compounds, John Vlissides makes the following observation [Vlis98a]:

> COMPOSITE-STRATEGY-OBSERVER, better known as Model-View-Controller, from the Smalltalk world. Buschmann & Co. wrote this up as an architectural pattern [POSA1], but casting it as a composite pattern yields a more compact discussion with little or no disadvantage.

What and when we choose to identify a pattern as a compound depends on the choice of ground level of pattern description. By definition, any nameable and commonly recurring design fragment at a coarser level of granularity is a candidate for being a compound. For a pattern collection documented at a finer level, the atoms split: for one documented at a coarser level, the compounds transmute into atoms.

In practice the notion of pattern compound is not quite so slippery and alchemical. We have a tendency to cling to names and perspectives that are recognized and already useful in some way. As an analytical method, however, the concept of a pattern compound is a good tool for identifying the consistency, grouping, or ordering of patterns within a given collection. As a synthetic method it also offers new ways of presenting design ideas in terms of constituent parts with which designers may already be familiar.

Although there is a degree of relativism in identifying them, it is worth reiterating that pattern compounds are not arbitrary recurring collections of patterns [Rie98]:

> A composite pattern is first of all a pattern: it represents a design theme that keeps recurring in specific contexts. I call it a composite pattern, because it can best be explained as the composition of some other patterns. However, a composite pattern goes beyond a mere composition: it captures the synergy arising from the different roles an object plays in the overall composition structure. As such, composite patterns are more than just the sum of their constituting patterns.

Looking back over our examples and descriptions, the linguistic metaphor of compounds is perhaps more successful than the chemical one. Compound words and phrases—and indeed the way that words and phrases evolve in natural language—offer a slightly less mystical or quantum-mechanical perspective than the chemical metaphor of elements and compounds, which calls on the splitting of atoms or transmutation of elements for each shift in perspective. The consideration of patterns as the basis of a design vocabulary and the elements of design dialog certainly invites these more linguistic comparisons.

7   **Pattern Sequences**

> *I cordially dislike allegory in all its manifestations, and always have done so since I grew old and wary enough to detect its presence. I much prefer history, true or feigned, with its varied applicability to the thought and experience of readers. I think that many confuse 'applicability' with 'allegory'; but the one resides in the freedom of the reader, and the other in the purposed domination of the author.*
>
> J.R.R. Tolkien

This chapter builds on the pattern relationships discussed thus far in this part of the book. Pattern stories offer a presentation form that describes how patterns have been (or might be) applied concretely to construct a particular system, implement a specified feature, or transform a given situation. Pattern sequences generalize this narrative into something more fundamental, distilling out the actual sequence of patterns applied so that the same sequence can be considered elsewhere. The discussion of pattern sequences allows us to revisit the question of context once again.

7.1   Patterns Tell Software Engineering Success Stories

There is no single privileged view of what a software system is or how it was developed. Each perspective highlights one aspect that may not be visible from another point of view and communicates a slightly different message. For example:

- A *code-centric view* emphasizes detail and precision. Although modern programming languages have support for expressing modular structure, many of the relationships present in the code are not obvious at this level. For example, classes and inheritance are emphasized in languages that support object orientation. Object-to-object associations between classes, however, do not receive the same syntactic honor, requiring careful reading or a suitable tool to uncover them.

- A *diagrammed class model view* casts its net over a system differently, emphasizing classes and all relationships, whether association or inheritance, and de-emphasizing detail within the class. The goal is to see dependencies and macrostructure, but this is inevitably at the expense of precision and fine structure. The attempt to introduce such detail into class diagrams is a common failing of CASE tools and modelers alike. Whether a class model is sketched on the back of an envelope or presented on screen from an underlying stored model, its human audience will lose interest (and perhaps even the will to live) if bombarded with distracting details that are better abstracted away.

- A *pattern-based view* emphasizes the problems addressed and roles introduced that together comprise a software system, by describing its structure *and* rationale. This view may be related to—and may annotate—other models and views of the software. It can also be something that lives as a separate description, either in a document, or retold in part on a whiteboard whenever some description of the system is needed.

The pattern-based view typically cuts across the units of the code-centric and class-model views, focusing on combinations, qualities, and interactions. It does not necessarily focus on blocks from which you can build up a system, but on the ingredients that go to make up a system—the roles that blocks will fulfill. In some ways, the metaphor of cooking has more to offer us than the metaphor of construction: ingredients blend and affect one another in a way that lacks convenient parallels in the world of steel, glass, bricks, and wood.

This short list of three views is intentionally demonstrative rather than exhaustive—a whole book could be filled with possible views [Kru95] [Zach]! Each view just described overlaps with, extends, or omits features of the others in some way. They also have something more fundamental in common: they are all static. They show a snapshot of something as it appears at a single point in time. This snapshot can capture various things, such as:

- The code that resides in the version control system.

- The class relationships as they reflect code already written or anticipate code to be written.

- The patterns as they have been used.

As it happens, class models are also considered static, in that they do not show the behavior of a running system with respect to time. The static–dynamic distinction we are interested in, however, is the one concerned with system development rather than system runtime.

7.2   Pattern Stories

Hearing that a system uses sixty-seven well-known and forty-two proto-patterns in its implementation is impressive... but essentially useless. It may be better than just being handed an alphabetical listing of its classes, but comprehending the system from a laundry list of patterns is a daunting prospect. Where does one start?

There are many ways to approach such a task of comprehension, such as the various organizational schemes described in *Chapter 8, Pattern Collections*. Another approach is storytelling, which has become popular for both its educational qualities and its user friendliness. Storytelling treats the development of a system as a narrative in which the progressive application of patterns creates the system.

Returning to the cooking metaphor, the sequence of preparation and combination of ingredients is as critical to the outcome as the ingredients themselves. As the story unfolds, so does the system, its design, and its rationale. This sequencing is certainly more accessible and reasonable than presenting a system's architecture as a laundry list of patterns.

A Short Story

We can present a simple short story by revisiting and extending the second run of our request-handling experiment from *Chapter 4*, drawing out the progression of decisions made in the design:

> *We are developing an extensible request-handling framework. How can requests be issued and handled so that the request-handling framework can manipulate the requests explicitly?*

Objectify requests as COMMAND objects, based on a common interface of methods for executing the client requests. Command types can be expressed within a class hierarchy. Clients of the system issue specific requests by instantiating concrete Command classes and calling the execution interface. This object then performs the requested operations on the application and returns the results, if any, to the client.

> *The chosen language for implementing the framework is statically typed. There may be some implementation common to many or all COMMAND classes. What is the best form for the COMMAND class hierarchy?*

Express the root of the hierarchy as an EXPLICIT INTERFACE. Both the framework and clients can treat it as a stable and published interface in its own right, decoupled from implementation decisions that affect the rest of the hierarchy. Concrete COMMAND classes implement the root EXPLICIT INTERFACE. Common code can be expressed in abstract classes below the EXPLICIT INTERFACE rather than in the hierarchy root, and concrete classes are expressed as leaves in the hierarchy.

> *There may be multiple clients of the system that can issue commands independently. How can command handling be coordinated generally?*

A COMMAND PROCESSOR provides a central management component to which clients pass their COMMAND objects for further handling and execution. The COMMAND PROCESSOR depends only on the EXPLICIT INTERFACE of the COMMAND hierarchy.

The COMMAND PROCESSOR also makes it easy to introduce a rollback facility, so that actions performed in response to requests can be undone. The EXPLICIT INTERFACE of the COMMAND is extended with the declaration of an undo method, which will affect the concreteness of any implementing classes, and the COMMAND PROCESSOR handles the management.

In introducing an undo mechanism, there is also a recognized need to offer a redo facility, so that previously undone COMMAND *objects can be re-executed. How can the* COMMAND PROCESSOR *best accommodate both undo history and redo futures for* COMMAND *objects?*

Add COLLECTIONS FOR STATES to the COMMAND PROCESSOR, so that one collection holds COMMAND objects that have already been executed—and can therefore be undone—and another collection holds COMMAND objects that have already been undone—and can therefore be re-executed. Both collections are sequences with 'last in, first out' stack-ordered access.

Some actions may be undone (or redone) quite simply, but others may involve significant state changes that complicate a rollback (or rollforward). How can the need for a simple and uniform rollback mechanism be balanced with the need to deal with actions that are neither simple nor consistent with other actions?

Optionally associate each COMMAND with a MEMENTO that maintains whole or partial copies of the relevant application state as it was before the COMMAND was executed. COMMAND types that require a MEMENTO will share common structure and behavior for setting and working with the MEMENTO's state. This commonality can be expressed in an abstract class that in turn implements the COMMAND's EXPLICIT INTERFACE. MEMENTO-based COMMAND types then extend this abstract class. COMMAND types that are not MEMENTO-based would not inherit from this abstract class, implementing instead the EXPLICIT INTERFACE directly or extending another abstract class suitable for their purpose.

The framework needs to provide a logging facility for requests. How can logging functionality be parameterized, so that users of the framework can choose how they wish to handle logging, rather than hardwired?

Express logging functionality as a STRATEGY of the COMMAND PRO-
CESSOR, so that a client of the framework can select how they want
requests logged by providing a suitable implementation of the
STRATEGY interface. Some users will want to just use standard logging options, so that the framework should provide some predefined logging types, whereas others may wish to define their own
custom logging.

*How can the optionality of logging be realized as transparently as
possible within the framework, given that it makes little functional
difference to the running of the framework?*

Provide a NULL OBJECT implementation of the logging STRATEGY.
This logging implementation does nothing when it is invoked, but
uses the same interface as the operational logging implementations. This selection through polymorphism ensures that the
framework need not modify its control-flow structure to accommodate this optional behavior.

*Compound requests that correspond to multiple requests performed
in sequence and as one, and similarly are undone as one, need to
be added to the framework. How can this be expressed without up-
setting the simple and uniform treatment of COMMANDs within the
existing infrastructure?*

Implement a compound request as a COMPOSITE COMMAND object
that aggregates other COMMAND objects. To initialize a COMPOSITE
COMMAND object correctly, other COMMAND objects, whether primitive or COMPOSITE themselves, must be added to it in sequence.

This pattern story has been expressed with simple prose, using a call–
response style that corresponds to problem–solution pairings. It could
be supplemented with code fragments and diagrams, either iconically
showing the sequence of patterns applied or schematically showing
the class diagram building up with each pattern. The story captures
and communicates the design narrative that can be said to lie behind
the structure of the framework, and does so with more depth, engagement, and reason than could be conveyed using a simple list of the
patterns used or classes involved.

Published Stories

There are many published examples of how stories have been used to unfold a design or reveal how a situation changed, demonstrating the decisions made and patterns used along the way. Pattern stories can do for a collection of patterns what simpler motivating examples can do for individual patterns: bring them to life and illustrate how they work in practice. The use of such interwoven examples dates back to Christopher Alexander's work in building architecture. For example, a brief, reportage-like example gives an account of the basic progression of a design in *A Pattern Language* [AIS77]. A longer form that includes more rationale can be found in the *The Oregon Experiment* [ASAIA75].

We also see a tradition of storytelling within software patterns. The aphysical nature of software development inevitably demands the use of examples to make the abstract concrete. In most cases stories are treated as educational and informative extras rather than as something integral to the pattern concept. However, just as we consider the use of examples as a matter of form and not just a formality, we take a similar view of the role played by pattern stories.

For example, the design of the Lexi document editor in *Design Patterns* [GoF95] is presented through a narrative form, highlighting a design progression that draws in the use of patterns. The following problem areas are addressed in order: document structure, formatting, embellishing the user interface, supporting multiple look-and-feel standards, supporting multiple windowing systems, user operations, and spell checking and hyphenation. The design moves forward through the application of the following patterns, addressing each problem in order: COMPOSITE, STRATEGY, DECORATOR, ABSTRACT FACTORY, BRIDGE, COMMAND, ITERATOR, and VISITOR, whose order of exposition matches the problem areas outlined above.

The goal of the Lexi story is to introduce the reader to the concept of patterns and how patterns can be applied in practice, as well as present actual design patterns. To keep the scope and the story manageable, however, only a few aspects and a few patterns are presented. A full treatment of all the design patterns involved in a document editor would have made for a much longer chapter and possibly a less engaging narrative.

In *The Design Patterns Smalltalk Companion* [APW98], the idea of an illustrative story is expressed quite literally: a short fictionalized drama:

> It consists of three vignettes: three days in the life of two Smalltalk programmers who work for MegaCorp Insurance Company. We are listening in on conversations between Don (an object newbie, but an experienced business analyst) and Jane (an object and patterns expert). Don comes to Jane with his design problems, and they solve them together. Although the characters are fictitious, the designs are real and have all been part of actual systems written in Smalltalk.

A first-person narrative, peppered with code, offers a personal tutorial approach to demonstrating patterns in action. For example, *Pattern Hatching* [Vlis98b] walks readers through the design requirements, issues, and C++ solutions for a hierarchical file system example. In *Smalltalk Best Practice Patterns* [Beck96] the reader is presented with the pattern-based evolution of Smalltalk code for handling multi-currency values.

Experience reports offer stories from the real world. In *Organizational Patterns of Agile Software Development* [CoHa04] four such stories are presented briefly to showcase each of the four documented collections of patterns. In *Fearless Change* [MaRi04] four separately authored stories are used to show how the documented patterns for introducing organizational change can be combined and used in practice.

Volumes in the POSA series also used pattern stories to show how patterns can be combined to produce applications:

- In *Patterns for Concurrent and Networked Objects* [POSA2] the architecture of the JAWS concurrent Web server framework is retold through a progression of patterns, each applied in context with problem and solution described.

- In *Patterns for Resource Management* [POSA3] two stories are told: a solution for ad hoc networking with mobile devices and distributed services is presented, along with an architecture for a mobile telecommunication network.

- In *A Pattern Language for Distributed Computing* [POSA4], a long and detailed story relates the development of a process control system for warehouse systems at various levels of abstraction, including its baseline application architecture and its communication middleware infrastructure.

- Finally, in the current volume we have told (more than once) the story of a request-handling framework.

7.3   From Stories to Sequences

The idea that we can capture the evolution of a system by understanding the patterns applied in a time-ordered sequence takes us from still photography to cinematography. It also raises an important question. Many stories are fiction, without necessarily having any firm basis in fact [PaCle86]. From an engineering perspective it is the facts about the system that we ultimately want to communicate. Is there a conflict here?

In one way we can say that many pattern stories exist as complete things in the real world. As with many stories, they capture the spirit—although not necessarily the truth—of the detail in what happens. It is rare that our design thinking will so readily submit itself to named classification and sequential arrangement, so there is a certain amount of retrospective revisionism. To recall a quote, used in both POSA2 and POSA3, from philosopher of science James Burke:

> History rarely happens in the right order or at the right time, but the job of a historian is to make it appear as if it did.

The fidelity of a story's sequence is not the issue here. The story serves its purpose as a communication tool if it ends up in the right place, having woven its way through the significant (and insignificant) decisions and details that made the system what it is today—the good, the bad, and the ugly. Like Galadriel's Mirror [Tolk04], these stories may be of systems that were, systems that are, and systems that yet may be. As an educational and architectural tool such an approach can reveal more than conventional case studies—and case studies can greatly benefit if they apply the kind of narrative we are prescribing.

Looking at the Pieces in Piecemeal Growth

The utility of pattern stories also suggests something deeper about piecemeal growth in design. If we can tell stories of system development in terms of growth through the progressive application of patterns, can we not also develop systems in this way, rather than as masterplanned, large-lump affairs? As shown above, the development of a system can be viewed as a single narrative example, in which design questions are asked and answered and structures are assembled for specific reasons. It is therefore also reasonable to consider this narrative as a proactive approach to development, one that is empirically based and responsive.

If we can view the progress of some designs as the progressive application of particular patterns, what about turning that idea around to focus once again on pattern relationships? The pattern relationships discussed so far in this part of the book have focused largely on containment and usage, with the occasional hint—as opposed to concrete suggestion—of sequencing. Although we previously used the story metaphor when describing patterns, there has been no deep guidance on the narrative connection between patterns. We have also used the metaphor of patterns as vocabulary, focusing on the suitability of application, but again without discussing the ordering that would make best use of the best words in the best sequence.

7.4   Sequences of Patterns

The application of one particular pattern after another is a piece of design that may occur across many systems, or a change in situation that may occur in many environments. The sequence has an effect—hopefully desired—that is repeated and can be recounted. There is no need necessarily to tell the story of a whole system to find its useful subsequences. These sequences, whether whole or partial, can be mined from existing systems—just as individual patterns can be—and presented as slices of architecture retold.

In terms of presentation, a pattern story is indeed a narrative: it may be supported by diagrams, but it is typically textual rather than notational. A simple sequence can embrace the notion of cooperating patterns we described earlier, demonstrating them in a larger context and showing how one leads to the next to meet a consequent design challenge. Where patterns compete, this can be considered either a matter of dramatic tension, as one option is actively considered with respect to another, or a matter of branching the story, where a different story unfolds on each branch.

In addition to the various styles used for pattern stories, there are various different approaches to presenting pattern sequences. They can be presented simply and linearly as a list of the patterns applied [AIS77] [BeCu87] [Hen05b], perhaps with some commentary to describe the pattern. A pattern sequence can alternatively be presented using a form, such as a thumbnail, that includes some description of the pattern being applied so that the specific problems and resolutions are visible [ASAIA75] [Ale04a].

An Early Example

Where it is present, the notion of applying patterns in a particular temporal sequence has often been understated or implicit, rather than presented as an artifact in its own right. Although it has not had the mindshare enjoyed by other pattern concepts, the importance of applying patterns in an orderly sequence has long been a part of the pattern tradition [AIS77] [Ale79], even within the realm of software patterns.

For example, the following description, taken from the earliest paper on patterns in software [BeCu87], is careful to outline a pattern sequence:

Consider a very small pattern language for designing Smalltalk windows. We suggest the following patterns:

1. Window Per Task

2. Few Panes Per Window

3. Standard Panes

4. Short Menus

5. Nouns and Verbs

We presented these patterns to a team of application specialists writing a specification for a special purpose programming environment. Without detailed understanding of any of Smalltalk's interface mechanisms (MVC for example) they were able to specify very reasonable interfaces after one day of practice. Note that we sorted and numbered the patterns. Pattern 1 must be addressed first. It decides what windows will be available and what will be done in them. Next patterns 2 and 3 divide each window into panes. Finally patterns 4 and 5 determine what selections and actions will do within each pane. This order was derived from the topology of influences between each pattern.

Where a pattern story provides a specific narrative, a pattern sequence provides the model of the narrative. It structures the stories we can tell and characterizes the stories we might regard as similar.

A Pattern Sequence is Both a Process and a Thing

There is more to pattern sequences, however, than just the telling and retelling of stories, valuable as these tales are. Just as each pattern is both a process and a thing, so to is a pattern sequence. A sequence represents a process made up smaller processes—its constituent patterns—arranged in an order that achieves a particular architecture, architectural feature, or change of environment with desired properties.

Just as an individual example can illustrate an individual pattern, we can consider a pattern story an extended example that not only illustrates a number of patterns, but also serves to illustrate a pattern sequence. A pattern sequence is therefore a successive progression of design decisions and transformations. In the limit, we might retrospectively consider the application of a single pattern as a sequence of one.

We have said that individual patterns may be whole or dysfunctional: does this characterization also apply to pattern sequences? Certainly, a pattern sequence based on dysfunctional patterns is unlikely itself to be whole. But what of sequences made up of whole patterns? A conclusion reached time and time again in our investigation into the pattern concept is that patterns cannot be applied arbitrarily, no matter how good the individual patterns might be in other situations. As a result, even pattern sequences made of patterns that are whole can be dysfunctional, just as a framework made up of classes that are simple and cohesive can itself be complex and ineffective.

When it comes to sequences, what distinguishes the good from the bad? Certainly, solving the wrong problem qualifies as a problem. For example, a successor pattern may address forces that are not present, or miss those that are. We can also look to the quality of what is built to determine at each stage in the process whether or not the design is in some way whole and stable.

A healthy pattern sequence is thus one in which each intermediate step represents a sensible and sufficiently stable structure. While it may not necessarily be a final design, it is not perched precariously in a half-way state that cannot be built or easily described, or that has no obvious follow-on step. A sequence represents a path through a design space, and we would prefer the sequence be based on intermediate steps that are as whole and stable as possible.

Again, what we have arrived at is incremental development through piecemeal growth. The development may be governed by a vision, whether ambitious and system-wide or modest and focused on a handful of classes. The steps taken to realize the vision, however, are each taken with a surer footfall than the large leap of faith taken in a big up-front design. Each point in the pattern sequence responds to the feedback and context created by the previous design. Following a pattern sequence is more like following a recipe than following a plan—improvisation and style are encouraged if you are a skilled cook or are familiar with a particular recipe.

Of course, just as we know that a given pattern is not good in all situations, the same is true of pattern sequences. How we choose between related pattern sequences will lead us to pattern languages, which is the subject of Part III of this book, *Into Pattern Languages*.

A Short Story Revisited

Returning to the request-handling story, we can uncover its underlying sequence. The sequence and the specific contextual details are already described in detail, but we can abstract the contextual detail to capture just the backbone of the process:

> COMMAND is expressed with EXPLICIT INTERFACE. COMMAND PROCESSOR is then introduced, to which COLLECTIONS FOR STATES is added. COMMAND is then augmented with MEMENTO. COMMAND PROCESSOR is then refined with STRATEGY, which leads to NULL OBJECT. COMPOSITE COMMAND is then introduced.

This outline is somewhat like summarizing the plot of a play by leaving out the specifics, talking about it in only the most abstract terms. For example, the plot of a three-act play could be summarized as an opening act in which the protagonist, supporting roles, and main theme of the play are introduced, a second act in which the protagonist is in conflict with the situation that has developed, and a closing act in which there is climax, catharsis, and resolution. Not exactly a summary to inspire would-be theatergoers to snap up tickets, but an honest rendition of the progression nonetheless.

It is even possible to precis the pattern sequence that summarizes our request-handling story a bit further and more formally:

> ⟨COMMAND, EXPLICIT INTERFACE, COMMAND PROCESSOR, COLLECTIONS FOR STATES, MEMENTO, STRATEGY, NULL OBJECT, COMPOSITE COMMAND⟩

Pattern sequences, however, are not just an exercise in brevity: they have a purpose. The sequence described above highlights only one aspect of the pattern sequence. To be useful in practice, we would need to describe more about the context at the start and the goal and desired properties of what we are trying to build. We would also want to summarize the interaction between the various roles introduced by each pattern—simply saying that one pattern follows another does not tell us how. We might even want to give the sequence a name, so that we could refer to it and convey it concisely to our colleagues.

7.5   Pattern Compounds and Complements Revisited

We have been here before. We can consider pattern compounds as subsequences: short stories in which the plot and plot elements are well-enough known, and the roles and interactions pretty much fixed, so that we need not be told all the details. This familiarity was certainly borne out when we compared the two ways of presenting COMPOSITE COMMAND in *Section 6.3, From Complements to Compounds.*

Recomposition

Building on the idea that sequence matters, we can see that COMPOSITE COMMAND is best captured by the couplet ⟨COMMAND, COMPOSITE⟩ and not by ⟨COMPOSITE, COMMAND⟩, despite the pattern compound's name. Why? Wholeness and stability. COMPOSITE refines COMMAND, which implies that COMMAND is introduced first. A COMMAND on its own is a stable design if command abstraction is what is needed, but without such an intentional context a COMPOSITE becomes a COMPOSITE of what? This is why this pattern is better described by the name COMPOSITE COMMAND and not by, say, COMMANDED COMPOSITE.

We can also see this question of progression played out in code. Starting with COMMAND is an easy and whole step, as is following it with a COMPOSITE implementation. Start with just a vague notion of COMPOSITE, conversely, and nothing can be written yet. Against a written COMMAND interface a COMPOSITE, or indeed any other kind of concrete command, can be implemented. Against a vague notion of a COMPOSITE, nothing can be written—a composition of what?

This short sequence also highlights the importance of role compatibility and integration. It is not simply that one pattern is applied after another, it is that their roles are compatible and can be integrated. For example:

• The COMPOSITE pattern defines a recursive whole–part arrangement for some kind of component type, in which concrete components form a class hierarchy with respect to the general component type.

- The COMMAND pattern defines a class hierarchy for objects whose primary purpose is execution of a task, in which different concrete commands can fulfill the command interface introduced at the root of the hierarchy.

By first introducing a COMMAND, we put in place not only the notion of a class hierarchy, but also of a definite and purposeful component type. By then introducing a COMPOSITE, we simply implement a concrete form of COMMAND, with possibly some feedback to modify the root interface. The roles dovetail and also suggest the sequence to follow.

If you re-examine *Section 4.3, A Second Design Experiment: Interwoven Patterns*, you may notice that although there was a class named CompositeCommand, the COMPOSITE COMMAND pattern was never actually mentioned by name: as the story was told, the pattern applied was COMPOSITE. Is this a different story? Or simply a different way of telling the same story?

The question to ask is whether or not the resulting design is any different. The answer is no: in the earlier account COMPOSITE was applied last and integrated with COMMAND, which was introduced first. In the latest account, COMPOSITE COMMAND was applied last, and integrated with COMMAND, which was introduced first. The resulting structure is identical. In applying COMPOSITE COMMAND, all the COMMAND roles were already present and integrated, and so only components for the COMPOSITE aspect needed introduction. The value of referring to the pattern compound is in clarity of presentation: it makes clearer which pattern roles were being added and integrated. Recall the sequence was summarized as follows:

⟨COMMAND, EXPLICIT INTERFACE, COMMAND PROCESSOR, COLLECTIONS FOR STATES, MEMENTO, STRATEGY, NULL OBJECT, COMPOSITE COMMAND⟩

Summarizing it as follows is no less accurate:

⟨COMMAND, EXPLICIT INTERFACE, COMMAND PROCESSOR, COLLECTIONS FOR STATES, MEMENTO, STRATEGY, NULL OBJECT, COMPOSITE⟩

In this case, the use of the pattern compound does not make any difference to the resulting design. It simply makes clear that the COMPOSITE's component role relates to COMMAND and not to, say, STRATEGY, which was also applied in the pattern sequence and whose roles would also have been compatible with COMPOSITE. Of course, we could come up with a fancier notation to show how roles combined, but recall that the goal was *clarity* rather than *cleverness*. If the progression of role introduction and integration is what we want to show, prose is likely to shed more light than angle brackets.

Iterator Rebatched

Revisiting where we first combined competing patterns intentionally, in *Section 5.4, Patterns in Combination*, we can see that sequence of pattern application was also important, even if not emphasized:

> Start with the core idea of an ITERATOR: an ITERATOR represents a position in a sequence of elements, one that can be moved for traversal of the elements. Follow on with the core idea of a BATCH METHOD: a BATCH METHOD represents a single service to pull across multiple elements. And now combine them: retain the notion of an ITERATOR as a position in a stream of elements, but refine its interface by defining traversal in terms of a BATCH METHOD.

In other words, BATCH ITERATOR can be summarized as ⟨ITERATOR, BATCH METHOD⟩ rather than ⟨BATCH METHOD, ITERATOR⟩. The first design represents the more stable progression: introduce an ITERATOR, then refine its interface with a BATCH METHOD.

In contrast, the second sequence involves more significant churn of the roles and code: introduce a BATCH METHOD onto a collection, then drop it in favor of an ITERATOR, and reimplement a BATCH METHOD on the ITERATOR. BATCH METHOD as the first step would set the wrong context for what was to follow. This is not to say that this sequence would never be followed in practice: it would be the sequence followed by someone who first introduced BATCH METHOD and later realized that it was not the right approach. The pattern sequence ⟨BATCH METHOD, ITERATOR⟩ is not one, however, that we would identify or promote as whole.

Reinterpretation

In *Section 6.4, Element or Compound?*, we examined INTERPRETER, decomposing it into the pattern triplet COMMAND, CONTEXT OBJECT, and COMPOSITE. This ordering happened to reflect the order of presentation, but what about the underlying sequence? The sequence, in this case, is the same, as we can demonstrate by elaborating the narrative behind the compound:

> *We need to develop an interpreter for a simple scripting language. The execution of a given script is to be accessed from within a client program. How can we programmatically manipulate and execute a script?*

Represent the whole script as a COMMAND object. Present an interface of methods for executing a script and performing whatever secondary queries and modifications may be required by a client application using a script.

> *A given script is likely to need to execute more than once, independently of any other scripts, over the lifetime of the client application. A script also needs to receive, and possibly pass back, environmental settings and operations that make it useful and allow it to execute correctly. How can an executing script gain access to this external state and behavior?*

Represent the relevant state and behavior in an object that encapsulates the needed context and pass it explicitly via an argument to the COMMAND object representing the script. If necessary, the state of an execution can be passed to another script or persisted for later use.

> *The scripting language follows a simple grammar, structured in terms of statements and/or expressions. The smallest script can be a single statement or the simplest expression possible. The syntax of the language may also have a context-free grammar. How can the script be expressed at runtime?*

Decompose the whole-script COMMAND object in terms of the grammar of the language, so that each executable construct is a COMMAND. Containment and recursion in the grammar are realized through a COMPOSITE. At runtime the current execution state is held and passed around in the CONTEXT OBJECT.

We can also illustrate this sequence diagrammatically, showing the progression of the design resulting from each of the three pattern steps, starting with COMMAND, then introducing a CONTEXT OBJECT, and then applying COMPOSITE to COMMAND:

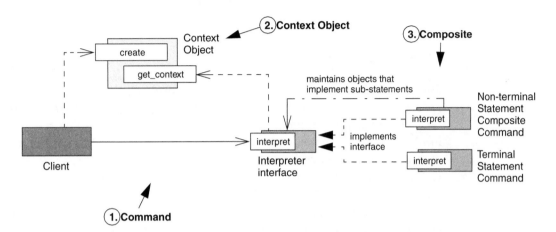

In a nutshell this figure represents the following tuple: ⟨COMMAND, CONTEXT OBJECT, COMPOSITE⟩. This path represents the optimal and most stable realization of the three patterns, while other routes can lead to the same result but will involve more refactoring detours.

Now, consider what would happen if we wished to add scriptable request handling to our request-handling framework. Leaving the pattern compounds intact, the resulting sequence would be as follows:

⟨COMMAND, EXPLICIT INTERFACE, COMMAND PROCESSOR, COLLECTIONS FOR STATES, MEMENTO, STRATEGY, NULL OBJECT, COMPOSITE COMMAND, INTERPRETER⟩

If we expand the compounds, this leads to the following pattern sequence:

⟨COMMAND, EXPLICIT INTERFACE, COMMAND PROCESSOR, COLLECTIONS FOR STATES, MEMENTO, STRATEGY, NULL OBJECT, *COMPOSITE*, *CONTEXT OBJECT*, *COMPOSITE*⟩

The INTERPRETER integrates with the roles of the existing COMMAND pattern, and so CONTEXT OBJECT relates back to the roles of the first pattern applied, COMMAND. What is interesting, however, is that COMPOSITE is repeated. In both cases it can be considered part of a

COMPOSITE COMMAND. The recursive composition in the second application, however, concerns the grammar of the script, not the composition of arbitrary COMMAND objects. It elaborates and integrates with the COMMAND object type responsible for representing scripts through their grammar, and is not necessarily related to the COMPOSITE introduced to allow grouping of arbitrary COMMANDs.

Realigning Architecture and Organization

Pattern compounds represent a restricted and relatively fixed form of pattern sequence. Other sequences may be more fluid in their formation. For example, *Section 5.2, Patterns in Competition* explored the implications of Conway's Law as a force between a development organization and its corresponding software architecture. The CONWAY'S LAW pattern proposed a general solution that could be better characterized as ALIGN ARCHITECTURE AND ORGANIZATION. Closer analysis, however, revealed that there were distinct, complementary concrete patterns within this high-level solution: ORGANIZATION FOLLOWS ARCHITECTURE and ARCHITECTURE FOLLOWS ORGANIZATION.

In practice, what are the possible pattern sequences that we could play against these two complements? At one extreme we could chose not to pursue either option, which would result in an empty sequence, ⟨⟩. If the architecture is stable and proven, however, it may make more sense to organize the development around the architecture, resulting in a somewhat lonely pattern sequence of one: ⟨ORGANIZATION FOLLOWS ARCHITECTURE⟩. Alternatively, an architecture that has not yet stabilized—but an organization that is resistant to change—might be better suited by the complementary approach: ⟨ARCHITECTURE FOLLOWS ORGANIZATION⟩.

A more open and feedback-driven response to the situation may be to 'align the structure of the architecture with the structure of the organization by making piecemeal changes to one or other' [CoHa04]. This solution gives rise to a family of sequences, rather than a single pattern sequence. The form of this family is of the form ⟨ORGANIZATION FOLLOWS ARCHITECTURE, ARCHITECTURE FOLLOWS ORGANIZATION, ORGANIZATION FOLLOWS ARCHITECTURE...⟩ or, leading with the other foot, ⟨ARCHITECTURE FOLLOWS ORGANIZATION, ORGANIZATION FOLLOWS ARCHITECTURE, ARCHITECTURE FOLLOWS ORGANIZATION...⟩.

7.6   Returning to the Question of Context

As we highlighted in *Chapter 1*, there is sometimes a debate about whether or not a pattern's context is part of the pattern itself. Now that we have examined pattern relationships more deeply we are now in a better position to revisit this issue.

If the context determines a pattern's applicability and is a part of it, there is the danger of losing the generality of the pattern and having it anchored to a single problem situation. But if the context is not a part of the pattern, what determines its applicability? A pattern is not just an arbitrary structure that can be applied anywhere, so without some guidance from context it is rudderless.

The strong emphasis on context can be seen in Christopher Alexander's work, from which we can perhaps find some clarification [Ale79]:

> Each pattern is a three-part rule, which expresses a relation between a certain context, a certain system of forces which occurs repeatedly in that context, and a certain software configuration which allows these forces to resolve themselves.

This definition certainly seems to state that the context is part of the pattern. But this is little more than argument by quotation. It does not resolve the dichotomy we outline above.

Defining Context

Closer inspection reveals that much of the perceived problem with context reduces to matters of terminology. The question is not really whether or not context is a part of a pattern: the question we need to address is 'what is context?'

Put simply, the context of a pattern is where it can be applied. But what does that mean? Given that a pattern addresses a problem arising from particular forces, those forces must be connected to the context. If the context is not part of the pattern, then neither are the forces. However, if the forces are part the pattern—which they must be, otherwise patterns just become solutions—they must be rooted in the context and have arisen from there. The context cannot therefore be divorced from the pattern. Yet the context for a pattern considered as a stand-alone pattern is in some way more generic than the context for a pattern considered within a pattern sequence.

So how do we define a pattern's context? As we explored in *Section 1.5, The Context: Part of a Pattern or Not?*, one way to do this is by exhaustive enumeration: describe all the programming situations that would lead to creating the design tension addressed by the pattern. Unfortunately, this could be a very long list, and one that, by induction, would never be finalized and complete. Moreover, it would never be comprehensible.

For example, our BATCH METHOD example from *Chapter 1* could be applied in many situations in which iterative access would be expensive. This breadth included distributed and concurrent systems, as well as in-memory database access, and even that range was by example rather than by exhaustive enumeration. As our interest was on distributed and concurrent systems, we intentionally focused on that context rather than others—better to be a master of one (or two) than a jack (or hack) of all.

If a pattern is applied in the context of another pattern, as it is in a pattern sequence, then we can narrow the description of the context to define it as that preceding pattern. In a given story, all of the specifics are nailed down, so the generality of the sequence is further narrowed. The context in question is now very concrete. This is not a description of the pattern in general, however, it is a description of the pattern within a specific sequence. We may therefore chose to make it more specific by omitting the description of forces and consequences that do not apply, and also by phrasing the solution more specifically.

For example, BATCH METHOD can be applied in the context of ITERATOR, which gives us the BATCH ITERATOR pattern compound. Of course, as we know, there is much more to BATCH METHOD than following ITERATOR. In the sequence of BATCH ITERATOR, however, other attributes of BATCH METHOD may not be relevant, and could even be considered a distraction.

For some pattern authors this is what context means: a concrete description of the situation through enumeration of the patterns that set up the pattern of interest. In a pattern sequence we know the list is short, because we have severely reduced the scope of interest of the pattern. In a different sequence the narrowed context would be different. We might also find that we rephrase, rename, or otherwise restructure the pattern to make it more direct and improve its fit.

While this view captures the situation within a particular constrained use of a pattern, it fails to address part of the 'pattern nature' of the pattern: its recurrence across different situations. What is it that is stable and invariant and can be referred to as *pattern*? Here are some choices:

- Is it the essence of the solution structure? Definitely.

- It is the essence of the conflicting forces? Certainly, because otherwise we have a recurring solution pattern without an understanding of the problem class that motivated it.

- Is it the essence of the context? This may be the key: it is the essential anatomy of the context, as opposed to a specific enumeration, that recurs. It is the class or characterization of the context, as opposed to a more specific instance in, say, a story or, looking ahead, a language.

Without some essential underlying features that can be seen as common, it is hard to claim that a pattern can identify a recurring set of forces without saying anything about the origin of these forces.

A pattern sequence, or even multiple pattern sequences that contain the same pattern, may pin down the scope of the context to the point at which it is nameable and enumerable, but it does not fully define the scope of the pattern in its own right. Of course, attempting a union of all possible uses of a pattern would defeat much of the practical side of the pattern concept, which is not what we are after! To provide a general context statement we aim to typify the kind of context by its common features—an intensional approach—rather than by defining the context class by listing its members—an extensional approach.

For example, we might in general define the context of some pattern in a sequence as '…you have used ACTIVE OBJECT to introduce concurrency of tasks into a BROKER and a MONITOR OBJECT to serialize access to common resources…' This locates a pattern more precisely within a specific sequence and its role within a design. A generalized view of the context, however, would be intentionally less specific but none-theless precise, for example, '...concurrent threads of activity exist in a system or part of a system, along with synchronized access to certain objects...' This view is less useful to the user focused on the sequence of patterns that includes ACTIVE OBJECT, BROKER, and MONITOR OBJECT, but more useful to someone looking at the pattern outside that pattern sequence, whether applying it freely or including it in a new story of their own.

As the presentation in which a pattern is found becomes more specific, so too can its context become more specific. Within a finite, enumerable set of patterns, then, enumerating precursor patterns as the definition of context is the simplest and most direct form of communication for the pattern. Presented outside a closed system, however, the appropriate form for the context is often the more general approach of characterizing the properties of the context that result from previous design steps, rather than the design steps themselves.

Specialization and Variation

Considering the context in terms of breadth of scope and specificity also provides a different insight into how patterns specialize. Consider PROXY, a general pattern that can be found playing a role in many parts of a distributed system, including:

- At the process level in firewalls, namely FIREWALL PROXY.

- At the class-hierarchy level, the classic Gang-of-Four PROXY example.

- In a distributed object model as a CLIENT PROXY, the stub clients use to invoke operations on remote objects.

- In the C++-specific form of a SMART POINTER that manages the lifetime or synchronization of in-process objects.

Each situation often has an associated name for the use of PROXY, but in general terms and parlance these are all still known as PROXY, in spite of such specific naming. How can PROXY be the same pattern in all these cases? The specifics, such as how you design the firewall proxy versus how you define a smart pointer class, are clearly quite different. The basic context is also quite different: processes connected on the Internet versus C++ code in a stand-alone program. The general metaphor of a proxy applies to all of them and it is possible to formulate a general description of context properties that make PROXY desirable. Such a description, however, is likely to be more abstract than would be useful for most developers or design situations.

Narrowing the scope—that is, the context—allows us to say more about the specific forces, the solution structure, and the consequences than in the most general case. It also allows relabeling the pattern as necessary, for example, FIREWALL PROXY and SMART POINTER. So, although such an idea is often understood in terms of specialization or generalization, it is perhaps sometimes more usefully driven from the perspective of narrowing or widening the context of applicability.

With the exception of the entry pattern, it is clear that the context of each pattern in a pattern sequence is very specific: the preceding pattern. For pattern descriptions written in the context of a pattern sequence this is sufficient context for readers. They are left free to generalize a pattern beyond that context, but such generalization may not be assisted by the pattern's description. For patterns documented individually, it is the contextual properties that are of most interest to readers, since they bound the scope over which the pattern applies.

7.7 Pattern Connections

This chapter focuses on the significance of sequencing in applying or thinking about patterns, where sequences represent 'sentences' of patterns. More broadly, Part II of the book, *Between Patterns*, underscores that patterns are outgoing, fond of company, and community spirited. Of course, the value of individual patterns should not be underrated, just as the power of individual words should not be underestimated. However, just as the potency of words arises from their context—in the sentences, paragraphs, sections, and chapters that contain them—the primary value of patterns occurs when they are brought together as a community.

It is this networking on the part of patterns that reflects the nature of design, of designs, and of the complexity of all systems whose design elements interact across more than one dimension. The notions of synthesis, overlap, reinforcement, and balance affect different design elements according to the roles they play. These notions reinforce what to some appears an initially counterintuitive view of design: that the components found in a design may not be the best representation of the design's history, rationale, or future.

Just as a house may be built from distinct parts, it is the interplay between them that makes the house a home, not the parts considered in isolation. What looks good and makes sense in one situation may be quite the wrong thing in another. For example, a new set of shelves may make a previously positioned picture look askew. Similarly, the addition of a new class of events may make an existing event-handling model hard to program or optimize. In these types of situations, parts cannot be considered in isolation from one another without also missing some valuable perspective.

Connections with Conviction

It is not enough to say that patterns simply get along with each other, that they relate well with their companions. There must be some precision to this notion of relationships. Looking back over the relationships discussed in this and previous chapters in Part II, it appears that there are two fundamental types of relationships between patterns that help most in expressing an architecture or characterizing a situation:

- A *spatial relationship*, that of connection by inclusion, which describes a form.

- A *temporal relationship*, that of sequencing in time, which describes a process.

These basic ingredients, when combined with optionality, opposition, and abstraction, allow us to move from just a simple passive vocabulary of design to something more profound: an active language for genuine communication, with meaning, dialog, and reflection. Part III of the book describes the form, contents, and properties of such languages.

8 Pattern Collections

Science is facts; just as houses are made of stones, so is science made of facts; but a pile of stones is not a house and a collection of facts is not necessarily science.

Henri Poincaré

The previous chapters have explored how patterns can connect to form a design and inform the activity of design. This chapter looks at the general issue of collecting, organizing, and considering many patterns together, in part in response to the challenge of how a handbook of software architecture might be assembled. The theme of this chapter is pattern collections and catalogs, which act as repositories of patterns. In helping to organize such repositories, we also explore *problem frames* as a technique for capturing the context and problems in which patterns may be applied, and examine a semiotic perspective on pattern structure and relationships.

8.1   Toward a Handbook

Patterns are gregarious by nature. Any significant design will inevitably draw on many patterns, whether consciously or otherwise, which suggests that in practice a lone pattern is something of a curiosity. The most obvious presentation of multiple patterns is in the form of a collection.

To date, the most ambitious collection of patterns we know of is Grady Booch's *Handbook of Software Architecture* [Booch]. This project aims to fulfill much of Bruce Anderson's original vision of an architecture handbook, which we outlined in *Section 0.1, Beginnings...* At the time of writing, the *Handbook of Software Architecture* lists on the order of 2,000 patterns, many of which are thumbnail sketches.

Most collections, however, are more modest in size and ambition, often focusing on a particular kind of problem, context, or system, and numbering at most a few tens of patterns. The goal and medium for presentation vary from collection to collection. Some collections are general and are published in book form, such as the *Pattern Languages of Program Design* series [PLoPD1] [PLoPD2] [PLoPD3] [PLoPD4] [PLoPD5], others are based around a community and can be found online, such as the *Pedagogical Patterns Project* [PPP].

Collections, Catalogs, and Repositories

There are various terms that are sometimes used when describing patterns collections. The term *collection* itself is perhaps the most common and general purpose. It is often used in the context of a single paper that presents a number of patterns. By contrast, the term *catalog* is more typically used for larger works, such as books or Web sites, and stresses the importance of indexing. For online catalogs, particularly where multiple authors may contribute, the term *repository* is also common, as in the original Portland Pattern Repository [PPR]. These terms are not strict, however, and their precise intent is normally obvious from the context.

The focus of the previous chapters has moved from individual patterns to simple families and communities of patterns. Each concept presented has a strong focus, typically on resolving a problem or a problem space. To move to anything that embraces the encyclopedic vision of an architecture handbook, however, requires more than just specific focus: it requires a method of organization.

8.2   Organizing Pattern Collections

Collections may be organized for personal reasons, for business reasons, or for reasons of publication: authors, may wish to collect patterns for themselves just to better understand a particular domain, a collection of patterns may have relevance for the business of an organization, while a published collection provides an opportunity for sharing domain knowledge. A collection may be put together as part of the act of writing the individual patterns within it. It is not just pattern authors, however, who compile collections. Pattern users can draw different, existing patterns together in a collection, for example to describe the particular set of design practices and styles used by a specific team working on a specific system. This approach reflects the original motivation of software patterns as architecture handbooks.

Whether there is a strong underlying organizational model to a collection is a matter for its compilers. There are various ways of organizing a catalog that are worth considering. On one hand, patterns can form an ad hoc collection, with no overarching scheme or unifying theme: for example, a collection of proceedings from a conference. On the other hand, a collection can be pulled together for a particular purpose, such as presenting the patterns within a particular architecture, so it could be organized by the problems or partitions that characterize that architecture. Different approaches are not necessarily mutually exclusive, so that a collection can be sliced both vertically by intent and horizontally across levels. Similarly, a perspective based on scale and abstraction can complement a view of patterns based on problem domains.

8.3   Ad Hoc Organization

An ad hoc collection of patterns does not necessarily imply that the patterns are organized arbitrarily. It does suggest, however, that the organization and inclusion of patterns is more reactive than proactive: given some set of patterns, what organizational scheme would best group and separate the patterns?

Each of the *Pattern Languages of Program Design* books [PLoPD1] [PLoPD2] [PLoPD3] [PLoPD4] [PLoPD5] answers this question, and answers it slightly differently in each case. The contents of each volume are drawn from submitted patterns that have been workshopped at one of the PLoP conferences, so it is unlikely that they will fit automatically within some predefined taxonomy. Some patterns are grouped by domain, some by level, some by intent, and so on, and each volume is different. Beyond that, the structure of these catalogs is loosely coupled: there is little cross-linking between patterns or consistency in their presentation.

Indexing is useful for any collection. For an ad hoc catalog that does not have an overall organizational theme that would naturally guide the reader, the index is particularly important—and the larger a catalog, the more important the index becomes. The *Pattern Almanac* [Ris01] is perhaps the ultimate index and catalog of its time. Its goal was not the presentation of patterns, but the organization by reference, with summaries, of a majority of the patterns published up to the end of the millennium. Clearly there is no overall schematic vision or ambition that binds these patterns other than the vision and ambition needed to create the almanac and the fact that all its contents are patterns. As a catalog, the almanac has no choice but to be ad hoc in its organization, reacting to and working with the available set of patterns.

Thus organization of a collection may be ad hoc but still support simple access and readability for the reader. The patterns, considered as a whole, cannot necessarily be said to form a society, more of a ragged and coincidental collection of individuals or other distinct groups.

A potential liability of ad hoc collections is that they can be seen to encourage patterns for the sake of patterns. They do not necessarily have a specific, target readership—just the pattern-interested—and they do not necessarily address specific domains, such as distributed systems development, project management, or programming with threads in Java. It is unlikely that an organization would benefit greatly from an ad hoc pattern collection. However, although we would not encourage them as a general scheme, ad hoc collections have legitimate practical uses, such as conference proceedings and general reference resources.

8.4   Organization by Level

One of the earliest pattern classification schemes was in terms of levels of abstraction, granularity, or scale. Perhaps the commonest scheme of this sort is found in *A System of Patterns* [POSA1], the first volume of the *Pattern-Oriented Software Architecture* series. This scheme grades patterns in terms of granularity, differentiating between *architectural patterns*—sometimes called *framework patterns*—at the most coarse-grained level, *design patterns* in the middle, and *idioms* at the most fine-grained level. The collection is organized primarily in terms of these sections: the same three-level model has since been used elsewhere, such as the distinction between architecture patterns and general-purpose design patterns found in the *Pattern Languages of Program Design* series [PLoPD1] [PLoPD2] [PLoPD3].

Clarifying 'Design' and 'Architecture'

There are some valid objections to this three-level scheme based simply on terminology. Establishing an architecture and applying programming language idioms successfully are both acts of design, therefore surely they are also *design patterns*? In truth, now that we have examined the pattern concept more deeply, we can see that the term *design pattern* can be considered a general clarification, distinguishing the patterns we are discussing from organizational or pedagogical patterns, for example, or even unrelated uses of the term 'pattern,' such as knitting patterns, patterns on wallpaper, pattern matching with regular expressions, pattern recognition in image processing, and so on. The notion that they are *design* patterns, however, does not necessarily distinguish one kind of pattern concerning design from another kind.

In hindsight it would be fairer to describe the patterns classified as *design patterns* in POSA1 as 'of a similar nature and granularity to the patterns found in the Gang-of-Four *Design Patterns* book,' but what this gains in precision it rather loses in brevity. Similarly, given that patterns are often considered intrinsically architectural in nature, how can one level of granularity be considered *architectural* and not others? Surely they all have the potential to be architectural in some sense? Unless one subscribes to a view of architecture that equates with so-called 'PowerPoint architecture'—'architecture is the big boxes on a presentation slide'—then favoring one level of granularity as *architectural* over others does not make consistent sense. Architecture ultimately embraces and cuts across all levels of detail: it cannot be considered so separately.

The following definition of *design* and *architecture* offers a useful clarification [Booch06]:

> As a noun, design is the named (although sometimes unnameable) structure or behavior of a system whose presence resolves or contributes to the resolution of a force or forces on that system. A design thus represents one point in a potential decision space. A design may be singular (representing a leaf decision) or it may be collective (representing a set of other decisions).

> As a verb, design is the activity of making such decisions. Given a large set of forces, a relatively malleable set of materials, and a large landscape upon which to play, the resulting decision space may be large and complex. As such, there is a science associated with design (empirical analysis can point us to optimal regions or exact points in this design space) as well as an art (within the degrees of freedom that range beyond an empirical decision, there are opportunities for elegance, beauty, simplicity, novelty, and cleverness).

> [...]

> All architecture is design but not all design is architecture. Architecture represents the significant design decisions that shape a system, where significant is measured by cost of change.

So if one considers architecture to be primarily concerned with the most significant decisions in a system's design, and not necessarily with all design, then it becomes clear that sometimes a given pattern will qualify as *architectural* and sometimes it will not. It is, therefore, not necessarily an intrinsic property of a pattern as to whether it can be considered *architectural*, it becomes a property of application. In this sense it is sometimes better to distinguish between patterns playing a *strategic* role versus playing a *tactical*—or even *logistical*—role.

For example, in the implementation of a state-machine interpreter the OBJECTS FOR STATES pattern can be used strategically, forming a core role in shaping the architecture of the program. In realizing the private representation and lifecycle of some kind of connection object, however, the use of OBJECTS FOR STATES would be considered tactical: replacing it with METHODS FOR STATES would be a local change with little ripple effect on other architectural decisions. Of course, many patterns will tend to fall predominantly into one category or another: NULL OBJECT is rarely likely to be strategic in its application, whereas PROACTOR is almost always going to be strategic.

Clarifying 'Idiom'

Questions also arise with respect to *idioms*, which relate to language usage and vernacular style [Booch94]:

> An *idiom* is an expression peculiar to a certain programming language or application culture, representing a generally accepted convention for use of the language.
>
> [...]
>
> One defining characteristic of an idiom is that ignoring or violating the idiom has immediate social consequences: you are branded as a yahoo or, worse, an outsider, unworthy of respect.

The concept of an idiom is common in natural language: the idea of *idiom* referring to design techniques for working with a programming language was popularized by Jim Coplien [Cope92]. Subsequently, the term has also come to be associated with patterns that are specific to a given programming language. However, in some cases *idiom* retains its original linguistic sense of indicating a merely conventional sign as opposed to a solution to a problem. In many cases, moreover, *idiom* refers to something that qualifies as both. Thus there is already ambiguity in the term, because sometimes it refers to a problem-solving practice, while at other times it describes just a matter of convention.

Another issue is that on closer inspection the term *idiom* can refer to more than just patterns within a programming language, which is the sense in which it was used in POSA1. In particular, it can legitimately refer to patterns that are used within a specific context, whether domain, coarse-architectural partition, or technology. A programming language is simply one example of a solution domain in which some practices represent part of a vernacular body of practice, so *programming language idiom* would be the more specific term when that is what is intended.

There are also practices that are idiomatic in a particular context, but which do not qualify as programming language patterns. For example, the use of BATCH METHOD for iteration is idiomatic in a distributed object computing system design, but might not necessarily be as appropriate in other contexts. Moreover, there are some patterns that are often considered general rather than idiomatic, but actually come across as idiomatic with a slight change of programming context. For example, the use of ITERATOR for iteration is considered general, yet in Smalltalk iteration is idiomatically expressed through an ENUMERATION METHOD. This would reclassify ITERATOR as an *idiom* specific to, say, C++ and Java rather than a *design pattern*, according to the original classification. Of course, there are also cases in which the notion of idiom does refer to something that differs between specific languages. For example, the idiomatic expression of ITERATOR is different in the C++ standard template library than in Java.

There is also some abuse of the term *idiom* with respect to our understanding that, in natural language, an idiom represents a common pattern of usage specific to a cultural group. Some patterns branded as idioms are actually uncommon, and even unknown, within the solution domain they target. They may be patterns if there is at least some recurrence, but branding them as idioms when they are not idiomatic is at best a little confusing and at worst a little disingenuous—it is as if the word 'idiom' is being used simply to mean 'good.' It is not uncommon to hear of authors proposing 'new idioms,' which is a curious contradiction. They may be proposing new techniques, but until they become culturally accepted it is perhaps premature to label them as 'idioms.'

Mixing Levels

Jim Coplien also identifies issues with the three levels [Cope96]:

> Splitting patterns into three levels of abstraction [...] is arbitrary in the sense that abstraction falls along a continuum without clear boundaries. This makes classification subjective.

> But there is a deeper issue as well. Many patterns transcend all three levels of architecture. Consider MODEL-VIEW-CONTROLLER, which started as an idiomatic artifact of the Smalltalk culture. As it became more broadly understood, it became a design staple for object-oriented user interface design. Buschmann et al [POSA1] use it as framework-level pattern because it is the primary structuring principle at the highest levels of the system. Patterns this broad are difficult to characterize according to this three-level abstraction taxonomy.

We can find many patterns that exist, in one form or another, at each of the three levels. For example, in a distributed system we find that PROXY can recur at each of the three levels identified. If we focus more on the specific variants, it becomes clearer that at the system-wide level we can have a FIREWALL PROXY, within the infrastructure we could find CLIENT PROXY, and in the programming language API we may find SMART POINTER. So there is also a question not just of granularity, but also of resolution in deciding how we choose to describe an architecture in terms of patterns.

On the Level

Although the three-level approach is appealing and there are many examples that fit, it is not sufficiently general or flexible to accommodate the many cases that do not fit. We can conclude that it is nearly impossible to squeeze patterns into a generalized, consistent, and fixed hierarchical scheme without bending either the patterns or the hierarchical organization. There is nothing wrong with the individual terms used, just the fixed way they are used to distinguish disjoint categories. For example, *architecture* and *architectural, design,* and *idiom* and *idiomatic* are useful terms, but not necessarily to describe distinct levels of patterns.

If we focus on a particular context of application, however, the notion of hierarchy and containment is more likely to make sense. For a given kind of system it can become easier to distinguish levels that are stable in terms of the patterns they would contain. Against a particular context it is more likely that a given pattern qualifies as *strategic, tactical,* or *logistical* in scope. It is also more likely in such situations that organizing patterns by architectural partition or by intent makes just as much—if not more—sense, as we shall see.

8.5   Organization by Domain

The notion of a domain is sometimes a loose one, but in its most common interpretation it defines an area under one rule. Playing on the various meanings of the word *rule,* this fits well with its various applications in the world of software development.

In the broadest sense we can distinguish *problem* domain from *solution* domain. Under problem domain—also known as *application* domain—we find a classification of patterns that relate to undertakings visible in the real world, such as telecommunications, finance, healthcare, avionics, logistics, teaching, etc. Some patterns may be specifically suited either to the decomposition of problems or to the establishment of architectures in each of these problem domains. We might consider these patterns to be more user- or customer-centric in their outlook and application. When we look to the domain of the solution we are looking at the realm of the (virtual) *machine,* the internal structure of the software, and are reflecting primarily software-centric concerns. Patterns in the solution domain include idioms that are related to specific programming languages, platform technologies, architectural styles, object-oriented frameworks, etc.

These two coarse groupings are intended to be more complementary than mutually exclusive. A development team creating an online healthcare system may wish to consult both the patterns that relate to the design of healthcare systems and the patterns for the design of multi-tier Web systems. Another domain that may be of interest to the team is the domain of software development processes, where we find many agile development practices documented and reasoned through in pattern form [Cun96] [BDS+99][CoHa04]. In each case a domain can be considered a projection of a system or its development with respect to specific criteria—technology, process, business, etc.

Revisiting our ongoing discussion of the role of context in patterns, a domain defines some or all of a context in which a pattern is applied. So the notion of organizing patterns by domain is tantamount to organizing patterns by some aspect of their context. Organization by domain or context also finds a sympathetic elaboration in the form of problem frames, which we will examine later in this chapter.

From the perspective of any kind of handbook, organization by domain presents a convenient alignment between the work of a developer, an architect, or a project manager and the patterns of immediate interest. On the other hand, such an organizational scheme de-emphasizes and potentially obscures patterns that cut across domains. A great deal of programming, architectural, and management insight can be derived by generalizing from common experiences in different domains. A potential liability of a domain-organized collection is therefore an overly narrow or prescriptive view.

8.6 Organization by Partition

Narrower than the general notion of domain is the classification of patterns with respect to the part of an architecture in which they are seen to apply. Where an architecture introduces partitioning, each partition may be based on a different technology or concern than the other partitions, and therefore different patterns are applicable within each partition for elaborating design detail. Examples of partitions include layers, tiers, components, and packages.

In a given architecture different partitions exist to fulfill different roles, and will therefore follow a different set of patterns to define their internal micro-architecture. For example, one component may represent a framework, whereas another may represent application logic. The patterns used for *constructing* extensible libraries are often quite different than those used for building applications *using* extensible libraries.

Architecture with Tiers

Perhaps the commonest coarse-grained architectural partitioning is LAYERS. A specific application of the LAYERS pattern assigns different responsibilities to each layer, so each layer defines a different context for the patterns that will be used within it. An example of this approach can be found in the *Core J2EE Patterns* catalog [ACM03]. Described as the *tiered approach*, five logically separate layers of concern are identified—client tier, presentation tier, business tier, integration tier, and resource tier—and used as the basis for grouping the patterns. Patterns are documented for the three middle tiers:

> *Presentation Tier.* The presentation tier encapsulates presentation logic required to service clients. It is responsible for generating UI elements—the UI elements are actually executed in the client tier. JSPs and Servlets are used in this tier and take advantage of many patterns, including FRONT CONTROLLER and CONTEXT OBJECT.

> *Business Tier.* The business tier provides the underlying business services required by application clients. The business tier is where business objects reside. Business objects may be implemented as EJBs and may rely on many patterns, including BUSINESS DELEGATE and TRANSFER OBJECT.

> *Integration Tier.* The integration tier handles communication with non-local resources and external systems, such as legacy systems and data repositories. JDBC, JMS, and various other middleware technologies are often used in this tier. The patterns of benefit in this layer include DATA ACCESS OBJECT and DOMAIN STORE.

The benefit of this approach to organizing patterns in a collection is that it makes quite clear where each pattern fits within an overall architectural style, namely that of multi-tier enterprise Java systems.

Road to Partition

Sometimes an architectural partition overlaps with the idea of a domain. For example, the domain of user-interface design is also distinct when considered in terms of architectural partitioning: the user interface is part of the presentation layer. The same alignment between domain and partition is also true of database design. In both cases, the domain of interest and the partitioning in the architecture establish a context for organizing patterns that provide appropriate solutions. However, although there is often some overlap, it is not as common to find perfect alignment between domain and partition, so organizing by partition does not subsume organizing by domain, nor vice versa.

As with organizing by domain, the benefit for pattern readers of organizing by partition is being able to offer a ready-to-use, handbook-like arrangement of patterns that matches the architecture in which they are working. However, in spite of such habitability, it is possible that the scope of applicability for patterns may be narrowed unnecessarily. For example, there may be a number of patterns that cover design and coding style that are common to all partitions. In which partition would these be documented? Thus organizing by partition cannot necessarily be used as the only criterion for organizing all the patterns. Similarly, but in the manner of Russell's paradox[16], patterns that describe the overall partitioning do not themselves fit within any partition.

8.7 Organization by Intent

A pattern collection can be organized with respect to the common intent of groups of patterns, where the intent may identify an architectural characteristic, a common goal or responsibility, and so on.

---

16. Russell's paradox in set theory can be posed thus: 'There is a barber in town who shaves all men who don't shave themselves. Does the barber shave himself?'

POSA by Intent

Categorizing patterns with respect to intent has been success-fully as the dominant scheme in the second, third, and fourth vol-umes of the *Pattern-Oriented Software Architecture* series, *Patterns for Concurrent and Networked Objects* [POSA2], *Resource Management Patterns* [POSA3], and *A Pattern Language for Distributed Computing* [POSA4]. Many of the intention-based categories used in POSA4 are drawn from those used in the previous volumes, sometimes renamed, sometimes regrouped, sometimes further divided.

In POSA2, patterns were divided across four groups:

- Service Access and Configuration
- Event Handling
- Synchronization
- Concurrency

In POSA3 there were three categories:

- Resource Acquisition
- Resource Lifecycle
- Resource Release

In POSA4 there were thirteen categories:

- From Mud to Structure
- Distribution Infrastructure
- Event Demultiplexing and Dispatching
- Interface Partitioning
- Component Partitioning
- Application Control
- Concurrency
- Synchronization
- Object Interaction
- Adaptation and Extension
- Object Behavior
- Resource Management
- Database Access

Classification by intent is also used for parts of POSA1, so that LAYERS, PIPES AND FILTERS and BLACKBOARD are all grouped together under the common banner *From Mud to Structure*. Similarly, *Interactive Systems* classifies both MODEL-VIEW-CONTROLLER and PRESENTATION-ABSTRACTION-CONTROL, *Communication* classifies FORWARDER-RECEIVER and OBSERVER, and *Management* classifies COMMAND PROCESSOR and VIEW HANDLER. The intention scheme used in POSA1, however, is subordinate to the classification by level of abstraction and the naming is not always consistent. For example, *Interactive Systems* is more of a domain-related name than an intention-based name, for which *Interaction* would be a better candidate. This is perhaps a minor point, but one that becomes more obvious when the question of classification is discussed in detail and reflected upon, as we have done in this chapter.

GOF by Intent

Perhaps the most enduring intention-based scheme is the one found in *Design Patterns* [GoF95]. Patterns are grouped according to whether their purpose is considered to be *creational, structural,* or *behavioral.*

Popular as it is, however, it is not always clear what is meant or why this scheme is useful—or, indeed, whether it even works. Certainly, *creational* properly captures an identifiable intent and is the one category that is clear, useful, and works. But what is really meant by *behavioral* in contrast to *structural?* Ultimately all object-oriented design is about achieving behavior through structure, so there is nothing at this level that distinguishes, say, COMPOSITE—which is considered structural—from INTERPRETER—which is considered behavioral. Similarly, CHAIN OF RESPONSIBILITY, a name with strong overtones of structure, is classified as behavioral, whereas DECORATOR, a name with strong overtones of behavior, is classified as structural. All of these examples propose and describe structures that are intended to support a particular set of behaviors as well, and vice versa.

One of the few recurring themes that one can find is that in the *structural* patterns the behavior is typically expressed through some form of direct forwarding, whether to one—for example, in PROXY—or to many—such as in COMPOSITE. This would be a classification of common solution structure, however, not of intent, and it is not consistent across all the patterns. The behavioral category, moreover, seems worse off, often acting as a catch-all for patterns that did not quite fit into either creational or structural categories.

DDD by Intent

Of course, organizing patterns with respect to intent is not the strict preserve of patterns focused directly on designed artifacts, such as objects and components. Such an intentional approach applies equally to more process-related patterns, amongst others. *Domain-Driven Design* [Evans03] offers an approach to system conceptualization and development centered around domain models. The articulation of *Domain-Driven Design* is based on patterns that are grouped by intent. For example, the categories include the following: *Binding Model and Implementation, Isolating the Domain, Supple Design*, and *Maintaining Model Integrity*. The naming of these groups of patterns is strongly intentional, and gives the reader a clear notion of where to look depending on the kind of problem they are trying to solve.

Reflection on Intent

It seems that intent offers a stable approach to organizing a collection, and indeed one that reflects part of the structure of patterns themselves. By focusing on the nature of the problem being solved, intention-based categories offer a good match and a prelude to the patterns they contain. They follow a goal-oriented perspective that is likely to be a good match for many pattern readers. However, there is a subjective element here as well that the pattern collection compiler should be aware of: the characterization of a pattern's intent is not necessarily unique and objective.

8.8   Organizing Pattern Collections (Reprise)

The question of where and why we wish to use a particular set of patterns motivates the organization of a pattern catalog. A pattern anthologist has many choices in this presentation, and the various styles of grouping together by common context, such as domain or partition, or common purpose (that is, intent), seem to offer the most coherent schemes. The applicability of a pattern springs from an intention in a specific situation: the desire to create something to achieve a particular goal in a particular context. This combination of situation and intention can also be used successfully to characterize the organization of pattern collections.

Where a pattern collection is intended in some way to be general purpose, a broad situation and vague intent are unlikely to be helpful. However, where the situation is in some way more precise, and likewise the intention, this combination of situation and intention can offer insight to the pattern anthologist about how to organize patterns, and clarity to the pattern reader in navigating the patterns. For example, thread-safe design in Java with the goal of thread safety, good performance, and minimal intrusion on the code, offers a concrete goal within a clearly defined scope.

A situation can be characterized both in terms of its problem domain and in terms of a solution domain. This notion of organization by problem domain, specifically the problem domain in which a software system sits, bridges the different perspectives associated with analysis and design. It casts further light on the role and meaning of context for a pattern and how its forces arise. This interest in the nature of the problem being solved as a means of organization also suggests that a related approach—that of *problem frames*—may be relevant to the distillation and presentation of patterns.

8.9   Problem Frames

A criticism often leveled at software development is that, individually and culturally, it is often too solution-centric [BTN06]:

> Software developers solve problems in code. It's part of our nature to decompose, resolve, or drive toward a solution quickly and efficiently. We naturally gravitate to 'the solution space' where our architectures, designs, patterns and idioms combine to resolve the plaguing problems that our clients continually push on us.

Either the world of the solution absorbs software developers to the detriment of the problem be solved or, in more extreme cases, solutions precede the problems that they might solve: there sometimes appears to be an abundance of 'solutions' in search of a problem.

Design-focused patterns offer one bridge between the problem and solution domains, highlighting a design relationship between solution structures and their roles and the problem context and its forces. Although unrefined and imprecise, even the original soundbite definition of a pattern we started with in *Chapter 1* makes explicit the two sides that a pattern brings together: 'a pattern is a solution to a problem that arises within a specific context.' Yet in spite of this, many developers and pattern commentators see patterns solely as solution-oriented constructs. They are perhaps forgetful or unaware of the problem-motivated nature of a pattern, accidentally mistaking the solution structure proposed by a pattern for the whole pattern. Consequently they can find themselves wrestling with the ambiguities of different patterns that have seemingly identical solution structures.

So, even within the world of patterns, which intentionally promote friendly relations between the worlds of the problem and the solution, there is often still a lingering solution bias that assumes a proper understanding of the problem domain [BTN06]:

> Patterns work like a ladder in the 'Snakes and Ladders' board game—given a known context and problem (square on the board) they give us a leg-up to a higher place. Design patterns fall squarely in the middle of the solution space and provide object-oriented fragments of structure to resolve solution space forces [Jac95]. But they do assume that the problem and context are sufficiently well understood so that a sensible selection of the appropriate

pattern can be made. So what if we don't yet have this orientation? What if we find ourselves washing around in the amorphous problem space, unable to get a foothold on anything to bear the weight of a pattern or to anchor a fragment of architecture?

The common, stock answer to all of this is to adopt a prescribed method that has, within its lifecycle, an extensive analysis activity that follows one specific particular school of thought. For example, 'the world is made up of objects' and 'the world is made up of processes' offer two contrasting views of analysis. Many such approaches, however, can end up resembling more of a synthesis (composing a solution to a problem) than an analysis (understanding the problem), trying to shoehorn a problem into a view that does not fit comfortably.

Framing the Problem

Michael Jackson's concept of problem frames [Jac95] [Jac01] aims to cut across the one-size-fits-all analysis-and-design methods and engage in a more genuine analysis: understanding the problem domain on its own terms, and without the adoption of metaphors and structures from the world of programming. Although the real world can be said to have both objects and processes, neither bears anything more than a superficial resemblance to the concepts of the same name in software development. Indeed, to equate one with the other is often a category error with amusing and expensive consequences. The map is not the territory.

A problem frame names, bounds, and describes a recurring kind of problem [Jac95]:

> A problem frame is a generalization of a class of problem. If there are many other problems that fit the same frame as the problem you're dealing with, then you can hope to apply the method and techniques that worked for those other problems to the problems you're trying to solve right now.

Five fundamental problem frames—'far from a complete or definitive set'—are identified and described [Jac01]:

> *Required behaviour:* there is some part of the physical world whose behaviour is to be controlled so that it satisfies certain conditions. The problem is to build a machine that will impose that control.

Commanded behaviour: there is some part of the physical world whose behaviour is to be controlled in accordance with commands issued by an operator. The problem is to build a machine that will accept the operator's commands and impose the control accordingly.

Information display: there is some part of the physical world about whose states and behaviour certain information is continually needed. The problem is to build a machine that will obtain this information from the world and present it at the required place in the required form.

Simple workpieces: a tool is needed to allow a user to create and edit a certain class of computer-processable text or graphic objects, or similar structures, so that they can be subsequently copied, printed, analysed or used in other ways. The problem is to build a machine that can act as this tool.

Transformation: there are some given computer-readable input files whose data must be transformed to give certain required output files. The output data must be in a particular format, and it must be derived from the input data according to certain rules. The problem is to build a machine that will produce the required outputs from the inputs.

The result of each frame is a clear description of a problem rather than a proposal of a solution. What distinguishes one frame from another is the kind of problem that is described and the way that it is described, and consequently the way that you might then solve it. Different problem frames suit different modes of description. For example, a Transformation frame problem is best described using data-flow techniques or Jackson Structured Programming (JSP), whereas Simple Workpieces are better considered in terms of class or entity models, along with use cases and dynamic models. Realistic problems tend not to fit tidily within a single frame, giving rise to the notion of *multi-frame* or *composite frame* problems [Jac95]:

> Problem frames are always simple. That's their role in life. They cut out all the nasty inconvenient complications that plague realistic problems, and leave you with something simple: a problem that you can understand, and an effective method for solving it.
>
> When you're faced with a problem of realistic complexity you need to decompose it into a number of simple problems. That means decomposing it into problems you can solve—there's not much point

in decomposing one problem you can't solve into several more problems that you still can't solve. And that means decomposing it into problems for which you have well-understood problem frames and methods.

Just as we can recognize and name pattern compounds, some common composite frames can also be identified, for example, Workpieces with Command Display [Jac01].

Problem frames seem to be in tune with patterns—'kissing cousins,' even [BTN06]—in their attempt to focus on specifics, reacting against the tendency of overgeneralization found in many methods. There is more than one way to design, and more than one way to a view a problem.

Contrasting Problem Frames and Patterns

Bounding the problem is an important ingredient in successful software development. A pattern-based approach aims to do this by understanding the forces within a given context that give rise to the problem that the pattern's solution part resolves. There is no formal guidance, however, for identifying the context, its forces, and the motivation that gives rise to the problem.

In contrast, problem frames propose a discipline for talking about and delimiting the world of the problem without involving or being distracted by solution specifics. Within a given problem frame there are likely to be some patterns that are readily applicable at a strategic level and some that are not. For example, within a composite frame comprising Simple Workpieces and an Information Display, MODEL-VIEW-CONTROLLER suggests itself as such a strategic pattern, defining the core shape and style of the architecture.

Michael Jackson states that 'a problem frame is a kind of pattern,' which begs the following question: exactly what kind of pattern is a problem frame? Even by the soundbite definition of pattern we introduced in *Chapter 1*, a problem frame cannot be considered to be quite the kind of pattern that we have focused on in this book: it does not propose a solution. The purpose of a problem frame is to understand the projections of a problem more precisely and more clearly based on recurrence of the problem class. It is this recurrence that gives us the 'kind of' pattern that they are, but it also tells us that although there is a useful kinship to explore further, problem frames are neither a specialization nor a subset of the pattern concept we are considering.

One could consider calling problem frames *problem patterns*. In the sense that they have a problem focus and a recurring form, this is certainly an accurate label. The imagery of 'framing the problem', however, is stronger and less misleading. One might also be tempted to rename *patterns* as *solution patterns*. This rebranding would be both too convenient and somewhat inappropriate, given our efforts so far to clarify that patterns are not a strictly solution-centric concept. That said, *solution patterns* is perhaps a good term for describing what some developers mistakenly assume patterns to be: common structures found in code or class diagrams, but otherwise free of intent and problem motivation. And although *problem–solution patterns* would be honest and accurate, it would also just be a more verbose restatement of what we have already said *patterns* means by itself!

What the problem frame and pattern approaches share is the notion of establishing a vocabulary and promoting understanding based on common occurrence of form. Their most suitable linkage is that a problem frame can provide the context of applicability for some key patterns. If we look to problem frames as being more like analysis patterns [Fow97], in which the resulting context does not involve so much a solution as an understanding of the problem situation, we also find a way in which we can think about them in pattern form— and even cast them into pattern form [BTN06].

Combining Problem Frames and Patterns

Where many methodologies of the past have sought to impose a single, grand narrative on development, exclusively favoring one style over others, problem frames try to define the applicability and boundaries of distinct architectural approaches.

For example, in the context of a Transformation problem, PIPES AND FILTERS suggests itself as a natural architecture, supporting the successive and direct transformation of input streams into output streams. A more localized and tactical view is to present input and output streams using ITERATOR and have the transformation code drive from one to the other. An alternative approach, based on inversion of control, is to use an ENUMERATION METHOD, perhaps in combination with a VISITOR, to traverse and transform the input range to the output range. These two variations can be seen in the world of XML parsers, where some APIs favor a pull model and others a push model. There are other variations and considerations in the pattern vocabulary and pattern sequences we may choose, but clearly the frame concept lives up to its name: it helps to define a suitable boundary within which we can focus our design efforts.

If not the specific problem frames identified by Jackson, then at least the approach of problem frames offers a useful way of organizing collections of patterns. The idea of a problem frame can be seen as a highly expanded and detailed intent, capturing the nature of a problem domain and the constraints it imposes on a solution.

Applied to the concept of an architecture handbook, the problem frames approach gives rise to a richly problem-focused approach, reinforcing the basic idea that catalogs organized by situation and intent are more coherent and useful than the other schemes discussed earlier.

8.10 Pattern Semiotics

If patterns define a vocabulary and a pattern description is a form of literature, perhaps some tools associated with linguistics and literary analysis can help us understand the relationships between patterns, how they are used, and thus how they may be organized effectively. Semiotics is the study of signs and symbols, particularly in language and especially in comprehending the role and meaning of symbols used in society.

In its earliest form, semiotics (née semiology) defines a sign as a two-part whole, a dyad, comprising a *signifier* and a *signified*. The signifier is the expression of a sign, its material aspect. The signified is the corresponding mental concept engendered by the signifier. For example, in English, the written signifier 'red' and the signified concept of redness together form a sign. The relationship between a signifier and a signified, however, is considered to be an arbitrary one, not a given. In German, the written signifier 'rot' plays the same signifier role but, although clearly different in its expression, redness is still the signified concept. The same signifier in English has a relationship with a quite different sign, one whose signified aspect is the concept of decay.

Patterns and Pattern Descriptions as Signs

In this model of semiotics we can say *sign = signifier + signified*. It is this decomposition of a sign that underpins the semiotic approach to pattern deconstruction explored by James Noble and Robert Biddle [NoBr02]:

> One of the biggest challenges in documenting patterns is to avoid their misinterpretation—that is, that someone reading a description of a pattern will not understand (or understand imperfectly) the solution and the intent of the pattern being described. When reading a program (or inspecting a building), we can similarly misunderstand the patterns we find—the 'cupboard' under the stairs is really a staircase to the basement, the door we expect to push must be pulled, and the code we think is the OBSERVER pattern is actually using MEDIATOR, or is just a random bad design, and so on.

> Our semiotic approach encompasses misinterpretation by making the possibility explicit. While signifiers, by their nature, are concrete, tangible, and therefore public, signifieds are abstract, intangible, and private mental concepts—when reading a program or exploring a building, each of us alone constructs signifieds of any signs we encounter. Due to this, it is perfectly possible to produce an 'incorrect' mental image of a signified for which a given signifier stands.

> [...]

> Semiotics makes clear that these kinds of misunderstandings can happen whenever you use signs, so it should not be surprising that such misunderstandings arise with patterns.

In this approach a pattern is considered to be a sign that combines a name (the signifier) with a pattern description (the signified). In turn, the pattern description itself is seen as a sign, comprising a solution that is visible in a design (the signifier) and the intent (the signified), defined broadly as the pattern's context, problem, rationale, and known uses, as opposed to just the *Intent* section associated with the Gang-of-Four pattern form. This perspective means that a pattern is considered to be defined by a second-order semiotic system with *pattern* and *pattern description* defining the two levels:

pattern = name + pattern description

pattern description = solution + intent

This two-level decomposition allows patterns, their variety of relationships, their meanings, and their misapplications to be understood within a conceptual framework different than the ones commonly used in discussing and reasoning about patterns. The semiotic approach appears to reinforce and, in some cases, make clearer some of the observations already made in previous chapters.

For example, the common problem of treating the solution part of the pattern as the whole pattern, excluding its intent, becomes easier to appreciate when viewed from a semiotic perspective. The pattern reader may have no association between the material expression of the pattern in code and the mental concept—context, problem, rationale, and exemplars—that lies behind the code. The pattern is thus seen as being a simple, one-level sign in which the pattern description is replaced by the solution, and not by the full combination of solution and intent. In other words, the reader sees:

pattern = name + solution

rather than:

pattern = name + pattern description

where *pattern description = solution + intent*

A common example of this problem occurs when only one aspect of the solution is considered, such as its expression in a class diagram. The solutions for both the STRATEGY and the OBJECTS FOR STATES patterns are expressed through identically structured class diagrams. This diagrammed form is also similar for the BRIDGE pattern, and identical when there is no handle hierarchy, so it is perhaps not surprising to find that implementations of these patterns are often mistaken for one another—as illustrated in the diagram below:

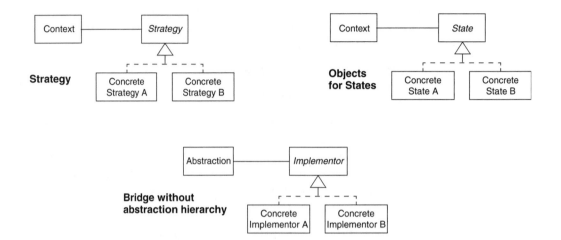

Of course, there are cases in which the complementary nature of these patterns means that a particular design does indeed implement more than one pattern: each design element plays different roles in each of the patterns, as shown in *Section 4.3, A Second Design Experiment: Interwoven Patterns*. This complementary overlap, however, is not true of all designs in which confusion arises over which pattern has been implemented.

Another and deeper example deals with the problematic meaning of ADAPTER in the Gang-of-Four catalog. The notion that there is a single pattern called ADAPTER is in practice present nowhere except in the table of contents of the Gang-of-Four book. It is not intrinsically a property of the pattern description, which admits to at least four quite distinct patterns: OBJECT ADAPTER, CLASS ADAPTER, TWO-WAY ADAPTER, and PLUGGABLE ADAPTER, which adds two further complementary patterns to the ones we had already identified in *Chapter 5*.

While these four patterns may have adaptation as a common theme, adaptation is better considered a category or family of patterns rather than an individual pattern in its own right. We can find further support for this view in the semiotic analysis of DECORATOR with respect to its synonym WRAPPER, which is also a synonym for ADAPTER. Taken together with the notion that FACADE is based on introducing a wrapper layer, we can determine that a more specific *adaptation* or *wrapping* category would offer a more useful and precise classification for these patterns than the somewhat all-embracing but vague umbrella of *structural*, which along with *behavioral*, as already noted earlier in this chapter, is a description that is ultimately true of all the design patterns in *Design Patterns* [GoF95]. This alternative categorization is both sufficiently precise and sufficiently general that we can see its applicability beyond just the context of *Design Patterns*. WRAPPER FACADE, for example, also falls within its scope.

The semiotic approach makes missing categories and connections more obvious. In this case, the semiotic perspective reveals a clear intentional category—adaptation—that would mean more to developers browsing a handbook than just considering the various patterns and variations to be a subset of a general structural category. Given the subjectivity and variability of any classification, and the importance of a clear organization in any pattern collection, understanding the possible interpretations and misinterpretations of patterns in a collection has value for the compiler of the collection. This kind of feedback and attention to detail appears to be a benefit of the semiotic approach.

8.11 Pattern Collections and Style

We noted in *Section 5.2, Patterns in Competition* that the choice between two or more patterns that have similar intent can amount to a question of style, all other things being equal. Favoring a simple ITERATOR for iteration is a default style that is idiomatic to C++, C#, and Java programs, whereas ENUMERATION METHOD is the more natural idiom for Ruby and Smalltalk programs, and BATCH METHOD and BATCH ITERATOR are the vernacular for distributed object computing systems.

The idea that patterns characterize style, however, is not just restricted to programming idioms or tiebreaking situations between one pattern and another. Style is more generally applicable to focused collections of patterns and corresponding architectures [Booch06]:

> In any given genre of systems, the same designs are found again and again. Insofar as we can name these designs and codify them in a relatively general fashion, they are the patterns of that domain.

> Sometimes we will speak of a particular style (or school) of design. A style is a named collection of a set of designs that is observably identifiable from other styles.

A style can be seen as the rules that are followed within a particular architecture or social structure that contribute to making that architecture or social structure what it is, and which are therefore distinct from other architectures and social structures.

Many collections of patterns can be seen to capture a style. For example, Erich Gamma's original thesis [Gam92] captured the design style of the ET++ framework in pattern form. The patterns in *Patterns for Concurrent and Networked Objects* [POSA2] capture the common design style found in object-oriented and broker-based middleware. Many evolved (and not so evolved) systems exhibit common architectural features and development-process characteristics, the style of which has been captured in the *Big Ball of Mud* patterns [FoYo97].

Unix Interface Design Patterns

The Art of UNIX Programming [Ray04] captures the history, culture, tools, and techniques of the Unix operating system. Included in this commentary is a list of interface design patterns that characterize the style of working with Unix through a command-line shell: FILTER, CANTRIP, SOURCE, SINK, COMPILER, ED, ROGUELIKE, SEPARATED ENGINE AND INTERFACE, CLI SERVER, and POLYVALENT-PROGRAM.

The descriptions of these patterns are too long to include here, but we can summarize them as follows:

> The FILTER pattern defines a non-interactive program or execution of a program that takes data on standard input, transforms it in some fashion, and sends the result to standard output. For example, the sort and grep programs can be executed as filters.

The CANTRIP pattern defines a non-interactive program that takes no input and generates no output, only a status result. A cantrip is invoked as a simple, stand-alone command. For example, the rm program for removing files can be cast as a cantrip.

The SOURCE pattern characterizes non-interactive programs that only emit data on the standard output stream and take no input. For example, the ls program for listing directories is a source.

The SINK pattern characterizes non-interactive programs that only take data on the standard input and emit no output. For example, the lpr program for spooling input to the print queue is a sink.

The COMPILER pattern represents non-interactive programs that transform files of one form into files of another form. They may emit messages on the standard error stream, but otherwise take no other input and offer no other output. For example, the cc C compiler and the gzip and gunzip compression utilities all qualify as compilers.

The ED pattern defines programs with a simple interaction model. They interpret a simple command language on the standard input, and are therefore scriptable. The non-visual ed line editor offers the canonical example, but there are others, including the GNU debugger, gdb.

The ROGUELIKE pattern defines programs that use the visual display more fully and are driven by keystrokes. They are interactive but not easily scriptable. The rogue dungeon-crawling game offers the original example, but more well-known examples include the vi and emacs editors.

The SEPARATED ENGINE AND INTERFACE pattern defines an architecture for programs that separates the *engine* part of the program, which holds the core logic for the application domain, from the *interface* part, which is responsible for presentation logic and user interaction. The engine and interface roles are normally realized in separate processes.

The CLI SERVER pattern characterizes programs that, when run in the foreground, offer a simple command-line interface on the standard input and output streams, but when run in the background take their I/O from a TCP/IP port. Many protocol-based servers follow this pattern, such as for POP, IMAP, SMTP, and HTTP.

The POLYVALENT-PROGRAM pattern characterizes programs whose architecture allows them to have a variety of interfaces, ranging from programmatic API to command-line and/or GUI, CANTRIP to ROGUELIKE.

In all cases the programs characterized by these patterns are also parameterized by their start-up environment, which includes any command-line arguments.

These patterns quite clearly characterize a native style of design and working that is quite distinct from, for example, an approach based on graphical user interfaces or the style of many other command-line shell environments, such as DOS or VMS. Essentially, the overarching pattern that forms the 'backbone' [Vlis98b] of this style is PIPES AND FILTERS. The patterns represent a specific and detailed—but still generic and generative—application of the PIPES AND FILTERS pattern in a particular context. The patterns can be characterized as offering solutions primarily against the Transformation problem frame, but there are also examples of patterns in the Simple Workpieces frame, such as the ED pattern, and the Information Display frame, such as ROGUELIKE.

Web 2.0 Design Patterns

The term 'Web 2.0' has come to characterize not so much a technology as an approach to doing design and business on the Web. This approach has been captured in terms of pattern descriptions [ORei05] [MuOr+07].

The following patterns and summaries are taken from the original pattern sketches [ORei05]:

THE LONG TAIL. Small sites make up the bulk of the internet's content; narrow niches make up the bulk of the internet's possible applications. *Therefore*: Leverage customer-self service and algorithmic data management to reach out to the entire web, to the edges and not just the center, to the long tail and not just the head.

DATA IS THE NEXT INTEL INSIDE. Applications are increasingly data-driven. *Therefore*: For competitive advantage, seek to own a unique, hard-to-recreate source of data.

USERS ADD VALUE. The key to competitive advantage in internet applications is the extent to which users add their own data to that which you provide. *Therefore*: Don't restrict your 'architecture of participation' to software development. Involve your users both implicitly and explicitly in adding value to your application.

NETWORK EFFECTS BY DEFAULT. Only a small percentage of users will go to the trouble of adding value to your application. *Therefore*: Set inclusive defaults for aggregating user data as a side-effect of their use of the application.

SOME RIGHTS RESERVED. Intellectual property protection limits re-use and prevents experimentation. *Therefore*: When benefits come from collective adoption, not private restriction, make sure that barriers to adoption are low. Follow existing standards, and use licenses with as few restrictions as possible. Design for 'hackability' and 'remixability.'

THE PERPETUAL BETA. When devices and programs are connected to the internet, applications are no longer software artifacts, they are ongoing services. *Therefore*: Don't package up new features into monolithic releases, but instead add them on a regular basis as part of the normal user experience. Engage your users as real-time testers, and instrument the service so that you know how people use the new features.

COOPERATE, DON'T CONTROL. Web 2.0 applications are built of a network of cooperating data services. *Therefore*: Offer web services interfaces and content syndication, and re-use the data services of others. Support lightweight programming models that allow for loosely-coupled systems.

SOFTWARE ABOVE THE LEVEL OF A SINGLE DEVICE. The PC is no longer the only access device for internet applications, and applications that are limited to a single device are less valuable than those that are connected. *Therefore*: Design your application from the get-go to integrate services across handheld devices, PCs, and internet servers.

Web 2.0, and the increased use of these patterns, has emerged in recent years and is characterized by a style that is considered distinct to what can retrospectively be termed 'Web 1.0' design and business models.

Style and Conceptual Integrity

A style helps to establish a culture, but it also lends integrity and character to a system. Conceptual integrity spans more than individual design decisions and embraces a common collection of design ideas [Bro95]:

> I will contend that conceptual integrity is the most important consideration in system design. It is better to have a system omit certain anomalous features and improvements, but to reflect one set of design ideas, than to have one that contains many good but independent and uncoordinated ideas.

We can relate this notion of a set of design ideas to a collection of patterns. Of course, and as we have seen, an arbitrary collection of patterns will not offer conceptual integrity: there must coherence in how their roles and resulting parts fit together, and they must fulfill some end goal [PP03]:

> Conceptual integrity means that a system's central concepts work together as a smooth, cohesive whole. The components match and work well together; the architecture achieves an effective balance between flexibility, maintainability, efficiency, and responsiveness.

The notion of character and coherence form an important part of being able to differentiate one style of work or architecture from another, and therefore style is important in guiding developers working on and within a given system.

For example, if we need to implement an operation that traverses a collection of objects in a particular way, and there can be more than one type of collection, candidate styles include classic object-oriented programming and generic programming. In the classic OO approach, commonality will be factored out with respect to class hierarchy. Thus a superclass will factor out the common parts of the algorithm, perhaps as a TEMPLATE METHOD, and access details will be deferred to implementing subclasses. Collection types that need to support the traversal operation are required to inherit from this superclass. In contrast, a generic programming style decouples collections from algorithms. The operation is expressed as a stand-alone function that works on a sequence of elements presented through an ITERATOR range. The collection type is orthogonal to additional operations on it, but it must support an interface that offers the necessary iterators. These two approaches have different trade-offs and characterize different styles [Hen05a] for guiding development.

8.12 Toward Pattern Languages

Organized collections offer a useful repository of knowledge that extends the reach of patterns in design beyond either individual patterns or the combinations of patterns considered in the previous chapters. In considering the structuring of such collections and the relationship between patterns, many of the ideas presented in Part II of this book, *Between Patterns*, offer starting points for organizing patterns and pattern constructs with respect to context and purpose.

Concepts such as pattern stories and pattern sequences help to animate a collection of patterns. Patterns can be framed with respect to common context or common purpose. For a particular system, architecture, or framework, a collection of patterns can capture the style of the system, architecture, or framework. This notion of style is particularly vivid when accompanied by illustrative pattern stories or common pattern sequences, such as the warehouse management process control chapters in POSA4. In essence, by capturing a style, patterns express the vernacular or idiomatic way that things are done in a particular system, making explicit the rules of good citizenship for any extensions and future work on that system.

The metaphor of language has featured prominently in our discussion of the pattern concept in the previous and current chapters, for example in the form of stories and in semiotics. Combined with a recurring emphasis on bringing more than a single pattern to bear on a design situation, and this chapter's exploration of pattern collections, we are now in a good position to fulfill the metaphor and consider pattern languages.

III Into Pattern Languages

Runic stone at Moesgård Museum in Aarhus
© Mai Skou Nielssen

In the third part of the book we build on the concepts and conclusions of the first two parts by introducing pattern languages. Pattern languages aim to provide holistic support for using patterns to develop software for specific technical or application domains. They achieve this goal by enlisting multiple patterns for each problem that can arise in their respective domains and weaving them together to define a generative and domain-specific software development process.

Successfully designing software with patterns was and still is the original vision of *Pattern-Oriented Software Architecture*. The concepts we introduced and discussed in Part I, *Inside Patterns*, and Part II, *Between Patterns*—stand-alone patterns, pattern complements, pattern compounds, pattern stories, and pattern sequences—contribute to this vision, but do not quite, perhaps, fully realize it. This part of the book, therefore, elaborates the concept of pattern languages, which aim to provide holistic, systematic, and constructive support for developing software with patterns—both regarding the concrete designs to create and the process to create those designs. Pattern languages fulfill this goal by integrating the concepts listed above and extending them with additional concepts, mainly in the area of processes.

This part of the book includes the following chapters:

- *Chapter 9, Elements of Language*, takes a first look at pattern languages in detail. We re-examine the pattern concepts introduced and applied thus far from the perspective of trying to establish a language of design.

- *Chapter 10, A Network of Patterns and More*, dives deeper into pattern languages. We start with an explanation and discussion of the fundamental notion and structure of pattern languages. We then address quality aspects of pattern languages, the role and importance of forces, context, and the genericity of a language's solution space. We next reflect on the use of diagrams, the naming of pattern languages, and their maturation over time.

- *Chapter 11, A Billion Different Implementations*, explores the process side of pattern languages. We first present and discuss the constituent elements of the process and show how pattern languages are applied in practice. We next explore how pattern languages compare or integrate with other approaches, such as refactoring, product-line architectures, and even individual patterns.

- *Chapter 12, Notes on Pattern Language Form*, addresses the documentation of pattern languages, which goes well beyond describing their individual patterns and collecting them together. We also discuss techniques for communicating the vision and details of a pattern language to readers effectively.

- *Chapter 13, On Patterns versus Pattern Languages*, explores the commonalities and differences of stand-alone patterns and pattern languages, and concludes that both concepts mutually need each other to unfold their fullest power.

The concept of pattern languages is not new in the software community—it has been portrayed and discussed since the beginning of the software pattern movement [Cope96]. These early treatments, however, have only been sparsely updated to reflect the latest conceptual insights or experiences in writing and using pattern languages [Hen05b]. As a consequence, not all the aspects of pattern languages we discuss in this part of the book are mature or well-established in the pattern community. For example, while fundamental aspects and properties of the process introduced by pattern languages, such as piecemeal growth, are widely accepted and practiced, other aspects and properties, such as the role of pattern sequences in defining a grammar for pattern languages, are considered as new or even subject to debate.

In addition, not all members of the pattern community consider pattern languages as a useful or practical concept. One camp advocates languages as the pinnacle of achievement in patterns. Another camp, in contrast, complains that pattern languages overly constrain their use of patterns by dictating a specific architectural style they find either useless or unfamiliar. Our own position in this discussion is pragmatic: we have used pattern languages successfully in a range of production software systems, so we think they are a useful concept. We do not, however, apply them blindly in situations in which they limit us unnecessarily or where other pattern concepts, such as pattern sequences or even stand-alone patterns, are more effective. In practice, we have found that situations in which pattern languages were too restrictive simply required a revision of the language we were applying, so the two views are often much less in conflict in practice than they may appear in theory.

Our goal with this part of the book is once again to be as complete and up-to-date as possible, according to the latest state of knowledge and experience in using patterns. We have therefore compiled a full portrait of the pattern language concept, regardless of the maturity of its various aspects or its universal acceptance in the pattern community.

Due to our areas of expertise, the examples used to show the concept of pattern languages are taken from the 'domain' of design patterns. The properties and aspects of pattern languages we explore, however, are relevant for any domain in software (patterns), as well as for pattern languages in general.

9 Elements of Language

We dissect language along lines laid down by our native language... Language is not simply a reporting device for experience but a defining framework for it.

Benjamin Whorf, linguist and anthropologist

This chapter takes the first step toward pattern languages. We re-examine the pattern concepts introduced and applied earlier in the book from the perspective of trying to establish a *language* of design that is more than just a *vocabulary* of design elements. Pattern collections, stories, and sequences provide part of the picture, but not all of it.

9.1 Designing with Patterns

In *Part II, Between Patterns*, we explored the space between patterns and discussed pattern complements, pattern compounds, pattern stories, pattern sequences, and pattern collections. A common theme that cuts across these various concepts is their support for *designing with patterns*. In particular, they acknowledge that a production software system must resolve many different design and implementation problems. For each problem it is necessary to compare available solution alternatives carefully and recognize that the chosen solutions can influence—and be influenced by—the potential solution spaces of other related problems.

Stand-alone patterns, as discussed in *Part I, Inside Patterns,* do not address such issues. By definition, they focus single-mindedly on resolving a single problem with a specific set of forces, without considering—or at best *briefly* considering—alternative solutions and their impact on other problems and their solutions. Software development, in contrast, must take a broader and more comprehensive view of both the general and the detailed design issues faced by a project. Without such oversight it is hard, if not impossible, to produce sustainable software architectures that meet and balance all their requirements.

A closer look at the concepts we explored in Part II reveals, however, that they address only specific or local aspects of designing with patterns. Each concept thus provides just a 'brief greeting,' a hint of what a software system based on patterns could look like:

- *Pattern complements* help explore the pattern space for resolving specific, focused problem families, but not the pattern space for designing an entire software system.

- *Pattern compounds* resolve a problem by using other, 'smaller' patterns and arranging their roles in particular configurations, thereby bringing individual patterns to life and giving them clearer context, purpose, process, and structure. Yet pattern compounds are only slightly larger in scope than pattern 'atoms,' so their impact on a whole software architecture is potentially limited in the same way. Pattern compounds also capture just one specific configuration of their constituent patterns, without looking beyond their borders to discuss other possibly useful combinations of the patterns.

- *Pattern stories* are like diaries that tell their readers how patterns guided the development of an entire software system, subsystem, or large component—as demonstrated nicely by the pattern story in *Chapter 7, Pattern Sequences.* Pattern stories also discuss what problems were resolved in what order during the construction of the software systems whose genesis they describe. In addition, they discuss what patterns were selected to resolve these problems and how the selected patterns were instantiated within the software architectures of these systems.

  Pattern stories, however, are tightly coupled to the context, requirements, and development constraints of a specific system. Two software systems from the same domain, but with different contexts, requirements, and development constraints, may follow different pattern stories simply because these differences suggest the use of different patterns or a different pattern ordering. Pattern stories are therefore of less help if the respective contexts, requirements, and constraints in these stories do not match with the contexts, requirements, and constraints of the systems being developed or refactored. Although developers can generalize from specifics, they may not draw the intended conclusions from the specific example.

- *Pattern sequences* essentially remove the *story* from pattern stories—in particular, the specific contexts and constraints of the systems described in them—to better emphasize the raw sequences of the applied patterns. Pattern sequences are therefore more general than pattern stories. If a software system shares the requirements addressed by a specific pattern sequence, it can be designed using this sequence or, at least, by applying relevant parts of it. If a software system's requirements are not met by a given pattern sequence, however, the design advice offered by the sequence is at best limited. Since each pattern sequence denotes only one possible system design and implementation under a given set of requirements, different designs and implementations would require alternative pattern sequences.

- *Pattern collections* can be organized in a variety of ways, of which the ad hoc approach is perhaps the least relevant here. To varying degrees, catalogs organized by domain, by partition, by level, and by intent offer ways of capturing a set of possible designs, even design styles. They offer potentially greater breadth than just pattern sequences, but they do so by offering less depth. What is missing in a conventional catalog is a strong sense of connection—something stronger than simply knowing that another pattern in the collection is related in some way. When collections are presented in conjunction with, for example, pattern sequences, we start to get a stronger sense of connection.

From this brief analysis we conclude that while our understanding and application of the pattern concept spans a broad range of useful approaches, they do not necessarily fulfill the promise of pattern-oriented software architecture. These concepts would provide useful entries in the software architecture handbook described in *Chapter 8, Pattern Collections*, but they may be no more instructive to a pattern-based approach to software development than a dictionary is to the teaching of proper grammar or effective speaking.

9.2   From Pattern Stories and Sequences to Pattern Languages

The 'missing link' we are seeking is a concept that supports the *systematic* application of patterns to:

- Create software for specific application domains, such as warehouse management or medical imaging, or

- Address relevant technical software development aspects, such as distributed computing, fault tolerance, or object-lifetime management in C++.

This holistic concept should provide explicit guidance on what problems can arise in a domain, inform the order to address these problems, and suggest one or more patterns to solve each specific problem. The concept should support the explicit consideration of complementing or conflicting pattern combinations to resolve a given problem, along with the integration of patterns into a concrete design. Moreover, the concept should continue and complete the conceptual path paved by pattern complements, pattern compounds, pattern stories, pattern sequences, and pattern collections.

It should also build on the same properties as stand-alone patterns, reinforcing them at the broader scope of a whole system, technical domain, or perspective on development.

Using such a concept, we could provide an entry in a software architecture handbook with a pattern-based development or solution approach for each topic of interest in software development. There would be entries for each application domain, such as various types of enterprise, pervasive, and embedded systems, as well as entries for technical aspects, such as distribution, concurrency, security, and fault tolerance, and programming in specific languages. Each root entry, 'frame,' or section in the handbook could be viewed as a special purpose *pattern language* that advises developers how to construct a specific type of software system or address a specific technical aspect under a specific set of requirements with the help of patterns.

An Incomplete Story

With this vision in mind, pattern stories and pattern sequences certainly come closest to the idea of pattern languages, at least intuitively. They describe how a specific type of system or technical concern was—or can be—systematically designed, implemented, or addressed with help of patterns. For example, the pattern story from *Chapter 7, Pattern Sequences*, described how we created a pattern-based design for a flexible request-handling framework: COMMAND, EXPLICIT INTERFACE, and COMMAND PROCESSOR define the fundamental structure of this mechanism, while COLLECTIONS FOR STATES, MEMENTO, STRATEGY, NULL OBJECT, and COMPOSITE specify its details.

The class diagram below outlines the design told by this pattern story.

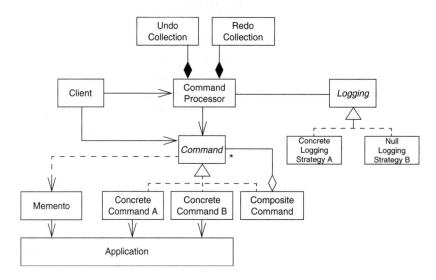

As outlined in *Section 9.1, Designing with Patterns* above, however, the main drawback of pattern stories is that they capture only one of potentially many pattern-based solutions for a specific type of application or technical concern. Had there been different contextual issues, constraints, or requirements involved when designing the request-handling framework, there would be a different story to tell.

For example, had we preferred inheritance over delegation to support variations in 'housekeeping' functionality, such as logging, the corresponding pattern story would feature COMMAND, EXPLICIT INTERFACE, COMMAND PROCESSOR, COLLECTIONS FOR STATES, MEMENTO, TEMPLATE METHOD, and COMPOSITE, with TEMPLATE METHOD replacing STRATEGY and NULL OBJECT.

The concrete design created by this alternative story is illustrated in the following class diagram.

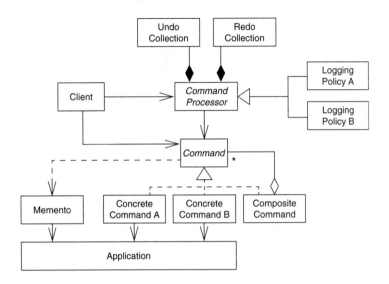

Yet another pattern story might describe how the request-handling framework receives request messages instead of procedural-style requests, which must first be transformed into executable commands. In this story, the patterns applied could be MESSAGE, COMMAND PROCESSOR, INTERPRETER, COMMAND, EXPLICIT INTERFACE, COLLECTIONS FOR STATES, MEMENTO, TEMPLATE METHOD, and COMPOSITE.

The class diagram for the corresponding design is shown below.

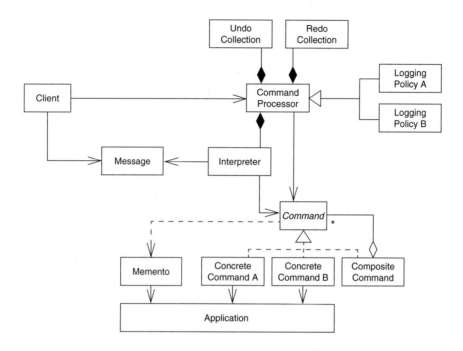

Now we already have three valid pattern stories for request-handling frameworks, but even more stories are possible—for example, if we had designed a thread-safe COMMAND PROCESSOR.

Nevertheless, each pattern story tells us exactly *why* a specific pattern sequence was chosen to realize a specific piece of software. Comparing different pattern stories helps us understand how and why different contexts and requirements result in different pattern-based solutions for the software. Pattern stories can therefore contribute to the concept of pattern languages, but their scope and purpose is simply too small to form a conceptual basis for pattern languages that meets all the requirements listed at the beginning of this section.

The following excerpt from one of the first works coining the term 'pattern story' supports this perspective [Hen99b]:

> Where pattern languages are narrative frameworks, the development of a system can be considered a single narrative example, where design questions are asked and answered, structures assembled for specific reasons, and so on. We can view the progress of some designs as the progressive application of particular patterns.
>
> What we can term *pattern stories* are narrative structures, that is, they exist as complete and in the real world. As with many stories, they capture the spirit and not necessarily the truth of the detail in what happens. It is rare that our design thinking will so readily submit itself to named classification and sequential arrangement, so there is a certain amount of retrospection and revisionism. As an educational tool, however, such an approach can reveal more than conventional case studies, as each example literally tells the story of a design. This exposition is a valuable aid in studying design through the study of designs.

Combining Sequences

A pattern sequence compresses and abstracts a pattern story so that developers can use it to create corresponding solutions in their own systems, in case they meet the same requirements addressed by the patterns in the sequence. Pattern sequences therefore switch the focus from example to essence. Yet from the perspective of our envisioned properties of pattern languages, they have similar limitations as pattern stories, as outlined at the beginning of this chapter.

What if, however, we take multiple pattern sequences that all describe solutions for the same domain and combine these pattern sequences with one another? Would this set of integrated sequences form the pattern language concept we are looking for? The hypothesis, at least, sounds promising:

- Multiple, integrated pattern sequences are likely to define a solution space for constructing software for a specific domain, addressing alternative designs for the same requirements and different designs for different requirements. If the individual sequences are combined carefully, this solution space could also cover more design paths than there were original, sample pattern sequences. The whole becomes more than the plain sum of its parts, and can therefore better embrace other applications of the same patterns in the same design space.

For example, integrating the pattern sequences that underlie the pattern stories described above results in a prototypical mini 'pattern language' with two variation points. First, if our request handling mechanism should receive request messages, we can start with the partial pattern sequence: MESSAGE, COMMAND PROCESSOR, INTERPRETER, COMMAND, and EXPLICIT INTERFACE. Second, if the mechanism receives procedural style requests, we can start with the partial pattern sequence: COMMAND, EXPLICIT INTERFACE, and COMMAND PROCESSOR. The COMMANDs in either partial pattern sequence can be refined further by MEMENTO and COMPOSITE, the COMMAND PROCESSOR by COLLECTIONS FOR STATES and, if we prefer inheritance to support variations in behavior, TEMPLATE METHOD, or if we prefer delegation, STRATEGY and NULL OBJECT. Note how this mini 'pattern language' describes four design alternatives, one more than suggested by the three pattern sequences of which it was composed.

- If building new software with the set of integrated pattern sequences results in new pattern sequences, and if these sequences were added to the set, the solution space defined by the set could evolve and always represent the latest state-of-the-art in building software for a particular application domain.

As a result of such continuous integration we could generate a pattern language whose constituent patterns and sequences define the entire—or least a sufficient—vocabulary and grammar for constructing a particular (aspect of a) software system [Cool02]. This language could also initiate a dialog with software architects and developers as to what pattern sequence is best for this type of system or system aspect for a given context, set of requirements, and constraints. With enough experience, we might even be able to anticipate sooner and with greater confidence which pattern sequences are likely to yield whole, balanced software architectures and which are likely to yield dysfunctional, unbalanced ones. We might also be able to provide a better foundation for determining the value of alternative software designs [BS00] [SCJS99] [SGCH01].

To summarize and sharpen our hypothesis:

- Pattern stories help us to understand and learn from specific examples.

- Pattern sequences help us to generalize what we learn from the pattern stories and see how to reapply such knowledge.

- Multiple integrated pattern sequences can form pattern languages that free us from trying to apply the same pattern sequences in contexts where they are not a perfect fit.

This hypothesis sounds promising enough. The following chapters, therefore, explore the concept of pattern language in detail. We also uncover whether pattern languages can achieve our ambitious expectations for *designing with patterns*, or what limitations they still have in reaching this goal.

10 A Network of Patterns and More

*Now we shall begin to see in detail how the rich and
complex order of a town can grow from thousands of
creative acts. For once we have a common pattern language
in our town, we shall have the power to make our streets
and buildings live, through our most ordinary acts. The
language, like a seed, is the generic system which gives our
millions of small acts the power to form a whole.*

Christopher Alexander, 'The Timeless Way of Building'

This chapter delves into pattern languages by re-examining our earlier
request-handling framework example and looking to see what language might surround it, rather than simply what sequence produced
it. We revisit the question of context and the relationships in a pattern
language. Grammar provides us with a useful and related metaphor
to make this connection.

10.1 A Network of Patterns

From a bird's-eye view, and as a conclusion from the discussion in *Chapter 9*, we might be tempted to characterize a software pattern language as:

> A network of tightly interwoven patterns that defines a process for systematically resolving a set of related and interdependent software development problems.

Although this characterization is in line with the relevant discussions and publications on pattern languages—for example [Cope96], [Gab96], [Cope97], [POSA2], [HaKo04]—it does not tell the whole story. Just as a stand-alone pattern is much more than 'a solution to a problem that arises within a specific context,' a pattern language is much more than 'a network of tightly interwoven patterns that defines a process for systematically resolving a set of related and interdependent software development problems.' This chapter therefore examines what a software pattern language is—and can be—in greater depth.

10.2 A Process and a Thing

Analyzing our draft pattern language for request handling from the previous chapter reveals that it reinforces an important property of stand-alone patterns: it provides both a *process* and a *thing*, where the 'thing' is created by the 'process' [Ale79]. The thing in our example is a request-handling framework. More generally, it is a specific kind of software system, system part, technical aspect, or development process of interest, such as distributed computing [POSA4], middle-tier resource management [POSA3], security [SFHBS06], object lifetime management in C++ [Hen01b], or development process for an entrepreneurial company [Cun96]. The process is jointly defined by the valid pattern sequences through the language and the creation processes of its constituent patterns.

Being both a process and a thing is an important property of pattern languages, otherwise they cannot support a *systematic* resolution of a set of related and interdependent software development problems, as claimed in the initial pattern language characterization above. Providing this support requires both procedural guidance for *how* to solve these problems, as well as information on *what* concrete solutions are suggested in terms of designs or implementations.

The Iterative Nature of the Process

Process and thing are tightly interwoven in a pattern language. One or more patterns define its 'entry points,' addressing the most fundamental problems that must be resolved when building the language's 'thing.' The entry-point patterns also define the starting points for the language's process: each use of the pattern language begins there.

For instance, our example pattern language for request handling that we laid out in *Combining Sequences* in *Chapter 9* by combining three different pattern sequences has two entry points: COMMAND if the mechanism receives procedural-style service requests, and MESSAGE if the mechanism receives request messages from remote clients. Both patterns address the problem of how to represent concrete service requests that clients can send to an application. For example, the description of COMMAND in *A Pattern Language for Distributed Computing* [POSA4] contains the following problem statement:

> Accessing an object typically involves calling one of its methods. It is sometimes useful, however, to decouple the sender of a request from its receiver. It may also be useful to decouple the selection of a request and receiver from the point of execution.

Since a pattern is both a process and a thing, each entry-point pattern then describes what concrete structure to create and what concrete activities to perform to resolve the problem. For example, COMMAND defines the following solution and associated creation process:

> Encapsulate requests to the receiving object in command objects, and provide these objects with a common interface to execute the requests they represent.

In addition to specifying the core solution and its fundamental implementation steps, the creation process for each entry-point pattern also suggests what other patterns in the language could be used to address subproblems of the original problem. If several alternative patterns are referenced when resolving a particular subproblem, the trade-offs for each alternative are described and hints given to select the 'right' alternative for a specific application.

Here is an excerpt from the corresponding discussion in the COMMAND pattern:

> To realize a COMMAND structure, first specify an EXPLICIT INTERFACE for uniform command execution. The interface will define one or more methods for execution, receiving arguments as necessary. Concrete commands implement this interface to reify particular requests. Each concrete command is initialized with whatever state is needed to support its execution, such as a receiver object or method arguments for later use. An INTERPRETER is a special form of COMMAND in which a script from a simple language is transformed into an executable runtime structure.
>
> Command objects can offer an undo mechanism by retaining the state necessary to roll back the behavior they execute. If the state is heavyweight or hard to restore, however, a MEMENTO that snapshots the receiver's state before executing the command may provide a simpler, more lightweight option.
>
> A COMPOSITE structure supports the construction and execution of macro commands, aggregating multiple command objects uniformly behind a single interface, and executing or rolling them back in a particular order. A separate COMMAND PROCESSOR that executes command objects on behalf of their sender can provide additional request-handling support, such as for multiple undo/redo, scheduling, and logging.

Note how this discussion of the COMMAND pattern suggests that some aspects of its realization are mandatory and others optional. An EXPLICIT INTERFACE is mandatory, because otherwise it is impossible to let all command objects share the same interface and decouple clients from a command objects' implementation. All remaining aspects of realizing COMMAND are optional. In a design that does not use macro commands, COMPOSITE is not applied.[17] In systems where requests cannot be undone because they change things in the physical world, such as formatting a disk or printing a document, COMMANDs do not

---

17. Though applying COMPOSITE is optional when realizing COMMAND, in practice it is a common configuration. In fact, this configuration is so common that it is documented as a pattern compound, called COMPOSITE COMMAND, as we discussed in *Chapter 6*.

need a MEMENTO. A COMMAND PROCESSOR is applied only if there is a need for a centralized command execution infrastructure. Last but not least, a COMMAND is only implemented as an INTERPRETER if it processes scripts—an aspect we have not yet considered in our example pattern language.

The description of the MESSAGE pattern [POSA4] provides corresponding information about the problem of representing requests, the core solution of this problem, and the solution's pattern-based realization:

> Distributed components collaborate like collocated components, invoking services on one another and exchanging data. However, on-the-wire protocols such as HTTP only support byte streams, the most basic form of data transmission, but not the notions of service invocations and data types.
>
> [...]
>
> Therefore:
>
> Encapsulate method requests and data structures to be sent across the network into messages: byte streams that include a header specifying the type of information being transmitted, its origin, destination, size, and other structural information, and a payload that contains the actual information.
>
> [...]
>
> A separate COMMAND PROCESSOR helps to transform a specific message (sequence) into a concrete method invocation on the message receiver, and can provide additional request handling support, such as for multiple undo/redo, scheduling, and logging.

In our example pattern language for request handling, knowing that some aspects of implementing COMMAND and MESSAGE are mandatory and others optional constrains the set of valid pattern sequences and facilitates new pattern sequences that we have not yet identified.

For example, a pattern sequence that does not contain EXPLICIT INTERFACE to realize a COMMAND is invalid with respect to the pattern description above. In contrast, the pattern sequence COMMAND, EXPLICIT INTERFACE is both valid and complete. This constraint does not mean that a COMMAND can only ever be implemented with respect to an EXPLICIT INTERFACE—the framework could be written in a dynamically typed language or by using a partially implemented abstract class. In the context of our example pattern language, however, the use of

EXPLICIT INTERFACE is a desirable and necessary property, as well as a design characteristic that forms part of the style of the language. Such strict loose coupling simplifies extension behavior across component and process boundaries. In contrast, a pattern sequence that does not contain COMMAND PROCESSOR to implement COMMAND is a valid sequence: the use of a COMMAND PROCESSOR is optional in the COMMAND description.

The creation process of a pattern in a pattern language, therefore, indicates explicitly which referenced patterns address mandatory implementation aspects and which address optional implementation aspects. To ensure a stable and sound pattern implementation, referenced patterns whose use is mandatory are presented in the suggested application order. Since optional referenced patterns just refine aspects of the pattern's core design, or extend it with aspects needed only for specific applications, they can be applied in any order that fits the mandatory pattern order. Without this explicit guidance on process, languages that fit the basic network of the patterns might not provide a suitable process that helps to ensure a sufficiently complete and well-formed design.

In the context of a pattern language, following a pattern reference in a pattern leads to another pattern and its associated creation process. This pattern can in turn be applied to resolve the problem that it addresses. This second pattern can reference still other patterns to resolve subproblems of the subproblem of the initial problem, as illustrated by the following path through our example pattern language for request handling:

> Both COMMAND and MESSAGE suggest using a COMMAND PROCESSOR to provide an infrastructure for advanced request handling functionality. COMMAND PROCESSOR references six other patterns: COLLECTIONS FOR STATES, TEMPLATE METHOD, INTERCEPTOR, STRATEGY, STRATEGIZED LOCKING, and MONITOR OBJECT.

> Some these patterns are alternatives to one another: TEMPLATE METHOD, INTERCEPTOR, and STRATEGY address the aspect of varying command handling helper functionality; STRATEGIZED LOCKING and MONITOR OBJECT the issue of thread-safety.

> Several patterns referenced by COMMAND PROCESSOR can also be further decomposed into other patterns. For instance, the STRATEGY pattern—one of three alternatives that helps vary helper

functionality in a COMMAND PROCESSOR—suggests two other patterns, EXPLICIT INTERFACE and NULL OBJECT, to consider for its realization.

The diagram below outlines this portion of our example pattern language for request handling:

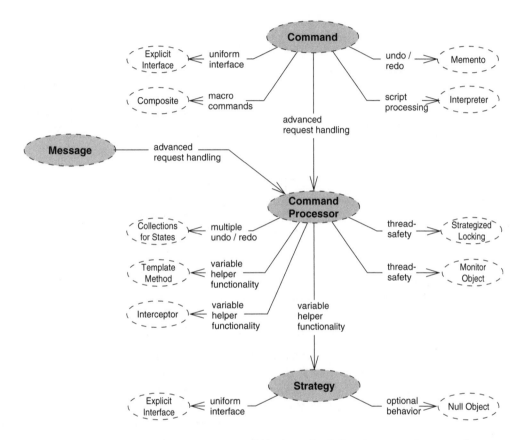

This iterative process of 'descent'—following a pattern reference and applying the referenced pattern's creation process—continues until there are no more pattern references to follow within the language. The complete path through the example pattern language defines a pattern sequence whose application results in one possible kind of design of our request-handling framework.

The processes defined by other pattern languages follow the same principles. For example, the pattern language for distributed computing described in POSA4 starts with the DOMAIN MODEL pattern, which references thirteen other patterns that help with its implementation [POSA4]. Two or more alternative patterns are suggested for five of the relevant implementation aspects of DOMAIN MODEL, as shown in the following diagram.

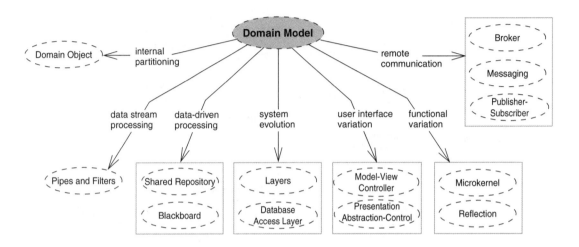

Each referenced pattern uses other patterns in the language, which themselves are composed of yet further patterns, and so on. In total, the language connects approximately 300 patterns in the pattern literature that are relevant for building distributed software systems.

Similarly, the *Organizational Patterns of Agile Software Development* collection comprises pattern languages on project management, development process, project organization, and people-and-code management [CoHa04]. Each pattern language consists of twenty-three to twenty-six tightly connected and integrated patterns, and mutually share some of their patterns with the other languages in the same book.

The diagrams included with many pattern languages often provide a concise overview of the topology they define. Examples include—but are certainly not limited to—the pattern languages for object lifetime management in C++ [Hen01b], context encapsulation [Hen05b], exception handling in Java [Haa03], telecommunication switching systems [HaKo04], user-interface design for searching [Wel05], session management in groupware systems [LS05], application-level communication gateways [Sch98], object request brokers [SC00], event-dispatching frameworks [POS05], distributed systems [POSA4], and agile software development [CoHa04].

Concrete and Domain-Specific Guidance

The process defined by a pattern language is significantly different than general-purpose software development processes, such as Waterfall [Boe82], V-Model [Drö00], Rational Unified Process (RUP) [Kru00], XP [Beck04], or Scrum [SB01]. The most striking difference is that a software design pattern language is highly domain specific. It gives *concrete and thoughtful guidance* for developing or refactoring a specific type of system or system aspect, including:

• What are the key problems to resolve.

• In what order should these problems be tackled.

• What alternatives exist for resolving a given problem.

• How should dependencies between problems be handled.

• How to resolve each individual problem most effectively in the presence of its 'surrounding' problems.

Gerard Meszaros states the need for concrete guidance even more strongly [Mes01]: 'a pattern language should guide the uninitiated in building a system.' A valid question in this context is, however, how uninitiated can one be and still build a working system with a pattern language? As we noted in *Chapter 0*, patterns are not a replacement for solid design and implementation skills. The same is true of pattern languages: people with little or no experience in software development are likely to fail to produce an effective working result even by applying a pattern language. Uninitiated does not equate to unskilled or without any appropriate foundation knowledge.

All of the above considerations on the process embodied within pattern languages, and the guidance such a process provides, also hold for pattern languages from domains other than software design. For example, the four pattern languages documented in *Organizational Patterns for Agile Software Development* [CoHa04] provide concrete domain-specific processes—and thus concrete and thoughtful guidance—on how to perform project management, organize (software) development processes, shape project organization, and manage code and people. Despite the guidance provided by these pattern languages, using them successfully on concrete software projects requires corresponding experience and skills. A project manager familiar with various organizational and process pattern languages still needs to have appropriate people and management skills.

It important to note, however, that although a pattern language may be generic in the sense that it covers different uses of its underlying process, it is not generic in the sense of being a one-size-fits-all for development as a whole. For example, design-focused pattern languages, such as our example pattern language for request handling, offer details about design, but say nothing about development organization, people management, use of tools, and so forth. Process and organizational pattern languages focus on these issues [Ker95] [Cun96] [CoHa04], but may say nothing about the concrete specifics of design.

Nevertheless, on concrete software projects, multiple pattern languages can be applied together, each of which addresses one specific concern in software development. For example, a project that develops a distributed system could use a pattern language for distributed computing to define the system's software architecture [POSA4], a pattern language for piecemeal growth to define the development process for the system [CoHa04], and a project management pattern language to steer it [CoHa04]. With such a mix, all issues of importance are addressed by a corresponding pattern language, and for each of these issues defined, domain-specific, and concrete guidance is provided in the form of a 'thing' to create and the process to create it.

General-purpose development processes, in contrast, target the construction of arbitrary software systems. Consequently, the processes *must be* so broad in scale and so general in nature that they can give only very basic advice. For example, RUP simply explains which overall software development activities to perform in what order and mixture, and which general technical concerns to consider when designing a software architecture [Kru00].

With such disconnected guidance, however, inexperienced software developers will still be largely uninformed about how to establish or refactor their software architectures, and they will receive no substantive hints or support on how to address specific architectural challenges. The process defined by pattern languages, in contrast, provides integrated and explicit guidance about how to design specific types of software systems and system aspects, or how to address other concerns of relevance in software development, such as project organization and management, development processes, and configuration, code, and people management. The trade-off, of course, is that each language is applicable effectively within its particular context, and less effectively or even ineffectively outside this context.

10.3 Best of Breed

Pattern languages also provide more than just a concrete and considered process for establishing and maturing a suitable software architecture or feature. They also support similarly concrete and considered software designs and implementations that is based on proven development experiences from successful production systems. Reinforcing and adapting our earlier statement on stand-alone patterns from *Chapter 1*, good pattern languages do not represent neat ideas that *might* work, but rather designs and implementations that *have been* repeatedly applied successfully in the past, which is what makes them *pattern languages*, as opposed to *design documents*.

Our example pattern language for request handling has also proven its worth in the line of duty: several production applications [Bus03a] [BGHS98] [Dorn02] realize request handling and (user) command execution as outlined by the design shown in the second part of our introductory experiment from *Section 4.3, A Second Design Experiment: Interwoven Patterns*.

The following three criteria should be followed to ensure that pattern languages support the creation of 'best of breed' solutions and effective development practices:

1 *Sufficient coverage.* Pattern languages must include the right patterns to address the various aspects and subproblems of their subject, otherwise they cannot support the creation of useful software.

2 *Sustainable progression.* Pattern languages must connect their patterns appropriately to ensure that challenges are addressed in the right order, which is essential to creating sustainable designs incrementally and via stable intermediate steps [Bus03b].

3 *Tight integration.* Pattern languages must integrate their constituent patterns tightly, based on the roles each pattern introduces and
   the inter-relationships between them.

The third criterion—tight integration—is necessary to ensure that
the resolution of different design and implementation challenges
mutually support and complement one another, reinforcing their
quality properties at an architectural level. For example, recall the
two designs we created by applying the same pattern sequence in the
experiments from *Chapter 4.* The first design (intentionally) considered patterns as isolated, self-contained building blocks that were
plugged together in a strictly modular fashion—a view that contradicts strongly with the third quality criterion above. This 'ignorance'
led to a suboptimal solution even though the experiment followed
the first of the three criteria above quite strongly, and the second
criterion weakly.

The second design, in contrast, reflected all three criteria, by virtue of
following the third criterion strictly, namely that patterns should act
as sets of interacting roles that can be combined and integrated in
accordance to their inter-relationships. The second criterion was also
met better and more strongly than in the first design.

The diagram on the next page revisits the resulting two designs. The
difference in quality between them is evident. The 'modular' design is
overcomplicated, inflexible, inefficient, and hard to understand, even
though each involved pattern can be identified clearly as a result of
the exaggerated 'modularity.' The 'integrated' design, conversely, is
lean, flexible, efficient, easier to understand, and well-balanced, although it is somewhat harder to discover and identify the contributing patterns due to their tight integration.

Without concrete guidance in the pattern descriptions, however, it
would be tempting to create the first design as a result of applying our
example pattern language. The description of each pattern in a language must therefore specify precisely what other patterns help realize which of its *roles.* Just describing what subproblems these other
patterns help to address is not sufficient.

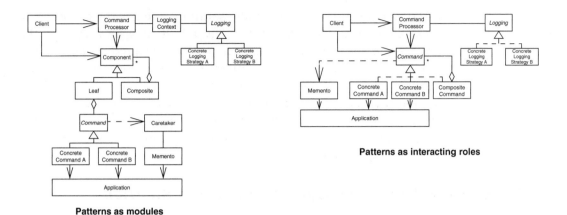

Patterns as modules

Patterns as interacting roles

The following is an excerpt from the COMMAND PROCESSOR description [POSA4]. Note how this description suggests other patterns to help implement the command processor *role*, not the realization of the COMMAND PROCESSOR *pattern* in general:

> Internally, the command processor can manage the requests it receives via multiple COLLECTIONS FOR STATES. For example, a do collection can hold all requests that have yet to execute, as well as all requests that have been undone and can now be redone. An undo collection can maintain all requests that have been executed on the component that can be rolled back. If the command processor receives requests as COMMAND objects, it can simply invoke these objects to execute the encapsulated requests on the component. If requests are received as MESSAGES, an INTERPRETER can help to transform their content into COMMANDS.

> Scheduling and other housekeeping functionality, such as logging and authorization, can be realized and configured via TEMPLATE METHOD, STRATEGY, or INTERCEPTOR. These patterns allow the configuration of a command processor with different request execution policies, considering different trade-off options in terms of binding time and looseness of coupling. [...]

Despite the quality criteria discussed above, there is no inherent assurance that pattern languages will be applied correctly, any more than we can guarantee the correct application of a single pattern. For example, although the designs that can be created with a pattern language have a proven track record, there is no guarantee that developers will choose the appropriate specific solution or follow the proposed solution steps and detail faithfully. The result may be a system that works somehow, but not quite as required or desired. Similarly, pattern languages may also be incomplete and fail to address a particular aspect of importance for their subject. Corresponding deficiencies in the software created with these languages is an inevitable consequence. Nevertheless, carefully and consciously written pattern languages help to reduce the scope for failure and actively support the creation of quality software.

Dysfunctional Pattern Languages Produce Poor Solutions

Misapplication and incompleteness of pattern languages are not the only causes of inappropriate solutions. Just as we can distinguish 'good' patterns from 'bad' or, better, whole patterns from dysfunctional ones, we can also distinguish whole pattern languages from dysfunctional ones. The dysfunctionality of a pattern language largely stems from not fulfilling one or more of the three quality criteria we outlined above, as follows:

1 *Insufficient coverage.* Dysfunctional pattern languages often include inappropriate patterns to address the various aspects and subproblems of their subject, or simply miss patterns to address aspects and subproblems of significant relevance for that subject.

2 *Unsustainable progression.* In dysfunctional pattern languages many patterns often stand alone or expose only few of the existing relationships to other patterns, rather than being fully connected pattern networks. Another common problem is the selection of inappropriate entry points: the root of a pattern language defines a starting point and assumption, but it is not uncommon to find pattern languages that start with an implementation detail before dealing with the domain problem they are addressing. Consequently it is hard to provide a process for addressing the subjects of the languages that provides concrete guidance to ensure that challenges are addressed in the right order, and to create sustainable designs incrementally and via stable intermediate steps. Instead, the possible pattern combinations and sequences make only little sense, and do not encourage stable, whole designs.

3 *Loose integration.* As a consequence of not supporting sustainable progression, dysfunctional pattern languages cannot support a tight, role-based integration of their patterns, which is likely to lead to designs in which patterns are handled as modular building-blocks with little or no overlap in their implementations. As a result, many quality properties that the individual patterns of these languages promise to fulfil, such as performance and adaptability, are not met by the designs created with the languages.

The consequence of applying a dysfunctional pattern language is obvious: the resulting software does not meet its functional, operational, and developmental requirements. In other words, dysfunctional pattern languages are likely to create dysfunctional solutions.

We are not aware of any formal metrics that help to distinguish whole from dysfunctional pattern languages. There is, however, an informal heuristic: the more a pattern language is created from, or comprises, successful pattern sequences, and the more pattern (success) stories are reported from production systems, the more likely it is that the language is whole. This simple insight revisits the opening argument for this section: good pattern languages build on proven knowledge and actual success stories, not on fairy tales: empiricism in contrast to idealism.

These considerations and statements about quality apply for pattern languages of all types, not just for pattern languages on software design. Applying a dysfunctional pattern language for project management, for example, would lead to poor project management.

10.4 Forces: the Heart of Every Pattern Language

A fundamental prerequisite for a successful design-focused pattern language is its ability to create and support a sustainable software architecture. Knowing that a pattern language addresses a specific subject well, however, is no guarantee for its successful use. It is ultimately a combination of the skills of the development team and the concrete requirements of production applications that determine the quality of any design or implementation created with a pattern language. If a specific solution does not address and meet the requirements of the software system in which it is integrated, the solution is of insufficient quality for that system. Moreover, a solution that works perfectly for an application in one domain may be inappropriate for others in different domains.

Pattern languages, therefore, describe their scope of applicability by enumerating the specific requirements they address for their subject, the constraints they observe, and the properties supported by the designs they can generate. Such precision helps to reduce misapplication of pattern languages. By comparing the requirements defined for an application or a specific application aspect with the requirements addressed by a corresponding pattern language, developers can decide whether a given pattern language is appropriate for their needs.

A useful pattern language will provide developers with working solutions for common design and implementation challenges. It may also suggest alternative pattern languages, or even non-pattern solutions. For example, a major concern in our example pattern language for request handling is flexibility: configurable command sets, command composition, and command scheduling and housekeeping functionality. An application that needs flexible command handling will therefore benefit more from this pattern language than one that just needs raw performance.

As described in *Section 1.4, Forces: the Heart of Every Pattern,* stand-alone patterns can use explicit forces to specify the concrete requirements, properties, and constraints they address, support, or consider in the context of their problem. Forces tell us why the problem that a pattern is addressing requires an 'intelligent' solution. They are also key to understanding the rationale for a particular solution. It therefore appears natural to specify forces for pattern languages that explicitly express the requirements addressed, properties supported, and constraints considered by the designs and implementations they can create.

The Three Levels of Forces

But what are the forces of a pattern language? The most direct answer to this question is that the forces of a pattern language are the union of all forces of the language's constituent patterns. This answer is certainly not incorrect: if a pattern is part of a language for a specific subject, the problem addressed by the pattern is relevant in the context of that subject, and thus so are the forces that influence the solution to that problem. Yet this understanding is only part of the answer, and perhaps not even useful at the level of the entire language.

A pattern language must also balance forces related globally to its subject as a whole, rather than just to individual problems that arise when creating specific designs or implementations for this subject. For example:

- The need for configurability is a global force for our example pattern language for request handling: control over quality of service is another.

- The pattern language for component design specified in *Server Component Patterns* [VSW02] addresses several global forces, such as support for independent component development, evolution, reusability, scalability, and availability.

- The POSA4 pattern language for distributed computing captures the variabilities in distributed software systems without compromising their operational qualities, such as performance and scalability [POSA4].

- The pattern language *Caterpillar's Fate*—which helps to transform detailed analysis documents into an initial software design—addresses the global force that this transition should be as seamless as possible [Ker95].

It is therefore the entirety of all patterns in a language that resolves the global forces, not just the forces in any given stand-alone pattern, which only contributes to part of the resolution.

Some pattern languages also address several problem areas that are relevant for their subject. For instance, the POSA4 pattern language for distributed computing comprises thirteen problem areas, which include distribution infrastructure, concurrency, event-handling, and database access. There are often general forces associated with the problem areas that are resolved by the entirety of the patterns they comprise. For example, the event-handling problem area in the POSA4 pattern language lists several forces associated with event throughput, asynchronous event arrival, and concurrent event handling. Similarly, the pattern language *Caterpillar's Fate* comprises four problem areas: concurrency, transactions, program shape, and data design [Ker95]. Each problem area addresses specific forces, such as how stimuli will be acquired and responded to in the program shape problem area, and downwards data compatibilty in the data design problem area. Our example pattern language for request handling could also distinguish two problem areas with their own set of forces:

- *Request representation.* The forces associated with this problem area are the requirement for configurable request composition and extensible request representation.

- *Request handling.* The force associated with this problem area is the requirement for variable request-handling behavior.

To summarize, forces of a pattern language can reside at three levels: system (part or aspect), problem area, and individual problem. Forces from a higher level summarize and compress the forces from the next lower level. Similarly, forces from a lower level unfold and describe some the forces from the next higher level. All forces are related, and gradually guide a pattern language user from a bird's-eye, system-level viewpoint to a worm's-eye, implementation-level perspective. Users are thus provided with the right level of detail about the forces to balance throughout the process of creating the software artifacts that arise from the pattern language.

The diagram below shows how the global force of configurable request handling in our example pattern language for request handling is characterized by the corresponding forces of its two problem areas, as well as by selected patterns in each of the two problem areas.

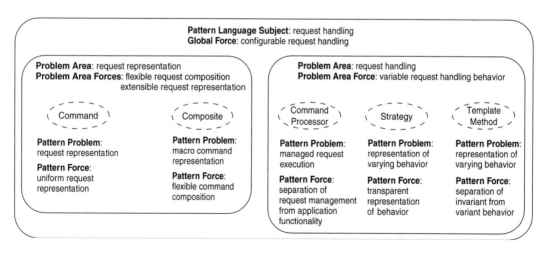

In addition to specifying requirements, constraints, and properties considered by pattern languages, forces also help users navigate through their topology. Whenever a pattern description in a pattern language references another pattern, it should convey to users the circumstances in which the referenced pattern is applicable. Such guidance is typically expressed as specific forces that arise in the context of resolving certain problems. This guidance is particularly helpful when several alternative patterns are referenced, because it is the forces associated with each alternative that influence which specific pattern is best in a given situation.

For example, the COMMAND PROCESSOR pattern in our example pattern language for request handling suggests three alternatives for realizing variations of request housekeeping functionality [POSA4]:

> Scheduling and other housekeeping functionality, such as logging and authorization, can be realized and configured via TEMPLATE METHOD, STRATEGY, or INTERCEPTOR. These patterns allow the configuration of a command processor with different request execution policies, considering different trade-off options in terms of binding time and looseness of coupling.

Which alternative to apply, or whether any alternative applies at all, is determined by the associated forces, as indicated by the guidance given in the COMMAND PROCESSOR example. If the forces of any of these patterns match the concrete requirements and constraints, the corresponding pattern can be applied appropriately, otherwise not. Consequently forces play an essential part in guiding the selection of a specific path through a pattern language. They act as road signs that direct users from pattern to pattern through the entire language, and to choose the most appropriate pattern sequence for the software system under development.

10.5 Pattern Contexts Define Topology and Architectural Style

In Part I, *Inside Patterns*, we explored the context of a stand-alone pattern and described the essential characteristics of situations in which the problem addressed by the pattern can arise. We showed how the context gives each pattern a precise and defined scope of applicability.

Context, problem, and forces of a stand-alone pattern also form a triad: the context must give rise to the problem addressed, and the forces specify the requirements that must be met to resolve the problem in its given context.

In Part II, *Between Patterns*, we continued the context discussion from the viewpoint of pattern sequences. Each pattern in a pattern sequence, except for the first, is applied when realizing one or more specific preceding patterns in that sequence. For example, in the pattern sequence that generated the design for our request handling mechanism, COMMAND PROCESSOR is applied following COMMAND, and STRATEGY is applied following COMMAND PROCESSOR. We can therefore narrow the context of a pattern in a sequence to the list of all its precursor patterns, or just its immediate precursor. This short list defines a precise scope of applicability and does not bother readers with situations that are not relevant for building the sequence's subject.

Listing precursor patterns is therefore a natural approach for specifying the context of patterns in a pattern language. For example, in our example pattern language for request handling, the context for STRATEGY would become quite simple, short, and precise:

> A COMMAND PROCESSOR is used to realize advanced request scheduling and housekeeping functionality.

Patterns in a pattern language may have more than one entry point, so, correspondingly, their context can enumerate more than one pattern. In our example pattern language, for instance, the context of EXPLICIT INTERFACE would list both COMMAND and STRATEGY.

Together, the contexts of all patterns in a pattern language jointly define the language's topology. This topology describes which patterns connect with other patterns. It also constrains the ordering in which patterns of the language can potentially be sequenced. These connections therefore form a partially ordered set of patterns [PCW05] [Hen05b].

A context such as the one for STRATEGY above is also specific to the particular language from which it is taken. For example, in a language for object–relational data mapping, STRATEGY would have a different specific context. Unlike relationships between patterns in an ad hoc pattern catalog, pattern languages do not provide a general connection scheme for patterns, but instead describe how their patterns connect within a particular domain.

A pattern language also defines one or more architectural styles, as opposed to 'the one true solution.' In addition to using other patterns, another pattern language for the same domain can also connect the same patterns differently. For example, compare the available pattern languages on mapping objects to relational databases [BW95] [KC97] [Kel99] [Fow02] with one another: despite many commonalities, they each propose different approaches to designing a database access layer. Just as the difference between complementary patterns often reduces to design style, the difference between complementary pattern languages is in their supported architectural styles. The difference between the two is that the design style of a pattern is defined primarily by its forces, as discussed in *Chapter 8, Pattern Collections*, whereas the architectural styles of a pattern language are defined by the contexts of its patterns.

Language Specific versus General Context

Language-specific contexts are clearly needed to understand how patterns connect to define a language's architectural styles. Such contexts, however, are often of little use when trying to understand a specific pattern by itself, regardless of its integration into the language. The context for STRATEGY described above is a good example. Although this context states precisely how STRATEGY is related to other patterns in our example language for request handling, it provides no information about when to apply it. Since the triad of context, problem, and forces feels incomplete, it is therefore hard to understanding the specific role STRATEGY plays in the language.

What is missing is some general information about when STRATEGY applies, independently of how it is integrated with the pattern language. This information would provide a starting point for understanding the pattern. In addition to listing the preceding patterns, therefore, the context of a pattern in a pattern language can be supplemented with the description it might have if documented as a stand-alone pattern:

> When using a COMMAND PROCESSOR to realize request scheduling and housekeeping…

> … we must consider that different applications may need to use different algorithms and policies for such functionality.

This context tells readers where they are in the language and informs them about the essential characteristics of the situations that motivate the use of a particular pattern. Readers can therefore understand each pattern in a language without having to read and digest all the possible precursor patterns. Moreover, the scope of applicability of each pattern in the language becomes unambiguous and precise: its triad of context, problem, and forces are more obviously balanced and tied together—triptych rather than cryptic.

Many pattern languages have adopted the form of context discussed above in their pattern descriptions. For example, the pattern language for distributed computing described in POSA4 follows it quite literally. The inbound patterns of the language whose implementations can benefit from the described pattern are listed first, followed by a description of the general situation that gives rise to the problem addressed by that pattern. The context form used in *Remoting Patterns* [VKZ04], *Server Component Patterns* [VSW02], or *Software Configuration Management Patterns* [BeAp02] is similar. Each pattern in these books lists both inbound patterns and the general situation giving rise to the addressed problem, but does not separate the two aspects explicitly from one another as POSA4 does.

10.6 Patterns Form Vocabulary, Sequences Illustrate Grammar

When connecting patterns together into a pattern language, the collective patterns play the role of the language's *vocabulary*, the language's range of principal words, with each pattern considered to be a 'word.' For each relevant problem in the context of a specific pattern language, at least one 'word' expresses the solution to the problem.

Alternative patterns for resolving a given problem are thus like synonyms in natural language: they share much of the same meaning but have a different sense or feel to them, expressed by the individual forces addressed by each alternative.

Vocabulary alone, however, is just one part of a proper and useful pattern language. Grammar is the other. But what is the grammar of a pattern language? One possibility, returning to the notion of a pattern language as a network, is that the grammar of a pattern language is defined by its topology. This topology in turn is defined by the contexts of the language's constituent patterns, as discussed above. This perspective is somewhat naïve, however, since topology is not grammar.

During the exploration of the process defined by a pattern language on *page 263*, we noted that if a pattern in a pattern language references multiple other patterns, these other patterns cannot always be applied in arbitrary order. In other words, not all paths through a pattern language that are possible from navigating its topology will create a sustainable and working design or situation. The potential solution space spawned by a pattern language considered only as a network therefore requires some narrowing, filtering out invalid or impractical paths.

Turning this around, not all sequences through a pattern language considered only as a network are grammatically well formed. It is perhaps better to start the understanding of grammar from a language's sequences rather than from its abstract topology. To continue with the natural language metaphor, each pattern sequence can be viewed as a properly formed sentence in a pattern language.

Our example pattern language for request handling, for example, includes the following pattern sequences:

> One valid pattern sequence is the empty sequence ⟨⟩, which implies not applying the pattern language for request handling. Useful, non-empty pattern sequences include ⟨COMMAND, EXPLICIT INTERFACE⟩, ⟨COMMAND, EXPLICIT INTERFACE, MEMENTO⟩, ⟨COMMAND, EXPLICIT INTERFACE, MEMENTO, COMPOSITE⟩, ⟨COMMAND, EXPLICIT INTERFACE, COMPOSITE⟩, ⟨COMMAND, EXPLICIT INTERFACE, COMPOSITE,

MEMENTO⟩, and ⟨COMMAND, EXPLICIT INTERFACE, MEMENTO, COMPOSITE, COMMAND PROCESSOR, COLLECTIONS FOR STATES, STRATEGY, NULL OBJECT⟩.

Further pattern sequences, which we omit for brevity, provide different orderings of the patterns in the last sequence, or involve the MESSAGE and TEMPLATE METHOD patterns.

The union of all pattern sequences supported by a pattern language can thus be understood as its full set of grammatically correct sentence forms. Yet the grammar of a pattern language is only implicitly visible in these pattern sequences, simply because they show the *results* of its application, not its *rules*.

There are two options for making the grammar of pattern languages explicit:

- *Direct integration.* The grammar rules can be integrated directly into the description of the language's constituent patterns, as shown in the discussion of the COMMAND pattern on *page 262*. It can be quite a complex and tedious activity, however, to phrase grammar rules unambiguously in pattern descriptions. In addition, embedding grammar rules directly in pattern descriptions does not give a 'big picture' view—an overview of the entire language grammar.

- *Use a separate notation.* One option for documenting the grammar of pattern languages is to use a formal notation. For example, key elements of the CSP model [Hoare85], a process algebra, are applied within and beyond the description of communicating sequential processes in concurrent systems [HoJi99]. There are a number of useful parallels with pattern languages: the patterns within a pattern language form the *alphabet* of its development process, the application of a pattern constitutes an *event*, the possible pattern sequences through a language forms the set of *traces* of the process. Alternatively, graphical or prose notations are also possible to capture pattern language grammars.

As an example of a simple formal notation, we can use $\emptyset$ to denote a starting state, $\rightarrow$ can denote a mandatory sequential composition, $\rightarrow^\circ$ can denote an optional sequential composition, $|$ can denote an alternation, and $(\,)$ can denote grouping. This notation leads to the following portion from the grammar of our example pattern language for request handling, derived from the pattern sequences presented above:

$$\varnothing \rightarrow^\circ (\text{COMMAND} \rightarrow \text{EXPLICIT INTERFACE} \rightarrow^\circ$$
$$(\text{MEMENTO} \rightarrow^\circ \text{COMPOSITE} \rightarrow^\circ \text{COMMAND PROCESSOR} \rightarrow$$
$$\text{COLLECTIONS FOR STATES} \rightarrow \text{STRATEGY} \rightarrow \text{NULL OBJECT})$$
$$\mid (\text{COMPOSITE} \rightarrow^\circ \text{MEMENTO}))$$

A BNF-derived notation [EBNF96], as used for specifying the syntax of programming languages, would be another way to present the grammar of a pattern language. A prose description offers yet another alternative:

> COMMAND may optionally be applied, but if applied it must be followed by EXPLICIT INTERFACE. EXPLICIT INTERFACE may optionally be followed by MEMENTO, which may optionally be followed by COMPOSITE, which may optionally be followed by COMMAND PROCESSOR, which if applied must be followed by COLLECTIONS FOR STATES, which must be followed by STRATEGY, which must be followed by NULL OBJECT. Alternatively, EXPLICIT INTERFACE may optionally be followed by COMPOSITE, which may optionally be followed by MEMENTO.

Graphical notations can also be used to illustrate the grammar of a pattern language. One possible option is feature modeling notation, which visually captures commonality and variability in a software design [CzEi02], and a variant of which is used to present the pattern language for context encapsulation [Hen05b]. In feature modeling a root *concept* is hierarchically decomposed into *features*, and the legal combinations of features with respect to one another is shown, such as whether two features are mutually exclusive, mandatory, or optional. In borrowing this notation, however, patterns should not be confused with features, though the notation can be applied to relate concepts via a simple visualization of valid combination options.

Another graphical presentation for pattern language grammars is the 'railroad' notation—a diagramming technique that has been popular since the 1970s for describing the syntax of programming languages, in particular Pascal [JeWi74].

The portion of our pattern language for request handling outlined above could be represented as follows using the 'railroad notation':

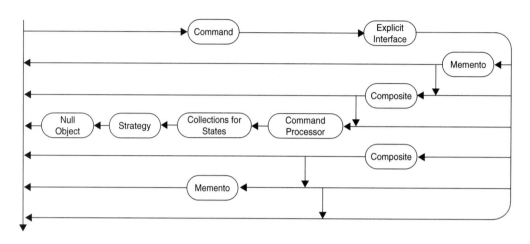

The preferences of pattern language authors or the demands of their target audience determine the specific expression of a grammar that works best—whether a list of pattern sequences, formal or semi-formal prose, or a graphical form of describing grammar rules, and whether interwoven with the pattern descriptions or separate. For example, the pattern language for distributed computing from POSA4 expresses grammar rules in prose, interwoven with the pattern descriptions [POSA4]. This option has been chosen by most pattern languages in the software area, from design-centric pattern languages [VSW02] [Fow02] [HoWo03] [VKZ04] to pattern languages for development process and organization, and project and people management [Ker95] [Cun96] [CoHa04].

Regardless of which grammar form is chosen, however, it is important that documented pattern languages actually offer guidance on the issue of meaningful paths through a language. Otherwise, it is hard to avoid the selection of ill-formed pattern sequences that create fundamentally broken software. The set of sensible sequences through a language is part of the language and not something accidental or separate. Thus making the grammars of pattern languages more explicit is one method for supporting their appropriate use. However, we must also recognize some practical limitations in this endeavor: the grammar for a large and richly interwoven pattern language will be difficult to express in a readily accessible form. In such cases the guidance on paths is perhaps better expressed more locally within each pattern description rather than externally in a single form.

10.7 Genericity

An essential property of stand-alone patterns is that they provide a solution space for resolving a given problem, rather than just a single solution. Whoever implements the pattern can respond to the specific needs of the situation effectively and concretely, while still following the essential guidance of the pattern and preserving the core of its proposed solution.

Pattern languages similarly spawn a design space for building a particular type of system, system aspect, or system part, rather than a single, fixed, one-size-fits-all solution. This property is absolutely essential for their success and usability in production software development, even more than for stand-alone patterns. Pattern languages would otherwise be unable to respond to the wide range of requirements and constraints that different instances of a specific type of application can have. But how do pattern languages achieve this genericity? We explore two answers to this question below that focus on the existence of many different pattern sequences through a pattern language, and societies of smaller patterns that can be composed to address a large scope.

Many Different Pattern Sequences

In *Section 10.2, A Process and a Thing*, we explained that a particular path taken through a pattern language results in a pattern sequence that creates a specific design or situation when applied. Almost all pattern languages offer alternatives for resolving some of the problems they address. Since some of these problems are not always relevant for all systems, many different pattern sequences are possible through a given language, each one producing a different design or implementation. For example, our example pattern language for request handling supports the creation of many alternative designs:

> The pattern sequence ⟨COMMAND, EXPLICIT INTERFACE⟩ realizes a simple request-handling mechanism that decouples senders of procedural-style service requests from the components providing the services. Additional request-handling functionality is not supported.
>
> The pattern sequence ⟨COMMAND, EXPLICIT INTERFACE, MEMENTO, COMPOSITE, COMMAND PROCESSOR, COLLECTIONS FOR STATES, STRATEGY, NULL OBJECT⟩ creates a design that supports advanced request handling functionality: multiple undo/redo, logging, and scheduling. Most functions can also be configured with different algorithms.
>
> The sequence ⟨MESSAGE, COMMAND PROCESSOR, INTERPRETER, COMMAND, EXPLICIT INTERFACE, MEMENTO, COMPOSITE, COLLECTIONS FOR STATES, STRATEGY, NULL OBJECT⟩ creates an alternative design in which clients deliver request messages instead of function calls.

Adapting a quote from Christopher Alexander [AIS77], we can summarize and conclude that 'each pattern language describes an entire solution space for realizing software of a particular application or technical domain, in such a way that you can instantiate this solution space a million—perhaps even a billion—times over without ever doing it twice the same.'

Societies of Patterns

Another reason for the genericity of pattern languages for software design stems from the fact that their patterns are not described in terms of fixed designs with associated concrete code, but are instead defined as *societies* of several 'smaller' patterns. These more local patterns define the solution space of their aggregating patterns implicitly rather than explicitly. They do this via their concrete arrangement in the containing patterns, their own individual genericity, and the number of possible combinations of their implementation variants.

When these local patterns are realized in a specific valid combination and instance, they automatically *generate* a specific instance of the 'larger' pattern.

> When realizing a request-handling framework with the help of our example pattern language, there are two options for implementing variant behavior of a COMMAND PROCESSOR using STRATEGY. The

first option is to introduce a separate strategy hierarchy for each varying algorithm: the second option is to have a separate strategy hierarchy for each group of related algorithms that can vary, as shown in the following two-part diagram.

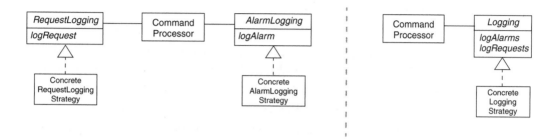

The 'smaller' patterns themselves can also be—and most often are—defined as societies of even smaller patterns. The genericity of the entire pattern language therefore grows through the depth of its topology. This genericity is also far more powerful than the sum of all genericities provided by the language's individual patterns. Each new pattern that is integrated into the pattern language increases this genericity even more.

10.8 A Whole Language Says More than a Thousand Diagrams

While it is useful to complement the textual description of a stand-alone pattern with a diagram that illustrates some possible configurations of its elements, providing a similar diagram for a pattern language is much harder. The reason for this extra complexity is the language's genericity and interwoven process. In particular, the number of different, concrete designs or implementations that are supported by a pattern language can be so large, and two specific designs or implementations can differ so much, that it is often not feasible to summarize them all in a single diagram, or even a small number of diagrams.

Even if the space embraced by a pattern language could be captured in a single diagram, it is likely that this diagram would be so unreadable as to be useless or even misleading. Only for very small pattern languages would such a visualization be possible at all. Hence most pattern languages do not attempt to provide a diagram that shows the entire solution space for their subject. A whole language is simply much more expressive than a thousand diagrams—or even a thousand and twenty four!

The inappropriateness of using a diagram to capture the solution space of a pattern language does not mean that pattern languages should contain no diagrams at all. Indeed, there are many aspects of pattern languages that can actually benefit from being explained and illustrated with diagrams. In particular:

- Each pattern in a language could provide a diagram that illustrates its proposed solution, as we discussed in *Chapter 1*.

- One or more diagrams could outline the topology of a pattern language, like those presented in *Section 10.2, A Process and a Thing*.

- One or more diagrams could visualize the grammar of a language, as discussed in *Section 10.6, Patterns Form Vocabulary, Sequences Illustrate Grammar*.

Nevertheless, all these diagrams address different concerns than attempting to visualize the entire solution space for the language's subject.

10.9 Domain-Oriented Names Help to Recall Pattern Languages

A successful pattern language must support more than just the creation of sound designs and implementations. For a language to play a role in our day-to-day work, we must also be able to identify and reference it precisely and unambiguously. If we cannot easily recall a pattern language, it cannot become a tool in our design toolkit, and will rarely be used faithfully in practice, regardless of its qualities.

As with a stand-alone pattern, therefore, each pattern language has a name. If someone references a pattern language by its name, everyone who knows the language should ideally be able to recall it easily. The name of memorable stand-alone patterns, such as PROXY, BROKER, and REACTOR, should be evocative and convey the essence of their solutions to the target audience [MD97]. Pattern languages, in contrast, are typically named after the domain that they cover.

For example, names like *Server Component Patterns* [VSW02] or *A Pattern Language for Distributed Computing* [POSA4] indicate the application domains or problem areas in which the corresponding languages apply. Even languages with more picturesque names that do not summarize their target domain, such as the *CHECKS* pattern language [Cun95], often come along with a clarifying subtitle, which for *CHECKS* is *A Pattern Language for Information Integrity*. From this perspective, the name of our language example, *A Pattern Language for Request Handling*, seems an appropriate choice.

At first glance, domain-related names can be considered the opposite of the solution-oriented naming practice for stand-alone patterns. Such a naming practice would name pattern languages after the core architectural characteristics of the solutions they introduce. For example, a structure-oriented name for the language *Patterns of Enterprise Application Architecture* would be *Three-Tier Architecture*. A solution-oriented name, however, often does not scope a language's applicability in a manner that helps developers choose the appropriate pattern languages for their system. For example, three-tier architectures are built for many types of system, but not all pattern languages that create three-tier architectures are useful in the enterprise application domain.

Pattern languages that do not provide domain-oriented names can be hard to remember and are therefore rarely referenced, regardless of their quality. A good example of such a 'forgotten' pattern language is *Caterpillar's Fate*, which describes a process for transforming from analysis to design [Ker95]. The name has no relationship to the language's application domain, but is a metaphor for the type of process that it introduces. Unfortunately, only relatively few people actually remember *Caterpillar's Fate*, and probably even fewer people really understand it. A more prosaic name might have been less exciting, but hindsight suggests that it would have been more memorable.

A domain-oriented naming approach is thus the most effective means of keeping a pattern language in everyone's mind and on their tongues, which is a first step toward more frequent and widespread use.

10.10 A Pattern Language Initiates Dialog and Tells Many Stories

The inherent properties of pattern languages we have discussed up to this point have an interesting consequence. By their nature, pattern languages do not simply present an unbounded set of sustainable solutions for a specific subject: they also initiate a dialog with their users to guide them through the solution spaces they span. This dialog outlines the challenges the languages address in their solution spaces, motivates potential design and implementation alternatives for resolving specific challenges, and encourages explicit decisions in the presence of such alternatives.

In other words, a pattern language should not be blindly copied, pasted, and adapted as a predefined reference solution for the software system being developed or refactored, the project organization to shape, the configuration management to establish, and so on. Instead, it invites its users to engage in a *creative* design process. The solutions that pattern languages help to create therefore result from many conscious and thoughtful decisions and considerations, rather than being an ad hoc and purely mechanical approach to software development.

The dialog initiated by pattern languages is also broader in scope and deeper in effect than those initiated by stand-alone patterns or other pattern organization forms. For example, stand-alone patterns present and discuss knowledge about resolving a specific, local problem. While this brief dialog is better than no discussion at all, it has limited effect beyond the scope and applicability of the pattern being discussed.

Pattern complements extend the dialog with users by reflecting about *alternatives* to resolve a given problem. This reflection offers better problem coverage than a stand-alone pattern because it considers the specific context in which the problem at hand arises. Pattern languages extend this brief exchange even further, toward an extended dialog about the design of an entire software system, system part, or system aspect. Readers of pattern languages therefore get a much deeper understanding of the issues relevant for developing the language subjects, and also about the subjects themselves.

Each concrete dialog initiated by a pattern language results in a specific pattern sequence that creates a specific pattern story when applied. In turn this story conveys how a design for a concrete system,

system part, or system aspect unfolded. This observation leads directly to the conclusion that the dialog itself is ultimately enabled by the integrated set of all pattern sequences included in a pattern language.

We can now refine our hypothesis from the end of *Chapter 9* on what pattern languages could be. We proposed that pattern stories help us understand specific examples, and that pattern sequences help us generalize what we learn from pattern stories and guide us in reapplying this knowledge. We further hypothesized that multiple integrated pattern sequences could form pattern languages, addressing the one-size-fits-all problem of trying to apply pattern sequences in contexts where they are not a perfect fit. It now appears that this hypothesis was a step in the right direction, which has been further supported by the discussions in this chapter.

10.11 Work in Progress

Pattern languages that are useful for production software development must be sufficiently complete and mature [HaKo04]. In particular, they must be complete regarding the coverage of the problem and solution spaces for their subjects, and must be mature regarding the quality and interconnection of their constituent patterns. Anyone who has ever appreciated wine, cognac, or single malt whisky knows that quality and maturity cannot be produced casually and hastily, but require great care and much time to age gracefully.

Pattern languages are no exception to the following timeless rule: each pattern language can only reasonably document the experience of the past and the present, and can cover competently only those problem and solution areas of which their authors are aware, or on which they have focused intentionally. Similarly, the quality of a pattern language is only as good as the quality and maturity of its constituent patterns (vocabulary) and the network (grammar) that they form. It is the practical experience gained over time—paired with hindsight—that ultimately confirms whether a pattern language is functional or dysfunctional, what deficiencies and gaps it has, and by what measures these drawbacks and holes can be addressed.

Pattern languages evolve in response to various events and insights, such as new experiences gained developing a specific type of system. Similarly, new technologies with corresponding patterns may arise to resolve specific problems relevant for a particular type of system. For example, Service-Oriented Architectures (SOA) gave rise to a new set of patterns for software integration and loose coupling [MaLu95], but also built on many well-known patterns for distributed computing [POSA1] [POSA2] [VSW02]. It is certainly desirable to integrate these new experiences and patterns into related existing pattern languages to keep them up to date. Consequently, all pattern languages, from the rawest to the most mature, should always be considered *works in progress* that are subject to continuous revision, enhancement, refinement, completion, and sometimes even complete rewriting. Our example pattern language for request handling is also a work in progress:

> Some applications must ensure that there is only one COMMAND PROCESSOR per subsystem, per container, or even for the entire software. An OBJECT MANAGER provides such a controlled object creation on behalf of a specific application instance or deployment. COMMAND PROCESSOR could thus be extended to reference OBJECT MANAGER for optional lifecycle control. Similarly, concurrent access to a COMMAND PROCESSOR can be supported by realizing it as a MONITOR OBJECT or providing it with STRATEGIZED LOCKING. Adding both patterns to the pattern language for request handling can make it more complete and mature.

Treating pattern languages as works in progress demands even more 'gardening' effort than is needed for stand-alone patterns. Writing an effective pattern language is an incremental process, since it takes a long time to understand a given domain—its scope, problems, and solutions—in sufficient depth. Similarly, pattern languages typically contain many patterns that can also be used as stand-alone patterns, each of which must itself be mature to form the basis for the pattern language.

Topology is another factor that drives the incremental maturation of pattern languages: understanding how stand-alone patterns connect in a specific pattern language typically requires extensive experience in building software. Similarly, extending pattern languages with missing patterns is not simply filling empty slots. Patterns and their relationships are not modular, so intensive integration and reworking of the languages and their patterns is often needed.

The effort ratio of documenting pattern languages versus documenting stand-alone patterns or pattern catalogs is similar to the effort ratio of developing object-oriented application frameworks versus developing stand-alone classes or class libraries. It takes time to generalize from a piece of software written individually for one specific customer to a framework that is configurable to meet the demands and requirements of many customers or even an entire market segment. Equally, it takes time to generalize from one specific pattern sequence to a pattern language that comprises and integrates many meaningful pattern sequences. For example, it took us nearly six years to document the pattern language for distributed computing in POSA4, even though we drew from many existing sources of mature patterns and pattern languages. Similarly, the first drafts of the *Organizational Patterns of Agile Software Development* [CoHa04], a book published in 2005, date back over a decade, and were initially captured in Jim Coplien's paper on a *Generative Development-Process Pattern Language* [Cope95].

The immense effort required to write and mature quality pattern languages is perhaps the main reason why the number of good pattern languages documented is disproportionately smaller than the corresponding number of good stand-alone patterns. The effort needed to document and maintain pattern languages, however, is rewarded by the satisfaction obtained from writing pattern languages, sharing them with other developers, and improving them over time.

10.12 Pattern Languages Reward Creative Human Intelligence

The discussions earlier in this chapter may have given the (mistaken) impression that after functional pattern languages are mature and complete they are an absolute, infallible means to develop quality software—that is, they always produce 'the right thing' [Hearsay02] regardless of how experienced or inexperienced their users. If this were true, of course, we would have solved the 'software crisis' [Dij72]! In reality, however, pattern languages are not 'silver bullets' [Bro86]

[Bell06]. They are also not 'sausage machines,' churning out tasty turn-key solutions that always work, even when applied without any technical knowledge or experience.

It is definitely true that mature pattern languages capture the collective experience of expert software developers, such as their insights into solutions that have worked well in the past to resolve specific problems, and how these solutions can be realized effectively. It is also true that pattern languages are founded in human ingenuity rather than in rigid software development methods. Although pattern language solutions often tackle problems indirectly, even counter-intuitively, they can be considered superior to much software created with traditional and wide-spread bureaucratic approaches, such as the Waterfall [Boe82] and V-Model [Drö00] processes.

For example, our example pattern language for request handling provides some ways of addressing core challenges in building request handling components that might seem unusual at first glance:

> Traditionally, clients invoke services by calling corresponding methods on them. Such procedural-style invocation, however, increases the structural complexity of an application: clients are directly coupled to the services they use, and become dependent on concrete service method signatures. The COMMAND pattern breaks this tight coupling by encapsulating requests as objects that provide a signature-agnostic interface to invoking an operation on a specific service. Yet COMMAND objects do not follow traditional object-oriented principles [Sch86], since they represent a logical, not a physical entity, and they primarily realize behavior, not necessarily state.

> Similarly, following the advice of the Gang-of-Four book [GoF95], it has been considered good design and programming practice to internalize modal behavior into an object using the (OBJECTS FOR) STATE(S) pattern. Such a design, however, can pollute a request-handling component with many small classes, which only realize do and undo behavior for each supported COMMAND. A more elegant and efficient solution is to externalize the state of a COMMAND using two COLLECTIONS FOR STATES in a COMMAND PROCESSOR. One collection holds all COMMANDS in the undo state and another collection all COMMANDS in the redo state.

Despite the expertise embodied in mature pattern languages, however, it would be wrong—though often tempting—to conclude that users of pattern languages can be completely inexperienced yet still produce good software. As discussed in *Section 10.2, A Process and a Thing*, it is unlikely that inexperienced software developers will produce anything meaningful with pattern languages. To quote Louis Pasteur: 'Fortune favors the prepared mind'—so while pattern languages celebrate human intelligence, they only reward those with a sufficient level of competence, preparation, and creativity.

Regardless of their backgrounds, of course, the study of pattern languages can help developers advance more rapidly from novitiates to masters. In particular, studying and applying patterns and pattern languages helps developers to avoid software traps and pitfalls that have traditionally been discovered only by prolonged and costly trial and error. The point we want to underscore, however, is that despite their many benefits, pattern languages are no substitute for creative human intelligence.

10.13 From a Pattern Network to a Pattern Language

Pattern languages that support our vision of *Pattern-Oriented Software Architecture* are clearly much more than a network of tightly interwoven patterns that define a process for systematically resolving a set of related and interdependent software development problems. While this brief summary is not 'wrong' per se, it is the inherent qualities we discussed in this chapter, paired with the individual quality of all contributing patterns, that define the essence of pattern languages. If a network of patterns does not expose these qualities, it may be a network of patterns, but not a pattern language that can be considered functional and whole.

There are many commonalities between the notion of pattern languages developed in this chapter and Christopher Alexander's original characterization in *A Timeless Way of Building* [Ale79] and *A Pattern Language* [AIS77], including:

- A pattern language is both is a process and a thing.

- The thing a language helps create must be of high quality.

- Forces and context are important.

- A language is always work in progress.

- A pattern captures experience and rewards creative human intelligence.

Like us, Christopher Alexander also noted that pattern languages are not a panacea and do not capture the ultimate truth in constructing a specific thing. These caveats are the reason why he called his pattern language for towns, buildings, and construction *A Pattern Language*, with an emphasis on the word *'A'* [AIS77].

Our coverage of pattern languages for software also goes beyond Alexander's work to address the integration of alternative patterns for resolving specific problems addressed by a pattern language, the aspect of mandatory and optional pattern application, the notion and role of topology and grammar, the relationships of pattern languages with pattern sequences, and the role of names and diagrams. These extensions are complementary, not contrary, to Christopher Alexander's understanding of pattern languages.

11 A Billion Different Implementations

Like snowflakes, the human pattern is never cast twice.
We are uncommonly and marvelously intricate in
thought and action, our problems are most complex
and, too often, silently borne.

Alice Childress (1887-1948), anthropologist

This chapter explores the process side of pattern languages. So far we have seen examples of individual patterns and groups of patterns applied through narrative sequences, but this chapter gives the first coverage of how pattern languages are applied. We also show how pattern languages compare with other approaches, such as refactoring, agile development, and product-line architectures, to help improve software understanding, sustainability, and reuse.

11.1 One Size Does Not Fit All

In *Chapter 2* we showed how each stand-alone pattern can be implemented in many different ways without ever being the same twice. This observation confirmed our claim that there is no such thing as a globally applicable and universally generic reference implementation for a pattern. This statement also holds true for pattern languages, for the simple reason that they connect many different patterns, each of which can be realized in a million different ways. In fact, the solution space spawned by a pattern language is even larger than the simple sum of all solution spaces of its constituent patterns. If a stand-alone pattern has a 'million different implementations,' therefore, a pattern language can certainly be instantiated in a 'billion different ways.' Instead of arguing *that* pattern languages actually cover whole solution spaces, therefore, this section explores *why* pattern languages offer such a huge instantiation variety.

11.2 Piecemeal Growth

Pattern languages can support such a broad solution space because they 'practice' a process of *piecemeal growth* [Ale79]. In particular, by using pattern sequences, a specific solution is developed stepwise through many creative acts until it is complete and consistent in all its parts. Each individual act within the process of piecemeal growth differentiates existing space. A given design or situation in which a particular problem arises is thus gradually transformed into another design or situation in which the problem is resolved by an appropriate pattern of the applied language.

System-Oriented and Evolutionary Design

Analyzing the process of piecemeal growth reveals that it is strongly *system-oriented* and *evolutionary*. It is system-oriented because it always focuses on the *wholeness* of the subject being created. This 'whole' is then unfolded, stepwise, to develop its constituent 'parts.' In particular, each pattern that is applied is integrated into the existing partial design such that it does not violate this design's vision and key properties. Instead, it resolves the problem that arose in accordance with that vision and properties. Applying a pattern is thus structure *transforming*, but vision and property *preserving*.[18] In addition, this stepwise unfolding process avoids architectural drift, because all design activities are governed by the larger structure in which they take place [Cool02] [Cool06].

For example, our pattern language for distributed computing [POSA4] starts with the vision of a DOMAIN MODEL for the distributed software being developed. This vision then governs and guides all subsequent development steps for that software, from specifying its baseline architecture to addressing details of synchronizing threads in a concurrent implementation, and much more. Similarly, the pattern language for defining development organizations described in *Organizational Patterns of Agile Software Development* [CoHa04] first describes an overall project organization, a COMMUNITY OF TRUST, before it focuses on defining organizational details, such as the profiles of specific roles in a project. Yet another example is the pattern language for creating documents [Rüp03], which first targets the global document shape and structure before it addresses details of formatting and typesetting. Put another way, in a pattern language, 'the whole always precedes its parts' [Ale79].

The process of piecemeal growth is also evolutionary, because it supports a stepwise adaptation and refinement of the artifact or 'thing' under development based on its individual needs and requirements. Evolution is achieved through *gradual stiffening*, where developers are 'weaving a structure which starts out globally complete, but flimsy; then gradually making it stiffer but still rather flimsy; and only finally making it completely stiff and strong' [Ale79].

---

18. At a first glance this statement appears to be in contrast to Christopher Alexander's understanding, where the term *structure preserving* is used in this context [Ale79] [Ale04a]. The term *structure preserving* can be applied in gist, but it cannot be applied strictly, because each pattern transforms structure and therefore cannot be considered wholly structure preserving. What is intended by this term, however, is that although each pattern transforms some elements of a given structure, the *essence* of that previous structure remains.

Pattern languages addressing software design, for example, first suggest the application of patterns that outline a concrete and complete architecture vision for the software under construction—a structural baseline. These 'baseline' patterns, however, do not prescribe any of the finer details of the architectural vision, they just suggest one or more patterns to unfold it. Which of the offered patterns applies is not prescribed up-front—this is decided just at the moment when a particular detail is addressed. Gradual stiffening therefore allows developers to respond to the latest relevant requirements concerning the currently addressed detail or topic. This process continues recursively and iteratively until all parts and aspects of the software being developed are completely defined and refined through one or more appropriate patterns.

The process of piecemeal growth is also supported by our example pattern language for request handling:

> The core structure of a request-handling framework is defined by a COMMAND and EXPLICIT INTERFACE arrangement that can optionally be extended by a COMMAND PROCESSOR, if advanced request-handling functionality is required, and by an INTERPRETER within the COMMAND PROCESSOR, if clients issue requests via MESSAGES instead of method invocations. Several other patterns help to unfold the baseline designs that can be created with these four patterns. STRATEGY and NULL OBJECT, or, alternatively, TEMPLATE METHOD, support variations in a COMMAND PROCESSOR's request execution and housekeeping functionality. MEMENTO helps in adding single undo/redo support to a COMMAND, COLLECTIONS FOR STATES allow a COMMAND PROCESSOR to realize a multiple undo/redo mechanism. COMPOSITE extends the request handling structure to support macro commands.

All designs that can be created with the example pattern language for request handling share the same structural core: a COMMAND arrangement with an EXPLICIT INTERFACE. Other patterns progressively extend or refine this core to address additional aspects and requirements. Alternative patterns, and also alternative implementations of the applied patterns, help to create request-handling frameworks for different purposes and with different functionality. In other words, a common baseline design is gradually stiffened via piecemeal growth until it defines a complete and working request-handling framework out of the many possible alternatives.

Similarly, our pattern language for distributed computing [POSA4] supports a gradual stiffening of software architectures for distributed software systems. Specific aspects and details of the core vision underlying each distributed system are decided—that is, *stiffened*—at the latest possible time in the design process. As a result, the design of the application being developed is largely decoupled from decisions about which communication middleware platform or concurrency model to apply for specific subsystems or components.

Another example of gradual stiffening appears in the pattern story that illustrates the project management pattern language described in *Organizational Patterns of Agile Software Development* [CoHa04]. This story relates how new roles were added to a project a while after it started because some unanticipated problems arose and needed immediate attention. In other words, a new situation in the project occurred that required an adaptation of the existing project management practices, but the pattern language for project management provided the appropriate 'response' to that new situation.

Piecemeal Growth and Agile Development

The process of piecemeal growth contrasts with other general-purpose software development processes. It is not a compositional process, such as visually assembling widgets in a graphical interface builder in which pre-formed parts are combined to create a whole. Nor is it a sequential process, such as Waterfall [Boe82] and V-Model [Drö00], that aim to develop a 'master plan', a 'large-lump' design that specifies all and every detail up-front before the system under construction is actually implemented.

These general-purpose processes are appropriate for their specific purpose, specific context, and specific constraints—just so long as their limits are understood and observed. In particular, these processes do not adequately address the development of software artifacts whose concrete structure or design depends on many requirements and constraints that are uncertain or can change. They also are poorly suited for developing software artifacts whose design resolutions are mutually dependent.

The process of piecemeal growth, therefore, shares many properties with agile (software) development processes [CoHa04], such as Extreme Programming (XP) [Beck04], Scrum [SB01], or Crystal [Coc01]. For example, deferring design decisions to the 'last responsible moment' in the process forms a cornerstone of *Lean Software Development* [PP03]. Agile software development processes are also designed to ensure that a system evolves over time through STABLE INTERMEDIATE FORMS [Hen04a], rather than through functionally incomplete and unintegrated steps. Different needs and requirements for each system yield different designs and implementations.

It is important to note at this point that piecemeal growth is not tied exclusively to software development or the application of pattern languages. Rather, its practices are generally applicable for any activity of construction and design—and they actually form a pattern language of their own [CoHa04]:

> Note, perhaps surprisingly, than none of these patterns [from the piecemeal growth pattern language] ties to software development. They are applicable to any design activity that involves a group of people building something to solve a problem. They are as applicable to software services as they are to building product, to hardware development as they are to software development. They are patterns about human nature and human organizations, about the ways that people come together to solve problems.

We conclude from this discussion that agile development processes share the same foundations of piecemeal growth as pattern languages: the underlying method is iterative, incremental, and based on generalizing from experience and using feedback to guide future actions. These development processes differ from others primarily in their scope, style, and detail. Knowing that the process of piecemeal growth is 'embedded' in high quality pattern languages also creates confidence that they really help us (humans) build sustainable 'things,' such as pieces of software, development organizations [CoHa04], parts of development processes [Ker95] [Cun96], or documents [Rüp03].

11.3 Refactoring Not Excluded

Although it may be comforting to know that all pattern languages include the 'right thing to do' in theory, this does not actually ensure that developers always 'do the right thing' when applying them in practice [Hearsay02]. There are ample opportunities to overlook important considerations when documenting or applying pattern languages. For example, an important variation or detail may have been omitted in a pattern language. Alternatively, a particular design decision may seem ambiguous or contradictory in a particular application. Moreover, something in the situation may change, such as customer priorities, a platform-specific consideration, knowledge concerning a technology, or organizational structure, in ways that are not anticipated or are covered incorrectly by a pattern language.

An inappropriate problem resolution may result from selecting an inappropriate pattern, or a pattern that becomes inappropriate due to other changes, or from implementing a pattern incorrectly. At best, only a small, localized portion of a system's implementation may be affected. At worst, the entire baseline architecture of the system being developed must change.

When developing software, a mismatch between the current design and the preferred design provides an opportunity for *refactoring* [Opd92] [FBBOR99], which involves rewriting a part of a program to improve its structure or readability while preserving its meaning. When applying a pattern language, refactoring involves identifying a misfit pattern and backtracking, so that within the pattern applied prior to selecting the 'wrong' pattern, an alternative is chosen instead. This refactoring process creates—in part—a different path through the pattern language and therefore a different, hopefully more appropriate pattern sequence, according to which the software design can be refactored to meet its requirements.

The following example illustrates such a need for refactoring:

In *Chapter 9* we illustrated that the pattern sequence ⟨COMMAND, EXPLICIT INTERFACE, COMMAND PROCESSOR, COLLECTIONS FOR STATES, MEMENTO, TEMPLATE METHOD, COMPOSITE⟩ creates a flexible framework for request handling. One flexibility point in this framework design is realized by TEMPLATE METHOD. The pattern supports configurability of the command processor with different policies for varying algorithms, such as scheduling and logging.

The class diagram below outlines this solution.

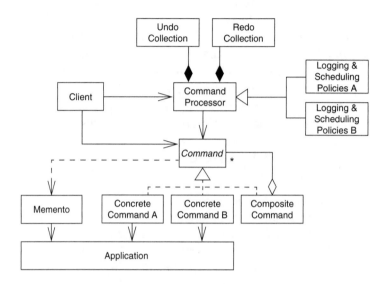

This solution works fine as long as none of the concrete policy classes derived from the command processor class share any hook method implementations with other policy classes. If this is not the case, there will be a maintenance and evolution cost to pay. For example, two policy classes could vary in their logging policies but support the same scheduling policy. Capturing this situation with TEMPLATE METHOD requires that the two policy classes share the same scheduling policy *implementation*. If the implementation of this scheduling policy evolves, two classes must be adapted, which is not only tedious but also error prone. First, all classes that need adaptation must be identified, then all classes must be changed in the same way. The more classes that share hook method implementations, the more this situation becomes a problem.

To avoid this problem, we could refactor the design of our request-handling framework by choosing a different solution for realizing adaptable command processor behavior than TEMPLATE METHOD. And in fact, the COMMAND PROCESSOR pattern description suggests two potential alternatives for this purpose: INTERCEPTOR and STRATEGY [POSA4]. Selecting STRATEGY instead of TEMPLATE METHOD results in a partly different pattern sequence than the one with which we started: ⟨COMMAND, EXPLICIT INTERFACE, MEMENTO, COM-POSITE, COMMAND PROCESSOR, COLLECTIONS FOR STATES, STRATEGY, NULL OBJECT⟩. Applying this 'refactored' pattern sequence creates the following design for our request-handling framework:

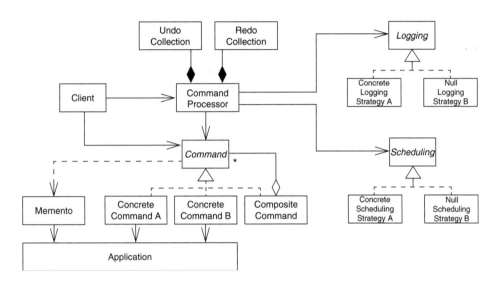

In this design, logging and scheduling policies are realized as pluggable types via concrete strategy classes, so that a specific instance of the request-handling framework can be configured with the particular policies it needs. Each concrete logging and scheduling policy is realized only once, thus the maintenance and evolution problem caused by applying TEMPLATE METHOD cannot occur. As a consequence, the refactored design meets the flexibility requirements for our request-handling framework better than the first design.

To conclude the discussion, any path through a pattern language results in a strictly ordered sequence in which to apply the patterns of the path. This ordering, however, does not imply a strict waterfall development process in which a concrete design or implementation, once specified, is never re-examined. If any part of a given pattern sequence proves inappropriate, it should be replaced with a more appropriate alternative: refactoring is the mechanism to move from one path—and thus one design—to another [Ker04].

Choosing an inappropriate pattern or pattern sequence from a pattern language is only one of several situations in which refactoring can offer help. Another situation was identified nicely by our first experiment in *Chapter 4, Pattern Islands?*. Here the right patterns for the job had been chosen, but their roles had not been properly integrated as a whole within the design. Refactoring the 'smelly' parts of such a design to regain the desired aromatic quality is the response that can lead to the result shown in our second experiment in *Chapter 4*.

Refactoring is thus an inevitable part of the process of piecemeal growth and, therefore, of creating and applying pattern languages for software design. This process acknowledges that humans learn through experience and feedback, can make mistakes, and that the devil is always in the details. All three factors make it impossible to guarantee the selection and correct implementation of the 'right' pattern sequence up front. Refactoring is therefore both the safety net that helps in such situations and the lubricant of change in supporting piecemeal growth.

11.4 One Pattern at a Time

Another reason that pattern languages support a broad design space is rooted in the 'mechanics' through which their patterns are applied. Most importantly, pattern languages are structured to support and encourage the application of *one pattern at a time*, in the order defined by the pattern sequences that result from the chosen paths through the language. This guideline ensures that the core property of piecemeal growth is preserved: the 'whole' always precedes its 'parts.' Each pattern that is applied differentiates and unfolds the architecture, design, structure, or implementation 'produced' by the patterns that come earlier in the sequence, one by one.

Clear Focus on the Problem at Hand

There is a sound rationale for applying only one pattern at a time: at any one time, all the focus should be on resolving the particular problem that the applied pattern addresses, a problem that obviously is present in the concrete context of realizing an instance of the language's subject. This problem should be resolved well and appropriately under a given set of forces. Applying multiple patterns at the same time, however, could require us to pay too much attention to their combination and integration with one another, rather than to resolving the problem at hand. This shift of focus is particularly undesirable when the problem to resolve is new or unknown, or its proper solution is critical for the success of the software being developed.

Applying one pattern at a time keeps our focus on the problem we are addressing—there is no distraction from it, even if we already know what other patterns will be applied as well. Only in the cases in which we have resolved a larger problem several times before, or can find a pattern compound that addresses the problem, should we take larger strides in confidence, applying multiple patterns at once. If we find our strides are too large for comfort, we can adjust our pace and take smaller steps to regain confidence in what we are building.

Priority-Driven Design Decisions

Another reason to apply just one pattern at a time is that users of a pattern language are encouraged to take explicit decisions about which problems are more important than others. Each design, structure, or implementation created by a pattern constrains and limits the solution space for the patterns applied thereafter. Applying multiple patterns at the same time therefore implies confusion or indecision over which problem is the most important to address next. Even if several problems are interrelated and their solutions thus overlap, the most important problem should be resolved first, and its solution should govern the solutions of subsequent problems. Otherwise there is a tendency to resolve too many issues simultaneously, which can lose sight of the 'whole' architectural vision.

The rule of applying one pattern at a time holds even if a pattern needs more patterns to help implement its solution. It may be tempting to apply these 'smaller' patterns together with the 'larger' pattern so as to slay many problems with a single stroke. Before we actually see how the larger pattern is integrated with the design being applied, however, it is hard to know whether it is appropriate to apply all, some, or none of the smaller patterns. Similarly, if the original pattern suggests several alternative patterns to resolve a sub-problem, it is hard to know which alternative to select before knowing what concrete forces drive this selection.

Without a holistic view of the design it is therefore likely that we will chose an inappropriate solution for the problem at hand—and thus fail to resolve it well. Only when we see how the roles of a pattern are arranged can we decide which of the suggested smaller patterns to use for its refinement or which alternative of a given set of patterns to chose. Again, applying one pattern at a time avoids being a jack of all trades but master of none.

Pattern Integration Precedes Pattern Implementation

The rule of applying one pattern at a time does not, however, necessitate that a pattern must always be fully implemented or completed before we can apply the next pattern. In many situations such an interpretation of this rule is not even useful!

For example, it is often more productive and reasonable to first integrate a set of patterns into a (partially) complete design or structure that is a useful and self-contained 'whole,' and to implement this design or structure after it becomes stable. In other words, the *design* of an artifact, such as the design of a software component or part of a software development organization, is created by applying one pattern at a time. In contrast, the *implementation* of this artifact can often be realized in one step. Such an approach minimizes the need to change or refactor implementation aspects of a pattern whenever we integrate a new pattern into a (partial) solution. It also allows us to reason and reflect about a design as a whole before we start to address its realization.

Another example where it might not be useful to complete a pattern before the next pattern is applied is the realization of a pattern that references multiple other patterns, some that are mandatory and some that are optional. To get a better feeling of what optional patterns to apply, it may instead be useful to integrate and realize the mandatory referenced patterns first, leaving the 'larger' pattern incomplete until its core parts are sound and solid. Nevertheless, such a procedure still complies with the guideline of applying one pattern at a time. In particular, when realizing a 'larger' pattern we initially follow a 'depth-first' approach to realize the specific patterns that define its core parts, and then a 'breadth-first' approach to complete its implementation by applying patterns that address selected optional aspects.

11.5 Role-Based Pattern Integration

As noted in *Section 11.2, Piecemeal Growth*, applying a pattern of a pattern language transforms an existing (partial) structure in which a specific problem occurs into a structure in which this problem is resolved. This resolution should preserve the vision and core properties of the original structure, as well as address the forces of the current problem. To achieve this transformation smoothly, patterns in pattern languages cannot be treated as self-contained modules that are plugged wholesale into designs. Such an approach would yield an incoherent and inconsistent patchwork of artifacts with no clear vision, inner coherence, or consistency—whether these artifacts are software, organizations, project management practices, or other 'things.' Instead the development process associated with a pattern language should ensure that patterns are integrated with the system's overall structure and design based on the specific roles that they introduce.

Option 1: Identify and Keep Already Implemented Roles

When applying a pattern of a pattern language, we recommend first identifying whether elements in the existing structure or design already provide (some of) the roles introduced by the pattern. If so—and if the pattern does not prescribe implementing these roles separately—then let these existing elements keep their roles and extend them with the missing role parts defined by the pattern.

The following example illustrates this type of situation in our pattern language for request handling:

> The COMMAND PROCESSOR pattern introduces a role, the command processor, that is responsible for executing COMMAND objects on behalf of clients, for example by using a specific scheduling algorithm.

If this algorithm can differ across concrete COMMAND PROCESSOR instances, STRATEGY can be applied to realize this variability. STRATEGY introduces three roles: context, strategy interface, and concrete strategy.

In terms of STRATEGY, however, the COMMAND PROCESSOR already plays the context role. Applying STRATEGY therefore involves refactoring the existing COMMAND PROCESSOR design so that it can be configured with different concrete strategies for different scheduling algorithms.

The following diagrams illustrate this situation:

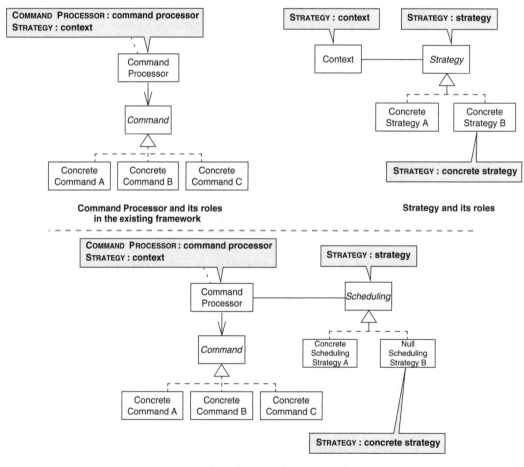

**Command Processor and its roles
in the existing framework**

Strategy and its roles

**Strategy integrated with Command Processor
in the evolved framework**

Option 2: Identify and Separate Already Implemented Roles

If, on the other hand, an element of the existing solution already realizes one or more roles introduced by the pattern, but the pattern prescribes implementing these roles separately from each other, refactor the existing solution accordingly:

COMMAND objects can offer a simple undo/redo mechanism, which requires them to capture a snapshot of the application's state before executing a request, and to restore this state in the application when their undo method is called. Implementing the undo/redo data structures directly within the COMMAND objects, however, would tightly couple them with the application on which they are executing. In particular, changes in the application's data structures would require corresponding changes in the COMMAND objects. The COMMAND pattern, therefore, suggests splitting its functionality into two parts: one part to realize the request execution functionality, and a separate MEMENTO to capture and maintain application-specific data.

The diagrams below illustrate this situation:

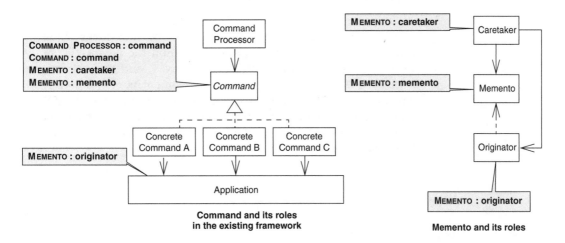

**Command and its roles
in the existing framework**

Memento and its roles

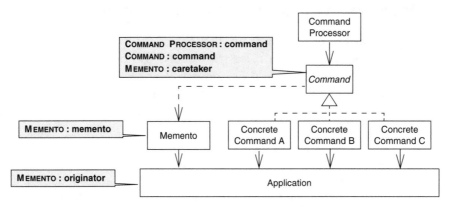

**Memento integrated with Command
in the evolved framework**

Option 3: Assign Missing Roles to Existing Design Elements

If the pattern introduces roles that are not yet realized by the existing solution, assign those of its roles that complement the roles of existing elements in that solution to the respective elements:

To support macro commands, a COMMAND arrangement can be realized as a COMPOSITE structure. COMPOSITE introduces three roles: component, composite, and leaf. From the perspective of COMPOSITE, the command objects are leaves, and their shared EXPLICIT INTERFACE is a component. The composite role, however, is not present in the COMMAND design. Yet to provide a meaningful macro command structure, one concrete command is extended with the responsibilities of the composite role specified by the COMPOSITE pattern.

The diagram illustrates this case:

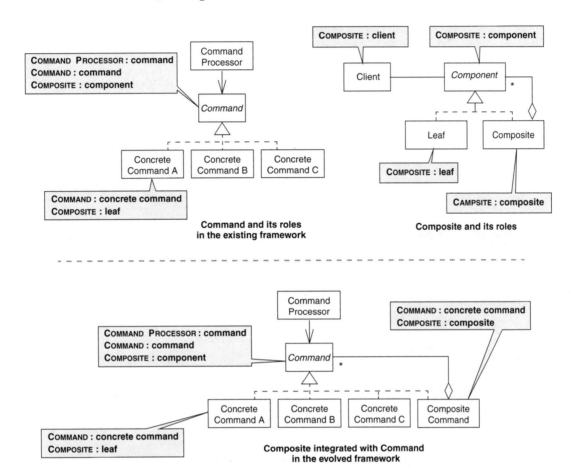

**Command and its roles
in the existing framework**

Composite and its roles

**Composite integrated with Command
in the evolved framework**

Option 4: Implement Missing Roles as New Design Elements

Finally, the roles of a pattern that, according to its description, *must be* implemented separately are integrated into an existing solution by evolving it with corresponding new elements:

The command processor role introduced by the COMMAND PROCESSOR pattern serves as a central entity for executing COMMANDs on behalf of clients, providing advanced request-handling functionality such as multiple undo/redo, scheduling, and command histories. When integrating COMMAND PROCESSOR into an existing COMMAND arrangement, the command processor role must be implemented as a separate entity, because otherwise it cannot fulfill its responsibilities effectively. This design is shown in the diagram below:

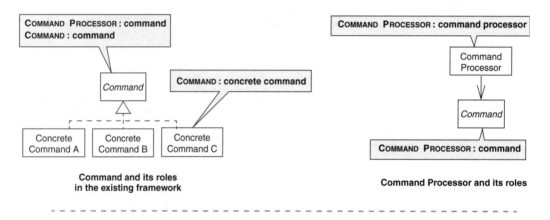

Command and its roles in the existing framework

Command Processor and its roles

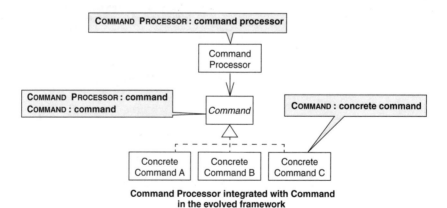

Command Processor integrated with Command in the evolved framework

Role-Based Pattern Integration and Piecemeal Growth

Following the principle of a role-based integration of patterns into a concrete design or solution helps to support successful pattern-based (software) development using the process of piecemeal growth. It also leads naturally to pattern realizations that are tailored toward the needs of the larger design, implementation, structure, or configuration of elements in which they are contained. Such realizations can thus address forces that are not yet resolved, complete or extend software to fill in missing features, and reinforce and balance the vision and properties of a software architecture [HaKo04].

As an example, recall the two designs we created in the experiment from *Chapter 4, Pattern Islands?* Transforming the first version of the request-handling framework—modular but unbalanced—to the second version—integrated and balanced—was only possible because our example pattern language for request handling supported the role-based integrations discussed earlier. Similarly, the original project management set-up outlined in the pattern story used to illustrate the project management pattern language in *Organizational Patterns of Agile Software Development* could only be extended and refactored because the pattern language integrated its constituent patterns tightly based on their roles [CoHa04].

11.6 Pattern Languages and Reference Architectures

A question that arises in the study of pattern languages for software design is whether or not they can 'produce' or 'characterize' *reference architectures* for their subject. Jazayeri, Ra, and van der Linden define the notion of reference architecture as follows [JRV00]:

> A reference architecture is the collection of concepts and patterns of structure and texture that allow the systems conforming to the same reference architecture to interoperate and to be managed by the same tools and procedures.

For example, our pattern language for distributed computing [POSA4] can be used to characterize the key design artifacts in the OMG's reference architecture for a CORBA Object Request Broker (ORB). Similarly, it can characterize the architectures of other middleware, such as .NET and J2EE [Stal03]. It can also create concrete 'instances' of a given reference architecture, such as the design of the TAO CORBA-compliant ORB [SC99] [POSA4].

Whether a pattern language is used to create a reference architecture or a project-specific architecture depends on the intent and the concrete requirements being satisfied. For example, an architect in a particular organization and situation may intend to create a reference architecture to form the basis for all concrete systems of that type or domain. Applying a suitable pattern language can help create this reference architecture, subject to other development forces and considerations. Other organizations can apply the same pattern language to realize different reference architectures for their systems. Conversely, if an architect intends to specify a concrete instantiation of a reference architecture, applying the pattern language can also help create that concrete instantiation. Finally, if an architect intends to create an architecture tailored for a specific project, applying the pattern language can once again result in this custom architecture.

The reason why pattern languages do not always provide a, or *the*, reference architecture for their respective domains is that they cover a *solution space*. In contrast, a particular reference architecture may cover just a specific *solution niche*. Of course, covering a solution space often includes covering multiple solution niches, and thus has the potential to create multiple reference architectures. As with standards, the good thing about architectures that emerge from pattern languages is that there are so many to choose from!

In conclusion, pattern languages are not blueprints that detail the design of one specific (reference) architecture. They provide a generative process to create a billion different software architectures, with each software architecture being 'tuned' to meet the particular requirements of the system it is built to serve.

11.7 Pattern Languages and Product-Line Architectures

Many researchers and practitioners from the software engineering community have noted that pattern languages help to create *product-line architectures* [Bosch00] [Coc97] [Bus03a] [Bus03b] [POSA4]. Bosch defines product-line architecture as follows [Bosch00]:

> A product-line architecture is a software architecture that serves as a common basis for a whole family of related software products.

In general, a product-line architecture consists of a stable baseline that captures the commonalities across all members of the product family, and a set of adaptable and configurable design parts hooked into the common baseline to capture their variabilities [Bus03b]. An instance of a product-line architecture for a specific member of the product family is defined by selecting concrete configuration and adaptation options for each variable design part.

Our pattern language for distributed computing [POSA4] is an example of a pattern language for creating product-line architectures. It provided, for example, the conceptual foundation for the product-line architecture used in a warehouse management process control system that supports different types, sizes, and organizational forms of warehouses [Bus03b]. The language also guided the product-line architecture for the TAO CORBA-compliant ORB, which can be configured [SC99] to support a broad range of deployment and quality-of-service scenarios for distributed real-time and embedded systems, including—but not limited to—the warehouse management process control system.

The following diagram and discussion from POSA4 provides an overview of the baseline architecture for TAO's server-side ORB Core.

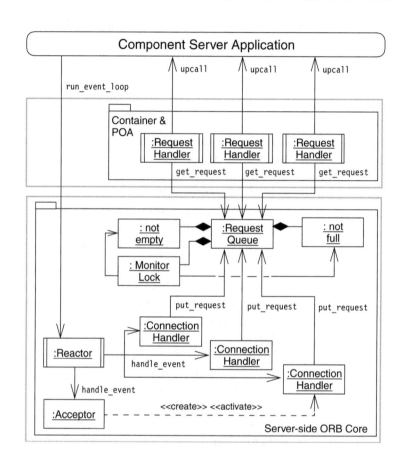

A key design goal for TAO's architecture was to address all issues necessary for communication middleware to support distributed real-time and embedded systems, including concurrency, synchronization, transports, fault tolerance, request and event demultiplexing, and (de)marshaling, in a coherent and robust manner, while also ensuring that the ORB was configurable, extensible, adaptable, and portable. TAO's architecture thus balanced the need to support stringent operational qualities with the need to support a broad range of customer and application requirements. Balancing these needs is a common theme in defining product-line architectures [Bus03a].

The pattern sequence that helped design TAO's server-side ORB Core is listed in the following table:

No.	Pattern	Challenges
1	BROKER	Defining the ORB s base-line architecture
2	LAYERS	Structuring ORB internal design to enable reuse and clean separation of concerns
3	WRAPPER FACADE	Encapsulating low-level system functions to enhance portability
4	REACTOR	Demultiplexing ORB Core events effectively
5	ACCEPTOR-CONNECTOR	Managing ORB connections effectively
6	HALF-SYNC/HALF-ASYNC	Enhancing ORB scalability by processing requests concurrently
7	MONITOR OBJECT	Efficiently synchronizing the HALF-SYNC/HALF-ASYNC request queue
8	STRATEGY	Interchanging internal ORB mechanisms transparently
9	ABSTRACT FACTORY	Consolidating ORB mechanisms into groups of semantically compatible strategies
10	COMPONENT CONFIGURATOR	Configuring consolidated ORB strategies dynamically

The first two patterns in this pattern sequence, BROKER and LAYERS, define the core structure for our CORBA-based ORB. BROKER separates application functionality from communication middleware functionality, whereas LAYERS separates different communication middleware services according to their level of abstraction. The third pattern, WRAPPER FACADE, helps to structure the lowest layer in the ORB's design—the OS Abstraction Layer—into modular and independently reusable building blocks.

Patterns three through seven in the sequence focus on the server-side ORB Core layer. REACTOR provides a demultiplexing and dispatching infrastructure that is independent of low-level demultiplexing mechanisms such as WaitForMultipleObjects and select, and can be extended easily to handle different event handling strategies. ACCEPTOR-CONNECTOR builds on REACTOR by introducing specialized event handlers for initiating and accepting network connection events, thereby separating connection establishment from communication in TAO's ORB Core. HALF-SYNC/HALF-ASYNC and MONITOR OBJECT augment REACTOR so that client requests can be processed concurrently, thereby improving TAO's server-side ORB scalability.

The final three patterns in the sequence address configurability within a common design framework, and thus support the essential capabilities needed to define a product-line architecture. STRATEGY is used wherever variability is possible in the ORB, such as alternative connection management, transport, concurrency, synchronization, and event/request demultiplexing mechanisms. To configure the ORB with a specific set of semantically compatible strategies, the client- and server-side ORB implementations use an ABSTRACT FACTORY. These two patterns work together to create variants of the ORB that are customized to meet the needs of particular users and application scenarios. COMPONENT CONFIGURATOR is used to orchestrate the (re)configuration of strategies and factories in the TAO ORB without modifying existing code, recompiling or statically relinking existing code, or terminating and restarting an existing ORB and its application component instances.

Although the TAO ORB was explicitly designed as a pattern-oriented product-line architecture, the result of applying a pattern language is not always a product-line architecture. In fact, most architectures or architectural features that are based on a pattern language—whether intentionally and explicitly or unconsciously and retrospectively—are *not* product-line architectures. Pattern languages help developers create architectures, but there is no inherent requirement that the results are *product-line* architectures: some are classic object-oriented frameworks, others are just one-off system designs.

If TAO were redesigned to restrict the application of specific patterns that enable flexibility, such as STRATEGY, ABSTRACT FACTORY, and COMPONENT CONFIGURATOR, the result would still be a design for communication middleware, but it would not be a product-line architecture. For example, some domains, such as deeply embedded systems, often only require a narrow set of variations and configurations. Restricting TAO's flexibility would be the right thing to do in these domains, and in full accord with the pattern language. Of course TAO's ability to create different configurations of the ORB would then be more limited in terms of its set of supported domains, the behavior of specific functions in this set, and its ability to support diverse operational requirements.[19]

The reason that pattern languages are not identical with product-line architectures is similar to the reason that pattern languages are not equivalent to, and do not prescribe, reference architectures. In particular, pattern languages cover a solution space for systems of a specific domain, and provide a generative process for creating specific solutions in that space. Pattern languages, however, specify neither one particular solution, such as a custom architecture, nor (just) a particular subset of this solution space, such as a product-line architectures.

Depending on the requirements and forces for a specific software system or software development project, applying a pattern language could create a product-line architecture or an application-specific architecture. Under different sets of requirements and forces, a pattern language can also inform the creation of more than one product-line architecture, with each product-line architecture being born of the language, but not an identical twin of any sibling. Similarly, a pattern language can inform the creation of more than one application-specific architecture, each of which is quite suitable for the role it was intended to fill.

Nevertheless, pattern languages *are* a powerful design tool for specifying sustainable product-line architectures, because their pattern networks explicitly capture the commonalities, variabilities, and design trade-offs in a given domain, as we discussed in *Chapter 10*. As the examples presented above indicate, many successful product-line architectures are created with the help of pattern languages. Pattern languages are thus a key enabler of product-line architectures, but the two concepts are complementary, not identical.

---

19. Advances in automated context-specific middleware specialization tools have made it possible to support product-line architectures whose variabilities can be customized offline [KGSHR06]. This approach helps to resolve the tension between the *generality* of standards-based middleware platforms, which benefit from commodity architectures designed to satisfy a broad range of application requirements, and *application-specific product variants*, which benefit from highly-optimized, custom middleware implementations. To resolve this tension, combining pattern languages and automated tools helps to retain the portability and interoperability afforded by standard middleware.

11.8 A Billion and One... and then Some

This chapter describes how the process of piecemeal growth embedded within each pattern language supports a stepwise, system-oriented, and evolutionary development of concrete designs and solutions for specific domains. We have also seen that the various paths through a pattern language open up a realization space for these designs and solutions that multiplies the solution spaces of its constituent patterns by an order of magnitude and more.

Consequently, pattern languages are not blueprints or reference architectures that work out of the box or after configuring a handful of parameters. Instead they encourage their users to *think* about the designs and solutions they want to create and to take *explicit, reasoned,* and *thoughtful* design decisions with every step in the process of their design. The goal of a pattern language is to support the development of an appropriate and sustainable solution for the situation at hand, not simply *a* solution. Quoting Dick Gabriel from his foreword to this book reinforces this perspective:

> Design is the thinking one does before building.

Although we agree with this statement, not all design work must be done from scratch, be novel and innovative, or be performed as a purely creative and generative act to make it useful for production software systems. There are many valid and reasonable ways to design a specific software system or organizational structure, as well as many ways to organize a (development) project or a system's code. In practice, however, some solutions recur more often than others because they are 'good enough' to serve the needs of many situations or users.

Capturing these recurring solutions into reusable reference and product-line architectures is the natural response to this observation. Pattern languages, therefore, support the creation of reference and product-line architectures, and thus help to limit the billions of potential solutions for a system to the few that are usable for many. Speaking in terms of 'thinking before building:' pattern languages encourage experienced designers and developers to think hard about the commonalities and variabilities of different solutions in specific domains, and to take explicit design decisions to capture their insights and lessons learned from this analysis into reference and product-line architectures.

If, however, these shrink-wrapped solutions do not work for you or in a given situation or context, pattern languages help you build a custom solution. In such a situation, it is the process of piecemeal growth that guides you systematically—and with your system and its specific requirements in permanent focus—through the almost infinite solution space that each pattern language can spawn.

12 Notes on Pattern Language Form

The notes I handle no better than many pianists.
But the pauses between the notes—ah, that is
where the art resides.

Artur Schnabel

Documenting pattern languages is not simply a case of documenting their individual patterns and collecting them together. Other considerations are needed to help communicate the vision and the detail of the language to readers. This chapter extends our discussion of form by considering the form of whole pattern languages.

12.1 Style and Substance

Chapter 3, Notes on Pattern Form, discusses how presentation is far from being a secondary detail in a pattern, which needs proper communication to fulfill its promise. The vehicle for this communication is a pattern's concrete, written form. It should be no surprise that form is also important in pattern languages, which consist of a whole network of tightly integrated patterns. Appropriate form is therefore even more crucial for communicating a pattern language. In general, our discussions on form for both stand-alone patterns and pattern compounds also hold for pattern languages. There are some additional issues to consider, however, regarding the elements and details of form in pattern languages, as we discuss below.

12.2 The Function of Form

There is little difference between patterns and pattern languages with respect to the function of form: the aesthetic and stylistic preferences of an author must be balanced with a language's technical message and the expectations of the target audience. All three 'parameters' of this 'formula' can vary, so as usual we conclude that no single form is suitable for all authors, pattern languages, and audiences. Despite their potential variations, however, all pattern language forms share a common theme, which is reflecting the general intent of pattern languages [BeCu87]:

> A pattern language guides a designer by providing workable solutions to all of the problems known to arise in the course of design. It is a sequence of bits of knowledge written in a style and arranged in an order which leads a designer to ask (and answer) the right questions at the right time. Alexander encodes these bits of knowledge in written patterns, each sharing the same structure. Each has a statement of a problem, a summary of circumstances creating the problem and, most important, a solution that works in those circumstances. A pattern language collects the patterns for a complete structure, a residential building for example, or an

interactive computer program. Within a pattern language, patterns connect to other patterns where decisions made in one influence the others. A written pattern includes these connections as prologue and epilogue. Alexander has shown that nontrivial languages can be organized without cycles in their influence and that this allows the design process to proceed without any need for reversing prior decisions [AIS77].

Questions of Form

The characterization of the purpose and structure of pattern languages above leads directly to a set of questions that a pattern language author must address. Ultimately, authors need to ensure the appropriate breadth and depth of technical content, and frame that content in a form suitable for the intended audience(s) of their pattern languages.

We addressed and summarized these questions for the individual patterns that make up a pattern language in *Section 3.2, The Function of Form*. Additional questions arise in the context of connecting the patterns within a language. The goals of these questions are to guide users to select appropriate pattern sequences from the language to support the construction or refactoring of specific designs, and to lead designers to 'ask (and answer) the right questions at the right time,' as noted in the quote above.

For example, at the level of the whole pattern language we can ask the following general questions that help us to understand its purpose:

- What is the specific domain that the language addresses?

- What are the key forces that arise in that domain?

- What are the different problem areas that are relevant in that domain?

At the level of connecting patterns in the language, we can ask more detailed questions that provide concrete design guidance, such as:

- Where does the language begin?

- What are the paths through the language?

- Where do paths branch and when to choose which branch?

Finally, at the level of the language's constituent patterns we can ask questions about the position of each pattern in the language, such as:

- What other patterns help in the realization of a specific pattern in the language?

- In the implementations of which other patterns is it, or can it be, used?

- Where in the realization process of a specific pattern in the language are decisions made that lead to other patterns in the language?

Authors of effective pattern languages must answer these questions precisely and unambiguously. At any point in the language the language's audience should know: where am I, what can I do here, where did I come from, and where can I go to?

No single pattern language form can address all these questions equally well for all audiences. Following a note we made in *Section 3.2, The Function of Form*: the healthy diversity of pattern language forms allows authors to exercise their own judgement with presentation form, while retaining some grounding and familiarity with other pattern languages in the literature.

12.3 The Elements of Form

The main concern of all pattern language forms is to make the languages tangible and comprehensible. The more patterns a language contains, the more important this concern becomes. A pattern language is of little use if its audience loses the big picture in an ocean of low-level details and, when reaching its end, has forgotten what was said in the beginning. Conversely, the essential information of each individual pattern within the language must also not be lost. Balancing both concerns equally well is hard!

Presenting the Big Picture

The need for comprehensibility and a clear 'big picture' requires a pattern language form to emphasize very explicitly its purpose and scope, as well as the relationships between its constituent patterns. Addressing these aspects explicitly and appropriately is the key to understanding a pattern language as a whole and the message it communicates. Without such a clear structure there is no story to tell, no dialog to lead, no lessons to learn about the design of a specific thing or subject. Instead, the audience of the language is lost in a maze of patterns, with no easy way in, no safe way through, and no clear way out: the language's message gets lost.

There are typically three acts to presenting the big picture of a pattern language, the first of which is its name. The name of a pattern language should clearly state what it is about and convey what can be done with the language, what is it good for, and what does it build? For instance, BATCH METHOD could be part both of a pattern language for API design and of a language for distributed computing.

The name of a pattern language also gives hints about the language's scope. For example, a pattern language for interface design has a much smaller scope than a pattern language for distributed computing. If a potential reader or user gets no hint about the *purpose* or *domain* of a pattern language, the motivation to read or use it decreases drastically. Many valuable pattern languages got lost or forgotten because their name did not provide this information, as evidenced by the fate of the *Caterpillar's Fate* pattern language we discussed in *Section 10.9, Domain-Oriented Names Help to Recall Pattern Languages*.

The second act in presenting the big picture of a pattern language provides a more detailed description of its domain, including an overview of the general forces that arise in that domain. This overview provides more information about the scope of a pattern language. For example, what specific areas or flavors of the domain are covered, and what are the key requirements, constraints, and desirable properties that drive the concrete designs supported by the language.

The third act in presenting the big picture of a pattern language is an overview of its content. This overview summarizes the patterns that it contains and how these patterns relate to one another. Often the patterns are outlined as thumbnails, as discussed in *Section 3.5, Aerial*

View, while diagrams depict the key relationships between them. The content overview also provides potential users with hints about the solutions they can expect from the pattern language, and what specific designs and solutions it helps to create.

Like individual patterns, pattern languages are empirical in nature. Using one or more examples to illustrate selected solutions supported by a pattern language can therefore complement the more general and conceptual description of its domain, scope, and content, and provide easy access to its use and understanding.

Brevity and Detail

The constraint for brevity naturally requires an author to provide only essential information about each pattern in a language. As explored in *Chapter 3*, this information typically includes a pattern's name, context, the core problem arising in that context, the main forces to be balanced when resolving the problem, the problem's core solution, and the consequences of this solution—in particular, how it addresses the forces. Lengthy solution descriptions or detailed implementation hints are typically omitted or relegated to appendices or references to other publications, since this information can distract readers from a language's primary message.

For example, we could provide the following more compressed version of BATCH METHOD for the purpose of integration into a pattern language, in contrast to the lengthier and more detailed description in *Section 3.2, The Function of Form* [POSA4]:

Batch Method

We may need to perform bulk accesses on an aggregate component.

Clients sometimes perform bulk accesses on an aggregate component, for example to retrieve all elements in a collection that match specific properties. If access to the aggregate is expensive, for example because it is remote or concurrent, accessing it separately for each element can incur significant performance penalties and concurrency overhead.

If the aggregate is remote, each access incurs latency and jitter, decreases the available network bandwidth, and introduces additional points of failure. If the aggregate is a concurrent component, synchronization and thread management overhead must be added to the cost of each access. Similarly, any other per-call housekeeping code, such as for authorization, further decreases performance. Nevertheless, it must be possible to perform bulk accesses to an aggregate efficiently and without interruption.

Therefore:

Define a single batch method that performs the action on the aggregate repeatedly. The method is declared to take all the arguments for each execution of the action, for example via an array or a collection, and to return results by similar means.

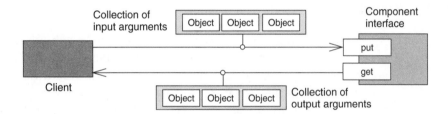

A batch method folds repetition into a data structure, rather than a loop within the client, so that looping is performed before or after the method call, in preparation or follow-up respectively.

A BATCH METHOD reduces the cost of accessing the aggregate to a single access or a few 'chunked' accesses. In distributed systems this can significantly improve performance, incur less network errors, and save precious bandwidth. Although by using a BATCH METHOD each access to the aggregate becomes more expensive, the overall cost for bulk accesses has been reduced. Bulk accesses can also be synchronized as appropriate within the method call.

This version of BATCH METHOD provides, in its essence, the same information about the pattern as the longer version from *Section 3.2, The Function of Form*. We know when we can consider its application, what problem is addressed and its associated forces, what the key aspects of the solution and its construction are, and the pattern's consequences. On the other hand, this abbreviated version omits concrete implementation hints, and summarizes context, problem, forces, solution, and consequences into short and concise paragraphs rather than providing detailed discussions and explorations of these aspects.

A small pattern language with only a few patterns could theoretically afford more detailed pattern descriptions. Pattern language authors, however, typically refrain from providing too much information, favoring short descriptions over longer pieces. When reading about more than a single pattern at once, there is a danger that readers could become confused about the language's intent: does it thread systematically through a domain, or is it just a bag of loosely related design gems and programming pearls? A pattern language should leave no doubt about having the first intent, thereby putting all design gems and programming pearls into their appropriate context, so that they serve a precise and practical purpose.

Pattern Connections

Successfully applying a pattern language in production software projects requires explicit enumeration and discussion of the inbound and outbound pattern connections for each of its constituent patterns. The context of a pattern in a pattern language is not only defined by the specific situation that gives rise to the problem it addresses, but also by all patterns in the language where this problem can arise. These inbound patterns can constrain the situation-oriented context of a pattern, because within a language it is only applied *within*, or in *conjunction* with, a limited set of other patterns of the same language. As such, specific forces that could arise in a more general setting for the pattern simply do not arise in the context of the language, and thus need not be discussed or addressed.

Adding the patterns to the general, language-independent context of BATCH METHOD from above would lead to the following language-specific context if it were part of a pattern language for distributed computing [POSA4].

Batch Method

Within an EXPLICIT INTERFACE, ITERATOR, or OBJECT MANAGER...

...we may need to perform bulk accesses on an aggregate component.

Clients sometimes perform bulk accesses on an aggregate component [...]

Similarly, the realization of a pattern in a pattern language can often benefit from other patterns of that language. Language users are therefore interested in what these outbound patterns are, where they can be applied in the realization process of the pattern, what aspects or problems they address and how, and whether alternative patterns are available for any given aspect or problem. Remember, a pattern language should guide its users to ask and answer the right questions and to take concrete decisions.

Typically the potential use of other patterns of a language is addressed in the discussion part of a pattern description, as in stand-alone patterns. For example, we could add the following paragraph to the BATCH METHOD description above to connect it to other patterns in our pattern language for distributed computing [POSA4]:

> Batch methods are often specific rather than general. That is, they are named for a particular action and their arguments reflect the inputs and results directly. For example, finding values that match keys can be expressed as a single method. If more generalization is required, however, further parameters that control the encapsulated loop are needed, such as finding all entries that are older than a particular date or greater than a particular value. The broadest generalization is to pass in a predicate or some control code, in the form of a COMMAND object, which makes a BATCH METHOD more like an ENUMERATION METHOD, with similar liabilities for a distributed environment.

The discussion of outbound patterns follows the same rules for brevity as the general pattern description. The focus is on connecting the patterns of a language together, not on specific details of concrete realizations and implementations of the outbound patterns.

Reviewing the Elements

The elements of pattern language form address at least three aspects: big picture, essential pattern description, and weaving the patterns of a language together. The more these three aspects are addressed explicitly and with sufficient clarity, the more likely the pattern language will be applied successfully in production software projects.

12.4 Details, Details, Details

While authors of stand-alone patterns have a variety of literary forms to chose from, from brief sketches to detailed explorations, pattern languages are typically documented using a short pattern form. Although short forms omit many pattern details, they are ideal for documenting pattern languages. In particular, they balance the need for capturing a language's big picture along with the essential core of each constituent pattern and the inter-relationships between patterns in the language.

Pattern Language Forms

The most prominent form for describing patterns in a pattern language is Alexandrian form [AIS77]. It has all the properties outlined earlier in this section:

- The core problem and core solution of a pattern build the form's skeleton.

- The discussion of the problem's forces and the solution's implementation and consequences augment this core.

- The context and 'outgoing' pattern references place the pattern within the language.

It is therefore not surprising that many software pattern languages are written either in the original Alexandrian form or in similar forms, such as the BATCH METHOD description in this chapter. Examples include the pattern language for distributed computing [POSA4], the *Server Components* pattern language [VSW02], the *Object-Oriented Remoting* pattern language [VKZ04], and the pattern language for *Human Computer Interaction* [Bor01].

Another form suitable for describing patterns in a pattern language is the Portland form, which is used by pattern languages like *CHECKS* [Cun95] and *Caterpillar's Fate* [Ker95]. Even more popular is the Coplien form, which is used in several pattern languages presented in the first and second volume of the *Pattern Languages of Program Design* series [PLoPD1] [PLoPD2]. Other forms are also used, but typically the differences between them and either the Alexandrian or the Coplien form tend to be minor.

As form is 'just' a communication vehicle, a pattern language can also be transformed to use another form. As was the case for a stand-alone pattern, however, moving a language to a new form is not just a simple matter of copy, paste, and modify 'a little.' Instead it is a translation, because different forms typically differ in style as well as in structure. For example, the Alexandrian form is purely prose-based, whereas the Coplien form is structured into labeled parts. The Alexandrian form does not require discussion of a 'resulting context,' whereas the Coplien form does. The Portland form follows the fundamental structure of the Alexandrian form, but neither requires a context nor an explicit separation between the problem and forces, or between the solution and solution discussion.

The appropriate form for a particular pattern language depends largely on the aesthetic and stylistic preferences of an author, the language's technical message, and the expectations of its audience. *Section 3.6, Different Pattern Forms* discusses the various trade-offs that can influence the selection of a specific form for documenting the patterns of a pattern language. Ultimately, however, the form that balances all three factors best, based on an author's perspective and experience, is probably the one to use.

Aerial View

Even with the shortest pattern form—or the most number of hyperlinks—it is not easy to comprehend pattern languages in their entirety, irrespective of the number of patterns they contain. As outlined in *Section 12.3*, most pattern languages therefore include a prologue whose purpose is to present an overview of the language. This bird's-eye view helps to guide the language's audience through the language's subject, its intent, its message, its big picture, and its content. The appropriate look-and-feel of such an overview depends—like the chosen pattern form itself—on author preferences, technical content, and audience expectations, as well as on the size of the language.

For small pattern languages it is often sufficient to provide a short introduction to their domain, completed by a list of thumbnails for each pattern in the language and a diagram that shows the core relationships between them. Good examples for such introductions are provided by the pattern languages *C++ Reference Accounting* [Hen01b] and *Java Exception Handling* [Haa03], or the languages in *Organizational*

Patterns For Agile Software Development [CoHa04]. For the latter, each pattern language's overview also features a short pattern story that shows how the language could be used to shape concrete organizations and projects.

This type of introduction is not always practical for larger pattern languages. Dozens of pages of pattern thumbnails, together with diagrams showing scores of pattern relationships, do not really provide meaningful information to readers—they are more likely to turn off than switch on.

Our pattern language for distributed computing [POSA4] follows another approach. It is partitioned into several groups of patterns, with each group representing an important intention-based problem area in the context of distributed computing. The overview of the language introduces each problem area briefly, lists the corresponding patterns, and presents a diagram that illustrates the core relationships between the problem areas, as outlined below:

> Our pattern language for distributed computing includes 114 patterns, which are grouped into thirteen problem areas. Each problem area addresses a specific technical topic related to building distributed systems, and contains all the patterns in our language that address the challenges associated with that technical topic. The main intent of the problem areas is to make the language and its patterns more tangible and comprehensible: patterns that address related problems are presented and discussed within a common and clearly scoped context. The problem areas are presented (roughly) in their order of relevance and applicability when building distributed systems, and include the following:
>
> • From Mud to Structure [Brief outline of the problem area].
>
> • Distribution Infrastructure [...]
>
> • Interface Partitioning [...]
>
> • Component Partitioning [...]
>
> • Application Control [...]
>
> • Concurrency [...]
>
> • Synchronization [...]
>
> • Object Interaction [...]
>
> • Adaptation and Extension [...]

- Modal Behavior [...]
- Resource Management [...]
- Database Access [...]

All thirteen problem areas outlined above complement and complete each other in terms of various technical aspects related to building distributed systems. The major relationships that connect the problem areas are illustrated in the following diagram.

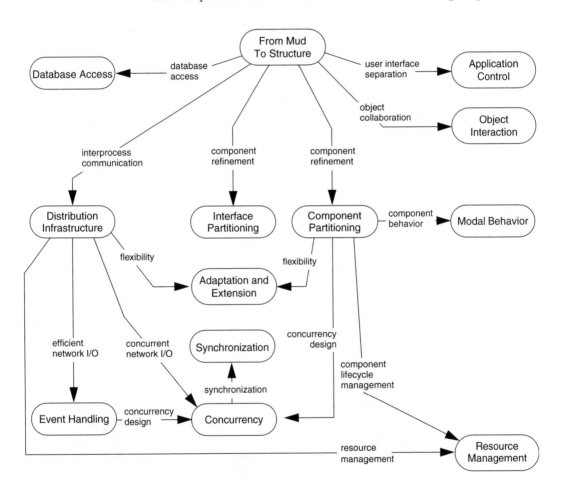

This highly compressed language overview is completed by more detailed problem area introductions, which follow the overview structure outlined above for short pattern languages. In other words, the pattern language for distributed computing uses a two-level introduction schema: a high-level overview to draw attention to the language as a whole, and several more detailed introductions to set the precise context for each problem area. Readers can thus chose how much overview information they want to bite off and digest before reading the patterns themselves. They can also chose what part of the language they want to explore in greater detail, or in what order they want to read the parts.

The following is an excerpt from the introduction to the event-handling patterns [POSA4]:

> Distributed computing is ultimately event-driven, even when middleware platforms offer applications with a more sophisticated communication model, such as request/response operations or asynchronous messaging. There are a number of challenges that differentiate event-driven software from software with a 'self-directed' flow of control:
>
> - Asynchronous arrival of events [Brief discussion of the challenge]
>
> - Simultaneous arrival of multiple events [...]
>
> - Non-deterministic arrival of events [...]
>
> - Multiple event types [...]
>
> - Hiding the complexity of event demultiplexing and dispatching [...]
>
> To master the challenges described above both elegantly and efficiently, event-driven software is often structured as a LAYERS architecture with an inverted flow of control. [...]
>
> Though a LAYERS approach decouples different concerns in event-driven software in a way that handles each concern separately, it does not explain how to resolve a particular concern optimally under a given set of forces. For example, an event-demultiplexing layer alone does not ensure efficient yet simple demultiplexing and dispatching of events to event handlers.

The four event-handling patterns in our pattern language for distributed computing help to fill this gap. They provide efficient, extensible, and reusable solutions to key event demultiplexing and dispatching problems in event-driven software:

- The REACTOR pattern [Pattern thumbnail]

- The PROACTOR pattern [...]

- The ACCEPTOR-CONNECTOR pattern [...]

- The ASYNCHRONOUS COMPLETION TOKEN pattern [...]

The following diagram illustrates how REACTOR and PROACTOR integrate into our pattern language.

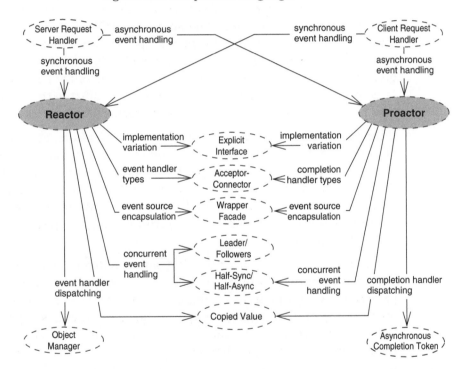

[A second diagram illustrates the integration of ACCEPTOR-CONNECTOR and ASYNCHRONOUS COMPLETION TOKEN into the pattern language for distributed computing.]

Regardless of how brief or comprehensive the introduction to a pattern language is, and regardless of how many levels of detail it contains, it must support the intended audience of the language in understanding and applying the language.

Sequence of Disclosure

The order in which the patterns of a language are presented is another important issue. An arbitrary order does not help to provide a clear story-line: the language will appear to degenerate into an ad hoc collection, losing its key message. One rule of thumb is to present the patterns in the order of their scope via a breadth-first approach, beginning with the entry patterns, recursively continuing with patterns that refine the preceding patterns, and ending with leaf patterns—those that are refined no further.

Most documented pattern languages, such as the languages in *Organizational Patterns For Agile Software Development* [CoHa04] and our pattern language for distributed computing [POSA4], order their constituent patterns according to their scope. It is not always possible, however, to organize all patterns that simply. For example, some languages have more than one entry pattern. If the entry patterns differ in scope, one possible presentation order is to start with the pattern that has the widest scope, followed by patterns with a narrower scope.

If the scope criterion is neither applicable nor feasible, an alternative is to begin with the pattern that is the easiest to access, presenting the more complex patterns thereafter. A pattern can also be used in different places in a language, having a different scope or impact at each place. In this case we could order such a pattern according to the broadest of all the scopes, the narrowest of all scopes, or the majority of all scopes.

Another rule of thumb for presenting patterns in a language is to pick one representative pattern sequence that visits all its patterns and present the patterns in the corresponding order. The more pattern sequences a pattern language supports, however, the less representative this one ordering becomes, and the more useful it is to arrange the patterns according to their scope.

Yet another approach to organizing patterns in a language is to present them with respect to criticality—strategic patterns first, followed by tactical patterns, followed by logistical patterns. This organization allows language authors to indicate clearly which patterns of their language shape the architecture or core structure of any solution, because they are presented first. The patterns that address local details of the architecture or solution are presented next, in accordance with our discussion in *Section 8.4, Organization by Level.*

In large pattern languages in which patterns are grouped into problem areas, as in our pattern language for distributed computing, the presentation could also be arranged group-wise, according to the main ordering of problem areas. Such partitioning into bite-sized language chunks ensures that patterns that address related problems are always presented together, which simplifies cross-referencing of alternative solutions and reduces reading ahead and section skipping. Within each problem area, the patterns could be arranged either according to their scope, the degrees to which they are strategic or tactical, their order of application, etc.

As usual, the form of pattern ordering that is most appropriate for a given language depends on its audience, scope, and size, as well as the personal preferences of its authors. An effective ordering, however, should guide users of the language to select appropriate pattern sequences from it that help them shape sustainable designs and solutions for the tasks at hand.

Leading by Example

Examples are essential for showing the proper use of pattern languages. They demonstrate how the language's patterns apply and connect to build production quality systems or solutions, bridging the gap from concepts and theory to daily practice. There are a variety of choices for examples, which we summarize below.

A running example that can show the use of each pattern in the language can nicely demonstrate the interplay of the patterns: how they connect, integrate, and support each other. If a running example is chosen, there are two options for its presentation:

- Integrate it with each pattern of the language. This option has the advantage that an example of the pattern is shown immediately.

- Separate it from the language and present it in its own section. Although this option presents the big picture view of the language as a whole, it may be hard to find a running example that uses all the patterns in a language.

Most pattern languages, therefore, present one or more pattern stories in separate sections that address selected areas of the language in detail.

For example, our pattern language for distributed computing presents a large pattern story from the domain of warehouse management. This story illustrates three aspects of building a distributed system: creating the baseline architecture, designing communication middleware, and detailing a specific component of the system. Although only around one third of all patterns in the language are covered by this example, nearly all problem areas are addressed. The example is thus sufficiently complete to represent the use of the language [POSA4]. As another example, each of the four pattern languages documented in the *Organizational Patterns For Agile Software Development* [CoHa04] present a short story, no more than a page in length, that outlines their use in concrete projects and organizations.

Some pattern languages also present multiple pattern stories, which together provide a complete coverage of the patterns in the respective pattern language. For example, the *Context Encapsulation* language [Hen05b] tells three stories, one in C#, one in C++, and one in Java.

If no representative example can be found, each pattern in the language can supply its own example. While this approach allows each pattern to be illustrated effectively, it can be hard to show how the patterns support one another in the context of the entire language. An example of a pattern language with individual examples for each of its patterns is that for *User Interface Design for Searching* [Wel05].

Yet another alternative for examples is possible if a pattern language is partitioned into several problem areas. For each group of patterns, it can tell an exemplary and illustrative pattern story that involves all patterns in the group.

Ideally, all three alternatives could be used together:

- Essential issues of each pattern in a pattern language are shown with very small examples woven into their descriptions.

- Larger, separated 'focus-stories' outline aspects that affect all patterns in a problem area or pattern group.

- A separate running example relates a selected pattern story from the entire language.

Thus all patterns are shown in detail and by example, but the big picture is not forgotten. This approach also brings out the diversity possible within a pattern language, in much the same way that more than one example for a stand-alone pattern can highlight its different aspects and applications. We get a balanced coverage both of the pattern language's subject and of the different paths criss-crossing it.

Pattern languages are written to support the construction of systems that work [Mes01]. Any examples employed should therefore be realistic enough to reinforce this message. Realistic examples should either be based on production systems or distilled from such systems. A production example lends credibility, because it tells a story that really happened. Similarly, an example that distills the essence of a production system helps to draw out and emphasize the key aspects of a pattern language and its patterns, while omitting unimportant or distracting details. Purely artificial examples, in contrast, can never mimic or replace reality, and are thus less convincing in showing the usefulness of pattern languages for production software development.

In addition to being realistic, the size and complexity of examples should match with the size and complexity of the languages or patterns they explain. An overly simple example is unlikely to motivate the need for a sophisticated and interwoven pattern language, or an advanced pattern in that language. Similarly, an overly complex example requires too much attention from readers to be understood, and thus distracts from the language or pattern itself, irrespective of whether it is small or large, simple or sophisticated. A good rule of thumb is that an example should be sufficient to show the issues an author wants to explain with it, but no 'better,' because this can detract from understanding of the language and its patterns.

Managing the Level of Detail

As with discussion about examples, the question arises as to whether design-focused pattern languages should present code. Obviously pattern languages about programming, such as *Smalltalk Best Practice Patterns* [Beck96], *C++ Reference Accounting* [Hen01b], *Java Exception Handling* [Haa03], and *Context Encapsulation* [Hen05b] would not be very convincing or useful without code. How much code is presented, however, depends on a language's level of detail.

As a general heuristic, the code should explain what is described, but no more. To keep the emphasis on the language and its patterns, it may also be helpful to show only key programming issues with code, whereas minor aspects are explained only by text. If a pattern language is not about code-related practices, but instead about general design or architecture, such as our pattern language for distributed computing [POSA4], then code, or too much code, can distract from its subject. In this case, authors should insert code sparingly or not at all.

One way to limit the amount of code in a pattern language while still conveying the key programming issues is to use a notation that assigns code snippets to design-centric elements such as classes. We use this approach throughout our pattern language for distributed computing, as the following PROACTOR pattern diagram shows:

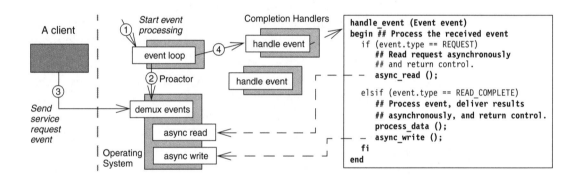

This approach allows us to present (pseudo)code where it is relevant or helpful to show a pattern's structure, complementary to showing the pattern's design structure.

The question of whether or not to present code is closely related to the broader question: how detailed should the patterns in a pattern language be? Earlier we argued that an author should present only essential information, as otherwise it is hard to balance the need for covering all important facts with the need for language comprehensibility and the communication of its big picture.

Even when an author achieves a fine balance for most readers, however, some may find that there is insufficient detail in the patterns for their taste. An author should think twice before adding more detail, however, since there is a danger of unbalancing other aspects. A better response may be to reference papers or code available on the Web that provide the missing information. This approach keeps the description of the language lean and focused while enabling readers to obtain the extra details if they need them.

Ideally, more in-depth descriptions of the patterns in a language are available that could be referenced. We took this approach for our pattern language for distributed computing in POSA4. Nearly all its constituent patterns are already documented as stand-alone patterns, mostly in very structured and detailed forms. Readers of the language who are interested in these details can therefore look them up easily and conveniently. The language complements these stand-alone descriptions with a bigger picture that binds them together. If more detailed descriptions of the patterns in a language are unavailable, referring to appropriate further reading or appendices that cover particular issues could be helpful.

Some readers may also complain about too much detail, however, even if a pattern language is described using a short form. For example, our POSA4 pattern language for distributed computing contains more than one hundred patterns, ties into several other pattern languages, and covers nearly 400 pages. The language uses a short form but is still too large to read in a single pass. An author's response to this problem should not be to remove more information from the patterns to shrink the footprint of the language, since that may make its content too shallow.

Christopher Alexander [AIS77] identified a simple yet elegant and effective way out of this dilemma, a technique that we also use in our pattern language for distributed computing: the pattern descriptions contain their own summaries. This summary consists of the core problem statement and the core solution statement, as shown in the description of BATCH METHOD on *page 330.* Both are written in bold font and thus form the essence of each pattern both visually and conceptually. Readers who just want to skim the language can start by reading the bold-face parts and only delve into detail—such as the forces associated with the problem and the explanation of the solution—where they are interested. Using this approach, even large pattern languages can be read quickly.

12.5 Style and Substance (Redux)

As with pattern descriptions, we can conclude that the form used for describing pattern languages matters both to language authors and language readers. The pattern language form defines a vehicle for presenting and communicating a message, along with a specific perspective and bias. Although the essence of a pattern language is independent of its description, the description frames how the language will be perceived, understood, and applied.

Nevertheless, all pattern language forms are only a means to convey the specific qualities of a pattern language to its intended audience. The form also establishes a dialog with the audience about the design of a specific subject, such as a software system, development organization, or residential building. Without substantive content, however, all considerations on form are meaningless. The quote from Kent Beck's and Ward Cunningham's original paper on patterns with which we opened this chapter reinforces this perspective [BeCu87]:

> A pattern language guides a designer by providing workable solutions to all of the problems known to arise in the course of design. It is a sequence of bits of knowledge written in a style and arranged in an order which leads a designer to ask (and answer) the right questions at the right time.

In a nutshell, pattern language form matters most when the language content actually describes something of substance. The best pattern languages, therefore, combine the appropriate form with good description and a whole and sound network of interwoven patterns.

13 On Patterns versus Pattern Languages

The leader has to be practical and a realist,
yet must talk the language of the visionary and the idealist.

Eric Hoffer, American social writer

This chapter compares and contrasts stand-alone patterns and pattern languages. Based on our explorations of both concepts, we summarize their commonalities and differences, and conclude that we have learnt valuable lessons of practice and theory from both concepts and their expression.

13.1 Patterns and Pattern Languages: Similarities

There are several questions that often arise when talking about patterns and pattern languages: in what ways are the two ideas similar? And in what ways do they differ? The answers to these questions help us to understand and appreciate the roles that each play in the pattern concept.

Common Core Properties

Comparing our exploration of patterns with that of pattern languages reveals that 'good' and whole patterns and pattern languages share almost all of their core properties, including their documented forms. In particular:

- Each defines a *process and a thing*. For example, in a design pattern the 'thing' is a particular design outline or code detail for a specific problem. For design-centric pattern languages, the 'thing' is the design or implementation of an entire system or a system aspect from a specific application or technical domain. For an organizational pattern, the 'thing' is a specific workflow or part of an organization. For an organizational pattern language, the 'thing' is the organization as a whole or many of its parts in concert. The process that comes along with a pattern or pattern language tells its users how to build this 'thing.'

- Each ensures that the 'thing' whose creation it supports is of *proven* and *sound quality* in its structure, behavior, and core properties.

- Each explicitly addresses the *forces* that can influence the concrete look-and-feel of the designs and the character of the environments that it helps to build.

- Each supports *genericity* by describing entire solution spaces, not (just) single point solutions.

- Each enables *communication*, *discussion*, and *dialog* about its subject to aid understanding of the nature, forces, and consequences of the solution presented.

- Each has a *concrete name* so that its audience can remember it and immediately know what subject or domain it addresses.

- Each is a *work in progress* that should constantly be updated toward new and evolved experiences and knowledge in its subject domain.

- Each can be *implemented in many different ways* without ever being 'twice the same'—dependent on the concrete requirements, constraints, and scope of the systems or environments in which it is applied.

Of course, it is not surprising that patterns and pattern languages share so many properties, since pattern languages consist of patterns! To provide their own qualities and characteristics, whole languages build upon and reinforce the properties of their constituent pattern elements.

Common Roots

Many pattern languages can be seen as elaborations and decompositions of their root patterns, which is another reason why they share such rich common ground. It is only natural that these languages build on and recursively unfold and strengthen their roots' core qualities. A prominent example of such a pattern language is *Remoting Patterns* [VKZ04], which decomposes the BROKER pattern into a fully fledged description of modern communication middleware architectures. When BROKER was described as a stand-alone pattern it could not be that expressive, but the remoting pattern language managed to reveal this generativity. Other examples are the decomposition of the Gang of Four's OBJECTS FOR STATES pattern into a state pattern language [DyAn97], and the decomposition of Allan Kelly's ENCAPSULATED CONTEXT pattern [Kel04] into a pattern language for context encapsulation [Hen05b].

The relationship between patterns and pattern languages is similar to the relationship between classes and frameworks. A class on its own is just a cohesive set of data and methods that operate on that data. It is the framework that brings the class into a more concrete and connected context, providing the whole, of which a class is a part.

Similarly, a stand-alone pattern is just a solution to a particular problem in a context, but in a pattern language it is an integral part of a larger whole.

Pattern Languages of One Pattern?

An interesting question in the context of comparing patterns and pattern language concerns cardinality. Can pattern languages of only one pattern be valid? Or does a pattern language necessarily require the presence of at least two patterns?

From a theoretical perspective there is no argument against pattern languages consisting of a single pattern. For example, we have seen that empty pattern sequences or sequences of a single pattern are possible. If a problem domain is so small that it includes only one problem, and if this problem has only one practical, recurring solution, then a pattern language for that domain would only include one pattern.

In practice, however, the real world is not that simple, regardless of what domain we analyze. We would be hard pressed even within the smallest domains to find only one possible problem of interest. Moreover, for any problem of interest, there is often more than one way to address it. Consequently, pattern languages that are useful in practice contain more than one pattern—atomic pattern languages are of more theoretical than practical interest.

Nevertheless, useful pattern languages can be small. The *CHECKS* pattern language for information integrity, for example, includes only eleven patterns [Cun95]. *Executing Around Sequences* [Hen01a] and *Context Encapsulation* [Hen05b] are even smaller: both language have only four patterns, yet they cover their constrained domains well. Smaller still is *Localized Ownership: Managing Dynamic Objects in C++* [Car96], which has only three patterns. A pattern language with just one pattern, however, has never been explicitly identified as such. Moreover, unless we promote pattern compounds from being pattern subsequences into languages, we are not aware of pattern languages with just two patterns.

In a nutshell: pattern languages of one pattern are possible in theory, but odds are stacked against them occurring in practice.

13.2 Patterns and Pattern Languages: Differences

The main differences between patterns and pattern languages lie in their scope, their emphasis, and their intent.

Patterns and Detail

Without any other considerations, an individual pattern stands alone. Each lone pattern focuses on one particular problem and its solutions, and is described more or less in isolation from other patterns and other problems. Some patterns have a larger scope and more strategic impact on a concrete design or solution than others, such as patterns typically used for structuring the baseline architecture of a system versus more localized programming-practice patterns, but still they address only a single problem. Consequently, the effect of stand-alone patterns on an overall system or situation may be rather limited, both with respect to the look-and-feel of the architecture and to its quality properties.

Since stand-alone patterns have such a narrow scope, however, they can focus on exploring solution implementation issues in full depth without becoming too broad and fuzzy. Using forms like the Gang-of-Four and POSA forms, many pattern descriptions therefore decorate and complement their essential problem–solution core with additional information about the structure and dynamics of the solution. They also provide hints for implementing the solution, use running examples to illustrate problem and solution, and discuss known uses in detail.

Stand-alone pattern descriptions often also use diagrams to show pattern details. Sometimes these diagrams use formalized notations like UML. Similarly, implementation hints are often accompanied by code fragments or other concrete construction details to show how the pattern can be realized. By providing these details, stand-alone patterns support concrete design and development activities in their respective domains. Readers should therefore not only get a synopsis of what the pattern is about, but should also be able to implement the pattern effectively in their own systems, solutions, and environments.

Pattern Languages and Interconnection

In contrast to the focused depth of stand-alone patterns, pattern languages describe how a family of patterns connect to build systems or solutions in a specific domain. Each pattern language provides a 'guided tour' through its respective domain. This domain characterizes the problems that can arise and their (alternative) solutions, the interdependencies between the problems and between the solutions, and also the order in which the problems should be resolved.

Within a pattern language, each pattern is narrower, addressing one particular problem that can arise in the domain and the context of its preceding patterns. The language as a whole ensures that this problem is not resolved in isolation, but under consideration of its surrounding problems and their solutions. Pattern languages therefore have a strong and deep impact on the architecture, design, implementation, and quality properties of a system or solution as a whole. Moreover, their scope can span the domain of software, as well as other domains, such as project management and development organizations.

Because pattern languages connect their patterns systematically and consistently, each language defines a certain architectural style or related family of styles. An architectural style usually affects the design and implementation of a system or solution at all levels of granularity, across its many forms of abstraction, and within all its parts. To achieve such a deep impact, pattern languages are documented typically in forms that focus on pattern networking, with less emphasis on pattern details than is common in stand-along patterns. These forms emphasize which pattern includes which other patterns and their ordering sequence. By providing such information, pattern languages intend to support the activity of (software) *design*. Readers should therefore obtain a thorough understanding of a particular domain and its challenges from the pattern language, and be able to use this information to portray these domains appropriately in their solutions and implementations.

Two Separate Worlds?

Some discussions and viewpoints in the software patterns community conclude that patterns achieve their (fullest) power only by being part of pattern languages. A conclusion we could draw from this perspective is that documenting stand-alone patterns is of little or no use, so authors should therefore solely focus on writing pattern languages. But is that really the case?

We do not share this perspective. We strongly believe that we need both: the documented forms of problem–solution focused stand-alone patterns *and* richer, interwoven domain focused pattern languages. Knowing and understanding a domain and the feasible structural arrangements that capture it is only one side of the coin. Any structure must also be realized for it to become concrete, but pattern language descriptions typically do not provide the necessary in-depth implementation information for their constituent patterns. Corresponding stand-alone pattern descriptions can do so, however, and the majority of such descriptions actually do. This simple insight holds for pattern languages and patterns on software design and implementation, as well for pattern languages and patterns for shaping software development and project organizations, design processes, documents, and so on.

We can also make two connected observations:

• Relatively few pattern languages have been documented. The number is increasing all the time, but they are still in a minority compared to the range of work undertaken in the name and domain of software development.

• Developers are intelligent and work best when empowered. They are able to combine many different patterns in their work. Stand-alone patterns document a broader context for their applicability that supports such combination.

Thus, although they may not provide deep advice on interconnection, stand-alone patterns leave developers free to improvise, compose, and rediscover pattern sequences that are not documented. This situation is reminiscent of the early days of object-orientation when the early adopters were still learning the skills needed to write effective reusable classes and stand-alone class libraries. It took years before the object-oriented community mastered the additional skills needed to connect groups of classes into frameworks that provided effective reusable architectures for families of related applications [John97].

13.3 Patterns versus Pattern Languages?

To summarize, we return to our original question from the beginning of *Chapter 9, Elements of Language* on how to best support a holistic approach to designing and building with patterns. Pattern languages help to define appropriate architectures and designs for systems and solutions in specific domains. Corresponding stand-alone descriptions for each applied pattern then ensure that these architectures and designs are constructed, realized, or implemented effectively and with appropriate means and measures.

In other words, the practical concept of patterns as a whole is incomplete if either ingredient is missing: the descriptive forms of stand-alone patterns and pattern languages complement one another, rather than being mutually exclusive. To set them in contradiction is, in many ways, a false dichotomy—when it comes to patterns and pattern languages, there is no 'versus.'

14 From Patterns To People

Now my understanding of what you are doing with patterns... it is a kind of a neat format, and that is fine. The pattern language that we began did have other features, and I don't know whether those have translated into your discipline. I mean, there was a root behind the whole thing—a continuous mode of preoccupation with under what circumstances is the environment good. In our field that means something.

Christopher Alexander,
keynote speech at OOPSLA 1996

People are the prime audience for patterns. From stand-alone patterns to pattern languages, patterns embody a strong human aspect, most obviously in the form of a pattern's reader, but also in other roles. This chapter investigates why patterns are so attractive for all parties who are interested in, or affected by, software. We also present the values often associated with the patterns community and the techniques used to support pattern authors in their writing.

14.1 Patterns are for People

Previous chapters mainly explored patterns from a content, property, and presentational perspective. But who is their target audience? For whom is this immense effort of identifying and documenting good patterns made? Some pioneers of the pattern community such as Christopher Alexander [Ale79] and Jim Coplien [Cope00] are quite clear about the answer to this question: patterns are for people!

This answer may appear surprising at a first glance, given the technical context in which we have presented many patterns. A closer look at the properties of patterns that we have uncovered and emphasized so far, however, supports this claim: these properties are concerned with a human audience. Not every human, of course, but the people who deal with the design and development of—or who are affected by—the subject or domain of a concrete pattern or pattern language. For example, our pattern language for distributed computing [POSA4] was written primarily for software architects and developers of software for distributed systems. A pattern language for project management could, in contrast, address project managers, project staff, the head of development, human resources, etc.

Well-documented patterns enable their intended human target audience to understand a particular problem, the situation in which the problem arises, the forces that influence its solution, the potential solutions to the problem, and the concrete realizations and trade-offs of each solution alternative. Much effort is also invested in presenting patterns in a form that is better than just human-readable. What we aspire to is a form that tells a story and initiates a dialog.

After digesting a pattern, its (intended) readership should be able to judge whether the problem addressed is one that they have in their (software) systems or (organizational) environment. Assuming the problem applies, the pattern description should help them select the most feasible solution from the solution space offered. Pattern compounds, pattern sequences, and pattern languages support similar goals to stand-alone patterns, but with the additional, broader ambition of guiding their audience through the problem and solution spaces of larger—yet specific—domains.

Pattern Value System

The focus of patterns on humans is supported by the pattern value system, which stems from a session run by Norm Kerth at the first Pattern Languages of Programming conference in 1994. It ties back to ethical concerns that the early software pattern advocates deemed crucial to the success of patterns. Jim Coplien published the following summary of the pattern value system [PPR]:

> We don't value new ideas for their own sake. Other communities should and do value novelty, but we want patterns to be a haven for ideas that have repeatedly proven effective and useful in actual use.

> We believe in giving credit where credit is due. If you are using someone else's pattern, cite it; if you are writing a pattern based on an idea you got from others, credit them.

> We believe patterns are one tool in our software toolkit; they are not a panacea; they will not lead to wild jumps in productivity. They are about building competence. To hype patterns beyond these modest roles in software development is irresponsible.

> We value 'real stuff.' Patterns are based in experience and convey real direction and structure for solving problems. They don't tell how to find solutions to problems; they *are* solutions to problems. We'd rather write patterns than talk about writing patterns. We can learn a lot by writing and critiquing patterns, and that's our focus.

> We strive for 'The Quality Without a Name.' We care about aesthetics.

> We care about the human side of software. All software serves some human need or want, and patterns should make explicit how they improve the quality of life for someone as a result of the pattern being applied. And we believe that patterns can never replace the experts whose knowledge they encode, nor the programmers who expertly interpret the knowledge to engineer, craft, and sculpt wonderful works of programming.

> We believe the constraints of the pattern form are in fact liberating, as they allow us to focus on important aspects of design beyond the form.

> We believe that there is high value in the work of coders, of those who touch the end-user deliverable artifacts. We believe they contribute as much or more to the design soundness, functionality,

and aesthetics of a software system than those who usually are viewed as having all the insight and influence, such as architects and methodologists.

We believe that users should participate in the design of the systems they are using, including the software they will be using. In general, the pattern community fosters a sense of community, and strives—and sometimes struggles—to build an open community. We believe we can learn a lot from other disciplines; software is an awfully inbred community.

The Human Audience

The explicit focus on a human audience distinguishes patterns from other tools and techniques such as Unified Modeling Language, Model-Driven Software Development, and Aspect-Oriented Software Development in the software development domain. Artifacts created with such techniques are also intended to be read by humans, but they can also feed tools that execute formal consistency and correctness checks on these artifacts, simulate them, and even generate code from them. From one point of view these techniques may seem superior to patterns because they have an apparently broader audience: both human and (virtual) machine.

These techniques all aim to support developers and development in some way. What distinguishes patterns from the others, however, is the nature of that support. For example, the panoply of available software techniques and technologies is targeted largely at the world of the artifact: the mechanisms that make up specifications or code and that create concrete solutions to specific problems. In real-world practice, therefore, these techniques are most useful for *implementing*, *documenting*, and *tuning* a system.

In contrast, patterns—and even more so pattern languages—aim to acknowledge their readers in the role of architect, and work with them in that capacity to *design*, *understand*, and *communicate* a system. What solutions are most appropriate for a given problem in a given context? What are the effects of the solution on the system's quality, in the small and in the large? Is the solution well balanced and easy to understand and communicate? Patterns and pattern languages help to answer such questions and support the architect in taking explicit and thoughtful design decisions. Returning to the essence of Dick Gabriel's foreword for this book:

> Pattern languages can encompass lots of design space. They are part of our software design and construction toolboxes. They work by helping people design better. Reflection on good design is how pattern languages are written down. Design, design, design, design.

The idea, however, that there is an 'exclusive or' between patterns on one hand and all other software techniques on the other is a false dichotomy. Each approach has well-defined and useful goals, and within the process of developing software there is a dedicated place for it. Patterns even support and contribute to generative technologies that aim to (semi-)automate selected software development activities, such as Aspect-Oriented Software Development [KLM+97] and Model-Driven Software Development [SVC06], as we discussed in various places in this book.

The same discussion also applies for technologies versus patterns, and for pattern languages in domains other than software design and development. For example, a range of systems and measures exist for *implementing*, *controlling*, and *improving* development organizations and processes, including the Capability Maturity Model (CMM) and its successor, Capability Maturity Model Integration (CMMI) [CKS06], and the organizational and process advice in RUP [Kru00]. The corresponding pattern languages, however, support *designing* a concrete organization and process that suits the needs of a particular business and project.

The remainder of this chapter explores the human nature of patterns in more depth, focusing on the domain of software design and development, since our core expertise lies there. Nevertheless, similar discussions can be had for patterns and pattern languages for other domains, including development or business organizations and processes, documents, residential architecture, and so on.

14.2 In Support of Software Developers

The people that most software patterns support are *developers*: those who practice 'the science and art of designing and making—with economy and elegance—applications, frameworks, and other similar structures so that they can safely resist the forces to which they may be subjected' [Hen03b]. Speaking metaphorically, patterns support the people who live and work *inside* the designs and code of the systems they create, refactor, and maintain. It is therefore important that developers feel at home, safe, and comfortable there, rather than alienated, lost, and awkward in the systems they work on. Patterns are an excellent means of creating such habitability [Gab96].

From a technical perspective, most developer-centric patterns help designers and programmers to build high-quality software systems by guiding them through key decisions during the construction of these systems. Such patterns also enable developers to explore particular software-related problems effectively, as well as study and evaluate their solution detail and alternatives. Another set of developer-centric patterns supports the understanding and application of third-party software such as communication middleware and service-oriented architecture platforms. Studying the patterns that underpin such software helps developers to customize, extend, and use the software appropriately.

There are also a range of patterns and pattern languages that support the development process itself, including day-to-day activities and environment around the code [Cun96] [CoHa04]. These patterns focus less on the workpiece created through craft and more on the craft and the crafter.

Human-Driven Development

Patterns are not just hard-edged and technical. They also address several softer, more obviously human-oriented aspects of software development:

- *Communication.* Patterns form a specialized but common vocabulary that software architects and developers can use to discuss particular problems that arise in their projects. This common vocabulary helps people to exchange ideas about how to resolve these problems, and even to communicate entire software architectures and implementations to their colleagues. Broadening the vocabulary that developers can use to express what they are doing or plan to do leads to a better joint understanding of particular problems and their solutions, and also of concrete software architectures and their realizations.

- *Confidence and consideration.* By using patterns, software developers can take advantage of proven, existing knowledge, which gives them confidence that they are on safe technical ground and are making the proper design and implementation decisions for their systems. In project meetings developers can use the forces and consequences of the applied patterns to explain the rationale and trade-offs behind their designs and to appreciate and reflect on the same qualities in the designs of others.

- *Understanding, responsibility, and control.* Patterns allow software developers to reason about important design and implementation problems *before* attempting to resolving them. In addition, they can use *concepts* for resolving these problems that *lead* to effective implementations. As a consequence, developers are more involved, responsible, and in control of what they are doing. If, on the other hand, developers implement solutions with little knowledge about the larger context in which the problems arise, they may feel frustrated and in the dark over precisely what, for whom, and why they are doing so.

- *Interest and fun.* Patterns help resolve problems constructively, which keeps software developers interested in their work, because they need not spend the bulk of their time creating ad hoc solutions for their problems and hacking at these solutions until they work, which is tedious and error-prone. In addition, most patterns do not just 'technically' resolve the problems they are addressing: they exhibit a certain aesthetic and elegance. Developers can be proud of their designs and implementations, and can enjoy them, which further increases the interest they have their work.

In a nutshell, developer-centric patterns offer technical advice and more: they encourage, confirm, and support software developers as *humans* in their job. This, in turn, helps developers to be effective both as individuals and in teams—a key factor in successful software development organizations.

14.3 In Support of Software Users

Some software patterns target a different audience than people who build and *live within* software. Instead, they address people such as end users, customers, and product managers, who are affected by or *live with* software. Too often such groups are not deeply enough involved in the development of software, even though it is they who must use it, pay for it, and market it. The goal of user-centric patterns is to bring these people back in and help them engage in meaningful conversations with software developers about their interests in a software system.

User-centric patterns intentionally do not address technical issues related to software systems internals, such as event-handling models or concurrency design. Nor do they simply recast and rebrand the developer-centric patterns for a different audience. Developer-centric topics are often not relevant for end users, customers, or product managers, who must rely on developers to 'do the right thing' [Hearsay02]. Instead, user-centric patterns focus on properties of software systems that are externally visible and observable, such as their look-and-feel, feature set, and operational qualities. These usability properties define the experience of applying and living with the software, and are therefore of interest to anyone affected by them.

User Interfaces

The look-and-feel of a software system intimately determines how easy and comfortable it is to operate the system. It also plays a key role in whether or not the software will be accepted by its customers and end users. Getting end users, customers, and product managers involved with software developers in the design and implementation of a user interface is therefore essential for the success of a software project.

An outstanding example of user-centric patterns that promote this dialog is Jan Borchers' human-computer interaction (HCI) patterns [Bor01]. For example, INVISIBLE HARDWARE and DOMAIN APPROPRIATE DEVICES stress the importance of hiding complex and unfamiliar hardware technologies from system users, allowing them instead to communicate with the system using devices and 'abstractions' that they know from their own domains. Other HCI patterns, such as FLAT AND NARROW TREE and INFORMATION JUST IN TIME strike the narrow balance between providing insufficient information and not overwhelming users with too much information.

The patterns in [Bor01] can be applied effectively by different groups in a software project. For example, system engineers and product managers can use the HCI patterns to specify how information should be presented in a system's user interface, or what collaborative work facilities a system should provide. Similarly, software developers can use the same patterns to introduce and educate end users, customers, and product managers to the behavior and look-and-feel of software systems they are building.

While usability and a human-centric view of patterns may seem like a new direction for the patterns community, this was actually the original driving force for introducing patterns to the domain of software development! The first software patterns documented, Kent Beck's and Ward Cunningham's WINDOW PER TASK, FEW PANES PER WINDOW, STANDARD PANES, NOUNS AND VERBS, and SHORT MENUS [BeCu87], instructed developers about how to create software that end users can understand and use effectively, which is clearly a human-centric view and ambition.

User Requirements

Beneath the surface of a systems's look-and-feel should be the confidence that the system satisfies user requirements within their application domain. Conveying these requirements from users to developers and back again is just as much a part of involving end-users, customers, and product managers as designing a meaningful user interface.

Customers or product managers may enlist skilled analysts to assist in this process, but patterns in this world of analysis are still considered more user-centric than developer-centric due to their user-facing stance.

For example, patterns for writing use cases [Coc00] help users and developers clearly articulate functional requirements from a scenario-driven perspective. Other analysis patterns, such as those for health care and corporate finance domains [Fow97], allow domain experts to engage software developers in discussions about how to model an application domain within a software system and what features are needed to fulfill its functional requirements properly. Aligning the vocabulary of development with that of the domain to create a common language for developers and domain experts is one goal of *Domain-Driven Design* [Evans03]. Domain-driven design patterns [Niel06] help analysts and developers to create models of a domain that support the effective definition and validation of business rules.

In the Hands of the User

Alexander expressed the ideal that patterns should ensure that 'all decisions about what to build, and how to build it, will be in the hands of the user' [ASAIA75]. 'The architect-builder is responsible for making sure that the actual design is in the hands of the family' [ADMC85]. User-centric software patterns are thus more closely and obviously related to Christopher Alexander's ideal than developer-centric patterns. Depending on factors like the environment, budget, and technical ambition, however, this ideal can be approximated to a greater or lesser extent in software projects, but is hard to meet fully. A division remains between those who have the intention and ownership in look-and-feel and usability concerns and those who have the expertise and experience of construction.

User-centric patterns and pattern languages can help to alleviate this division. By engaging end users, customers, and product managers more fully and explicitly throughout the software process, they will feel more responsible for—and more in control of—what is developed. In particular, they need not wait until the system is delivered before seeing the results, but instead can ensure that it is evolving to meet their needs. This iterative, feedback-driven approach is reflected in agile development processes and some of its associated patterns [CoHa04].

Applying user-centric patterns to the software development process helps to increase the confidence of end users, customers, and product managers in the software, as well as trust in the developers who build it. By enabling a dialog about a software system between all parties interested in or affected by its development, user-centric patterns have a strong human emphasis by their nature. It is not surprising, therefore, that user-centric patterns are popular in the field of participatory design [DFAM02], where end users, customers, and software developers collaboratively define the look-and-feel and the architecture of a software system.

14.4 In Support of Pattern Authors

Pattern authors are another group for whom patterns and their relationship with people matters. Good pattern writing does not spring forth, fully and perfectly formed, from a single author. In this book we have focused on questions of pattern form to show how the structure and style of pattern documentation can make a difference to readers. We have also shown through many examples that the process of writing a pattern—and especially a pattern language—is an iterative and incremental affair, which even when 'done' should still be considered a work in progress. What we have not mentioned is that behind the writing is more than just the author.

A number of innovations have emerged from the pattern community to support effective writing. These techniques emphasize collaboration and feedback, as described below.

Collaborative Writing

Many documented patterns are the work of more than one author. Rather than the current fashion of scientific papers, where it sometimes appears that anyone in the same corridor or on the same mailing list as the principal researchers is listed as an author, contribution to such joint works is more genuine.

Sometimes the coauthoring is face to face, at other times via e-mail. For example, the bulk of the POSA books after the first volume have been written by authors living in separate countries and on different continents. Often these author teams leverage the differences in time zones to conduct 'round the clock' writing sessions!

Beyond conventional coauthoring, pattern writing has also taken advantage of larger network effects to pull in more contributors. For example, most of the patterns included in *Fearless Change* [MaRi04] and *Design Patterns for Distributed Real-Time Embedded Systems* [DiGi07] were gathered and refined from workshops at conferences over a number of years. A more virtual example is the creation of the Wiki by Ward Cunningham. One of the original goals of the Wiki was to allow documentation, collaborative writing, and browsing of patterns, as demonstrated in the *Portland Pattern Repository* [PPR]. Wikis have grown beyond these humble beginnings to include some of the largest collaborative works seen to date [Wiki], but the original vision of using them for patterns is still alive [Shir].

Writers' Workshops

There are many different approaches to reviewing written works. Anonymous peer review is used in academic publication. Market-focused reviews are used by publishers. Unstructured reviews—calls for comments—are often used by authors with colleagues they can trust. It is in trust and openness that pattern writers' workshops are based [Cope96]:

> A good review can help ensure that the pattern is readable, that it hits its audience, and that it does its job. Patterns are literature, and we believe they deserve more than the dry design reviews we typically afford other software documents. Richard Gabriel, himself a poet (in addition to being one of the inventors of CLOS), taught us how poetry is reviewed at poetry conferences. We adapted that approach and call these sessions *writers' workshops*.

> The participants in a workshop are all pattern authors. The author reads a selection from the pattern, and then sits down and becomes invisible until the very end of the session. One of the reviewers summarizes the pattern. There is then open discussion on why the pattern works and what is good about it. Next,

reviewers can make suggestions on how to improve the pattern: content, form, usage anything is fair game. Finally, the author can ask for clarification.

There are many further details and variations on this basic format [CoWo99] [Gab02], but the essential process is simple. Such workshops form the backbone of the PLoP series of conferences, but they have also been applied by user groups, within companies, and in ad hoc meetings of interested parties.

Shepherding

Shepherding is another form of structured review that is used within the pattern community. It offers a structured and guided form of reviewing whose goal is the improvement of a pattern-based work. In contrast to traditional reviews, the approach is intentionally iterative [Har99] rather than packed into a single shot. It is also respectful: the shepherd is not the author, so suggestions are just that—suggestions, not copy-edits or demands.

Shepherding is normally used for papers submitted to PLoP conferences in preparation for writers' workshopping. It is also used in the publication of some pattern books (such as [POSA4]) and also informally between colleagues (such as [Kel04]). In recent years, academic conferences have also begun to use shepherding to improve the quality of accepted papers prior to their publication.

14.5 Technology for Humans

The previous sections in this chapter emphasized that the prime goal of patterns is to make design and technology accessible and comprehensible for a human audience. The goal is to ensure people—both users and developers—consciously and thoughtfully choose the appropriate expression or development approach for their systems and environments.

In contrast to other techniques, however, patterns address not only the roles played in a concrete project, such as project manager, software architect, and programmer in software development, but also explicitly address the people behind these roles. In this, patterns acknowledge that despite technological advances such as automated software construction and the benefits that derive from it, software and other things are still built largely by humans and—most of all— for humans.

15 The Past, Presence, and Future of Patterns

*A painting is never finished;
it simply stops in interesting places.*

Paul Gardner, painter

You seldom get a chance to reflect on your predictions about the future. It is even less common to get three chances to review (and revise) your predictions! But that is one benefit of writing a series of books, as we have done with the POSA volumes.

This chapter revisits our forecasts about the future of patterns that appeared in the third volume of the POSA series, *Patterns for Resource Management*, in 2004. We discuss the directions that patterns have taken in the past three years, analyze where they are now, and—with the benefit of hindsight—once again revise our vision about the future of patterns.

15.1 The Past Three Years at a Glance

Over the years we have become better at determining the future of patterns. In contrast to our forecasts in the first and second volume of the POSA series, nearly all the forecasts we made in the third POSA volume came true, or are coming true. We start by summarizing what has happened during the past three years, referencing much of the relevant work during that period, though our list is not exhaustive. Additional references are available at http://hillside.net/patterns/.

Patterns and Pattern Languages

Our main prediction from three years ago was that pattern languages would grow in importance and popularity: 'authors will focus largely on documenting pattern languages instead of stand-alone patterns, and [that] the majority of all new patterns and pattern languages will be domain-specific rather than general-purpose' [POSA3]. A survey of recent literature shows the accuracy of this prediction, since the most relevant and influential pattern publications are concrete pattern languages rather than stand-alone patterns, and the specific topics and domains addressed correspond closely to our predictions:

- *Security*. Security has been a topic for patterns since the beginning of this millennium, mirroring the growing emphasis on security in software systems in general [GSS03]. Key players in the field recently published a book, *Security Patterns*, [SFHBS06] that documents a range of patterns and pattern languages for security-related areas, such as authentication, authorization, integrity, and confidentiality. Many of these patterns and pattern languages had been documented in earlier pattern publications, mostly in the proceedings of pattern conferences during past three years. A key contribution of *Security Patterns* is therefore reworking these pattern descriptions in a common form based on the POSA form, and integrating the patterns with one another to provide a consistent and coherent pattern language for security in software systems. *Core Security Patterns* for J2EE Web Services [SNL05] is another pattern book published in the area of networked software security.

- *Fault tolerance and fault management*. Patterns on fault tolerance and fault management have been an active focus over the past decade [ACGH+96] [IsDe96] [FeRu98] [BRR+00] [SPM99] [Sari02] [Sari03]. As software is increasingly integrated into mission- and safety-critical systems—particularly large-scale distributed systems—it is clear that robust fault-management is needed to meet user requirements. Several recent books and papers contain patterns and pattern languages that address or relate to fault tolerance and fault management [Han04] [LoWo04] [Sari05] [Utas05] [POSA4] for systems with stringent operational quality requirements. A book that documents patterns for fault tolerant software is also in preparation [Han07].

- *Distributed systems.* Distributed systems are still a popular focus for pattern authors, despite the fact that distribution topics have been covered by pattern writers for many years. The fourth volume of the POSA series, for example, presents an extensive pattern language for building distributed software systems [POSA4]. The language contains 114 core patterns, with links to over 150 further patterns, that address topics ranging from defining and selecting an appropriate baseline architecture and communication infrastructure, to specifying component interfaces, their implementations, and their interactions, as well as to key technical aspects of distributed computing such as event handling, concurrency, synchronization, resource management, adaptation and extension, and database access.

  Other recent publications in the area of distribution document patterns for reliability, availability, and scalability in the context of so-called 'carrier grade' telecommunication systems [Utas05], and key principles and practices of distributed object computing [VKZ04], peer-to-peer computing [GrMü05], and time-triggered distributed embedded systems [HKG04].

- *Language- and domain-specific idioms.* Several programming styles have evolved and emerged over the past decade, including aspect-oriented software development [KLM+97] [Ladd03], domain-driven [Evans03] [Niel06] and model-driven software development [Fra03] [GSCK04] [SVC06], and generative programming [CzEi02]. Each of these styles has its own idioms, which distinguish programming in that style from other programming styles. It is thus not surprising that patterns and pattern catalogs have been documented for the most popular of these styles, in particular aspect-oriented software

development [Sch04a] [GCKL05a] [GCKL05b] [ScHa05] [Sch06b]
and model-driven software development [VöBe04] [Vö05a] [Vö05b]
[Vö06]. Programing language idioms continue to be documented and
published for mainstream languages, such as for Java [Hen04b], C#
[Nash06], C++ [AbGu05], and Python [Chr01].

- *Process.* Though many areas of software development processes
  have been described by patterns [Cope95] since the early days of
  the software patterns community, several new process pattern
  works have been published in the past three years. Some publications address specific types of software development processes,
  such as distributed, agile, test-driven, and domain-driven development [BHCY+04] [Evans03] [Ber05] [BrJo05] [HCSH05] [NoWe05]
  [Mes07]. Other publications integrate existing patterns on software
  development processes and organizations into interconnected pattern languages [CoHa04].

- *Education.* In recent years, patterns and pattern languages have
  become a widely accepted vehicle for teachers and consultants to
  exchange their knowledge on the art of teaching programming and
  software engineering. Consequently, a number of patterns published in the past three years are pedagogical patterns. The fifth
  volume of the PLoPD series [PLoPD5] includes some of these papers. In addition, recent papers [StFl04] [CiTy04] [LRP04] [Chr04]
  [PoCa04] [BSDM05] [TZP05] [VeSa06] cover other dimensions of using patterns in undergraduate education. Key researchers and
  practitioners in this field also founded the 'pedagogical patterns
  project' [PPP], which is a Web site that publishes pedagogical patterns and provides a forum for discussing teaching patterns, with a
  focus on teaching good software practice.

In addition to topics we predicted would attract attention from pattern
authors, patterns and pattern languages have also been published in
several other areas of software development, such as (general) software architecture [Mar04a] [Mar04b] [Zdun04] [AvZd06] [Mar05] and
group interaction [LS04] [Sch04b] [LS05] [SFM05] [SL06].

We were confident in the 2004 POSA3 forecast that many patterns and
pattern languages for mobile and pervasive computing would be published. Although there were some initial forays into these areas [Hon04]
[Bor06], the coverage has been sparse, despite growing demand for mobile and pervasive software systems. We continue to believe that both

areas will be attractive for software experts and pattern writers. There are many technical and social challenges to master for both types of systems, such as managing low and variable bandwidth and power and adapting to frequent disruptions in connectivity and service quality. Time-proven patterns are therefore needed to help developers create systems that are available whenever and wherever they are needed, but which also respect privacy and do not try to be overly prescriptive or proscriptive.

Theory and Concepts

Three years ago POSA3 predicted that the 'time has come to reflect on the past and, with hindsight, adjust and evolve the common understandings about patterns: what they are (really), what properties they have, what is their purpose, who is their audience, and what are the do's and don'ts of using them.' At that time, we expected that books and papers would be published on the concept of patterns and pattern languages, but were also aware that the circle of potential authors for such work was rather small.

Nevertheless this forecast largely turned out correct: thought leaders in the pattern community have begun writing more about the concepts of patterns, pattern sequences, and pattern languages. As expected, only a handful of papers have been published in this area [PCW05] [Hen05b], but these publications were important milestones that codified knowledge about, and understanding of, the pattern concept in software. The largest work in this area is the book you are holding—the fifth volume of the POSA series—which is a comprehensive exploration of the pattern concept that integrates its many different facets into a coherent whole.

Refactoring and Integration

With growing experience and hindsight in using patterns, the pattern community became aware that many existing pattern descriptions needed revisiting and revision to cover the current and expanded state of the art, in terms of advances in both software design and pattern concepts. An 'early' work from 2003 [BuHe03] therefore refactored some of the best-known patterns to capture what we know about them today. Based on the reception this work received in the patterns community, POSA3 predicted that 'more of such pattern refactoring would follow, specifically of the patterns published in the classic pattern books.' This forecast proved accurate: many new books and papers have been published recently that provide revised versions of existing patterns, rather than describing new patterns.

For example, of the 114 patterns documented in the fourth volume of the POSA series, *A Pattern Language for Distributed Computing* [POSA4], over a hundred of the patterns were already documented in other pattern sources, but were revised to fit into the context of distributed computing and the format of the book. Similarly, most patterns in *Security Patterns* [SFHBS06] had already been published in the proceedings of various pattern conferences, but were reworked for *Security Patterns* toward a common pattern form, writing style, and technical depth. Other work on pattern refactoring focused on the Gang-of-Four [VK04] [POSA4] and POSA patterns [VKZ04] [KVSJ04] [Ort05] [MoFe06].

Some patterns were actually revised multiple times, such as the BROKER pattern from the first volume of the POSA series, *A System of Patterns* [POSA1], as we described in *Section 1.9, Patterns are Works in Progress*. There are even reworkings and refinements of patterns that were published relatively recently. For example, although CONTEXT OBJECT's early known uses include the environment parameter of Scheme's eval procedure and the fact that it can be seen playing a key role in the INTERPRETER pattern, it was only recently documented as a pattern on its own. In 2003 it was documented both as a J2EE-specific design practice [ACM03] and in more technology-neutral terms [Kel04], and in 2005 it was both specialized for distributed computing [KSS05] and decomposed into a small pattern language [Hen05b].

As predicted, pattern authors have paid more attention in recent years to integrating their patterns more tightly [SFHBS06] [VKZ04] [POSA4]. This integration process is a natural and direct consequence of the trend toward publishing pattern languages instead of stand-alone patterns.

The Gang-of-Four

Although *Design Patterns* [GoF95] was published over a decade ago, it is still the most influential pattern work. Although this book is clearly seminal and has influenced much of our thinking about software design, much has changed since 1994. Today we know more about patterns and software development in general, and the Gang-of-Four patterns in particular. In addition, C# and Java have become mainstream programming languages, and the popularity of scripting languages such as Python and Ruby has grown to the point where they too are mainstream. The examples in the original *Design Patterns* publication, however, are predominantly C++, with some Smalltalk. POSA3 therefore predicted that authors would continue to feed the unquenchable demand for ruminations about Gang-of-Four patterns.

This forecast was borne out in many ways. Since 2004 several books and papers have been published that address the Gang-of-Four patterns in various ways. Some publications are companions describing how to implement the patterns in other programming languages [Met04], other publications rework and integrate the Gang-of-Four patterns for specific application contexts [VK04] [VKZ04] [SFHBS06] [POSA4].

OOPSLA 2006 held a touching memorial service for John Vlissides. During this service the remaining members of the Gang-of-Four reminisced about many aspects of their book, including its impact on the field of object-oriented software and the essential role John played in the original writing process. Although they remain committed to producing a second volume, the time frame for its release has not been finalized.

15.2 Where Patterns Are Now

After more than a decade of growth and evolution, the presence of patterns is now firmly established in the mainstream of software development. Patterns are used consciously in many production software projects [YaAm03] and university curricula [Hor06], often in isolation to resolve specific problems, but sometimes holistically to analyse, design, and implement entire programs and systems based on patterns and pattern languages. One of the original goals of the patterns community, to document and promote good software engineering practices, appears to have been met.

With respect to domain coverage, we have seen significant growth during the past three years. Over a decade ago, most published patterns were general-purpose and design focused: specific topic areas, such as distribution or requirements analysis, were rarely addressed. Today the situation is quite different. Patterns and pattern languages have been published for many domains, including but not limited to: concurrency, resource management, distribution, transaction processing, messaging, security, fault management, event handling, user interface design, enterprise application integration, Internet applications, music, requirements analysis, e-commerce, and many more. We are pleased with this growing body of documented patterns and pattern languages, because it demonstrates the utility and expressiveness of patterns in practice.

More importantly, software developers in general seem to have a better grasp of patterns than three years ago, both in terms of their experience using patterns effectively on software projects and their understanding of the pattern concept in its various facets and aspects. The quality of the published patterns and pattern languages has also generally increased. Most of the patterns and pattern languages we referenced in *Section 15.1, The Past Three Years at a Glance* are far more expressive, more comprehensive, more precise, and more readable than many patterns and pattern languages published in the past. In many ways it appears that software patterns have finally gone beyond the hype and reached their 'golden age' [ReRi85].

15.3 Where Will Patterns Go Tomorrow?

If patterns have indeed reached their golden age, that begs the question 'What is there now left to say about patterns?' Many software developers have some familiarity with the concept of patterns and with some of the patterns that apply in their domains. We expect that the proportion of developers familiar with the basics will increase, and we expect that the proportion of developers already familiar with the basics who go on to deepen their pattern knowledge to also increase. Beyond this question of uptake, we present below our prognostications on the future of patterns.

Patterns and Pattern Languages

First and foremost we expect that more technology- and domain-specific patterns and pattern languages will be documented. Not all technologies and domains of software development are yet addressed by patterns, and it may take decades to cover them all. The technologies and domains we predict will be addressed first include:

- *Service-Oriented Architecture (SOA).* SOA is a style of organizing and utilizing distributed capabilities that may be controlled and owned by different organizations or groups. The term was coined originally in the mid-1990s [SN96] as a generalization of the interoperability middleware standards available at the time, such as RPC-, ORB-, and messaging-based platforms. Service-oriented architectures have evolved to integrate middleware and applications that form larger, enterprise-level IT infrastructures, as well as to provide a platform for applications and product-line architectures in other domains, such as third-generation wireless systems [Par06] and defense systems [Lau04]. The SOA approach builds on many principles and technologies known from distributed computing and enterprise system integration, and can thus draw from a broad spectrum of existing patterns and pattern languages [CI01] [Fow02] [HoWo03] [MS03] [ACM03] [POSA4].

  Some SOA technologies, such as business process modeling, service orchestration, and ultra-large-scale systems [NFG+06], are still unexplored, however, and are not yet covered by corresponding documented patterns. We have recently seen an increased interest by pattern authors to fill these gaps, and expect corresponding pattern publications in the future.

- *Distributed real-time and embedded systems.* Some of the most challenging problems facing developers are those associated with producing software for distributed real-time and embedded systems in which computer processors control physical, chemical, or biological processes or devices. Examples of such systems include automobiles, airplanes, air traffic control systems, nuclear reactors, oil refineries, chemical plans, and patient monitoring systems. In most of these systems, the right answer delivered too late becomes the wrong answer, so achieving predictable end-to-end real-time performance is essential. Moreover, embedded devices often have limited memory available for the platform and applications (64–512 kilobytes).

Developing high-quality distributed real-time and embedded systems is hard and remains somewhat of a 'black art.' A forthcoming book [DiGi07] documents patterns for developing distributed real-time and embedded software, based on material from workshops at the OOPSLA [DRE02] and PLoP [DRE03] conferences. Some recent papers [Kon05] have also focused on validating such systems. We expect the body of patterns for distributed real-time and embedded systems to continue to grow in the future, since progress in this domain is essential for developing viable mission- and safety-critical applications.

- *Group interaction.* The world is becoming increasingly networked, as the Internet and Web makes information available at any location and at any time. E-mail and Internet forums, chatrooms, and communities allow people to connect, interact, and stay in contact with family, friends, and business partners. Instant messaging, computer telephony, and collaboration tools like Wiki, NetMeeting, and Webex allow people from different locations, cultures, countries, and continents to work together on projects such as global software development [SBM+06] and even writing volumes in the POSA series!

Group interaction in a virtual electronic environment differs considerably, however, from group interaction in a face-to-face, physical environment. For example, people lack immediate expression or representation of personality or self, and the means of communication are limited to those supported by computers and other electronic devices. In addition, interaction across a network is subject to delays, errors, and misunderstanding, even if group members share a common culture and work in the same time zone. Supporting effective group communication and interaction in such environments, therefore, demands specialized solutions that alleviate the penalties of an electronic collaboration infrastructure and mimic as many 'human' forms of interaction as possible, for example (visual) personality, feelings, and gestures.

Although many patterns for human-computer-human interaction have been published in recent years [Sch03] [LS04] [Sch04b] [LS05] [SFM05] [SL06], no integrated view of these patterns is yet available. Moreover, not all areas of group interaction in an electronic environment are covered by patterns yet—for example, virtual worlds and games that support massive numbers of players. Given the growing demand for electronic collaboration support, we therefore predict that more patterns and pattern languages will be published in the area of human-computer-human interaction in the near future.

Group interaction over the Web also encompasses the more dynamic and open business models being used, where 'harnessing collective intelligence' [ORei05] becomes the means of business and Web 2.0 becomes the medium. The initial set of Web 2.0 patterns, described in *Section 8.11, Pattern Collections and Style*, captures the emerging and proven practices in this space. We predict that as experience in this domain grows, so too will the documented patterns that capture it.

- *Software architecture.* Despite an increase in the number of documented pattern languages, the software industry has no parallel to the comprehensive handbooks found in other design disciplines. Although the *Design Patterns*, *Pattern-Oriented Software Architecture*, and *Pattern Languages of Program Design* books have made steady progress toward creating handbooks for software engineers, we have still not reached our goal. Recently Grady Booch joined this effort and is collecting thousands of patterns to create a *Handbook of Software Architecture* [Booch]. He is codifying the architecture of a large collection of interesting software-intensive systems, presenting them in a manner that exposes their essential patterns and permits comparisons across domains and architectural styles.

- *Mobile and pervasive systems.* As discussed in *Section 15.1, The Past Three Years at a Glance*, we still believe that patterns and pattern languages for mobile and pervasive systems are an important topic for pattern authors. Despite the fact that we failed twice with a corresponding prediction in earlier POSA volumes, we renew our forecast once again. If you work in these areas and are familiar with their best practices and patterns, please help our prediction come true this time around!

- *Process.* We predicted—correctly, this time—in *Section 15.1, The Past Three Years at a Glance* that software development processes would receive the attention of pattern authors [BoGa05] [MaRi04] [Ker04], and we predict that this trend is set to continue. The growing adoption of agile development processes and experience with such processes suggests that we will continue to see a growth in corresponding pattern literature. Some of this literature will focus on macro-process aspects, such as overall lifecycle and interaction with the business, and some will focus on micro-process aspects, such as Test-Driven Development, refactoring, and tool usage.

It is likely that patterns, pattern collections, pattern sequences, and pattern languages will also be published for areas other than those listed above. As we said in the beginning of this section, however, these topics appear the most promising based on our current knowledge of work on patterns and pattern languages.

Theory and Concepts

Although we think that most aspects of the pattern concept are sufficiently well explored and fundamentally understood, work on the underlying theory of the pattern concept will continue over the coming years. From today's perspective we foresee two areas of focus:

- Deepening the knowledge about known facets of the pattern concept, in particular pattern sequences.

- Exploring new and recent views on it further, such as the problem frame perspective outlined in *Section 8.9, Problem Frames*.

More generally, we expect clarifications and progress in those areas of the pattern concept that are either fairly new or still subject of debate.

Although Christopher Alexander has extended the depth and reach of his work with four books on *The Nature of Order* [Ale03a] [Ale04a] [Ale04b] [Ale03b], we do not expect *The Nature of Order* to define a major area of focus. Its contributions will be primarily to support deepening of our understanding of pattern concepts such as pattern sequences and the notion of 'centers' in design. Some researchers and practitioners will undoubtedly chose to go further in applying the other concepts presented in *The Nature of Order*, but we do not expect this to be a main focus of work.

Nevertheless, we consider the fundamental knowledge about, and understanding of, the pattern concept and its various facets and aspects as reasonably mature. Consequently, although we expect these ideas to spread further and be adopted more widely than they have been to date, we do not expect major breakthroughs in this area in the future.

Refactoring and Integration

We also expect the work on refactoring and integrating patterns to continue, in accordance with concrete usage experience and the latest knowledge of their (conceptual) understanding, as well as the state-of-the-art and practice in software design and implementation. Patterns and pattern languages are always work in progress, so this forecast is not really surprising.

Support for Other Software Development Approaches

The vast majority of design patterns documented since the early 1990s have been mined from object-oriented software written in third-generation programming languages. Patterns and pattern languages, however, have already started to influence and support other software development approaches, in particular aspect-oriented software development (AOSD) and model-driven software development (MDSD). In fact, we measure the maturation and acceptance of these approaches in terms of the degree to which their patterns and best practices are published in the literature.

For example, during the past several years, MDSD technologies [SVC06] have increasingly become mainstream, particularly in the embedded systems domain [KLSB03]. MDSD technologies are based on domain-specific languages (DSLs) [GSCK04], whose type systems formalize the application structure, behavior, and requirements within particular domains, such as software-driven radios, avionics mission computing, online financial services, warehouse management, or even the domain of middleware platforms. DSLs are described using metamodels, which define the relationships between concepts in a domain and precisely specify the key semantics and constraints associated with these domain concepts. Developers use DSLs to build applications using elements of the type system captured by metamodels and express design intent declaratively, rather than imperatively using third-generation programming languages. Transformation engines and generators then analyze specific aspect of models and synthesize various types of artifacts, such as source code, simulation inputs, XML deployment descriptions, or alternative model representations [Sch06a].

There have been some initial efforts [VöBe04] [Vö05a] [Vö05b] to capture MDSD patterns associated with process and organization, domain modeling, tool architecture, and application platform development. Discovering and documenting more basic and more elaborate patterns and pattern languages for MDSD technologies, however, is fertile ground for future pattern authors. We see two areas of pattern-related work regarding such technologies:

• Patterns and pattern languages that support the design and development of software systems using the respective approaches. For example, we can imagine more patterns [Vlis96] that help to integrate software written manually in third-generation languages with model-driven tools or software architectures that maximize the amount of possible generation.

• How best to take advantage of existing patterns and pattern languages within these software development approaches. For example, in an MDSD approach, the generators that transform domain-oriented and technology-independent models of applications into models that are more technology-specific or represent concrete application architectures could be designed using appropriate patterns and pattern languages. Similarly, patterns and pattern languages could guide and inform the specific kind of transformation that the generators perform, for example, generating a target architecture that is based on (technology-) specific instances of concrete patterns [SVC06].

We expect that the influence of patterns and pattern languages on aspect-oriented software development will be similar to that on model-driven software development. Some preliminary work has been published, as discussed above [HaKi02] [GSF+05] [CSM06] [CSF+06], but there is much left to do.

Influencing Other Disciplines

In what may come as a surprise to the software community, other disciplines are scrutinizing our practices for their potential in their own work. Ironically, building architecture is one such discipline, even though software engineering in general—and software architecture specifically—borrowed, adopted, and adapted many approaches and methods from there, including the pattern approach itself [Ale79]. Another discipline that has started to borrow insights from the software pattern community is music composition [Bor01].

On the other hand, it is fair to say that of the disciplines that have taken an interest in patterns, the pattern approach is most successful within that of software development. Consequently, there is a rare opportunity for the software community to cross-fertilize other disciplines in adopting the pattern approach, and perhaps even return its experience-based knowledge about patterns and pattern languages back to building architecture—a sort of homecoming.

Whether or not this comes to pass depends not only on the uncertainty of making any form of prediction, but a great deal on factors beyond our own control as software developers—but at least the chance is there.

Influence From Other Disciplines

As we note above, the software patterns community has long been influenced by Christopher Alexander's work on the architecture of buildings. There are also influences from other disciplines, such as music [AGA06], cultural anthropology [Mead60], and computer-human interaction [Bor01]. One of the more intriguing influences is from natural science, where biologists are now beginning to understand the basic elements and patterns within DNA sequences that are shared between organisms, as well as those that make each unique.

One contribution of POSA5 fulfills part of a prediction from our long-term vision in POSA2. At that time, we forecast that research and development on patterns and pattern languages would yield breakthrough discoveries of core software properties akin to biologists deciphering the genetic code of organisms. The notions of grammatically formed pattern sequences in *Section 10.6, Patterns Form Vocabulary,*

Sequences Illustrate Grammar represent our initial attempts to specify the basis for 'software DNA.' As more progress—particularly systematic controlled empirical studies—is made on defining the syntax and semantics of well-formed pattern sequences, we expect the results will enable architects and developers to engineer the complexity of large-scale software more effectively than is possible with the current state of the art.

15.4 A Brief Note about the Future of Patterns

The predictions—or, more modestly, forecasts—in this chapter are drawn from our experience and in-depth analysis of more than a decade of past and present work in the patterns community. Although we expect many of our forecasts will be realized, they should be taken with a healthy dose of skepticism and uncertainty.

The future of patterns may take directions that we have not imagined today. Therefore consider the forecasts in this chapter as one possible vision among many in the ongoing dialog on patterns and their future, and not as the prophecies of infallible oracles.

16 All Good Things...

May the forces be with you.

Grady Booch

In this final chapter we reflect upon our fifteen-year mission to fulfill the vision of *Pattern-Oriented Software Architecture*. We provide a retrospective that reaches back to where we started and outlines the paths we took to reach the destination of our long journey.

In this sequence of chapters, there is one last thing from our queue to say: all good things come to an end. The POSA series has run its course. For a decade and a half we have been working on and with patterns—mining, documenting, applying, and teaching them, and exploring their conceptual foundations. This effort started modestly in 1992 as an effort to document the development experiences we encountered in software projects just for ourselves, to help us to avoid reinventing the wheel in subsequent projects. Over time the POSA endeavor grew in scope, with many people from the patterns community joining the project, contributing to it, or otherwise supporting us with their advice and help. The results of our work have been published in a series of books, of which this is the fifth and last. It provides a capstone to our work that connects the patterns and pattern languages we published in the four earlier volumes.

From its inception, our work on patterns has followed the vision of *Pattern-Oriented Software Architecture*, which serves as both the name and the theme of our series of books. This theme underscores our belief that patterns should not just be applied independently of one another to resolve local or isolated design and development problems, but instead should be used systematically to guide the development of entire software systems. Articulating this vision was a step in the right direction: elaborating the vision so that it could be applied successfully in production systems was a much more ambitious goal that took us the better part of two decades.

When writing the first volume of the POSA series, *A System of Patterns*, we thought, perhaps a little naively, that we could address the conceptual foundations of patterns and building software with patterns in several short chapters. We soon discovered that there was much more to say about patterns and their effective use than we could possibly cover in a book that focused simply on documenting a system of patterns. Moreover, the more experience we gained with patterns, the more we realized how much else there was say about patterns, and how much more we needed to learn to convey the pattern concept effectively. As a result, with the benefit of hindsight we can see that the first volume of the POSA series just provided a basic—but self-contained—introduction to patterns.

Nevertheless, we did not lose sight of our original vision of *Pattern-Oriented Software Architecture*. When working with patterns on production software projects, mining 'new' patterns, presenting and discussing patterns at conferences, or documenting patterns in other POSA volumes, we always reflected on what we learned (by doing) about the pattern concept itself.

Step by step we collected different bits and pieces, perspectives and opinions, on the pattern concept, observing how they integrated and related to one another to form a coherent and whole picture. The evolution of our understanding of the pattern concept and the progress in mining, investigating, and integrating its different facets is also visible in the four previous POSA volumes:

- In POSA1, *A System of Patterns*, we had a relatively limited understanding of what designing with patterns could be, hence we more modestly called our approach a pattern system, not a pattern language. Although we understood and emphasized the importance of relationships between patterns to support their systematic use in software construction, we considered only the usage relationships between patterns, where one pattern uses another to support its implementation—but not pattern complements, alternatives, or compounds. We also did not explore the process aspects of patterns and pattern languages. Although context and forces were present in the patterns, the details and broader role of context and forces in pattern languages was not explored. We therefore just provided a brief hint about what patterns were and what designing with patterns could be, but did not focus on these topics in detail.

- In POSA2, *Patterns for Concurrent and Networked Objects* and POSA3, *Patterns for Resource Management*, we took the first steps toward documenting our knowledge in the form of pattern languages. These two volumes connect the patterns they contain to form small pattern languages. Although the languages do not cover all the available patterns in their domains, they nevertheless expose important properties of the pattern language concept. For example, both languages provide a process for designing systems or system components in their domain. Both languages also consider more relationships between the connected patterns than just usage, including alternatives and other complements. On the other hand, the aspects of context and forces were not as explicit and complete in the languages as they could have been.

- In POSA4, *A Pattern Language for Distributed Computing*, we finally covered the aspects of pattern languages and designing with patterns that were absent or incompletely addressed in the first three volumes. POSA4 documents an extensive pattern language for building distributed software systems that we believe reveals all the properties that useful pattern languages should expose. This language—or key parts of it—have been used in production software projects covering a broad range of domains, including distributed process control and factory automation systems, telecommunication management network systems, real-time avionics applications, and communications middleware. Documenting the pattern language in POSA4 helped us complete and refine our knowledge and understanding of patterns and designing software with patterns, as well as reinforcing the lessons about the pattern concept we learned while writing earlier POSA volumes.

After completing POSA4—ten years after the publication of POSA1—we felt we were prepared take the last step in our work on patterns: to explore the pattern concept in detail and document what patterns are, what they are not, and how patterns can support the systematic and constructive design of software. The results is this volume, which covers our latest insights and experience on the conceptual foundations of patterns, as well as our perspective on what supporting methods, techniques, and tools are needed to support *Pattern-Oriented Software Architecture*. We believe we have realized our original vision from 1992.

The fact that the final chapter of our work on *Pattern-Oriented Software Architecture* has come to an end, however, does not mean that there is nothing more to say about patterns. Nor does it mean that the pattern concept has reached its ultimate maturity or that no more patterns remain to be discovered and documented. Instead, we see the work in this book as a forward step, a STABLE INTERMEDIATE FORM, in the study of patterns that forms a solid foundation for the next steps, whatever they may be and wherever they may lead. Just as each pattern and pattern language is a work in progress, so too is the work on the pattern concept itself.

We will continue to participate in and contribute to this ongoing work, but we have no plans to write further POSA volumes... at least for now. All good things truly do come to an end, and we think it is time for the next generation of researchers to explore new domains, to seek out new patterns and new pattern languages, and to boldly document solutions to problems that no one has documented before.

May the forces be with you.

Pattern Concept Summary

This appendix summarizes key pattern terms that we use and define in greater detail within the book. When a definition consists of other terms also defined here, we italicize these terms. The focus here is explicitly on software and its development, otherwise terms such as 'architecture' and 'design' would obviously have far broader scope.

Analysis Pattern   A *pattern* that describes how to model a particular kind of problem in a business domain.

Anti-Pattern   See *Dysfunctional Pattern*.

Architectural Style   The key *software architecture* decisions common across a number of different architectures that are considered at one level equivalent. Architectural style allows the characterization and comparison of similar and dissimilar architectures.

Architecture   See *Software Architecture*.

Benefits   The *consequences* of a pattern that are considered beneficial.

Code Smell   A code-level *problem* that creates the motivation and *context* for *refactoring*. A code smell may have arisen from or be equivalent to a *dysfunctional pattern*.

Composite Pattern   See *Pattern Compound*.

Compound Pattern   See *Pattern Compound*.

Consequences   The results of applying a *pattern*. Consequences may be characterized in terms of *benefits* and *liabilities*.

Context   The situation in which a *pattern* is applied. The context can be characterized in general terms, describing general properties of an environment or, in specific terms, describing the preceding patterns that might
have been applied within a *pattern language* or *pattern sequence.*

Design   A creational and intentional act: the conception and construction of a
structure on purpose for a purpose. Design embraces the activities
performed by software developers that results in the *software architecture* of a system. Often the term 'design' is also used as a name for
the result of these activities.

Design Pattern   A design *pattern* provides a scheme for refining elements of a software
system or the relationships between them. It describes a commonly-
recurring structure of interacting *roles* that solves a general design
problem within a particular context.

Dysfunctional   A *pattern* whose *problem* and *solution* are not well aligned, so that the
Pattern   *consequences* of the pattern are a comparable or worse problem situation rather than a resolution. A pattern may be dysfunctional because
it does not correctly or completely characterize a problem or because
its solution is simply a poor one for the problem identified.

Example   See *Motivating Example.*

Forces   The features or characteristics of a situation that, when brought together, find themselves in conflict and create a *problem*. To consider
any *solution* to the problem effective, the forces must be balanced.

Generative   The quality possessed by a general process or rule that allows it to
create specific solutions.

Idiom   An idiom is a *pattern* specific to a programming language or programming environment. An idiom describes how to implement particular
behavior or structures in code using the features of the given language or environment. The term is also used more generally to refer
to common practices associated with a programming language or environment, without necessarily being patterns.

Liabilities   The *consequences* of a pattern that are considered problematic.

Literal Pattern   A literal pattern name is a direct description of a *pattern* using termi-
Name   nology in its primary sense, rather than in a metaphorical way.

Metaphorical Pattern Name A metaphorical pattern name creates an association between a *pattern* and another concept, for example a concept from everyday life, with which readers are hopefully familiar.

Motivating Example A concrete example used to demonstrate the type of problem a particular *pattern* resolves and how its solution can be implemented.

Noun-Phrase Pattern Name Noun-phrase names describe the result created by a *pattern*. They typically describe the solution structure of the pattern, and in some cases may explicitly enumerate the key *roles*. The emphasis of a noun-phrase name is on the artifact resulting from applying a pattern rather than the process of the pattern.

Organizational Pattern An organizational *pattern* addresses the structure of a development organization. It describes a commonly-recurring structure of interacting human or departmental *roles* that solves a development process problem.

Patlet An abbreviated description of a *pattern*, often, but not necessarily, associated with a simple diagram.

Pattern A pattern describes a particular recurring design problem that arises in specific design contexts and presents a well-proven solution for the problem. The solution is specified by describing the *roles* of its constituent participants, their responsibilities and *relationships*, and the ways in which they collaborate.

Pattern Catalog See *Pattern Collection*.

Pattern Collection Any organized grouping of *patterns*. The contents of a collection may be ad hoc or they may have been collected together to address a particular domain, problem, or level of abstraction. The organization of a collection may be unstructured or structured.

Pattern Compound A *pattern* that is made up of a community of patterns. A commonly recurring subcommunity of patterns that can be identified as a distinct pattern in its own right. Pattern compounds are also known as *compound patterns* and *composite patterns*.

Pattern Description A description of a *pattern* expressed in some *pattern form*. A pattern description describes the *problem* solved by a pattern and the *solution* proposed to resolve it. Ideally, a pattern description should make

clear the *context* in which the pattern applies, the *forces* that characterize the problem, and the *consequences* of applying the solution. A
pattern description may also include other detail as appropriate, such
as source code and diagrams.

Pattern Form   The documented structure and style used to describe a *pattern*.

Pattern Language   A network of interrelated *patterns* that define a process for resolving software development problems systematically.

Pattern Name   The name by which a pattern is known. The most common grammatical style for naming patterns is to use a *noun-phrase pattern name*, but *verb-phrase pattern names* are also popular. In terms of description, pattern names typically fall between *literal pattern names* and *metaphorical pattern names*. A pattern may be known by more than one name, depending on the technical context and the history of different pattern descriptions.

Pattern Repository   See *Pattern Collection*.

Pattern Sequence   A sequence of *patterns* applied to create a particular architecture or design in response to a specific situation. From the point of view of a *pattern language*, a pattern sequence represents a particular path through the language.

Pattern Story   A narrative that captures a *pattern sequence* and specific *design* issues involved in constructing a concrete system or creating a particular design example.

Pedagogical Pattern   A *pattern* that captures a recurring practice used in teaching, typically the teaching of software development.

Piecemeal Growth   The process of building a system in stable increments, responding to feedback, in contrast to a large-lump, master-planned approach, in which all design occurs before any kind of construction.

Problem   The undesirable situation within a *context* that a *pattern* proposes to address with a *solution*. A problem can be understood in terms of conflicting *forces* that need to be balanced.

Problem Frame   A problem frame names, bounds, and describes a recurring kind of problem. It is a generalization of a class of problem and the techniques that are used to understand and reason about that kind of problem.

Proto-Pattern A *problem–solution* pairing that is considered to have recurrence, but which is not yet fully understood in terms of a *pattern description* or the nature of the *problem* it solves.

Quality Without A Name (QWAN) See *Wholeness*.

Refactoring An incremental activity that improves the internal structure of software through successive, behavior-preserving transformations.

Relationship An association between *design* elements. A relationship may be static or dynamic. Static relationships show directly in source code. They deal with the placement of components within an architecture. Dynamic relationships deal with the interaction between components. They may not be easily visible from source code or diagrams.

Role The responsibility of a *design* element within a context of related elements. For example, an object-oriented class defines a single role that all its instances support. Another example is an interface that defines a role that all implementations support. If an element supports a given role it must provide an implementation of the interface defining the role. Elements expose different roles by implementing different interfaces. Different elements may expose the same role by implementing the same interface, which allows clients to treat them polymorphically with respect to that particular role. An implemented element may take different roles, even within a single *pattern*.

Running Example A concrete example used to illustrate the kind of problem a particular *pattern collection*, *pattern sequence*, or *pattern language* addresses and how the patterns can be applied in practice. A running example is built up incrementally within each individual *pattern description*.

SEP Somebody Else's Problem, Software Engineering Process, or Software Engineering with Patterns, whichever you prefer.

Software Architecture A software architecture represents the set of significant *design* decisions within a system. Such decisions can include, but are not restricted to, a description of the subsystems and components of a software system and the *relationships* between them. Subsystems and components are often specified via different views to show the relevant functional, operational, and developmental properties of a software system. The software architecture of a system is an artifact that results from software *design* activities.

Solution   The structure or activity that a *pattern* proposes to resolve the *problem* and *forces* the pattern addresses.

Thumbnail   A summary of a *pattern*, normally containing a brief *problem* statement and a summary of the essence of the pattern's *solution*.

Verb-Phrase   Verb-phrase names are imperative, giving an instruction that describes
Pattern Name   how to achieve a *pattern's* desired *solution* state. The emphasis of a verb-phrase name is on the process of the pattern rather than the solution artifact.

Wholeness   The quality possessed by a design that is considered in some way complete, sustainable, sufficient, habitable, and pleasing.

Referenced Patterns

This chapter presents extended abstracts for all patterns referenced in this book. All pattern abstracts also reference the original pattern source(s), which allows you to look up more details. Patterns are listed in alphabetical order. Patterns known by more than one name—or that are so closely related as to be interchangeable in many cases—have a full definition under one entry and a cross reference from any other names. For patterns whose quality or classification is considered questionable by us or by the software patterns community as a whole, we also explain briefly what their specific problems are or why they are considered to be of low quality.

Abstract Factory The ABSTRACT FACTORY pattern [GoF95] [POSA4] provides an interface for creating and deleting families of related or dependent objects without coupling clients to concrete classes. A concrete factory implements the factory interface for a given type of object family.

Acceptor-Connector The ACCEPTOR-CONNECTOR pattern [POSA2] [POSA4] decouples the connection and initialization of cooperating peer services in a networked system from the processing performed by the peer services after they are connected and initialized.

Active Object The ACTIVE OBJECT pattern [POSA2] [POSA4] decouples service requests from service execution to enhance concurrency and simplify synchronized access to objects that reside in their own threads of control. A PROXY represents the interface to the active object, so that service invocations are executed in a client's thread. A servant object executes requests in its own thread, and represents the active part.

Adapted Iterator The ADAPTED ITERATOR pattern (*Chapter 6, Pattern Compounds*) expresses an ITERATOR through an OBJECT ADAPTER.

Adapter The ADAPTER pattern [GoF95] converts the interface of a class into another interface that clients expect. Due to fundamental differences between its variations, however, adaptation is better considered a family of complementary patterns rather than a single pattern [NoBr02]. Members of this family include CLASS ADAPTER, DECORATOR, FACADE, OBJECT ADAPTER, PLUGGABLE ADAPTER, TWO-WAY ADAPTER, and WRAPPER FACADE.

Align Architecture and Organization See CONWAY'S LAW.

Application Controller The APPLICATION CONTROLLER pattern [Fow02] [POSA4] separates user interface navigation from the control and orchestration of an application's workflow. An application controller receives service requests from the application's user interface, decides which concrete service to invoke on its functionality dependent on the current state of its workflow, and determines which view to present at the user interface in response to the executed service.

Architect Also Implements The ARCHITECT ALSO IMPLEMENTS pattern [CoHa04] ensures that architects do not become disconnected from the consequences of their decisions or the reality of practice. Rather than treating an architect as having an ivory-tower role, ensure that architects are involved in day-to-day implementation.

Architecture Follows Organization The ARCHITECTURE FOLLOWS ORGANIZATION (*Chapter 5, Pattern Complements*) pattern recommends aligning the structure of the architecture with the structure of the development organization to ease the tension that can arise if they are mismatched.

Asynchronous Completion Token (ACT) The ASYNCHRONOUS COMPLETION TOKEN pattern [POSA2] [POSA4] allows event-driven software to demultiplex and process the responses of asynchronous operations it invokes on services efficiently.

Automated Garbage Collection The AUTOMATED GARBAGE COLLECTION pattern [POSA4] provides a safe and simple mechanism for reclaiming memory used by objects that are no longer needed. Objects in memory that are no longer referenced by live objects in an application can be reclaimed automatically.

Batch Iterator The BATCH ITERATOR pattern (*Chapter 6, Pattern Compounds*) implements an ITERATOR with a BATCH METHOD to step through multiple elements at a time.

Batch Method The BATCH METHOD pattern [Hen01c] [POSA4] folds together repeated accesses to the elements of an aggregate object to reduce the costs of multiple individual accesses.

Blackboard The BLACKBOARD pattern [POSA1] [POSA4] is useful for problems for which no deterministic solution strategies are known. Several specialized subsystems can use a blackboard to assemble their knowledge to build a possibly partial or approximate solution.

Bridge The BRIDGE pattern [GoF95] [POSA4] decouples an abstraction from its implementations so that the two can vary independently. It partitions an object into a handle, which represents the abstraction, and a body, which contains the implementation.

Broker The BROKER pattern [POSA1] [POSA4] [VKZ04] underpins distributed software systems whose components interact by remote method invocations. A federation of brokers manages key aspects of interprocess communication between components, ranging from forwarding requests to transmitting results and exceptions.

Build Prototypes The BUILD PROTOTYPES pattern [CoHa04] mitigates the risk associated with trying to build a product against unvalidated requirements. Building a prototype of the product allows gathering and clarifying of requirements to better assess risk and scope.

Builder The BUILDER pattern [GoF95] [POSA4] separates the construction and destruction of a complex object from its representation, so that the same construction and destruction process can create and delete different representations.

Bureaucracy The BUREAUCRACY pattern [Rie98] helps to implement hierarchical object or component structures that allow interaction with every level of the hierarchy and maintain their inner consistency themselves.

Business Delegate   The BUSINESS DELEGATE pattern [ACM03] [POSA4] encapsulates infrastructure concerns associated with access to a remote component, such as lookup, load balancing, and network error handling, from clients that use the component. A business delegate enables location transparency when invoking components in a distributed application.

Cantrip   The CANTRIP pattern [Ray04] defines a non-interactive program that takes no input and generates no output, only a status result. A cantrip is invoked as a simple, stand-alone command.

Chain of Responsibility   The CHAIN OF RESPONSIBILITY pattern [GoF95] [POSA4] avoids coupling the sender of a request to its receiver by giving more than one object a chance to handle the request. The receiving objects are chained together and the request is passed along the chain until an object handles it.

Class Adapter   The CLASS ADAPTER pattern [GoF95] converts the interface of a class into another interface that clients expect. Adaptation lets classes work together that could not otherwise collaborate due to incompatible interfaces. Class adapters are realized by subclassing the adaptee implementation and implementing the adapted interface—which may also be in terms of subclassing—to yield a single object, which avoids an additional level of indirection.

CLI Server   The CLI SERVER pattern [Ray04] characterizes programs that, when run in the foreground, offer a simple command-line interface on the standard input and output streams, but when run in the background take their I/O from a TCP/IP port.

Client Proxy   The CLIENT PROXY pattern [POSA1] [POSA4] [GoF95] [VKZ04] offers clients the same programmatic interface as a remote component with which they interact. Clients can access the remote component in a location-independent manner, as if it were collocated with the client.

Collections for States   The COLLECTIONS FOR STATES pattern [Hen99a] [POSA4] externalizes the state of an object by associating each state of interest with a separate collection that refers to all objects in that state. State transitions become transfers between collections.

Combined Method   The COMBINED METHOD pattern [Hen01c] [POSA4] arranges methods that are commonly used together into a single method to ensure correctness and improve efficiency in multi-threaded and distributed environments.

Command   The COMMAND pattern [GoF95] [POSA4] encapsulates a request as an object, thereby enabling the parameterization of clients with different requests and support for undo-able objects.

Command Processor   The COMMAND PROCESSOR pattern [POSA1] [POSA4] separates the request for a service from its execution. A command processor manages requests as separate COMMAND objects, schedules their execution, and provides additional services, such as logging and storage of request objects for later undo/redo.

Command Sequence   See COMPOSITE COMMAND.

Community of Trust   The COMMUNITY OF TRUST pattern [CoHa04] provides an organizational framework in which people in a team can trust each other to achieve a common goal. In particular, all things and actions are done explicitly and visibly for everybody on the team to demonstrate that they are working toward the common goal and not for themselves.

Compiler   The COMPILER pattern [Ray04] represents non-interactive programs that transform files of one form into files of another form. They may emit messages on the standard error stream, but otherwise take no other input and offer no other output.

Completion Headroom   The COMPLETION HEADROOM pattern [CoHa04] helps to estimate completion dates using the remaining effort estimates in a work queue report. The earliest possible completion date of each contributor is calculated, and the latest of these identified and compared to the hard delivery date for the project. The difference is the completion headroom.

Component Configurator   The COMPONENT CONFIGURATOR pattern [POSA2] [POSA4] allows an application to load and unload its component implementations at runtime without having to modify, recompile, or statically relink the application. It also supports the reconfiguration of components into different application processes without having to shut down and restart running processes.

Composite   The COMPOSITE pattern [GoF95] [POSA4] defines a partitioning for objects representing whole-part hierarchies composed of similar types of
objects. Classes for individual objects and for compositions of objects
implement a common interface, so that clients can treat individuals
and compositions uniformly.

Composite   The COMPOSITE COMMAND pattern (*Chapter 6, Pattern Compounds*) en-
Command   capsulates requests as an object, hiding the difference between single
requests and multiple requests behind a common interface.

Composite-   See MODEL-VIEW-CONTROLLER.
Strategy-
Observer

Context Object   The CONTEXT OBJECT pattern [ACM03] [Kel04] [KSS05] [Hen05b]
[POSA4] captures environmental services and information in component object form that can be passed to services or plug-in component
objects that need to access their surrounding execution context.

Conway's Law   The CONWAY'S LAW pattern [Cope95] [CoHa04] recommends aligning
the architecture and the development organization to ease the tension
that can arise if they are mismatched. Thus, ORGANIZATION FOLLOWS
ARCHITECTURE, or ARCHITECTURE FOLLOWS ORGANIZATION, or some combination of both.

Cooperate, Don't   The COOPERATE, DON'T CONTROL pattern [ORei05] advises Web appli-
Control   cations to open up through the use of Web Services and content syndication, and to build on equivalent services offered by others.

CORBA-   The CORBA-CGI GATEWAY pattern [MM97] introduces a gateway be-
CGI Gateway   tween a CORBA object model and a non-CORBA aware Web front-end
using the Common Gateway Interface (CGI). The scope of this pattern,
however, is unnecessarily restrictive with respect to CORBA, and the
same reasoning applies to interfacing between many different technologies that a simple Web interface will be unaware of.

Data Access   The DATA ACCESS OBJECT pattern [ACM03] supports encapsulating
Object (DAO)   the access and manipulation of persistent data in a separate layer
from the application logic.

Data is the Next Intel Inside The DATA IS THE NEXT INTEL INSIDE pattern [ORei05] [MuOr+07] focuses on the ownership of distinctive data rather than functionality as the business advantage for a Web application.

Data Transfer Object (DTO) The DATA TRANSFER OBJECT pattern [ACM03] [Fow02] [POSA4] reduces the number of update or query calls made to a remote component object by packaging groups of attributes into a simple object for passing or returning in single calls.

Decorator The DECORATOR pattern [GoF95] [POSA4] supports dynamic attachment of additional behaviors to an object. Decorators provide a flexible alternative to subclassing for adapting and extending class functionality at the instance level.

Disposal Method The DISPOSAL METHOD design pattern [Hen02b] [POSA4] encapsulates the details of object disposal by providing a method for destroying or otherwise finalizing an object, instead of having clients destroy the objects themselves or leaving them to a garbage collector.

Distributed Callback The DISTRIBUTED CALLBACK pattern [MM97] takes advantage of asynchrony by introducing an EXPLICIT INTERFACE for callbacks in a CORBA environment, in which each callback method on the interface is defined in IDL to be a oneway operation. The default semantics of CORBA oneway operations are not well defined, so the advice of this pattern should generally be ignored in favor of expressing asynchrony via more suitable MESSAGE mechanisms, such as asynchronous method invocations or so-called 'reliable' oneway operations.

Domain Appropriate Devices The DOMAIN APPROPRIATE DEVICES pattern [Bor01] simplifies human computer interaction by using input devices that resemble real objects from the application domain of the interactive system.

Domain Model The DOMAIN MODEL pattern [Fow02] [POSA4] defines a precise model for the structure and workflow of an application domain—including their variations. Model elements are abstractions meaningful in the application domain; their roles and interactions reflect domain workflow and map to system requirements.

Domain Object The DOMAIN OBJECT pattern [POSA4] encapsulates a self-contained, coherent functional or infrastructural responsibility into a well-defined entity that offers its functionality via one or more explicit interfaces, while hiding its inner structure and implementation.

Domain Store   The DOMAIN STORE pattern [ACM03] separates persistence from the
core domain object model to allow transparent persistence for the object model. The persistence mechanism is non-intrusive with respect
to the object model.

Don't Flip The   The DON'T FLIP THE BOZO BIT pattern [McC96] helps to improve team
Bozo Bit   communication by getting everyone in a team involved in contributing
ideas about any subject and matter of relevance for the success of the
project and tasks on which the team is working.

Dynamic   The DYNAMIC INVOCATION INTERFACE pattern [POSA4] offers a supple-
Invocation   mentary interface to a statically typed interface. DII allows clients to
Interface (DII) invoke methods on objects more dynamically, composing the calls at
runtime rather than selecting them statically from declarations.

ed   The ED pattern [Ray04] defines programs with a simple interaction
model. They interpret a simple command language on the standard
input, and are therefore scriptable.

Encapsulated   See CONTEXT OBJECT.
Context

Engage   The ENGAGE CUSTOMERS pattern [CoHa04] helps development organi-
Customers   zations ensure and maintain customer satisfaction by encouraging
communication between customers and key development roles, such
as developer and architect.

Enumeration   The ENUMERATION METHOD pattern [Beck96] [Hen01c] [POSA4] encap-
Method   sulates iteration over an aggregate component to execute an action on
each element of the component into a method on the aggregate. The
action is passed in as an object by the caller.

Explicit Interface The EXPLICIT INTERFACE pattern [POSA4] separates component usage
from realization details. Clients depend only on the contract that the
component interface defines, but not on the component's internal design, implementation specifics, location, synchronization mechanisms, and other realization details.

External Iterator See ITERATOR.

Facade   The FACADE pattern [GoF95] [POSA4] provides a unified, higher-level
interface to a set of interfaces in a subsystem that makes the subsystem easier to use.

Factory Method   The FACTORY METHOD design pattern [GoF95] [POSA4] encapsulates the concrete details of object creation by providing a method for object creation, rather than letting clients instantiate the concrete class themselves.

Few Panes Per Window   The FEW PANES PER WINDOW pattern [BeCu87] ensures that users of a windowing application are not overwhelmed with complex windows.

Filter   The FILTER pattern [Ray04] defines a non-interactive program or execution of a program that takes data on standard input, transforms it in some fashion, and sends the result to standard output.

Firewall Proxy   The FIREWALL PROXY pattern [SFHBS06] [POSA1] [POSA4] helps protect an application from external attacks by introducing a proxy for its services that inspects the payload of service requests to detect and block suspicious content.

Flat And Narrow Tree   The FLAT AND NARROW TREE pattern [Bor01] avoids large information hierarchies in user interfaces of interactive systems by organizing system content via a tree-structured hierarchy that is no more than five levels deep and has no more than seven branches in any node.

Forwarder-Receiver   The FORWARDER-RECEIVER pattern [POSA1] provides transparent interprocess communication for software systems with a peer-to-peer interaction model. It decouples the peers from the underlying communication mechanisms.

Front Controller   The FRONT CONTROLLER pattern [Fow02] [POSA4] establishes a single entry point into an application—the front controller—that consolidates the handling and execution of service requests issued through its user interface.

Half-Sync/Half-Async   The HALF-SYNC/HALF-ASYNC pattern [POSA2] [POSA4] decouples synchronous and asynchronous service processing in concurrent systems, to simplify programming without unduly reducing performance. The pattern introduces two intercommunicating layers, one for synchronous and one for asynchronous service processing.

Harnessing Collective Intelligence   The HARNESSING COLLECTIVE INTELLIGENCE pattern [ORei05] [MuOr+07] ensures an open 'architecture of participation' in the design of Web applications, so that users can add value to an application by adding data.

Immutable Value   The IMMUTABLE VALUE pattern [Hen00] [POSA4] sets the internal state of value objects at construction and disallows subsequent changes of their state by supporting methods that can at most query the private state. Immutable values can be shared between threads in a concurrent program without the need for additional synchronization.

Information Just In Time   The INFORMATION JUST IN TIME pattern [Bor01] avoids overwhelming users of interactive systems with usage instructions. These instructions are deferred until users need to know about them to proceed, and they are kept as short as possible.

Interceptor   The INTERCEPTOR pattern [POSA2] [POSA4] allows the transparent configuration of event-related processing into a framework and the automatic triggering of this processing when specific events occur.

Internal Iterator   See ENUMERATION METHOD.

Interpreter   The INTERPRETER pattern [GoF95] [POSA4] defines an interpreter for a simple language by modeling the grammar in terms of objects and making the grammar's representation directly executable with respect to a CONTEXT OBJECT that carries invocation state.

Invisible Hardware   The INVISIBLE HARDWARE pattern [Bor01] hides as much of the computer-related hardware of an interactive system as possible. Users see only devices that generate images relevant for the application domain of the interactive system.

Involve Everyone   The INVOLVE EVERYONE pattern [MaRi04] tries to make the introduction of a new idea across an organization successful by ensuring that everyone has an opportunity to contribute and support.

Iterator   The ITERATOR pattern [GoF95] [POSA4] provides a way to access the elements of an aggregate component sequentially without exposing its underlying representation. A separate, controllable iterator object is used to traverse the aggregate.

Layers   The LAYERS pattern [POSA1] [POSA4] helps to structure applications that can be decomposed into groups of subtasks in which each group of subtasks is at a particular level of abstraction, granularity, hardware-distance, rate of developmental change, or other partitioning criteria.

Leader/ Followers The LEADER/FOLLOWERS pattern [POSA2] [POSA4] provides an efficient concurrency model in which multiple threads take turns to share a set of event sources in order to detect, demultiplex, dispatch, and process service requests that occur on the event sources.

Leveraging the Long Tail The LEVERAGING THE LONG TAIL pattern [ORei05] [MuOr+07] suggests that the value of much of the Web, and therefore of many sites and applications, is in the niches, not just the obvious applications in the 'center.'

Macro Command See COMPOSITE COMMAND.

Manager See OBJECT MANAGER.

Mediator The MEDIATOR pattern [GoF95] [POSA4] promotes loose coupling between a group of objects by being the only object that has detailed knowledge of the methods of other objects. Objects communicate with each other through the mediator, rather than referring to each other directly.

Memento The MEMENTO [GoF95] [POSA4] pattern captures and externalizes the internal state of an object without violating its encapsulation. This externalized state can be used to later reset the object's state.

Message The MESSAGE pattern [HoWo03] [POSA4] encapsulates the information that two application objects can exchange into a data structure that can be transmitted across a network.

Methods for States The METHODS FOR STATES pattern [Hen02c] [POSA4] realizes all the behavior of an object as internal methods within a single class, rather than across multiple classes. Groups of method references are used to define the object's behavior in a particular mode.

Mock Object The MOCK OBJECT pattern [MFP00] [Beck03] is used for unit testing of code that interacts with external dependencies. The mock is primed to behave in a way that is appropriate for the unit test case and, if appropriate, to allow inspection by the test of its usage by the code under test.

Model-View-Controller (MVC) The MODEL-VIEW-CONTROLLER pattern [POSA1] [POSA4] [Fow02] divides an interactive application with respect to three roles. The model contains the core functionality and data. Views display information to the user. Controllers handle user input. Views and controllers together comprise the user interface. A change-propagation mechanism ensures consistency between the user interface and the model.

Monitor Object The MONITOR OBJECT pattern [POSA2] [POSA4] synchronizes concurrent method execution to ensure that only one method at a time runs within an object. It also allows an object's methods to schedule their execution sequences cooperatively.

Mutable Companion The MUTABLE COMPANION pattern [Hen00] supports the creation, through progressive modification of state, of value objects whose state is immutable.

Network Effects by Default The NETWORK EFFECTS BY DEFAULT pattern [ORei05] advises that instead of relying on users to add value to an application, set inclusive defaults that aggregate user data as an additional consequence of using the application.

Nouns and Verbs The NOUNS AND VERBS pattern [BeCu87] defines a user-interface model that addresses the balance between elements that need to persist and elements that are transient. Lists of things, the nouns, are offered in a list pane, which persists through interactions. The actions, the verbs, are offered in menus, which pop up and then disappear as the action commences.

Null Object The NULL OBJECT pattern [And96] [Woolf97] [Hen02a] [POSA4] encapsulates the absence of an object by providing a substitutable alternative that offers suitable default 'do-nothing' behavior.

Object Adapter The OBJECT ADAPTER pattern [GoF95] [POSA4] converts the interface of a class into another interface that clients expect. Adaptation lets classes work together that could not otherwise because of incompatible interfaces. The use of an object relationship to express wrapping ensures that the adaptation is encapsulated.

Object Manager The OBJECT MANAGER pattern [POSA3] [POSA4] separates object usage from object management, to support explicit, centralized, and efficient handling of components, objects, and resources.

Objects for States	The OBJECTS FOR STATES pattern [GoF95] [DyAn97] [POSA4] separates an object into two parts: the mode-dependent behavior of an object and the representation of the normal instance data. The object holding the instance data forwards method calls to a mode object, which is an instance from a class hierarchy that represents the behavior in a particular state.
Observer	The OBSERVER pattern [GoF95] [POSA4] helps to synchronize the state of cooperating component objects by enabling one-way propagation of changes from a subject to its observers. The observers of a subject object are notified by the subject when its state changes.
Organization Follows Architecture	The ORGANIZATION FOLLOWS ARCHITECTURE pattern (*Chapter 5, Pattern Complements*) recommends aligning the structure of the development organization with the structure of the architecture to ease the tension that can arise if they are mismatched.
Page Controller	The PAGE CONTROLLER pattern [Fow02] [POSA4] introduces a defined entry point, the page controller, for each form in a form-based user interface, to consolidate the handling and execution of service requests issued through each form.
Perpetual Beta	THE PERPETUAL BETA pattern [ORei05] [MuOr+07] treats applications as evolvable services rather than static software artifacts. Instead of monolithic releases, features are added on a regular and incremental basis.
Pipes and Filters	The PIPES AND FILTERS pattern [POSA1] [POSA4] [HoWo03] provides a structure for systems that process data streams. Each processing step is encapsulated in a filter component. Pipes are used to pass data between adjacent filters.
Pluggable Adapter	The PLUGGABLE ADAPTER pattern [GoF95] realizes a flexible form of adaptation, parameterizing an ADAPTER with a STRATEGY.
Pluggable Factory	The PLUGGABLE FACTORY pattern [Vlis98c] [Vlis99] provides a configurable factory. The creation of individual product types is parameterized through PROTOTYPE instances or some form of STRATEGY.

Polyvalent-
Program
The POLYVALENT-PROGRAM pattern [Ray04] characterizes programs whose architecture allows them to have a variety of interfaces, ranging from programmatic API to command-line and/or GUI, CANTRIP to ROGUELIKE.

Presentation-
Abstraction-
Control (PAC)
The PRESENTATION-ABSTRACTION-CONTROL pattern [POSA1] [POSA4] defines a structure for interactive software systems in the form of a hierarchy of cooperating agents. Each agent is responsible for a specific aspect of the application's functionality and consists of three components: presentation, abstraction, and control. This subdivision separates the human-computer interaction aspects of an agent from its functional core and its communication with other agents.

Proactor
The PROACTOR pattern [POSA2] [POSA4] allows event-driven software to demultiplex and dispatch service requests triggered by the completion of asynchronous operations efficiently, thereby achieving the performance benefits of concurrency without incurring some of its liabilities. Events are handled asynchronously, but completion is handled in the application's thread of control.

Prototype
The PROTOTYPE pattern [GoF95] specifies the type(s) of object to create using a prototypical instance and allows the creation of new objects by copying this prototype.

Prototype–
Abstract Factory
See PLUGGABLE FACTORY.

Proxy
The PROXY pattern [POSA1] [POSA4] [GoF95] enables clients of a component to communicate transparently via a surrogate rather than with the component itself. This surrogate can serve many purposes, including simplified client programming, enhanced efficiency, and protection from unauthorized access.

Publisher-
Subscriber
The PUBLISHER-SUBSCRIBER pattern [POSA4] structures distributed software systems whose services or components interact by exchanging events asynchronously in a one-to-many configuration. Publishers and subscribers of events are generally unaware of one another. Subscribers are interested in consuming events, not in knowing their publishers. Similarly, publishers just supply events, and are not interested in knowing who subscribes to them.

Reactor The REACTOR pattern [POSA2] [POSA4] allows event-driven software to demultiplex and dispatch service requests that are delivered to an application from one or more clients. An event-handling infrastructure waits on event multiple sources simultaneously, but only demultiplexes and dispatches one event at a time.

Reflection The REFLECTION pattern [POSA1] [POSA4] provides a mechanism for dynamically changing the structure and behavior of software systems. It supports the modification of fundamental aspects, such as type structures and function call mechanisms. This pattern separates an application into two parts. A base level includes the core application logic. The runtime behavior of the base level is observed by a meta level, which maintains information about selected system properties to make the software aware of its runtime context. Changes to information kept in the meta level can thus affect and guide subsequent base level behavior.

Remote Proxy See CLIENT PROXY.

Resource Lifecycle Manager See OBJECT MANAGER.

Roguelike The ROGUELIKE pattern [Ray04] defines programs that use the visual display more fully and are driven by keystrokes. They are interactive but not easily scriptable.

Separated Engine and Interface The SEPARATED ENGINE AND INTERFACE pattern [Ray04] defines an architecture for programs that separates the *engine* part of the program, which holds the core logic for the application domain, from the *interface* part, which is responsible for presentation logic and user interaction. The engine and interface roles are normally realized in separate processes.

Short Menus The SHORT MENUS pattern [BeCu87] ensures that pop-up menus can be searched conveniently by making them short, fixed, and single-level.

Singleton The SINGLETON pattern [GoF95] ensures that a class has only one instance and provides a global point of access to it. This pattern, however, has a long history of abuse and subtlety. It commonly plays the role of a global variable rather than enforcing a genuine creation constraint. In addition, it is hard to evolve SINGLETON-based designs, since singletons are often tightly coupled to a particular context, just like global variables.

Sink
The SINK pattern [Ray04] characterizes non-interactive programs that only take data on the standard input and emit no output.

Smart Pointer
The SMART POINTER pattern for C++ [Mey96] [Hen05a] helps to control access to objects accessed through a level of indirection. A class defines conventional pointer operations, such as `operator*` and `operator->`, so that access to the target object is provided but is also managed.

Software Above the Level of a Single Device
The SOFTWARE ABOVE THE LEVEL OF A SINGLE DEVICE pattern [ORei05] [MuOr+07] increases the value of Web applications by ensuring that they are designed with integration and multiple targets in mind, rather than from a PC-centric perspective.

Some Rights Reserved
The SOME RIGHTS RESERVED pattern [ORei05] encourages the use of existing standards and nonrestrictive licenses for Web sites to increase experimentation, collective adoption, aggregation, and mixing.

Source
The SOURCE pattern [Ray04] characterizes non-interactive programs that only emit data on the standard output stream and take no input.

Stable Intermediate Forms
The STABLE INTERMEDIATE FORMS pattern [Hen04a] reduces the risk involved in a process of change. Any change from one state of affairs to another that cannot be characterized as atomic inevitably involves a number of steps, any one of which could fail for one reason or another, leaving the change incomplete and the circumstances uncertain. Risk can be reduced by ensuring that each intermediate step in the process of change expresses a coherent state, one that in some meaningful way represents a whole rather than a partial state of affairs.

Standard Panes
The STANDARD PANES pattern [BeCu87] alleviates the need for users to learn how to operate every type of pane offered in a window. Each pane is cast into the format offered by one of a few standard panes.

State
See OBJECTS FOR STATES.

Strategized Locking
The STRATEGIZED LOCKING pattern [POSA2] [POSA4] parameterizes a component to enable user selection of the most appropriate synchronization mechanism to serialize the component's critical sections.

Strategy
The STRATEGY pattern [GoF95] [POSA4] captures a family of operations that vary together. Each variant is encapsulated within an object that shares a common interface with other variations. The use of these pluggable behavior objects is independent of the implementation variant.

Template Method
The TEMPLATE METHOD pattern [GoF95] [POSA4] defines a skeleton of an algorithm within an operation, deferring some steps to subclasses. This pattern allows subclasses to redefine specific steps of an algorithm without changing the algorithm's structure.

Template View
The TEMPLATE VIEW pattern [Fow02] [POSA4] introduces a template that predefines the general structure of how dynamically produced data should be presented to a user. A template view eliminates the need to hard code a number of separate view implementations.

The Long Tail
See LEVERAGING THE LONG TAIL.

The Perpetual Beta
See PERPETUAL BETA.

Transfer Object
See DATA TRANSFER OBJECT.

Transform View
The TRANSFORM VIEW pattern [Fow02] [POSA4] introduces a dedicated transform view component that transforms data received from an application in response to specific user requests into concrete views onto the data.

Two-Way Adapter
The TWO-WAY ADAPTER pattern [GoF95] implements a CLASS ADAPTER so that both the adapted and adaptee interfaces are accessible, allowing the adaptee to be used wherever the adaptee is expected and vice versa. Thus two different clients can view the object differently.

Users Add Value
See HARNESSING COLLECTIVE INTELLIGENCE.

View Handler
The VIEW HANDLER pattern [POSA1] helps to manage all views that a software system provides, coordinating dependencies between views and organizing their updates.

Visitor
The VISITOR pattern [GoF95] [POSA4] allows an operation to be performed on the elements of an object structure in which the objects can be of different types. The operation can be specialized for each

type visited, without actually needing to modify the types visited. The types visited provide a method that accepts a visitor. The visitor role selects its behavior according to the type of the visited object.

Window Per Task The WINDOW PER TASK pattern [BeCu87] ensures that all information needed to complete a task is available and obvious to a user. For each task a specific window is created.

Wrapped Class Adapter The WRAPPED CLASS ADAPTER pattern (*Chapter 6, Pattern Compounds*) encapsulates a CLASS ADAPTER within an OBJECT ADAPTER.

Wrapper See ADAPTER and DECORATOR.

Wrapper Facade The WRAPPER FACADE pattern [POSA2] [POSA4] encapsulates the functions and data provided by existing non-object-oriented APIs within more concise, robust, portable, and cohesive object-oriented class interfaces.

References

[AbGu05]   D. Abrahams, A. Gurtovoy: *C++ Template Metaprogramming: Concepts, Tools, and Techniques from Boost and Beyond*, Addison-Wesley, 2005

[ACGH+96]   M. Adams, J. Coplien, R. Gamoke, R. Hanmer, F. Keeve, K. Nicodemus: *Fault-Tolerant Telecommunication System Patterns*, in [PLoPD2], 1996

[ACGN01]   H. Albin-Amiot, P. Cointe, Y.G. Guéhéneuc, N. Jussien: *Instantiating and Detecting Design Patterns: Putting Bits and Pieces Together*, Sixteenth IEEE International Conference on Automated Software Engineering (ASE '01), IEEE Computer Society, Los Alamitos, CA, 2001

[ACM03]   D. Alur, J. Crupi, D. Malks: *Core J2EE Patterns: Best Practices and Design Strategies*, Second Edition, Prentice Hall, 2003

[Ada79]   D. Adams: *The Hitch Hiker's Guide To The Galaxy*, Pan Books, 1979

[Ada82]   D. Adams: *Life, the Universe and Everything*, Pan Books, 1982

[ADMC85]   C. Alexander, with H. Davis, J. Martinez, D. Corner: *The Production of Houses*, Oxford University Press, New York, 1985

[AGA06]   P. Arumi, D. Garcia, X. Amatriain: *A Data Flow Pattern Language for Audio and Music Computing*, Proceedings of the Pattern Language of Program Conference, Portland, OR, October 21–23, 2006

[AIS77]   C. Alexander, S. Ishikawa, M. Silverstein with M. Jacobson, I. Fiksdahl-King, S. Angel: *A Pattern Language – Towns · Buildings · Construction*, Oxford University Press, 1977

[Ale79]   C. Alexander: *The Timeless Way of Building*, Oxford University Press, 1979

[Ale03a]   C. Alexander: *The Nature of Order, Book 1: The Phenomenon of Life*, The Center for Environmental Structure, Berkeley, California, 2003

[Ale03b]   C. Alexander: *The Nature of Order, Book 4: The Luminous Ground*, The Center for Environmental Structure, Berkeley, California, 2003

[Ale04a]   C. Alexander: *The Nature of Order, Book 2: The Process of Creating Life*, The Center for Environmental Structure, Berkeley, California, 2002

[Ale04b]   C. Alexander: *The Nature of Order, Book 3: A Vision of a Living World*, The Center for Environmental Structure, Berkeley, California, 2003

[And96]   B. Anderson: *Null Object*, presented at the First European Conference on Pattern Languages of Programming (EuroPLoP 1996), 1996

[App96]   B. Appleton: *Patterns and Software: Essential Concepts and Terminology*, http://www.cmcrossroads.com/bradapp/docs/patterns-intro.html, 1996

[APW98]   S.R. Alpert, K. Brown, B. Woolf: *The Design Patterns Smalltalk Companion*, Addison-Wesley, 1998

[ASAIA75]   C. Alexander, M. Silverstein, S. Angel, S. Ishikawa, D. Abrams: *The Oregon Experiment*, Oxford University Press, 1975

[Aus99]   M.H. Austern: *Generic Programming and the STL*, Addison-Wesley, 1999

[AvZd06]   P. Avgeriou, U. Zdun: *Architectural Patterns Revised: A Pattern Language*, Proceedings of the Eleventh European Conference on Pattern Languages of Programming (EuroPLoP 2006), Irsee, Universitätsverlag Konstanz, July 2007

[Bat79]   G. Bateson: *Mind and Nature: A Necessary Unity*, Bantam Books, 1979

[BCC+96]   K. Beck, R. Crocker, J.O. Coplien, L. Dominick, G. Meszaros, F. Paulisch, J. Vlissides: *Industrial Experience with Design Patterns*, Proceedings of the Eighteenth International Conference on Software Engineering 1996 (ICSE '96), Berlin, March 1996, also available in [Ris98]

[BDS+99]   M. Beedle, M. Devos, Y. Sharon, K. Schwaber, J. Sutherland: *SCRUM: A Pattern Language for Hyperproductive Software Development*, in [PLoPD4]

[BeAp02]   S.P. Berczuk, B. Appelton: *Software Configuration Management Patterns: Effective Teamwork, Practical Integration*, Addison-Wesley, 2002

[Beck96]   K. Beck: *Smalltalk Best Practices*, Prentice Hall, 1996

[Beck03]   K. Beck: *Test-Driven Development: By Example*, Addison-Wesley, 2003

[Beck04]   K. Beck: *Extreme Programming Explained: Embrace Change*, Second Edition Addison-Wesley, 2004

[BeCu87]   K. Beck, W. Cunningham: *Using Pattern Languages for Object-Oriented Programs*, submission to the OOPSLA '87 workshop on Specification and Design for Object-Oriented Programming, October 1987

[Bell06]   A.E. Bell: *Software Development Amidst the Whiz of Silver Bullets...*, ACM Queue Volume 4, No. 5, June 2006

[Ber05]   J. Bergin: *Patterns for Agile Development Practice,* Proceedings of the Tenth European Conference on Pattern Languages of Programs (EuroPloP 2005), Irsee, Universitätsverlag Konstanz, July 2006

[Ber06]   J. Bergin: *Active Learning and Feedback Patterns*, Proceedings of the Thirteenth Conference on Pattern Languages of Program Design, Portland, Oregon, October 2006

[BGHS98]   F. Buschmann, A. Geisler, T. Heimke, C. Schuderer: *Framework-Based Software Architectures for Process Automation Systems*, self-contained Proceedings of the Ninth IFAC Symposium on Automation in Mining, Mineral, and Metal Processing (MMM '98), Cologne, Germany, 1998

[BGJ99]   A. Berner, M. Glinz, S. Joos: *A Classification of Stereotypes for Object-Oriented Modeling Languages*, Proceedings of "UML" '99 – *The Unified Modeling Language: Beyond the Standard*, R. France, B. Rumpe (eds.), Lecture Notes in Computer Science, 1723, Springer, 1999

[BHCY+04]   V. Bricot, D. Heliot, A. Cretoiu, Y. Yang, T. Simien, L.B. Hvatum: *Patterns for Managing Distributed Product Development Teams*, Proceedings of the Ninth European Conference on Pattern Languages of Programs (EuroPloP 2004), Irsee, Universitätsverlag Konstanz, July 2005

[BMMM98]   W.J. Brown, R.C. Malveau, H.W. McCormick, T.J. Mowbray: *AntiPatterns: Refactoring Software, Architecture, and Projects in Crisis*, John Wiley & Sons, 1998

[Boe82]   B.W. Boehm: *Software Engineering Economics*, Prentice Hall, 1982

[BoGa05]   T. Bozheva, M.E. Gallo: *Framework of Agile Patterns,* Proceedings of the Twelfth European Software Process Improvement Conference, EuroSPI 2005, Budapest, Hungary, November 9-11, 2005

[Booch]   G. Booch: *Handbook of Software Architecture*, http://www.booch.com/architecture/index.jsp

[Booch94]   G. Booch: *Object-Oriented Analysis and Design with Applications*, Second Edition, Benjamin Cummings, 1994

[Booch06]   G. Booch: *On Design*, Handbook of Software Architecture blog, March 2006, http://www.booch.com/architecture/blog.jsp?archive=2006-03.html

[Boost]   Boost C++ Libraries, http://www.boost.org/

[Bor01]   J. Borchers: *A Pattern Approach To Interaction Design*, John Wiley & Sons, 2001

[Bor06]   M. Bortenschlager: *A Flexible Coordination Language for Pervasive Computing Environments*, T. Pfeifer et al. (eds.), Advances in Pervasive Computing. Adjunct Proceedings of the Fourth International Conference on Pervasive Computing, Dublin, Ireland, 2006

[Bosch00]   J. Bosch: *Design and Use of Software Architectures: Adapting and Evolving a Product-Line Approach,* Addison-Wesley, 2000

[Box97]   D. Box: *Essential COM*, Addison-Wesley, 1997

[BRJ98]   G. Booch, J. Rumbaugh, I. Jacobsen: *The Unified Modeling Language User Guide*, Addison-Wesley, 1998

[BrJo05]   K. Braithwaite, T. Joyce: *XP Patterns: Patterns for Distributed eXtreme Programming*, Proceedings of the Tenth European Conference on Pattern Languages of Programs (EuroPloP 2005), Irsee, Universitätsverlag Konstanz, July 2006

[Bro86]   F.P. Brooks, Jr.: *No Silver Bullet: Essence and Accidents of Software Engineering*, in Information Processing '86. H.J. Kugler, ed., Elsevier Science Publishers B.V. (North Holland): 1069–1076, invited paper, International Federation of Information Processing (IFIP) Congress '86, Dublin, Ireland, September 1986.

[Bro95]   F.P. Brooks, Jr.: *The Mythical Man Month*, Twentieth Anniversary Edition, Addison-Wesley, 1995

[BRR+00]   D. Beder, A. Romanovsky, B. Randell, C. Snow, J. Stroud: *An Application of Fault Tolerance Patterns and Coordinated Atomic Actions to a Problem in Railway Scheduling*, SIGOPS Operating Systems Revue 34, 4 (October 2000), 21–31

[Bry02]   B. Bryson: *Troublesome Words*, Third Edition, Penguin Books, 2002

[BS00]   B.W. Boehm, K.J. Sullivan: *Software Economics: A Roadmap*, The Future of Software Engineering, Association for Computing Machinery, 2000 http://portal.acm.org/toc.cfm?id=336512&type=proceeding&coll=portal &dl=ACM&CFID=8740310&CFTOKEN=83178635

[BSDM05]   L.N. de Barros, A.P. dos Santos Mota, K.V. Delgado, P.M. Matsumoto: *A Tool for Programming Learning with Pedagogical Patterns*, Proceedings of the 2005 OOPSLA Workshop on Eclipse Technology eXchange, San Diego, California, October 16–17, 2005, Eclipse '05, pp. 125–129, ACM Press, New York,

[BTN06]   R. Wirfs-Brock, P. Taylor, J. Noble: *Problem Frame Patterns*, Proceedings of the Thirteenth Conference on Pattern Languages of Program Design, Portland, Oregon, October 2006

[BuHe03]   F. Buschmann, K. Henney: *Beyond the Gang-of-Four*, tutorial at the ACM OOPSLA 2003 Conference, Anaheim, CA, October 2003

[Bus03a]   F. Buschmann: *Patterns at Work*, Tutorial at OOPLSA 2003, Anaheim, CA, USA, 2003

[Bus03b]   F. Buschmann: *Notes on The Forgotten Art of Building Good Software Architectures*, Tutorial at the Eighth Conference on Java and Object-Oriented Technology, JAOO 2003, Aarhus, Denmark, 2003

[Bus05]   F. Buschmann: *Model-Driven Software Development – Hype or Hope?*, invited talk at the Tenth Conference on Java and Object-Oriented Technology, JAOO 2005, Aarhus, Denmark, 2005

[BW95]   K. Brown, B. Whitenack: *Crossing Chasms: A Pattern Language for Object-RDBMS Integration*, in [PLoPD2], 1995

[Car96]   T. Cargill: *Localized Ownership: Managing Dynamic Objects in C++*, in [PLoPD2]

[CH00]   A. Cornils, G. Hedin: *Tool Support for Design Patterns Based on Reference Attribute Grammars*, Proceedings of WAGA '00, Ponte de Lima, Portugal, 2000

[Chr01]   T. Christopher: *Python Programming Patterns*, Prentice Hall, 2001

[Chr04]   H. Christensen: *Frameworks: Putting Design Patterns into Perspective*, Proceedings of the Ninth Annual SIGCSE Conference on Innovation and Technology in Computer Science Education, Leeds, UK, ITiCSE '04, June 28–30 2004, ACM Press, New York, pp. 142–145, 2004

[ChVö02]   E. Chtcherbina, M. Völter: *P2P Patterns, Results from the EuroPLoP 2002 Focus Group*, 2002, http://www.voelter.de/data/pub/P2PSystems.pdf

[CHW98]   J.O. Coplien, D. Hoffman, D. Weiss: *Commonality and Variability in Software Engineering*, IEEE Software, Volume 15, No. 6, November 1998

[CI01]   R. Cattell, J. Inscore: *J2EE Technology in Practice: Building Business Applications with the Java 2 Platform, Enterprise Edition,* Addison-Wesley, 2001

[CiTy04]   M. Cinnéide, R. Tynan: *A Problem-Based Approach to Teaching Design Patterns,* Working Group Reports from ITiCSE on Innovation and Technology in Computer Science Education, Leeds, UK, June 28–30, 2004, ITiCSE-WGR '04. ACM Press, New York, pp. 80–82, 2004

[CKS06]   M.B. Chrissis, M. Konrad, S. Shrum: *CMMI(R): Guidelines for Process Integration and Product Improvement,* Second Edition, The SEI Series in Software Engineering, Addison-Wesley, 2006

[Coc97]   A. Cockburn: *Surviving Object-Oriented Projects,* Addison Wesley Object Technology Series, Addison-Wesley, 1997

[Coc00]   A. Cockburn: *Writing Effective Use Cases,* Addison-Wesley, 2000

[Coc01]   A. Cockburn: *Agile Software Development,* Addison-Wesley, 2001

[CoHa97]   J.O. Coplien, B. Hanmer: *Writing Patterns, A Short Course and Workshop,* Lucent Technologies, Bell Labs Innovations, 1997

[CoHa04]   J.O. Coplien, N.B. Harrison: *Organizational Patterns of Agile Software Development,* Prentice Hall, 2004

[Cool97]   W. Cool: *Personal Communication,* Hillside Inc. Meeting, Portland, Oregon, May, 1997

[Cool98]   W. Cool: *Personal Communication,* Hillside Inc. Meeting, Vancouver, Canada, October 1998

[Cool02]   W. Cool: *Personal Communication,* OOPSLA 2002 Conference on Object-Oriented Programming, Systems, Languages, and Applications, Seattle, Washington, October, 2002

[Cool06]   W. Cool: *Personal Communication,* OOP 2006 Conference on Object-Oriented Programming, Munich, Germany, January, 2006

[Con68]   M.E. Conway: *How Do Committees Invent?,* Datamation, April 1968

[Cope92]   J.O. Coplien: *Advanced C++ Programming Styles and Idioms,* Addison-Wesley, 1992

[Cope95]   J.O. Coplien: *A Generative Development-Process Pattern Language,* in [PLoPD1], 1995

[Cope96]   J.O. Coplien: *Software Patterns*, SIGS Books, New York, New York, 1996. See also http://users.rcn.com/jcoplien/Patterns/WhitePaper/

[Cope97]   J.O. Coplien: *The Column Without a Name: Pattern Languages*, C++ Report, Volume 9, No. 1, pp. 15–21, January 1997

[Cope98]   J.O. Coplien: *Multi-Paradigm Design for C++*, Addison-Wesley, 1998

[Cope00]   J.O. Coplien: quotation from *Beyond the Hype: The Sequel to the Trial of the Gang of Four*, OOPSLA '00, Minneapolis, 2000

[CoWo99]   J.O. Coplien, B. Woolf: *A Pattern Language for Writer's Workshops,* in [PLoPD4]

[CRW01]   A. Carzaniga, D.S. Rosenblum, A.L Wolf: *Design and Evaluation of a Wide-Area Event Notification Service*, ACM Transactions on Computer Systems, Volume 19, No. 3, pp. 332–383, August 2001

[CSF+06]   N. Cacho, C. Sant'Anna, E. Figueiredo, A. Garcia, T. Batista, C. Lucena: *Composing Design Patterns: a Scalability Study of Aspect-Oriented Programming*, Proceedings of the Fifth International Conference on Aspect-Oriented Software Development, Bonn, Germany, March 20–24 2006

[CSM06]   C.A. Cunha, J.L. Sobral, M.P. Monteiro: *Reusable Aspect-Oriented Implementations of Concurrency Patterns and Mechanisms*, Proceedings of the Fifth International Conference on Aspect-Oriented Software Development, Bonn, Germany, March 20–24 2006

[Cun95]   W. Cunningham: *The CHECKS Pattern Language of Information Integrity*, in [PLoPD1], 1995

[Cun96]   W. Cunningham: *EPISODES: A Pattern Language for Competitive Development*, in [PLoPD2], 1996

[CzEi02]   K. Czarnecki, U. Eisenecker: *Generative Programming, Methods, Tools and Applications,* Addison-Wesley, 2000

[DFAM02]   A. Dearden, J. Finlay, L. Allgar, B. McManus: *Using Pattern Languages in Participatory Design,* CHI 2002 Patterns in Practice Workshop, Minneapolis, 2002

[DiGi07]   L. DiPippo, C. Gill (eds.): *Design Patterns for Distributed Real-Time Embedded Systems*, Springer, 2007

[Dij72]   E.W. Dijkstra: *The Humble Programmer*, ACM Turing Award Lecture, 1972, available at http://www.cs.utexas.edu/users/EWD/ewd03xx/EWD340.PDF

[DLS05]   G. Deng, G. Lenz, D.C. Schmidt: *Addressing Domain Evolution Challenges in Model-Driven Software Product-line Architectures*, Proceedings of the ACE/MODELS 2005 workshop on MDD for Software Product-Line Architectures, Jamaica, October 2005

[Dorn02]   K.H. Dorn: *Vom Programmieren zum Konfigurieren von Software*, (From Software Programming to Software Configuration), OBJEKTspektrum, 1/02, SIGS DATACOM, January 2002

[DRE02]   *Patterns in Distributed Real-Time and Embedded Systems*, OOPSLA 2002 workshop, Washington State Convention and Trade Center, Seattle, November 5, 2002

[DRE03]   *Patterns and Pattern Languages for Distributed Real-Time and Embedded Systems*, Tenth Conference on Pattern Languages of Programs, Allerton Park, Illinois, USA, September 8–12, 2003

[Drö00]   W. Dröschel: *Das V-Modell 97*, Oldenbourg, 2000

[DyAn97]   P. Dyson, B. Anderson: *State Patterns*, in [PLoPD3], 1997

[EBNF96]   EBNF: *Information technology — Syntactic metalanguage — Extended BNF*, ISO/IEC 14977, 1996

[ECOOP97]   M. Aksit, S. Matsuoka (eds.): *ECOOP '97 – Object-Oriented Programming*, Proceedings of Eleventh European Conference on Object-Oriented Programming, Jyväskylä, Finland, June 1997, Lecture Notes in Computer Science 1241, Springer, 1997

[ECOOP98]   E. Jul (ed.): *ECOOP '98 – Object-Oriented Programming*, Proceedings of the Twelfth European Conference on Object-Oriented Programming, Brussels, Belgium, July 1998, Lecture Notes in Computer Science 1445, Springer, 1998

[ECOOP99]   R. Guerraoui (ed.): *ECOOP '99 – Object-Oriented Programming*, Proceedings of the Thirteenth European Conference on Object-Oriented Programming, Lisbon, Portugal, June 1998, Lecture Notes in Computer Science 1628, Springer, 1999

[ECOOP02]   B. Magnusson (ed.): *ECOOP '02 – Object-Oriented Programming*, Proceedings of the Sixteenth European Conference on Object-Oriented Programming, Málaga, Spain, July 2002, Lecture Notes in Computer Science 2374, Springer, 2002

[EGHY99]   A. H. Eden, J. Gil, Y. Hirshfeld, A. Yehudai: *Motifs in Object Oriented Architecture*, IEEE Transactions on Software Engineering, 1999

[EGKM+01]   S.G. Eick, T.L. Graves, E.F. Karr, J.S. Marron, A. Mockus: *Does Code Decay? Assessing the Evidence from Change Management Data*, IEEE Transactions on Software Engineering, Volume 27, No. 1, pp 1–12, January, 2001

[Evans03]   E. Evans: *Domain-Driven Design*, Addison-Wesley, 2003

[FBBOR99]   M. Fowler, K. Beck, J. Brant, W. Opdyke, D. Roberts: *Refactoring: Improving the Design of Existing Code*, Addison-Wesley, 1999

[FeRu98]   L. Ferreira, C. Rubira: *Reflective Design Patterns to Implement Fault Tolerance*, Proceedings of OOPSLA '98 Workshop on Reflective Programming in C++ and Java, Vancouver, Canada, October 18, 1998

[FJS99a]   M. Fayad, R. Johnson, D.C. Schmidt (eds.): *Implementing Application Frameworks: Object-Oriented Frameworks at Work*, John Wiley & Sons, New York, 1999

[FJS99b]   M. Fayad, R. Johnson, D.C. Schmidt (eds.): *Implementing Application Frameworks: Object-Oriented Frameworks at Work*, John Wiley & Sons, New York, 1999

[Fow97]   M. Fowler: *Analysis Patterns*, Addison-Wesley, 1997

[Fow02]   M. Fowler: *Patterns of Enterprise Application Architecture*, Addison-Wesley, 2002

[FoYo97]   B. Foote, J. Yoder: *Big Ball of Mud*, in [PLoPD4]

[Fra03]   D. Frankel: *Model Driven Architecture: Applying MDA to Enterprise Computing*, John Wiley & Sons, 2003

[Fri06]   T.L. Friedman: *The World is Flat: A Brief History of the Twenty-First Century*, expanded and updated version, Farrar, Straus and Giroux, 2006

[Gab96]   R.P. Gabriel: *Patterns of Software: Tales from the Software Community*, Oxford University Press, 1996

[Gab02]   R.P. Gabriel: *Writers' Workshops and the Work of Making Things*, Addison-Wesley, 2002,
             http://www.dreamsongs.com/Files/WritersWorkshopTypeset.pdf

[Gam92]   E. Gamma: *Objektorientierte Software-Entwicklung am Beispiel von ET++: Design-Muster*, Klassenbibliotheken, Werkzeuge, Springer, 1992

[Gam95]   E. Gamma: *personal communication*, 1995

[GCKL05a]   A. Garcia, C. Chavez, U. Kulesza, C. Lucena: *The Interaction Aspect Pattern*, Proceedings of the Tenth European Conference on Pattern Languages of Programs (EuroPloP 2005), Irsee, Universitätsverlag Konstanz, July 2006

[GCKL05b]   A. Garcia, C. Chavez, U. Kulesza, C. Lucena: *The Role Aspect Pattern*, Proceedings of the Tenth European Conference on Pattern Languages of Programs (EuroPloP 2005), Irsee, Universitätsverlag Konstanz, July 2006

[GoF95]   E. Gamma, R. Helm, R. Johnson, J. Vlissides: *Design Patterns: Elements of Reusable Object-Oriented Software*, Addison-Wesley, 1995

[GrMü05]   D. Grolimund, P. Müller: *A Pattern Language for Overlay Systems*, Proceedings of the Eleventh European Conference on Pattern Languages of Programs (EuroPLoP 2006), Irsee, Universitätsverlag Konstanz, July 2007

[GSCK04]   J. Greenfield, K. Short, S. Cook, S. Kent: *Software Factories: Assembling Applications with Patterns, Models, Frameworks, and Tools*, John Wiley & Sons, 2004

[GSF+05]   A. Garcia, C. Sant'Anna, E. Figueiredo, U. Kulesza, C. Lucena, A. von Staa: *Modularizing Design Patterns with Aspects: a Quantitative Study*, Proceedings of the Fourth International Conference on Aspect-Oriented Software Development, Chicago, pp. 3–14, March 14-18 2005

[GSS03]   S. Garfinkel, G. Spafford, A. Schwartz: *Practical UNIX and Internet Security*, Third Edition, O'Reilly and Associates, February 2003

[GTK+07]   J. Gray, J.P. Tolvanen, S. Kelly, A. Gokhale, S. Neema, J. Sprinkle: *Domain-Specific Modeling,* in *Handbook of Dynamic System Modeling*, P. Fishwick (ed.), CRC Press, December 2007

[Gun04]   B. Venners and B. Eckel: *A Conversation with E. Gunnerson: Insights into the .NET Architecture*, February 2004, http://www.artima.com/intv/dotnet.html

[Haa03]   A. Haase: *Java Idioms: Exception Handling*, Proceedings of the Seventh European Conference on Pattern Languages of Programming (EuroPloP 2002), Irsee, Universitätsverlag Konstanz, July 2003

[HaKi02]   J. Hannemann, G. Kiczales: *Design Pattern Implementation in Java and AspectJ*, Proceedings of the ACM OOPSLA 2002 Conference, Seattle, pp. 161–173, November 2002

[HaKo04]   R.S. Hanmer, K.F. Kocan: *Documenting Architectures with Patterns*, Bell Labs Technical Journal, Volume 9, No. 1, pp. 143–163, 2004

[Han04]   R.S. Hanmer: *Detection Techniques for Fault Tolerance*, Proceedings of the Eleventh Conference on Pattern Languages of Program Design, Monticello, Illinois, September 2004

[Han07]   R.S. Hanmer: *Patterns For Fault Tolerant Software*, John Wiley & Sons, 2007

[Har99]   N.B. Harrison: *The Language of Shepherding*, in [PLoPD5]

[Hat98]   L. Hatton: *Does OO Sync with the Way We Think?*, IEEE Software, 15(3), 1998

[HCSH05]   L.B. Hvatum, A. Creotia, T. Simien, D. Heliot: *Patterns and Advice for Managing Distributed Product Development Teams*, Proceedings of the Tenth European Conference on Pattern Languages of Programs (EuroPloP 2005), Irsee, Universitätsverlag Konstanz, July 2006

[Hearsay01] Kloster Hearsay (the daily EuroPLoP newspaper), Issue 02/2001: *Close to Heresy*, Irsee, Germany, 2001

[Hearsay02] Kloster Hearsay (the daily EuroPLoP newspaper), Issue 02/2002, Joe Bergin: *Do the Right Thing*, Irsee, Germany, 2002

[Hed97]   G. Hedin: *Language Support for Design Patterns Using Attribute Extensions*, Proceedings of the Workshop on Language Support for Design Patterns and Frameworks, June, 1997

[Hen97]   K. Henney: *Java Patterns and Implementations*, BCS OOPS Pattern Day, October 1997, London

[Hen99a]   K. Henney: *Collections for States*, Proceedings of the Fourth European Conference on Pattern Languages of Programming (EuroPloP 1999), Irsee, Universitätsverlag Konstanz, July 2001

[Hen99b]   K. Henney: *Substitutability: Principles, Idioms and Techniques for C++*, JaCC Conference, 1999

[Hen00]   K. Henney: *Value Added*, Java Report 5(4), April 2000

[Hen01a]   K. Henney: *C++ Patterns – Executing Around Sequences*, Proceedings of the Fifth European Conference on Pattern Languages of Programming (EuroPloP 2000), Irsee, Universitätsverlag Konstanz, July 2001

[Hen01b]   K. Henney: *C++ Patterns – Reference Accounting*, Proceedings of the Sixth European Conference on Pattern Languages of Programming (EuroPloP 2001), Irsee, Universitätsverlag Konstanz, July 2002

[Hen01c]   K. Henney: *A Tale of Three Patterns*, Java Report, SIGS Publications, October 2001

[Hen02a]   K. Henney: *Null Object*, Proceedings of the Seventh European Conference on Pattern Languages of Programming (EuroPloP 2002), Irsee, Universitätsverlag Konstanz, July 2003

[Hen02b]   K. Henney: *Patterns in Java: The Importance of Symmetry*, JavaSpektrum, Issue 6, 2002, SIGS–DATACOM GmbH, Germany

[Hen02c]   K. Henney: *Methods for States*, Proceedings of the First Nordic Conference on Pattern Languages of Programming, VikingPLoP 2002, Helsingør, Denmark Universitätsverlag Konstanz, July 2003

[Hen03a]   K. Henney: *The Good, the Bad, and the Koyaanisqatsi*, Proceedings of the Second Nordic Pattern Languages of Programs Conference, VikingPLoP 2003, 2003

[Hen03b]   K. Henney: *Beyond Metaphor*, endnote of the Eighth Conference on Java and Object-Oriented Technology, JAOO 2003, Aarhus, Denmark, 2003

[Hen04a]   K. Henney: *Stable Intermediate Forms*, Proceedings of the Ninth European Conference on Pattern Languages of Programming (EuroPloP 2004), Irsee, Universitätsverlag Konstanz, July 2005

[Hen04b]   K. Henney: *Relative Values — Defining Comparison Methods for Value Objects in Java*, Proceedings of the Third Nordic Pattern Languages of Programs Conference, VikingPLoP 2004, 2004

[Hen05a]   K. Henney: *STL Patterns: A Design Language of Generic Programming*, SD West 2005

[Hen05b]   K. Henney: *Context Encapsulation – Three Stories, A Language, and Some Sequences*, Proceedings of the Tenth European Conference on Pattern Languages of Programming (EuroPloP 2005), Irsee, Universitätsverlag Konstanz, July 2006

[HJE95]   H. Hueni, R. Johnson, R. Engel: *A Framework for Network Protocol Software*, Proceedings of the ACM OOPSLA 1995 Conference, Austin, Texas, October 1995

[HKG04]   W. Herzner, W. Kubinger, M. Gruber: *Triple-T (Time-Triggered-Transmission)*, Proceedings of the Ninth European Conference on Pattern Languages of Programming (EuroPloP 2004), Irsee, Universitätsverlag Konstanz, July 2005

[HLS97]   T. Harrison, D. Levine, D.C. Schmidt: *The Design and Performance of a Real-Time CORBA Event Service*, Proceedings of OOPSLA '97, ACM, Atlanta, GA, October 6–7 1997

[Hoare85]   C.A.R. Hoare: *Communicating Sequential Processes*, Prentice Hall, 1985

[HoJi99]   C.A.R. Hoare, H. Jifeng: *A Trace Model for Pointers and Objects*, in [ECOOP99], 1999

[Hon04]   S. Honiden: *A Pattern Oriented Mobile Agent Framework for Mobile Computing*, First International Workshop on Mobility Aware Technologies and Applications (MATA2004), pp. 369–380, Florianópolis, Brazil, October 20–22 2004

[Hor06]   C.S. Horstmann: *Object Oriented Design and Patterns*, John Wiley & Sons, 2006

[HoWo03]   G. Hohpe, B. Woolf: *Enterprise Integration Patterns – Designing, Building, and Deploying Messaging Solutions*, Addison-Wesley, 2003

[HvKe05]   L. Hvatum, A. Kelly: *What Do I Think about Conway's Law Now?*, Proceedings of the Tenth European Conference on Pattern Languages of Programming (EuroPloP 2005), Irsee, Universitätsverlag Konstanz, July 2006

[IsDe96]   N. Islam, M. Devarakonda: *An Essential Design Pattern for Fault-Tolerant Distributed State Sharing*, Communications of the ACM, Volume 39, No. 10, pp. 65–74, October 1996

[Jac95]   M. Jackson: *Software Requirements & Specifications: a Lexicon of Practice, Principles and Prejudices*, Addison-Wesley, 1995

[Jac01]   M. Jackson: *Problem Frames: Analyzing and Structuring Software Development Problems*, Addison-Wesley, 2001

[JeWi74]   K. Jensen, N. Wirth: *Pascal: User Manual and Report*, Springer, 1974

[JGJ97]   I. Jacobsen, M. Griss, P. Johnsson: *Software Reuse: Architecture, Process, And Organization for Business Success*, ACM Press, 1997

[John97]   R. Johnson: *Frameworks = Patterns + Components*, Communications of the ACM, Volume 40, No. 10, October 1997

[JRV00]   M. Jazayeri, A.C.M. Ran, F. van der Linden: *Software Architecture for Product Families*, Addison-Wesley, 2000

[Kaye03]   D. Kaye: *Loosely Coupled – The Missing Pieces of Web Services*, Rds Associates, 2003

[KC97]   W. Keller, J. Coldewey: *Accessing Relational Databases*, in [PLoPD3], 1997

[Kel99]   W. Keller: *Object/Relational Access Layer*, in Proceedings of the Third European Conference on Pattern Languages of Programming (EuroPloP 1998), Irsee, Universitätsverlag Konstanz, July 1999

[Kel04]   A. Kelly: *Encapsulated Context,* Proceedings of the Eighth European Conference on Pattern Languages of Programming (EuroPloP 2003), Irsee, Universitätsverlag Konstanz, July 2004

[Ker95]   N. Kerth: *Caterpillar's Fate: A Pattern Language for the Transformation from Analysis to Design*, in [PLoPD1], 1995

[Ker04]   J. Kerievsky: *Refactoring to Patterns*, Addison-Wesley, 2004

[KGSHR06]   A.S. Krishna, A. Gokhale, D.C. Schmidt, J. Hatcliff, V.P. Ranganat: *Context-Specific Middleware Specialization Techniques for Optimizing Software Product-Line Architectures*, Proceedings of EuroSys 2006, Leuven, Belgium, April 18–21, 2006

[KLM+97]   G. Kiczales. J. Lamping, A. Mendhekar, C. Maeda, C. Lopes, J.-M. Loingtier, J. Irwin: *Aspect-Oriented Programming*, in [ECOOP97], 1997

[KLSB03]   G. Karsai, J. Sztipanovits, A. Ledeczi, T. Bapty: *Model-Integrated Development of Embedded Software*, Proceedings of the IEEE, Volume 91, No. 1, pp.145–164, January 2003

[Koe95]   A. Koenig: *Patterns and Antipatterns*, Journal of Object-Oriented Programming, 8(1), 1995

[Kon05]   S. Konrad: *Assurance Patterns for Distributed Real-Time Embedded Systems*, Proceedings of the Twenty-Seventh international Conference on Software Engineering, St. Louis, pp. 657–657, ICSE '05, May 15–21, 2005

[Kru95]   P. Krutchen: *Architectural Blueprints: The '4+1' View Model of Software Architecture*, IEEE Software 12(6), pp. 42–52, 1995

[Kru00]   P. Kruchten: *The Rational Unified Process: An Introduction*, Second Edition, Addison-Wesley, 2000

[KSS05]	A. Krishna, D.C. Schmidt, M. Stal: *Context Object: A Design Pattern for Efficient Middleware Request Processing*, Proceedings of the Twelfth Pattern Language of Programming Conference, Allerton Park, Illinois, September 2005
[KTB98]	R.K. Keller, J. Tessier, G. von Bochmann: *A Pattern System for Network Management Interfaces*, Communications of the ACM, Volume 41, No. 9, pp. 86–93, September 1998
[KVSJ04]	M. Kircher, M. Voelter, C. Schwanninger, K. Jank: *Broker Revisited*, Proceedings of the Ninth European Conference on Pattern Languages of Programming (EuroPloP 2004), Irsee, Universitätsverlag Konstanz, July 2005
[Ladd03]	R. Laddad: *AspectJ in Action*, Practical Aspect-Oriented Programming, Manning Publications, 2003
[Lau04]	Y. Lau: *Service-Oriented Architecture and the C4ISR Framework*, CrossTalk: The Journal of Defense Software, September 2004
[LBG97]	K. Lano, J. Bicarregui, and S Goldsack: *Formalising Design Patterns*, in First BCS-FACS Northern Formal Methods Workshop, Electronic Workshops in Computer Science, Springer, 1997
[LC87]	M.A. Linton, P.R. Calder: *The Design and Implementation of InterViews*, Proceedings of the First USENIX C++ Workshop, November 1987
[Lea00]	D. Lea: *Concurrent Programming in Java, Design Principles and Patterns*, 2nd Edition, Addison-Wesley, 2000
[LK98]	A. Lauder, S. Kent: *Precise Visual Specification of Design Patterns*, in [ECOOP98], 1998
[LoWo04]	A. Longshaw, E. Woods: *Patterns for Generation, Handling and Management of Errors*, Proceedings of the Ninth European Conference on Pattern Languages of Programming (EuroPloP 2004), Irsee, Universitätsverlag Konstanz, July 2005
[LRP04]	T. Lewis, M. Rosson, M. Pérez-Quiñones: *What Do the Experts Say?: Teaching Introductory Design from an Expert's Perspective*, Proceedings of the Thirty-Fifth SIGCSE Technical Symposium on Computer Science Education, Norfolk, Virginia, USA, pp. 296-300, SIGCSE '04, ACM Press, New York, March 03–07, 2004

[LS04]   S. Lukosch, T. Schümmer: *Patterns for Managing Shared Objects in
            Groupware Systems*, Proceedings of the Ninth European Conference on
            Pattern Languages of Programming (EuroPloP 2004), Irsee, Universitätsverlag
            Konstanz, July 2005

[LS05]   S. Lukosch, T. Schümmer: *Patterns for Session Management in Groupware
            Systems*, Proceedings of the Tenth European Conference on Pattern
            Languages of Programming (EuroPloP 2005), Irsee, Universitätsverlag
            Konstanz, July 2006

[MaLu95]   D. Manolescu, B. Lublinsky: *Orchestration Patterns in SOA*,
            http://orchestrationpatterns.com

[Mar02a]   K. Marquardt: *Patterns for the Treatment of System Dependencies*,
            Proceedings of the Seventh European Conference on Pattern Languages of
            Programming (EuroPloP 2002), Irsee, Universitätsverlag Konstanz, July 2003

[Mar02b]   K. Marquardt: *Diagnoses from Software Organizations*, Proceedings of the
            Seventh European Conference on Pattern Languages of Programming
            (EuroPloP 2002), Irsee, Universitätsverlag Konstanz, July 2003

[Mar03]   K. Marquardt: *Performitis*, Proceedings of the Eighth European Conference on
            Pattern Languages of Programming (EuroPloP 2003), Irsee, Universitätsverlag
            Konstanz, July 2004

[Mar04a]   K. Marquardt: *Ignored Architecture, Ignored Architect*, Proceedings of the
            Ninth European Conference on Pattern Languages of Programming (EuroPloP
            2004), Irsee, Universitätsverlag Konstanz, July 2005

[Mar04b]   K. Marquardt: *Platonic Schizophrenia*, Proceedings of the Ninth European
            Conference on Pattern Languages of Programming (EuroPloP 2004), Irsee,
            Universitätsverlag Konstanz, July 2005

[Mar05]   K. Marquardt: *Indecisive Generality*, Proceedings of the Tenth European
            Conference on Pattern Languages of Programming (EuroPloP 2005), Irsee,
            Universitätsverlag Konstanz, July 2006

[MaRi04]   M.L. Manns, L. Rising: *Fearless Change: Patterns for Introducing New Ideas*,
            Addison-Wesley, 2004

[McC96]   J. McCarthy: *Dynamics of Software Development*, Redmond, Washington,
            USA, Microsoft Press, 1995

[MD97]   G. Meszaros, J. Doble: *A Pattern Language for Pattern Writing*, in [PLoPD3],
            1997

[Mead60]   M. Mead: *Cultural Patterns and Technical Change*, New American Library, 1960

[Mes96]   G. Meszaros: *A Pattern Language for Improving the Capacity of Reactive Systems*, in [PLoPD2], 1996

[Mes01]   G. Meszaros: *Introduction to Patterns and Pattern Languages*, presented at the Workshop on Patterns for Distributed, Real-Time, Embedded Systems at OOPSLA 2001, Tampa, Florida, 2001

[Mes07]   G. Meszaros: *XUnit Test Patterns: Refactoring Test Code*, Addison-Wesley, 2007

[Met04]   S.J. Metsker: *Design Patterns in C#*, Addison-Wesley, 2004

[Mey88]   B. Meyer: *Object-Oriented Software Construction*, First Edition, Prentice Hall, 1988

[Mey96]   S. Meyers: *More Effective C++*, Addison-Wesley, 1996

[Mey97]   B. Meyer: *Object-Oriented Software Construction*, Second Edition, Prentice Hall, 1997

[MFP00]   T. Mackinnon, S. Freeman, P. Craig: *Endo-Testing: Unit Testing with Mock Objects*, Proceedings of the XP 2000 Conference, 2000

[Mik98]   T. Mikkonen: *Formalizing Design Patterns*, Proceedings of the Twentieth International Conference on Software Engineering, pp. 115–124, IEEE Computer Society Press, 1998

[MK97]   A. Mester, H. Krumm: *Formal Behavioural Patterns for the Tool-Assisted Design of Distributed Applications*, IFIP WG 6.1 International Working Conference on Distributed Applications and Interoperable Systems (DAIS 97), Cottbus, Germany, September–October 1997, Chapman & Hall, 1997

[MM97]   R.C. Malveau, T.J. Mowbray: *CORBA Design Patterns*, John Wiley & Sons, 1997

[MoFe06]   P. Morrison, E.B. Fernandez: *Securing the Broker Pattern*, Writing Workshop paper at the Eleventh European Conference on Pattern Languages of Programs (EuroPloP 2006), Irsee, July 2006

[MS03]   Microsoft Corporation: *Enterprise Solution Patterns using Microsoft .NET*, Microsoft Press, 2003

[MuOr+07]   J. Musser, T. O'Reilly, O'Reilly Radar Team: *Web 2.0 Principles and Best Practices*, O'Reilly, 2007

[Nash06]   T. Nash: *Accelerated C#*, Apress, 2006

[NFG+06]   L. Northrop, P. Feiler, R. Gabriel, J. Goodenough, R. Linger, T. Longstaff, R. Kazman, M. Klein, D. Schmidt, K. Sullivan, K. Wallnau: *Ultra-Large Scale Systems: The Software Challenge of the Future*, The Software Engineering Institute, 2006, `http://www.sei.cmu.edu/uls/`

[Niel06]   J. Nilsson: *Applying Domain-Driven Design and Patterns: with Examples in C# and .NET*, Addison-Wesley, 2006

[NoBr02]   J. Noble, R. Biddle: *Patterns as Signs*, in [ECOOP02], 2002

[NOF92]   D. Flanagan (ed.): *X Toolkit Intrinsics Reference Manual: Volume 5*, O'Reilly, 1992

[NoWe05]   J. Noble, C. Weir: *Amethodology*, Proceedings of the Tenth European Conference on Pattern Languages of Programs (EuroPloP 2005), Irsee, Universitätsverlag Konstanz, July 2006

[OMG03]   Object Management Group: *Unified Modeling Language: OCL Version 2.0*, Final Adopted Specification, OMG Document ptc/03-10-14, October 2003

[OMG04a]   Object Management Group: *Common Object Request Broker Architecture*, Version 3.0.3, March 2004

[Opd92]   W. F. Opdyke: *Refactoring Object-Oriented Frameworks*, Ph.D. Thesis, University of Illinois at Urbana Champaign, 1992

[ORei05]   T. O'Reilly: *What is Web 2.0: Design Patterns and Business Models for the Next Generation of Software*, September 2005, `http://www.oreillynet.com/pub/a/oreilly/tim/news/2005/09/30/what-is-web-20.html`

[Ort05]   J.L. Ortego-Aronja: *The Pipes and Filters Pattern. a Functional Parallelism Architectural Pattern for Parallel Programming*, Proceedings of the Tenth European Conference on Pattern Languages of Programming (EuroPloP 2005), Irsee, Universitätsverlag Konstanz, July 2006

[PaCle86]   D.L. Parnas, P.C. Clements: *A Rational Design Process: How and Why to Fake It*, IEEE Transactions on Software Engineering 12(2), pp. 251–257, 1986

[Par94]   D.L. Parnas: *Software Aging*, Proceedings of the Sixteenth International Conference on Software Engineering (ICSE–16), Sorrento, Italy, May 1994

[Par06]   The Parlay Group: *Parlay X Web Services Specification*, Version 2.0, 2006

[PB01]   D.S. Platt, K. Ballinger: *Introducing Microsoft .NET*, Microsoft Press, 2001

[PCW05]   R. Porter, J.O. Coplien, T. Winn: *Sequences as a Basis for Pattern Language Composition*, Science of Computer Programming, Elsevier, 2005

[Pet05]   N. Pettersson: *Measuring Precision for Static and Dynamic Design Pattern Recognition as a Function of Coverage*, Proceedings of the Third International Workshop on Dynamic Analysis (WODA), ACM Press, pp. 1–7, St. Louis, May 2005

[PK98]   L. Prechelt, C. Krämer: *Functionality versus Practicality: Employing Existing Tools for Recovering Structural Design Patterns*, Journal of Universal Computer Science (J.UCS), 4(11), pp. 866–882, December 1998

[PLoPD1]   J.O. Coplien, D.C. Schmidt (eds.): *Pattern Languages of Program Design*, Addison-Wesley, 1995 (a book publishing the reviewed Proceedings of the First International Conference on Pattern Languages of Programming, Monticello, Illinois, 1994)

[PLoPD2]   J.O. Coplien, N. Kerth, J. Vlissides (eds.): *Pattern Languages of Program Design 2*, Addison-Wesley, 1996 (a book publishing the reviewed Proceedings of the Second International Conference on Pattern Languages of Programming, Monticello, Illinois, 1995)

[PLoPD3]   R.C. Martin, D. Riehle, F. Buschmann (eds.): *Pattern Languages of Program Design 3*, Addison-Wesley, 1997 (a book publishing selected papers from the Third International Conference on Pattern Languages of Programming, Monticello, Illinois, USA, 1996, the First European Conference on Pattern Languages of Programming, Irsee, Bavaria, Germany, 1996, and the Telecommunication Pattern Workshop at OOPSLA '96, San Jose, California, USA, 1996)

[PLoPD4]   N.B. Harrison, B. Foote, H. Rohnert (eds.): *Pattern Languages of Program Design 4*, Addison-Wesley, 1999 (a book publishing selected papers from the Fourth and Fifth International Conference on Pattern Languages of Programming, Monticello, Illinois, USA, 1997 and 1998, and the Second and Third European Conference on Pattern Languages of Programming, Irsee, Bavaria, Germany, 1997 and 1998)

[PLoPD5]   D. Manolescu, M. Völter, J. Noble (eds.): *Pattern Languages of Program Design 5*, Addison-Wesley, 2006 (a book publishing selected papers from the Pattern Languages of Programming conference series from 1999–2004)

[PoCa04]   R. Porter and P. Calder: *Patterns in Learning to Program: an Experiment*,
                Proceedings of the Sixth Conference on Australasian Computing Education,
                Volume 30, Dunedin, New Zealand, R. Lister, A. Young (eds.), ACM
                International Conference Proceeding Series, Volume 57, pp. 241–246,
                Australian Computer Society, Darlinghurst, Australia, 2004

[POS05]   I. Pyarali, C. O'Ryan, D.C. Schmidt: *A Pattern Language for Efficient,
                Predictable, Scalable, and Flexible Dispatching Components*, in [PLoPD5]

[POSA1]   F. Buschmann, R. Meunier, H. Rohnert, P. Sommerlad, M. Stal: *Pattern-
                Oriented Software Architecture, Volume 1: A System of Patterns*, John Wiley &
                Sons, 1996

[POSA2]   D.C. Schmidt, M. Stal, H. Rohnert, F. Buschmann: *Pattern-Oriented Software
                Architecture, Volume 2: Patterns for Concurrent and Networked Objects*, John
                Wiley & Sons, 2000

[POSA3]   P. Jain, M. Kircher: *Pattern-Oriented Software Architecture, Volume 3:
                Patterns for Resource Management*, John Wiley & Sons, 2004

[POSA4]   F. Buschmann, K. Henney, D.C. Schmidt: *Pattern-Oriented Software
                Architecture, Volume 4: A Pattern Language for Distributed Computing*, John
                Wiley and Sons, 2007

[PP03]   M. Poppendieck, T. Poppendieck: *Lean Software Development: An Agile Toolkit
                for Software Development Managers*, Addison-Wesley, 2003

[PPP]   *Pedagogical Patterns Project*, http://www.pedagogicalpatterns.org

[PPR]   *The Portland Pattern Repository*, http://www.c2.com

[Prec97]   L. Prechelt: *An Experiment on the Usefulness of Design Patterns: Detailed
                Description and Evaluation*, Technical Report 9/1997, Universität Karlsruhe,
                Fakultät für Informatik, Germany, June 1997

[PUS97]   L. Prechelt, B. Unger, D.C. Schmidt: *Replication of the First Controlled
                Experiment on the Usefulness of Design Patterns: Detailed Description and
                Evaluation*, Technical Report wucs-97-34, Department of Computer Science,
                Washington University, St. Louis, December 1997

[Ray91]   E.S. Raymond (ed.): *The New Hacker's Dictionary*, MIT Press, 1991

[Ray04]   E.S Raymond: *The Art of Unix Programming*, Addison-Wesley, 2004

[RBGM00]   D. Riehle, R. Brudermann, T. Gross, K.U. Mätzel: *Pattern Density and Role Modeling of an Object Transport Service*, ACM Computing Surveys, Volume 32, Issue 1es, Article No. 10, 2000

[RBV99]   M. Robinson, P.A. Vorobiev: *Swing*, Manning Publications Company, 1999

[ReRi85]   S. Redwine, W. Riddle: *Software Technology Maturation*, Proceedings of the Eighth International Conference on Software Engineering, pp. 189–200, May 1985

[RG98]   D. Riehle, T. Gross: *Role Model Based Framework Design and Integration*, Proceedings of the 1998 Conference on Object-Oriented Programming Systems, Languages and Applications (OOPSLA '98), pp. 117–133, ACM Press, 1998.

[Rie97]   D. Riehle: *Composite Design Patterns*, Proceedings of the 1997 ACM SIGPLAN Conference on Object-Oriented Programming Systems, Languages and Applications (OOPSLA '97), pp. 218–228, ACM Press, October 1997

[Rie98]   D. Riehle: *Bureaucracy*, in [PLoPD3], 1997

[Ris98]   L. Rising (ed.): *The Patterns Handbook*, SIGS Reference Library No. 13, Cambridge University Press, 1998

[Ris01]   L. Rising: *Design Patterns in Communications Software*, SIGS Reference Library No. 19, Cambridge University Press, 2001

[RJB99]   J. Rumbaugh, I. Jacobsen, G. Booch: *The Unified Modeling Language Reference Manual*, Addison-Wesley, 1999

[Rüp03]   A. Rüping: *Agile Documentation: A Pattern Guide to Producing Lightweight Documents for Software Projects*, John Wiley & Sons, 2003

[RWL96]   T. Reenskaug, P. Wold, O.A. Lehne: *Working with Objects: The OOram Software Engineering Method*, Manning Publications Company, 1996

[Sari02]   T. Saridakis: *A System of Patterns for Fault Tolerance*, Proceedings of the Seventh European Conference on Pattern Languages of Programs (EuroPloP 2002), Irsee, Universitätsverlag Konstanz, July 2003

[Sari03]   T. Saridakis: *Design Patterns for Fault Containment*, Proceedings of the Eighth European Conference on Pattern Languages of Programs (EuroPloP 2003), Irsee, Universitätsverlag Konstanz, July 2004

[Sari05]   T. Saridakis: *Design Patterns for Graceful Degradation*, Proceedings of the Tenth European Conference on Pattern Languages of Programs (EuroPloP 2005), Irsee, Universitätsverlag Konstanz, July 2006

[SB01]   K. Schwaber, M. Beedle: *Agile Software Development with SCRUM*, Prentice Hall, 2001

[SB03]   D.C. Schmidt, F. Buschmann: *Patterns, Frameworks, and Middleware: Their Synergistic Relationships*, Proceedings of the Twenty-Fifth IEEE/ACM International Conference on Software Engineering (ICSE), Portland, Oregon, pp. 694–704, May, 2003

[SBM+06]   R. Sangwan, M. Bass, N. Mullick, D.J. Paulish, J. Kazmeier: *Global Software Development Handbook*, Auerbach, 2006

[SC99]   D.C. Schmidt, C. Cleeland: *Applying Patterns to Develop Extensible ORB Middleware*, IEEE Communications Magazine, special issue on Design Patterns, April 1999

[SC00]   D.C. Schmidt, C. Cleeland: *Applying a Pattern Language to Develop Extensible ORB Middleware*, in [Ris01]

[Sch86]   K.J. Schmucker: *Object-Oriented Programming for the Macintosh*, Hayden Books, 1986

[Sch95]   D.C. Schmidt: *Experience Using Design Patterns to Develop Reusable Object-Oriented Communication Software*, Communications of the ACM (Special Issue on Object-Oriented Experiences), ACM, Volume 38, No. 10, pp. 65–74, October 1995

[Sch98]   D.C. Schmidt: *Applying a Pattern Language to Develop Application-Level Gateways*, in [Ris01], 1998

[Sch03]   T. Schümmer: *GAMA: A Pattern Language for Computer-Supported Dynamic Collaboration*, Proceedings of the Eighth European Conference on Pattern Languages of Programming (EuroPloP 2003), Irsee, Universitätsverlag Konstanz, July 2004

[Sch04a]   A. Schmidmeier: *Patterns and an Antiidiom for Aspect-Oriented Programming*, Proceedings of the Ninth European Conference on Pattern Languages of Programs (EuroPloP 2004), Irsee, Universitätsverlag Konstanz, July 2005

[Sch04b]   T. Schümmer: *Patterns for Building Communities in Collaborative Systems*, Proceedings of the Ninth European Conference on Pattern Languages of Programming (EuroPloP 2004), Irsee, Universitätsverlag Konstanz, July 2005

[Sch06a] D.C. Schmidt: *Model-Driven Engineering*, IEEE Computer, Volume 39, No. 2, pp. 41–47, February 2006

[Sch06b] A. Schmidmeier: *Configurable Aspects*, Proceedings of the Eleventh European Conference on Pattern Languages of Programs (EuroPloP 2006), Irsee, Universitätsverlag Konstanz, July 2007

[ScHa05] A. Schmidmeier, S. Hanenberg: *Cooperating Aspects*, Proceedings of the Tenth European Conference on Pattern Languages of Programs (EuroPloP 2005), Irsee, Universitätsverlag Konstanz, July 2006

[SCJS99] K.J Sullivan, P. Chalasani, S. Jha, V. Sazawal: *Software Design as an Investment Activity: A Real Options Perspective*, in *Real Options and Business Strategy: Applications to Decision Making*, L. Trigeorgis (ed.), Risk Books, 1999

[SFHBS06] M. Schumacher, E. Fernandez-Buglioni, D. Hybertson, F. Buschmann, P. Sommerlad: *Security Patterns: Integrating Security and Systems Engineering*, John Wiley & Sons, 2006

[SFM05] T. Schümmer, A. Fernandez, M. Myller: *Patterns for Virtual Places*, Proceedings of the Tenth European Conference on Pattern Languages of Programming (EuroPloP 2005), Irsee, Universitätsverlag Konstanz, July 2006

[SGCH01] K.J. Sullivan, W.G. Griswold, Y. Cai, B. Hallen: *The Structure and Value of Modularity in Software Design*, Proceedings of the Eighth European Software Engineering Conference, pp. 99–108, 2001

[SGM02] C. Szyperski, D. Gruntz, S. Murer: *Component Software: Beyond Object-Oriented Programming*, Second Edition, Addison-Wesley, 2002

[SH02] D.C. Schmidt, S.D. Huston: *C++ Network Programming, Volume 1: Mastering Complexity with ACE and Patterns*, Addison-Wesley, 2002

[SH03] D.C. Schmidt, S.D. Huston: *C++ Network Programming, Volume 2: Systematic Reuse with ACE and Frameworks*, Addison-Wesley, 2003

[Shir] C. Shirky: *Moderation Strategies*, http://social.itp.nyu.edu/shirky/wiki/?n=Main.PatternLanguage

[SL06] T. Schümmer, S. Lukosch: *READ.ME -- Talking About Computer-Mediated Communication*, Proceedings of the Tenth European Conference on Pattern Languages of Programming (EuroPloP 2005), Irsee, Universitätsverlag Konstanz, July 2006

[SN96]   R.W. Schulte, Y.V. Natis: *Service Oriented Architectures*, Part 1, SSA Research
              Note SPA–401–068, Gartner, 12 April 1996

[SNL05]   C. Steel, R. Nagappan, R. Lai: *Core Security Patterns: Best Practices and
              Strategies for J2EE Web Services, and Identity Management*, Prentice Hall,
              2005

[SPM99]   A. Silva, J. Pereira, J. Marques: *Object Recovery Pattern*, in [PLoPD3]

[Stal03]   M. Stal: *Reverse Engineering Architectures using Patterns*, tutorial notes,
              Seventeenth European Conference on Object-Oriented Programming (ECOOP
              2003), Darmstadt, Germany, July 2003

[StFl04]   S. Stuurman, G. Florijn: *Experiences with Teaching Design Patterns*,
              Proceedings of the Ninth Annual SIGCSE Conference on Innovation and
              Technology in Computer Science Education (ITiCSE '04), Leeds, UK,
              pp. 151–155, June 28–30 2004, ACM Press, 2004

[StLe95]   A. Stepanov, M. Lee: *The Standard Template Library*, Technical Report HPL-
              95–11 (R.1), Hewlett-Packard Laboratories, 1995

[Sun97]   Sun Microsystems: *Java Beans*, version 1.01, 1997
              http://www.java.sun.com/

[SVC06]   T. Stahl, M. Völter, K. Czarnecki: *Model-Driven Software Development:
              Technology, Engineering, Management*, John Wiley & Sons, 2006

[Tal94]   Taligent Inc.: *Taligent's Guide To Designing Programs – Well-Mannered Object-
              Oriented Design in C++*, Addison-Wesley, 1994

[Thu81]   Thucydides: *The Peloponnesian War*, Translation by R. Crawley, Random
              House, 1981

[Tolk04]   J.R.R. Tolkien: *The Lord of the Rings*, Fiftieth Anniversary Edition, Houghton
              Mifflin, 2004

[TZP05]   W. Tsai, L. Yu, F. Zhu, R. Paul: *Rapid Embedded System Testing Using
              Verification Patterns*, IEEE Software, Volume 22, No. 4, pp. 68–75,
              July–August 2005

[Utas05]   G. Utas: *Robust Communications Software: Extreme Availability, Reliability
              and Scalability for Carrier-Grade Systems*, John Wiley & Sons, 2005

[VeSa06]   Z. Velart, P. Šaloun: *User Behavior Patterns in the Course of Programming in C++*, Proceedings of the Joint International Workshop on Adaptivity, Personalization, and the Semantic Web (APS '06), Odense, Denmark, August 23–23, 2006, pp. 41–44, ACM Press, 2006

[VK04]   M. Völter, M. Kircher: *Command Revisited*, Proceedings of the Ninth European Conference on Pattern Languages of Programming (EuroPloP 2004), Irsee, Universitätsverlag Konstanz, July 2005

[VKZ04]   M. Völter, M. Kircher, U. Zdun: *Remoting Patterns: Foundations of Enterprise, Internet and Realtime Distributed Object Middleware*, John Wiley & Sons, 2004

[VlHe99]   J. Vlissides, R. Helm: *Compounding Command*, C++ Report, April 1999

[Vlis96]   J. Vlissides: *Generation Gap*, C++ Report, November–December 1996

[Vlis98a]   J. Vlissides: *Composite Design Patterns (They Aren't What You Think)*, C++ Report, June 1998

[Vlis98b]   J. Vlissides: *Pattern Hatching: Design Patterns Applied*, Addison-Wesley, 1998

[Vlis98c]   J. Vlissides: *Pluggable Factory*, Part I, C++ Report, November/December 199

[Vlis99]   J. Vlissides: *Pluggable Factory*, Part II, C++ Report, February 1999

[Vö05a]   M. Völter: *Patterns for Handling Cross-Cutting Concerns in Model-Driven Software Development*, Proceedings of the Tenth European Conference on Pattern Languages of Programs (EuroPloP 2005), Irsee, Universitätsverlag Konstanz, July 2006

[Vö05b]   M. Völter: *The Role of Patterns in Modern Software Engineering*, Presentation at the Tenth Conference on Java and Object-Oriented Technology, JAOO 2005, Aarhus, Denmark, 2005

[Vö06]   M. Völter: *Software Architecture — A Pattern Language for Building Sustainable Software Architectures*, Proceedings of the Eleventh European Conference on Pattern Languages of Programs (EuroPloP 2006), Irsee, Universitätsverlag Konstanz, July 2007

[VöBe04]   M. Völter, J. Bettin: *Patterns for Model-Driven Software Development*, Proceedings of the Ninth European Conference on Pattern Languages of Programming (EuroPloP 2004), Irsee, Universitätsverlag Konstanz, July 2005

[VSW02]   M. Völter, A. Schmid, E. Wolff: *Server Component Patterns: Component Infrastructures Illustrated with EJB*, John Wiley & Sons, 2002

[Wake95]   W.C. Wake: *Account Number: A Pattern*, in [PLoPD1]

[WaKl98]   J.B. Warmer, A.G. Kleppe: *The Object Constraint Language: Precise Modeling with UML*, Addison-Wesley, 1998

[Wel05]   T. Wellhausen: *User Interface Design for Searching – A Pattern Language*, Proceedings of the Tenth European Conference on Pattern Languages of Programming (EuroPloP 2005), Irsee, Universitätsverlag Konstanz, July 2006

[Wiki]   Wikipedia: http://wikipedia.org/

[Woolf97]   B. Woolf: *Null Object*, in [PLoPD3], 1997

[XBHJ00a]   S. Xia, A. Black, J. Hook, M. Jones: *JPat, A Pattern Definition Language*, Technical Report of Department of Computer Science and Engineering, Oregon Graduate Institute, 2000

[XBHJ00b]   S. Xia, A. Black, J. Hook, M. Jones: *Describing Patterns Using Index Types*, ECOOP '01 submission, 2000

[YaAm03]   S.M. Yacoub, H.H. Ammar: *Pattern-Oriented Analysis and Design: Composing Patterns to Design Software Systems*, Addison-Wesley, 2003

[Zach]   J.A. Zachman: *Zachman Framework*, The Zachman Institute for Framework Advancement, http://www.zifa.com

[Zdun04]   U. Zdun: *Some Patterns of Component and Language Integration*, Proceedings of the Ninth European Conference on Pattern Languages of Programming (EuroPloP 2004), Irsee, Universitätsverlag Konstanz, July 2005

Index of Patterns

Index of Names

Index